C0-ATV-954

A GLOBAL AGENDA

Issues Before
the 54th
General Assembly
of the
United Nations

A GLOBAL AGENDA

Issues Before the 54th General Assembly of the United Nations

An annual publication of the United Nations Association of the United States of America

John Tessitore and Susan Woolfson,
Editors

Rowman & Littlefield Publishers, Inc.
Lanham • New York • Boulder • Oxford

ROWMAN & LITTLEFIELD PUBLISHERS, INC.

Published in the United States of America
by Rowman & Littlefield Publishers, Inc.
4720 Boston Way, Lanham, Maryland 20706

12 Hid's Copse Road
Comnor Hill, Oxford OX2 9JJ, England

Copyright © 1999 by the United Nations Association of the
United States of America, Inc.

All rights reserved. No part of this publication may be reproduced,
stored in a retrieval system, or transmitted in any form or by any
means, electronic, mechanical, photocopying, recording or
otherwise, without prior permission of the publisher.

ISSN 1057-1213

ISBN 0-8476-9830-0 (cloth : alk. paper)
ISBN 0-8476-9831-9 (paper : alk. paper)

Cover design by Douglas Tait, Inc.

∞ ™ The paper used in this publication meets the minimum
requirements of American National Standard for Information
Sciences—Permanence of Paper for Printed Library Materials,
ANSI Z39.48–1984.

Contents

Acknowledgments

The editors wish to thank the many individuals who have been a part of this volume. First among these are our contributors, without whose effort and dedication there could be no *Global Agenda*. These talented men and women take time from their many other commitments, and somehow manage to meet a most demanding deadline. It is this yeoman performance that ensures the timeliness of our volume as it comes off the press each year in early September.

We are also deeply indebted to our Communications Interns, who have volunteered countless hours over a period of several spring and summer months. Each of these young scholars has assisted in research, proofreading, fact-checking, and even writing, and has been generally indispensable to the project. Our deep thanks and fond wishes go to Daniel Butenschøn, Eric A. Friedman, Nina Stechler Hayes, Elizabeth A. Lynch, Lara Saxman, and Susana Urra Calzada.

Finally, as in years past, we thank Lynn Gemmell of Rowman & Littlefield for her unflagging good spirits and her keen editorial stewardship.

John Tessitore
Susan Woolfson

New York, August 1999

Contributors

Nick Birnback (Beyond Peacekeeping; Africa; Central America and the Caribbean; The Commonwealth of Independent States; Cyprus) is currently serving as an Information Officer for UNAMET (United Nations Mission to East Timor). He has worked in U.N. peacekeeping operations in Bosnia-Herzegovina, Liberia, and Sierra Leone, and from 1993 to 1996 served as Manager of Media Relations for UNA-USA.

Derek Boothby (Arms Control and Disarmament) is an independent consultant and a Visiting Lecturer at Yale. He worked in the United Nations Department for Disarmament Affairs for 11 years, followed by service as the Deputy Director of Operations, UNSCOM, for weapons inspections in Iraq. From 1993 to 1998 he was Director of the Europe Division in the Department of Political Affairs, interrupted in 1996–97 by service as the Deputy Transitional Administrator of UNTAES, the peacekeeping operation in Eastern Slavonia.

Frederick Z. Brown (Cambodia) is Associate Director of Southeast Asia Studies at the Paul H. Nitze School of Advanced International Studies, Johns Hopkins University.

Daniel Guss Butenschøn (Health), a Fulbright Scholar from Norway, served as a UNA-USA Communications Intern while pursuing a degree at Columbia University's School of International and Public Affairs, where media and communications are his concentration.

Roger A. Coate (The United Nations and Development) is Professor of International Organization at the University of South Carolina and is coeditor of the journal *Global Governance*.

Mark A. Drumbl (Legal Issues) is Assistant Professor of Law, School of Law, University of Arkansas-Little Rock. He maintains research and teaching interests in public international law, international trade, and the global environment.

Felice D. Gaer (Human Rights; The Advancement of Women) is director of the Jacob Blaustein Institute for the Advancement of Human Rights, the American Jewish Committee. Author, analyst, and advocate, she serves on the steering committees of Human Rights Watch/Helsinki and the International Human Rights Council of the Carter Center, is vice president of the International League of Human Rights, and was a public member of the U.S. delegations to the U.N. Commission on Human Rights from 1994 to 1999.

Gordon M. Goldstein (The Former Yugoslavia; The Middle East), Director of the Council on Foreign Relations Project on the Information Revolution, is editor of a forthcoming volume from Yale University Press on presidential decision-making and the Vietnam war.

Nina Stechler Hayes (Disabled Persons, with Elizabeth A. Lynch), a UNA-USA Communications Intern, has just completed a master's degree in International Affairs at Columbia University, with a concentration in international media and communication.

Gail V. Karlsson (Environment and Sustainable Development) is a New York-based attorney specializing in international environmental law. She is currently working as a consultant to the United Nations Development Programme on sustainable energy policies.

Lee A. Kimball (Law of the Sea, Ocean Affairs, and Antarctica) is a specialist in treaty development and international institutions relating to environment and development issues. She works independently as a consultant in Washington, D.C.

David Lynch (WTO and Trade) is an assistant professor of political science at Saint Mary's University, Minnesota.

Elizabeth A. Lynch (Disabled Persons, with Nina Stechler Hayes), a UNA-USA Communications Intern, will enter Columbia University's School of International and Public Affairs in the fall.

Anthony Mango (Finance and Administration) worked for the U.N. Secretariat from 1960 to 1987. Between 1970 and 1983 he headed the secretariat of the Advisory Committee on Administrative and Budgetary Questions, and in the period 1983–87 served as Secretary to the U.N. Pension Board. Since retirement he has done consultancy work for the United Nations.

Peggy Polk (Food and Population Issues) is a Rome-based journalist who often writes about U.N. agencies.

Lara E. Saxman (Children and Youth), a UNA-USA Communications Intern and former Fulbright Scholar in Hungary, will enter Columbia University's School of International and Public Affairs in the fall.

Fiona Shukri (Crime and Drugs) is Manager of Media Relations at UNA-USA.

John Tessitore (Co-Editor) is Executive Director of Communications at UNA-USA.

Susana Urra Calzada (Ageing), a UNA-USA Communications Intern, recently completed a dual master's degree—Journalism and International Affairs—at Columbia University.

Susan Woolfson (Co-Editor) is Managing Editor of Communications at UNA-USA.

I
Making and Keeping the Peace

1. Peacekeeping in the 21st Century
By Nick Birnback

As the United Nations prepares for the challenges of the next millennium, the Organization finds itself confronted with both a new generation of conflicts and the bloody resurgence of old ones. Almost without exception, every conflict in the post–Cold War era has been intra-state. In the words of U.N. Secretary-General Kofi Annan, "the new conflicts which have erupted since 1991 have been civil ones. Although, often, there is outside interference, the main battle is between people who are, or were, citizens of the same State" [U.N. press release SG/SM/6901, 2/23/99]. Following the brief euphoric period of "aggressive multilateralism" in the early 1990s (a casualty, for the most part, of the disastrous Somalia operation), the United Nations is now searching for ways to adjust and redefine the increasingly complex and interdisciplinary tasks that confront it.

Disunited Nations

While the need for U.N. intervention has increased, the Security Council's willingness to authorize new peacekeeping missions has not. The collegial atmosphere that had characterized the post–Cold War Security Council appears to be a thing of the past, replaced by frequently fractious statements from Beijing, Moscow, Paris, and Washington/London. At this time of increased global conflict, U.N. peacekeepers are conspicuously absent or their roles have been marginalized [see *Christian Science Monitor*, Opinion Piece, 1/20/99]. An example of the disconnect between rhetoric and action was the failure of the Security Council to extend the mandate of the U.N. Preventive Deployment Force in the former Yugoslav Republic of Macedonia (UNPREDEP). The U.N.'s sole preventive deployment mission, UNPREDEP was referred to by the Secretary-General in his 1998 annual report as "a success, inasmuch as war has so far been avoided. . . ." He noted that "the presence of UNPREDEP has undoubtedly had a positive effect, helping to diffuse tensions both within the country and in the wider region. This year's crisis in Kosovo underlined the vital role of UNPREDEP in preserving stability." Despite the Secretary-General's strong recommendations that the mission be extended six months beyond its February 28, 1999, expiration, the Chinese delegation vetoed the resolution, claiming that "the already insufficient resources of the United Nations should be used where they were most needed" [U.N. press release SC/6648, 2/23/99].

Peacekeeping-by-Proxy

Given the increasing politics and complexities that appear to be confounding the U.N.'s decision-making process in peace and security matters, powerful member states have increasingly demonstrated their willingness to address emerging crises unilaterally or through strategic coalitions. One consequence of this new political impasse has been the tendency of the Security Council in recent years to "subcontract" peacekeeping operations to regional organizations. The regional approach has been an appealing alternative for Council members unwilling to expend the political and pecuniary resources necessary for high-quality peacekeeping operations. However, reliance on regional organizations to police their own backyards clearly has had mixed results, at best.

In the Balkans, NATO has effectively performed a peacekeeping role in Bosnia-Herzegovina and Macedonia—despite the Secretary-General's assertion that "peacekeeping is not, and must not become, an arena of rivalry between the United Nations and NATO." However, other more insolvent and/or politically disunited organizations, such as the Economic Community of West African States (ECOWAS), the Southern African Development Community (SADC), and even the Commonwealth of Independent States (CIS), have not fared as well. The Secretary-General has acknowledged that "peacekeeping is often best done by people from outside the region who are more easily accepted as truly detached and impartial," and even asserted that the United Nations should not "nurture any illusions that regional or sub-regional bodies will be able to handle these problems on their own, without help from the United Nations" [U.N. press release SG/SM/6901, 2/23/99]. Clearly, regional peacekeeping has its place, but recent history has also shown that it likewise has its limits.

A Tough Year

From the peace and security point of view, the United Nations experienced one of the most trying years in its 54-year history, with even the usually upbeat Security Council describing the "overall global security landscape" as "grim" [U.N. press release SC/6626, 1/12/99]. This was a year that saw the eruption of the first recent full-scale interstate war in Africa (Eritrea/ Ethiopia); expansion of the civil conflict in the Democratic Republic of the Congo (DRC) to include no fewer than seven sovereign nations; resumption of full-scale war in Angola, despite an enormous U.N. investment in the peace process; continuing internal conflicts in Tajikistan, Sierra Leone, Indonesia, Afghanistan, Georgia, and Somalia, to name a few; and resumption of nuclear testing by both India and Pakistan.

Despite the Secretary-General's vocal assertions that "the Security Council has a central role when it comes to questions of peace and security around the world and that they must be involved in any decision to use force" [U.N. press release SG/SM/6993, 5/14/99], the international community's response to two major crises—Iraq and Kosovo—completely circumvented the U.N. Security Council. The United States, fearful of a Security Council veto, chose to act unilaterally or in a small coalition. Following the attack on U.S. embassies in Kenya and Tanzania, the United States launched retaliatory air strikes on alleged terrorist bases in Sudan and Afghanistan without officially bringing the matter before the Council. Likewise, when the United States, along with Britain, chose to launch a major air operation against Iraq, it was done without a Security Council vote. In response to this trend, the Russian representative to the General Assembly's Special Peacekeeping Committee complained that "attempts to bypass the Security Council by resorting to international intrusion . . . contradicted the very basis of the existing system of international relations and could have implications of a global character" [U.N. press release GA/ PK/158, 3/24/99].

Despite repeated requests by permanent Council members Russia and China, NATO powers effectively excluded the United Nations from their decision-making process regarding Kosovo. The Secretary-General actively tried to reintegrate the Organization into the security equation, commenting that "We have also discovered that even in Kosovo, to have any chance for real and long term solutions, we need to return to the Security Council . . . [which] would be very important in terms of reaffirming the central rule of the Council and acceptance of rule of law and established precedents and procedures" [U.N. press release SG/SM/6993, 5/14/99].

The news, however, was not all bad. The United Nations enjoyed a number of successes over the past year, including the completion of the mandate for a Police Support Group in the Danube region of Croatia (the follow-on to UNTAES) [S/1998/1004, 10/27/98]; the U.N.-brokered agreements on East Timor; the delivery for trial of the suspects in the Pan Am 103 bombing case; the conviction by the International Criminal Tribunal for Rwanda of the former Rwandan Prime Minister for the crime of genocide; the adoption of a treaty banning the manufacture, stockpiling, and use of anti-personnel landmines; and the adoption of the Statute of the International Criminal Court. But on the front pages, the U.N.'s seeming inability to convince powerful member states to conduct themselves within established norms of multilateralism overshadowed these encouraging developments. Three U.N. missions—UNPREDEP, UNSCOM (Iraq), and MONUA (Angola)—were closed down prematurely [U.N. press release GA/PK/161, 3/26/99], joining "the growing roster of missions that have failed because of standoffs between bitterly entrenched foes and because United Nations member governments have been unwilling to commit the huge military and economic resources necessary to take charge of developments" [*New York Times*, 1/19/99]. After a year replete with disappointments and setbacks, the Secretary-General conceded that "we must never again send a United Nations force, just for the sake of it, to keep a non-existent peace, or one to which the parties themselves show no sense of commitment" [U.N. press release SG/SM/6901, 2/23/99].

Internally, the United Nations has begun to look at peace and security issues along a more "holistic" continuum of preventive deployment, peacemaking, peace-enforcement, peacekeeping, and post-conflict peace-building [Report of the Secretary General on the Work of the Organization, 1998]. As the Secretary-General put it: "Peacekeeping cannot be treated as a distinct task complete in itself. . . . More than ever, the distinctions between political and military aspects of our work are becoming blurred" [SG/SM/6901]. This shift, promulgated by the Secretary-General in his report on "The Causes of Conflict and the Promotion of Durable Peace and Sustainable Development in Africa" [S/1998/318, 4/13/98] as well as his Annual Report on the Work of the Organization [A/53/1] and by the Council in several statements [S/PRST/1998/29, S/PRST/1998/38], affirms that the "efforts to ensure lasting solutions to conflicts require sustained political will and a long-term approach in the decision-making of the United Nations" [S/PRST/1998/38]. Unfortunately, political disagreements among the five permanent Security Council members have dictated that support for this progressive initiative remain largely academic. Ignoring many indications of an impending conflict, the Security Council failed to authorize a preventive deployment to the Eritrea/Ethiopia border. Likewise, despite repeated requests, the Secretary-General has not received funding to create a rapidly deployable peacekeeping mission headquarters.

2. Africa
By Nick Birnback

"No one—not the U.N., not the international community—[can] escape the responsibility for the persistence of African conflicts," U.N. Secretary-General Kofi Annan advised the Security Council in the spring of 1998 ["Report to the U.N. Security Council on the Causes of Conflict and the Promotion of Durable Peace and Sustainable Development in Africa," 4/98], but the United Nations and the larger international community waited on the sidelines while the continent of Africa experienced one of the worst years in its post-colonial history. On much of the continent, "insufficient accountability of leaders, lack of transparency in regimes, non-adherence to the rule of law, absence of peaceful means to change or replace leadership . . . [and] lack of respect for human rights" [ibid.] seemed the rule rather than the exception.

A new civil war in the Democratic Republic of Congo drew in no fewer than seven sovereign African nations and resisted all the international community's attempts at mediation. Ethiopia and Eritrea became embroiled in Africa's first *inter*state war in years. Sudan, the Central African Republic, Sierra Leone, Guinea-Bissau, and Lesotho saw an outbreak or continuation of civil conflict. Somalia remains the only nation on earth without a centralized government. Algeria, despite the U.N.'s dispatch of a high-level human rights mission, led by former Portuguese President Mario Soares, continues to reject any form of Western "interference" in its domestic affairs (an estimated 77,000 people have been killed in that North African country since the authorities cancelled a general election in 1992, 600 of those deaths during the three months January to March 1999 [Reuters, 3/26/99]). Western Sahara's referendum on self-determination remains stalled nearly eight years after the United Nations established a mission to oversee the process. And in Angola, which was enjoying a brief period of relative peace after a decade of international mediation efforts, civil war heated up again and the United Nations packed in its peacekeeping operations.

Although **Africa's regional organizations** did demonstrate an increased willingness to take responsibility for security in their own backyard, the actual results have disappointed the hopes of many. There *were* a number of successes: the Economic Community of West Africa's (ECOWAS) restoration to office of Sierra Leone's democratically elected government and stabilization of the situation in Guinea-Bissau for some months; the South African Development Community's (SADC) intervention to stabilize Lesotho; the U.N.-authorized Inter-African Mission's supervision of the surrendering of arms in the Central African Republic, paving the way for deployment of the U.N.'s own peacekeeping mission; and the continuing political involvement of the Organization of African Unity (OAU) and others in peace initiatives in East Africa. But the ECO-WAS force (acronym ECOMOG) is alleged to have committed widespread human rights abuses; and regional players sometimes pursued the national interest by supporting and "even instigating conflicts in neighboring countries." This, said the U.N. Secretary-General, "must be candidly acknowledged" [*New York Times*, 4/17/99].

The **rules, standards, and protocols for regional peacekeeping** have yet to be established; and such bodies as the OAU's Mechanism for Conflict Prevention and the SADC's Organ on Politics, Defense and Security are not addressing aggressively the long-term threats to peace and stability. There is no underestimating the size and difficulty of this task. Sub-Saharan Africa, for example, is home to fully two-thirds of the people affected by HIV/AIDS wordwide, and a third of all Africans are not expected to live past the age of 40; millions of Africans live in refugee camps or camps for the internally displaced (7.3 million, according to one recent report [ibid., 5/9/99]); and most of the 2 million or more children killed in armed conflicts over the past decade lost their lives in Africa's wars [Secretary-General's Report on the Work of the Organization, 1998].

Other members of the international community have lent their support to efforts at addressing the internal conflicts and humanitarian emergencies in the Great Lakes, Central and Southern Africa, and both East and West Africa. But that limited assistance usually takes the form of political pressure or humanitarian aid as the globe's major actors continue their retreat from the beleaguered continent—a retreat due in no small measure to raw memories of the U.N.'s telegenic failures in Somalia and Rwanda. The perceived apathy of those actors and their unwillingness to risk financial and political capital in Africa undermine African confidence in the United Nations, completing a vicious circle. The result, said U.N. Secretary-General Annan, is that African leaders have begun "to marginalize the United Nations from further political involvement in the region's affairs" [Secretary-General's report on Africa, 4/98]. In fact, he added, "the credibility of the United Nations in Africa to a great extent depends upon the international community's willingness to act and to explore new means of advancing the objectives of peace and security on the continent" [ibid.].

The Secretary-General's extensive report on **"The Causes of Conflict and the Promotion of Durable Peace and Sustainable Development in Africa"** in April 1998 was an attempt to focus world attention on the problems of the African continent. He called for increased support of African regional bodies, for better coordination of peacekeeping operations and related exercises, and for a more effective means of inhibiting the flow of arms into Africa.

The report was unusually frank, the Secretary-General going so far as to assert that "African leaders have failed the peoples of Africa; the international community has failed them; the United Nations has failed them." It was equally blunt in insisting that "Concrete action must be taken." The Secretary-General's recommendations did not, however, address the political agendas, institutional paralysis, and inadequate resources plaguing the regional organizations for which the report advocates increased support.

In response to the report, the U.N. Security Council passed four resolutions and issued several presidential statements. The resolutions focused on the regional arms embargo [S/Res/1196, 9/16/98], maintenance of peace and security in refugee camps and settlements in Africa [S/Res/1208, 11/ 19/98], the establishment of an early-warning system to deal with emerging crises [S/Res/1197, 9/18/98], and the need for action by African states to stem the illicit flow of arms into the region as well as to curb weapons proliferation within their own borders [S/Res/1209, 11/19/98]. The Presidential Statements spoke of the need to support African peacekeeping initiatives [S/ PRST/1998/28], to settle conflicts peaceably [S/PRST/1998/29], and (this directed at regional organizations that take actions in the field of peace and security) to do so with respect to the U.N. Charter and in accordance with "principles of sovereignty, political independence and territorial integrity" [S/PRST/1998/35]. African states and many observers welcomed the increased international attention to these issues, although some expressed disappointment that the U.N.'s "initiatives" were largely rhetorical rather than action-oriented.

U.S. President Bill Clinton made a high-profile visit to Africa in 1998, but the **United States** continued to confine its intervention in the continent's problems to political pressure, diplomatic good offices, humanitarian aid, and occasional logistical assistance. The August 7, 1998, bombing of the U.S. embassies in Dar es Salaam, Tanzania, and Nairobi, Kenya (two East African capitals previously considered friendly and low-risk by the U.S. Department of State), the August 25, 1998, bombing of a Planet Hollywood restaurant in Cape Town, South Africa, and the memory of American losses in Somalia continue to make any kind of robust intervention politically risky. U.S. disengagement from Africa has also served to reduce America's official interest in promoting its Africa Crisis Response Initiative, a Clinton administration program launched in late 1996 to assist the creation of a Western-trained indigenous peacekeeping capacity. A U.S.-Africa Partnership Ministerial Summit, held in Washington, D.C., March 16–18, 1999, did provide a forum for high-level officials of sub-Saharan nations to discuss issues of common concern, and President Clinton proposed a $70 billion debt-reduction plan for Africa, but the meeting failed to produce the type of monetary and other pledges for which some observers had been hoping. Likewise, the United States gave only minimal assistance to the two U.N. missions authorized by the Security Council in 1998: the U.N. Observer Mission in Sierra Leone and the U.N. Mission in the Central African Republic.

For Africa there were **a few bright spots** during 1998–99. South Africa, Botswana, Mozambique, and Mali made steady progress toward the rule of law and respect for human rights [Human Rights Watch, Africa Report 1999]. Burundi's steady progress toward ending a five-year civil war led to the lifting of regionally imposed sanctions on January 23, 1999. And, to the surprise of many, Africa's most populous nation, Nigeria—long infamous for systemic corruption and oppressive military dictatorship—joined the ranks of African democracies.

Central and Southern Africa

On March 1, 1999, armed gunmen kidnapped 31 foreign tourists in western Uganda's Bwindi National Park. Eight of them—four Britons, two Americans, and two New Zealanders—were later murdered. After investigation of the incident, authorities determined that the attack in Uganda was carried out by Hutu militia from Rwanda operating from camps in the dense jungle of the Democratic Republic of Congo. This tragic incident offers a hint of Central Africa's convoluted political, ethnic, military, and economic situation. In fact, by 1998, a total of 9 individual national armies and 12 "irregular" armed forces were participating in the hostilities within the territory of the DRC, and 20 distinct rebel groups were operating in the region [U.N. press release HR/CN/893, 4/1/99]. Genocide, reprisals, mass migrations of terrified populations, and a seemingly endless cycle of rebellions, insurgencies, and counterinsurgencies have left their mark on Central-Southern Africa—the most unstable and bloody region on the planet.

The U.N. Security Council, the usual forum through which the international community would deal with peace and security issues, remained reluctant to engage the situation directly—a posture that is viewed with alarm in many quarters. "The Council's 'hands off' approach isn't working," noted one critical op-ed; and "its reliance on the Southern African Development Community (SADC) and the Organization of African Unity (OAU) to resolve the crisis has only inflamed it" [Eric G. Berman and Katie E. Sams in *Christian Science Monitor*, 1/20/99]. Warned the Security Council-mandated International Commission of Inquiry (Rwanda):

> The situation in the Great Lakes region is rapidly heading towards a catastrophe of incalculable consequences which requires urgent, comprehensive and decisive measures on the part of the international community. The danger of a repetition of tragedy comparable to the Rwandan genocide of 1994, but on a subregional scale, cannot be ruled out. [S/1998/1096, 11/18/98]

The new civil war in the Democratic Republic of Congo (formerly Zaire) is in fact an extension of the regional war whose roots lie in the **1994 genocide of Rwanda's Tutsi minority by the Hutu.**

In January 1994, Hutu elements of the Armed Forces of Rwanda and irregular militias slaughtered up to a million Tutsis and moderate Hutus in less than 100 days—a genocidal spree that ended only when the Tutsi-led Rwandan Patriotic Front defeated the forces of the Hutu government, driving some 2 million of its supporters into exile. In 1996, joining the campaign of Laurent Kabila to unseat Zairean dictator Mobutu Sese-Seko, Tutsi forces massacred tens of thousands of Hutu refugees. As a result, many of the estimated million, mostly Hutu, refugees who returned to Rwanda in that year were committed to fighting Rwanda's Tutsi-dominated government and joined the rebel groups that form the **Army for the Liberation of Rwanda** [for background, see recent editions of *A Global Agenda: Issues Before the General Assembly of the United Nations,* especially *Issues/50–53*]. The International Commission of Inquiry (Rwanda) believes that the majority of these groups are currently operating out of the DRC; others are based in Burundi, the Central African Republic, the Congo (Brazzaville), Sudan, Uganda, Tanzania, Zambia, and Rwanda itself [S/1998/1096].

Democratic Republic of Congo (DRC)

In May 1997, longtime rebel leader **Laurent Kabila** succeeded in taking the Zairean capital of Kinshasa, driving dictator Mobutu into exile and renaming the country. He followed up with a series of shortsighted policy initiatives that largely squandered the copious reserves of international good will generated by Mobutu's ouster, and less than two years after Kabila's triumphant march into Kinshasa, the new head of state found *himself* accused of despotism and fighting a large-scale foreign-sponsored domestic insurrection.

Kabila soon alienated his **former allies Uganda and Rwanda,** and by August 1998 had ordered their troops out of the DRC. They, in turn, switched their support to a loose **rebel coalition composed of primarily Tutsi rebel groups based in the eastern and northern provinces**—the Congolese Rally for Democracy (RCD), the Movement for the Liberation of the Congo (MLC), former Mobutu loyalists, and the Banyamulange— and several others. The **Angolan rebel group UNITA** also reportedly sent troops to eastern Congo to join this somewhat unlikely coalition now fighting Kabila's forces [*Christian Science Monitor,* 8/27/98].

In August, in a move to prevent the rebel coalition from sacking Kinshasa, a number of **neighboring states**—among them Zimbabwe, Angola, Namibia, and Chad—sent troops and matériel to support the DRC government. In October the coalition supporting Kabila (now including Burundi, or so the DRC alleges [Statement of Representative of the DRC, U.N. press release GA/9549, 3/23/99]) launched a counteroffensive against rebel strongholds in the eastern regions of the DRC [*New York Times,* 10/22/98]. In spring 1999, as fighting continued, Rwandan and Ugandan-backed groups of the rebel coalition controlled much of the DRC's eastern territory.

The international community has launched a number of **peace initiatives,** primarily under the auspices of the Organization of African Unity and the Southern African Development Community. SADC, the more active of the two bodies, is led by Zambia's President, Frederick Chiluba, with ongoing support from the U.N. Secretary-General.

High-level talks among African leaders (and the Secretary-General) in Durban, South Africa, in September 1998 failed to secure a cease-fire agreement. The major sticking point was the DRC President's refusal to allow any of the rebel groups to participate directly in the peace negotiations, arguing that all negotiations should be carried out with their patron states—Uganda and Rwanda—directly. On October 26, at a meeting in the Zambian capital of Lusaka attended by representatives of the DRC and its allies and by representatives of Rwanda and Uganda, speaking on behalf of rebel groups within the DRC, a cease-fire was agreed to in principle. Follow-up meetings over the next several months in Botswana, France, and Burkina Faso failed to produce a signed accord. Angola, for its part, questioned Zambia's leadership of the process, accusing Lusaka of aiding and abetting UNITA. A late-April 1999 meeting in the Libyan town of Sirte, however, did produce an agreement that called for "an immediate cessation of hostilities" [U.N. Daily Highlights, 4/22/99]. A further meeting, designed to bring together the government, opposition parties, rebels, civil society, and observers, was scheduled for late spring.

Early in 1998 the United Nations withdrew from the DRC its "Secretary-General's Investigative Team" (SGIT) because of "persistent noncooperation and harassment from the authorities" [Secretary-General's Report on the Work of the Organization, 1998]. The SGIT, founded in July 1997, was itself a replacement for a team of experts dispatched by the U.N. Commission on Human Rights to investigate allegations of massacres in eastern Zaire/DRC since September 1996—an investigative trio that included Roberto Garretón, the Commission's Special Rapporteur on then Zaire, whose participation was opposed by DRC officials. At the request of the Kabila government, the mandate of the SGIT was expanded to include the period following the 1994 Rwandan genocide when Hutu refugees streamed into the country to escape retaliation. Among those refugees were many people who had participated in the genocidal acts [for a history of both missions, see A Global Agenda: Issues/53, pp. 182–85]. The Secretary-General team's final report found that genocide "may have taken place," but failed to inspire the Security Council to authorize an independent investigation and the prosecution of those responsible [S/1998/581, 6/29/98].

At the United Nations, Special Rapporteur Garretón continues to speak out on the human rights situation in the DRC. In his April 1999 report to the Commission on Human Rights in Geneva, he accused the troops on both sides of the conflict in the DRC—whether government forces, rebel groups, or foreign troops—of violating the human rights of civilians. "Both parties to the armed conflict have disregarded the rules of international humanitarian law, particularly the rebels," Garretón wrote, "and neither parties [sic] recognize their responsibility in their violations." He concludes that it is "vital," to establish serious negotiations to end the war and an International Criminal Tribunal to "investigate and bring to trial those responsible for gross human rights abuses" [E/CN.4/1999/ 31]. The Human Rights Commission, meeting in April 1999, adopted a resolution calling for a mission to the DRC "to investigate all massacres carried out on the territory, immediately after the signing of a cease-fire," and expressing concern "at the preoccupying situation of human rights, particularly in the east" [U.N. Daily Highlights, 4/27/99].

Throughout the year the U.N. Security Council and the Secretary-General issued a number of statements and a resolution calling for a cessation of hostilities, the "orderly withdrawal of all foreign forces," and the "reestablishment of the authority of the Government of the Democratic Republic of the Congo over the whole territory of the country" [see S/PRST/ 1998/26 and 36; U.N. press release SC/6609, 12/11/98; U.N. press releases SG/SM/6663, 8/5/98, 6672, 8/ 11/98, 6679, 8/21/98, 6680, 8/21/98, 6693, 9/8/98, 6773, 10/26/98; and S/Res/1234, 4/9/99]. Despite statements by both the Security Council and the Secretary-General that they were "prepared to consider the active involvement of the United Nations, in coordination with the OAU, including through concrete, sustainable and effective measures to assist in the implementation of an effective cease-fire agreement" [S/PRST/1998/36], the U.N. role remains largely advisory.

During the early months of 1999, the possibility of a political settlement seemed to increase as Kabila relaxed his position on the participation of rebel groups in the dialogue. Also encouraging was the acceptance by both the rebels and Kabila of the Secretary-General's proposal of a temporary truce to allow UNICEF and the World Health Organization to conduct a polio immunization campaign [Reuters, 3/9/99]. In a hopeful development in late March—this at the request of the DRC government—the Security Council held an all-day "intensive" debate on the situation in the DRC in which some 30 delegates took part [U.N. press release SC/6654, 3/ 19/99].

By April the peace process had picked up some steam. OAU Secretary-General Salim Ahmed Salim visited Kinshasa, emerging "encouraged . . . with respect to the preparation for the initiation of national dialogue but also with respect to the Lusaka [peace] process," and newly appointed Special U.N. Envoy Moustapha Niasse traveled to the DRC capital too, meeting with President Kabila and numerous other regional actors [Reuters, 4/15/99]. In mid-April another round of peace talks got under way in the Zambian capital [Integrated Regional Information Network (hereafter IRIN), 4/17/99].

In mid-July, in what the *New York Times* characterized as "Not Quite a Triumph in Congo" [7/12/99], six governments on both sides of the DRC civil war signed an ambitious cease-fire plan and awaited the signatures of the two main rebel groups—one of which had a dispute over who would sign. The plan also creates timetables for a national dialogue on the future of the DRC and for the removal of all foreign forces, and calls for an international peacekeeping force. At its most ambitious, the plan contemplates the disarmament of armed groups, such as the Hutu militia responsible for much of the 1994 genocide in Rwanda and now based in the DRC. The hope is to track down and bring before the International

War Crimes Tribunal for Rwanda those suspected of gross violations of human rights [ibid., 7/11/99].

Secretary-General Annan has made no secret of his hope that the Security Council will send peacekeepers to the region once conditions permit [Reuters, 3/2/99]. Security Council permanent member Great Britain has circulated a "discussion paper" that offers several **peacekeeping options,** among them an international force of up to 12,000 peacekeepers to monitor a cease-fire [AP, 3/3/99].

Some observers have questioned the willingness of the U.N.'s major contributors to the peacekeeping budget, prominently the United States, to pay for a large new peacekeeping mission in the DRC. Attracting troops from Western member states may also be a problem, admits the Secretary-General. "I do not think we have fully overcome **the Somali syndrome,**" he said in late 1998, referring to the no-win civil war situation in which the U.N. found itself embroiled in 1993, with the effect that many governments are wary of joining peacekeeping operations in that area of the world. "The Somali syndrome affected Rwanda, and it is likely to affect any operation in the Democratic Republic of the Congo" [press conference at U.N. Headquarters, 12/14/98]. U.N. officials indicate that any U.N. deployment to the DRC would likely be confined to a "classic Chapter VI" operation, designed solely to monitor the withdrawal of foreign troops and to observe the conduct of all parties to the cease-fire. Privately, one U.N. official lamented that the operation under discussion will be "late, costly, dangerous, and long term" [interview for *A Global Agenda: Issues/54*].

Rwanda

In April 1999, as Rwanda marked the **fifth anniversary of the genocidal events of 1994,** the International Criminal Tribunal for Rwanda (ICTR) in Arusha, Tanzania, handed down the first guilty verdict for the crime of genocide in the history of international jurisprudence. A year before, **U.S. President Bill Clinton** had traveled to Kigali and apologized to the Rwandan people for the "monumental" failure of the international community—and specifically of the United States—for failing to prevent the wholesale slaughter of Tutsis and moderate Hutus by members of the country's Hutu majority [*New York Times*, 5/10/98]. **U.N. Secretary-General Kofi Annan** also visited Rwanda, where he admitted that "the international community could not muster the resources or the will to come to Rwanda's aid" and was subjected to a barrage of attacks by Rwandan leaders, some of them personal. Annan was at the head of U.N. peacekeeping operations during the period of the Rwanda genocide.

For the first time, U.N. officials publicly acknowledged their role in failing to prevent the genocide, which U.N. military officials now described as "the consequence of the collapse of the UNAMIR [the U.N.

Assistance Mission in Rwanda] mission" [PBS News, "Frontline"—"The Triumph of Evil," aired 8/98]. The French, Belgian, and U.S. governments continued this self-analytical trend by launching official inquiries into their respective roles in the debacle; and in late March 1999 the U.N. Secretary-General announced his intention to set up an "independent inquiry into the actions which the United Nations took at that time" [S/1999/339, 3/26/99]. The work of the International Tribunal for Rwanda (see Chapter VI ["Legal Issues"] of the present volume) and of the Security Council's International Commission of Inquiry (Rwanda) continues. A late-1998 report of the Commission inquiry into the illegal flow of arms into Rwanda (based on visits to Ethiopia, Kenya, Burundi, Mozambique, and South Africa, among others) found that rebel groups, now a "significant part" of the coalition supporting DRC President Kabila, were receiving increased support from regional governments—this in violation of the embargo imposed by the Security Council in October 1995. The Commission's report asserted that regional support for these groups, composed primarily of elements responsible for the 1994 genocide and committed to the overthrow of the Rwandan government and the completion of the Tutsi genocide, served to legitimize them—"a profoundly shocking state of affairs" [S/1998/1096, 11/18/98]. Many of these armed groups have been directly involved in the narcotics trade, the Commission contends.

Within Rwanda itself, the seemingly endless cycle of civil wars continues. International organizations estimate the number of Rwandans killed or displaced by the ongoing conflict in the hundreds of thousands [Human Rights Watch, Rwanda Report 1999]. The U.N. coordinator for humanitarian assistance is nonetheless able to report that the Rwandan government has managed to resettle more than 475,000 people displaced by the civil war [AP, 3/10/99].

With the spotlight on its unwillingness and/or inability to take action in Rwanda five years ago, the international community has begun reaching into its pockets for larger amounts of financial aid—$250 million for Rwanda over the next three years. The Paris Club of creditor nations agreed to write off 67 percent of Rwandan debt, and to permit the conversion of 20 percent more into investment aid [Human Rights Watch, Rwanda Report 1999].

Angola

Despite a decade of the most intense peacekeeping efforts in U.N. history, Africa's longest-running civil war burst into flame again in 1998, all but incinerating the tentatively successful peace process anchored by the Lusaka Peace Protocol of 1994. The United Nations has been reduced to the role of bystander as the well-armed forces of the rebel National Union for Total Independence of Angola (UNITA), led by Jonas Savimbi, and the Angolan government, led by José Eduardo dos Santos, attack each other and unlucky civilians with impunity in one of the most beleaguered, and potentially one of the wealthiest, countries of Africa.

Following UNITA's March 6, 1998, announcement that it had "demilitarized" its forces, the government of President Dos Santos legalized UNITA as a political party, appointing three governors and seven vice-governors nominated by the rebel group, and announced a law granting "special status" to its veteran leader, Savimbi. But in September 1998, UNITA indicated its intention to end cooperation with the international monitors (Portugal, the Russian Federation, and the United States) of the Lusaka accords. President Dos Santos responded by excluding UNITA from parliament and the fragile government of national unity, and declared that he would no longer cooperate with the UNITA leader. Angola's feet were not as firmly planted on the road to peace as had been thought.

The death of the Special Representative of the Secretary General to Angola, Alioune Blondin Beye, in a plane crash in June 1998—just two days short of his fifth anniversary in the post—played a role in undermining the peace process. The integration of UNITA and government officials into unified regional administrations (the Lusaka accords-mandated "normalization of state administration") failed to take place in "strategic localities," and by late July the United Nations pronounced ten of the country's 18 provinces to be unsafe. Fighting escalated across the country throughout the summer.

In October the Security Council extended until December [S/Res/1202, 10/15/98] the **U.N. Observer Mission in Angola (MONUA)**—the successor to peacekeeping operations UNAVEM, UNAVEM II, and UNAVEM III—but by early December what little political unity remained had been shattered. That month, in an attempt to consolidate its power, government forces launched an offensive against Savimbi headquarters, and fighting broke out across the country. On December 3 the Security Council held Savimbi "personally responsible" for the safety of MONUA personnel but also extended the mission's mandate until late February 1999 [S/Res/1213]. Four days later, U.N. peacekeepers stationed in UNITA-held territory were evacuated to MONUA headquarters in Huambo, and the Council issued a Presidential Statement reminding both parties of their obligation "to guarantee the safety and freedom of movement of MONUA personnel" [S/PRST/1998/37]. Fighting continued unabated, and both UNITA and the Angolan government began to suggest publicly that the United Nations might have outlived its usefulness in Angola [New York Times, 1/18/99].

During one of the darkest weeks in the 40-year history of U.N. peacekeeping, December 27, 1998–January 2, 1999, **two U.N.-chartered C-130s crashed in UNITA-held territory,** apparently shot down by rebel forces. Despite several Security Council resolutions and statements condemning the acts and calling for action [see S/Res/1219, 12/31/98; S/Res/1221, 1/12/99; U.N. press release SG/SM/6820, 12/7/98], one of which "deplored the incomprehensible lack of cooperation"—among the most stridently worded resolutions in recent memory—the United Nations was denied immediate access to the crash site. For several days following the tragedy, the fate of the 20-plus passengers and crew was unknown. All personnel are now presumed dead.

Throughout the month of January 1999, U.N. officials, including newly appointed Special Representative Issa Diallo, warned of a "continued disintegration" of the security situation on the ground. On January 4 all U.N. workers were withdrawn from conflict areas; and on January 17, when the Organization found itself unable to carry out its mandate or even to guarantee the safety of its personnel, the U.N. Secretary-General reluctantly recommended **closing the U.N. operation in Angola** [S/1999/49]. Upon expiration of the mission's mandate on February 26, the Security Council ordered the liquidation of all MONUA assets and the repatriation of its approximately1,000 monitors, aid workers, and administrative staff, leaving behind only 260 staffers, mostly security personnel and human rights monitors [U.N. press release SC/6650, 2/26/99]. After ten years in the country and the deployment of over 5,000 U.N. personnel, at the cost of $1.5 billion and the lives of 60 staff members, "the conditions for a meaningful U.N. peacekeeping role ceased to exist," said the Secretary-General [*Washington Post*, 1/19/99]. He had sharp criticism for the Angolan government but assigned "primary" responsibility for the situation to UNITA's Savimbi.

Over half-a-million people have died in Angola's long-running civil war. The peacekeepers leave behind a nation with an estimated 1.5 million internally displaced citizens and the immediate prospect of famine—yet another humanitarian disaster in the heart of Africa. A sad conclusion to one of the most ambitious chapters in U.N. peacekeeping history.

Western Africa

The situation in West Africa remains precarious at best, and high-ranking international officials warn that "West African countries could face the threat of disintegration because of internal armed conflicts" [European Union's Director of International Aid, quoted by BBC "World News," 2/16/99].

Sierra Leone

The war in Sierra Leone is without a doubt the most brutal being waged anywhere in the world. [BBC "World News," 3/2/99]

In May 1997 a small group of soldiers, most of them members of the former ruling military junta, staged a coup in Freetown, capital of Sierra

Leone, overthrowing the country's **democratically elected President, Tejan Kabbah,** who fled to Guinea. This self-proclaimed **Armed Forces Revolutionary Council (AFRC)** immediately allied itself with the **Revolutionary United Front (RUF),** a group of insurgents who had been fighting against successive Sierra Leonean governments since 1991. The rebel group—whose murky objectives and ambiguous political ideology seem to revolve solely around bitter resentment toward city elites, and the desire to control the country's lucrative diamond mines—presided over nine months of anarchic terror and wholesale slaughter.

In March of 1998, **ECOMOG forces led by Nigeria** managed to retake Freetown and restore President Kabbah to power. But the rebels were by no means defeated, retaining control over large segments of the country and committing gross violations of human rights. By January 1999, rebel forces had consolidated their gains and were able to mount yet another attack on Freetown. As international organizations, including the United Nations, were evacuating their personnel, the capital fell to the rebels. Over 6,000 Sierra Leoneans were killed in the **four-day orgy of destruction** that followed—among them police officers, judges, human rights activists, journalists, civil servants, government officials, and ordinary citizens [Reuters, 3/25/99]—and during the first few days of occupation, the rebels are reported to have amputated the limbs of 1,500 more [BBC "World News," 3/18/99]. Also targeted were churches, mosques, hospitals, prisons, and U.N. headquarters; and 20 percent of all housing stock in Freetown was destroyed [U.N. press release SC/6653, 3/11/99]. A U.N. human rights assessment team found that "the ultimate responsibility for the fighting, for most of the civilian casualties and for the related humanitarian emergency in Freetown rested with the rebel forces" [S/1999/237, 3/4/99]. One media report described the January attack as "**less a battle than a crime against humanity,** the worst in recent times" [BBC "World News," 3/2/99].

ECOMOG succeeded in regaining control of the city on January 11, but international enthusiasm for the peacekeepers, and for the pro-government forces, was dampened by persistent and troubling reports of summary executions and human rights violations. By the time the smoke cleared, over a fifth of the population had been uprooted: 450,000 Sierra Leoneans had fled the country (350,000 of them seeking refuge in Guinea) and 700,000 were internally displaced. By spring 1999, the **rebels controlled roughly two-thirds of the country;** and the U.N. Secretary-General speculated that "unknown numbers of rebels might have infiltrated the city [Freetown] and remain there ready to launch further attacks." For this reason he advised that "the security situation in Freetown, despite recent progress, should still be considered volatile" [S/1999/237, 3/4/99]. One seasoned journalist employed by a global news organization described Sierra Leone, where the per capita income is $171 a year [New York

Times, 1/19/99], as "a country whose agony words can no longer describe" [BBC "World News," 3/2/99].

Nonetheless, prospects for peace are encouraging, if uncertain. President Kabbah indicated his commitment to a peace process by convening a peace conference in early April 1999 that enlisted everyone from regional actors, such as ECOWAS officials, to local civic groups. The President even agreed to free imprisoned **RUF leader Foday Sankoh,** who was in the process of appealing a death sentence [address by President Kabbah, 2/21/99, circulated as Security Council document S/1999/186]. Sankoh (described as "a former photographer who claims supernatural powers" [AP, in *New York Times,* 1/8/99]) has also been sounding a conciliatory note. "The government is seriously committed to peace, particularly President Tejan Kabbah," he declared in March [Reuters, 3/9/99]. If the Sierra Leonean government does release Sankoh permanently, as it has indicated it will [IRIN, 4/15/99], it may have little effect, since there is no guarantee that he retains operational control over his commanders (in fact, Sankoh was in prison in Nigeria during RUF's period of greatest success) or that RUF elements in the bush actually want peace.

The United Nations was largely content to let ECOWAS deal with the situation on the ground while it remained actively engaged at the political level. The Security Council sponsored a rare open Security Council meeting on the subject (on December 18, 1998), and the U.N. Department of Political Affairs held an all-day special conference (July 29, 1998) chaired by the U.N. Secretary-General himself. The July conference was designed to solicit support for disarmament, demobilization, and reintegration programs and to address humanitarian and rehabilitation needs. The United Nations has also issued numerous statements about the plight of children and the situation of the civilian population, among them an unusual, if not unprecedented, joint statement by the Executive Director of UNICEF, the High Commissioner for Refugees, the Special Representative of the Secretary-General for Children in Armed Conflict, the High Commissioner for Human Rights, and the Emergency Relief Coordinator. They condemned the "outrageous violations of the human rights of the victims and their families," requested an international tribunal for Sierra Leone, and warned that "it is no longer sufficient for humanitarian and human rights officials to denounce atrocities while unable to prevent their recurrence" [U.N. press release L/2880, 6/17/98].

The Secretary-General's **Special Representative for Children in Armed Conflict,** Olara A. Otunnu, recommended that Sierra Leone be made a pilot project for a "concerted response" to the needs of children in the context of post-conflict peace-building [U.N. press release SC/6626, 1/12/99]. The situation of children is particularly acute in Sierra Leone, where rebel forces abducted an unknown number—thousands, it must be supposed—for use as laborers, fighters, and (in the case of girls) cooks and sexual partners [Human Rights Watch, World Report 1999: Africa]. Between early January and midFebruary 1999, childcare agencies in Freetown reported that 2,000 children had disappeared from that city alone. In early April the intergovernmental U.N. Commission on Human Rights expressed alarm at the "horrifying violations" and called on High Commissioner for Human Rights Mary Robinson to report back on the situation [Reuters, 4/6/99]. UNICEF, acting in conjunction with the U.N. Special Representative to Sierra Leone, the U.N. Special Representative for Children in Armed Conflict, and the Sierra Leonean government, went on to create a task force for the demobilization of child combatants and to take steps to protect the rights of children.

Despite the horror of the situation, the **international community**'s initiatives were mostly limited to the financial, the diplomatic, and the humanitarian. Even the military and security observers dispatched to Sierra Leone [S/Res/1162, 4/17/98] and the follow-up—the approximately 180-member **United Nations Observer Mission in Sierra Leone (UNOMSIL)** [S/Res/1181, 7/13/98]—were confined to monitoring the security situation, assessing disarmament efforts, and urging respect for international humanitarian law. Some observers point out that this response proved ultimately irrelevant to the peace process, since UNOMSIL was evacuated in advance of the rebel assault in January 1999, leaving it to ECOMOG, the regional peacekeeping force, to stabilize the situation [S/1999/20, 1/7/99].

In fact, ECOMOG is credited with doing a fairly good job in restoring stability to Freetown, but persistent reports of both human rights violations and plundering by its troops highlight the drawbacks of subcontracting peacekeeping operations to regional organizations [*New York Times*, 2/12/99]. At the same time, **Nigeria—the largest troop contributor to ECOMOG**—has expressed doubt about its ability to continue shouldering the estimated $1 million-a-day expense of keeping its troops in Sierra Leone. Nigeria has lost an estimated 1,200 soldiers in Sierra Leone [ibid., 2/24/99]. Withdrawal of the Nigerian troops could seriously destabilize the situation in Sierra Leone, and indeed in all of the region.

The United Nations continues to engage in Sierra Leone at a modest level, with the Security Council extending the UNOMSIL mandate until June 13, 1999 [S/Res/1231, 3/11/99] and the Secretary-General recommending that UNOMSIL return to Freetown as soon as possible [S/1999/237, 3/4/99]. The U.N. Development Programme has already been authorized to reestablish a limited presence in Freetown [U.N. press release SC/6653, 3/11/99], and aid agencies have begun to return [Reuters, 3/31/99].

There are those who doubt that much can be gained from such a limited presence. Said one: "The Council's failure to authorize appropriate numbers of blue helmets with more robust mandates has had grave consequences. Sierra Leone is simply the latest example" [Eric G. Berman and Katie E. Sams in *Christian Science Monitor*, 1/20/99].

Liberia

In July of 1997, longtime rebel leader Charles Taylor was elected President of Liberia, handily defeating former UNDP officer Ellen Johnson-Sirleaf. The election marked the end of a brutal seven-year civil war that destroyed Liberian society and displaced over half the country's population. The successful exercise in democracy may have engendered some international goodwill, but such feelings were quickly dampened by the President-elect's horrific human rights record and by **widespread accusations that Liberia was supplying arms to the rebels in Sierra Leone.**

In December 1998, President Taylor informed the Secretary-General's Representative in Monrovia that he was deploying the Liberian military along the Sierra Leonean border to counter an "impending attack against the territory of Liberia" [S/1999/20, 1/7/99]. The **ECOWAS Committee of Five on Sierra Leone** responded by holding an "extraordinary meeting," and in its wake the ECOMOG Force Commander and the Sierra Leonean Foreign Minister **accused Liberia of providing military support to the rebels**—a charge echoed by many international observers [*New York Times*, 2/4/99] but vehemently denied by Liberia. In fact, it is widely believed that Taylor continues to exert a significant amount of control over the RUF rebel groups inside Sierra Leone [Reuters, 4/6/99].

In early March 1999 the President of the Liberian Senate resigned under pressure from the ruling National Patriotic party. He had called for an immediate inquiry into the international allegations of Liberian support for Sierra Leonean rebels, and advocated enacting a law that would make it a felony for a Liberian national to take part in an armed conflict in a foreign country [Reuters, 3/9/99]. Back-channel diplomacy seems to have eased the tension considerably, and by early April the Sierra Leonean government was calling on Taylor to play an active role in regional peace initiatives. "Considering the economic, cultural and social ties between our two nations," said the country's ambassador to Liberia, "Sierra Leoneans are convinced that with your personal intervention, the war in Sierra Leone can speedily come to an end" [quoted by Reuters, 3/4/99].

ECOMOG was not as charitable. Stating that "it will no longer watch this mischief by supposed leaders," ECOMOG called on the international community to "prevail on Charles Taylor and his colleagues to desist from this evil action if peace is to be restored" [IRIN, 4/8/99].

The **United Nations role in Monrovia** is an example of post-conflict peace-building. Following the completion of the United Nations Mission in Liberia (UNOMIL) in September 1997, the U.N. Department of Political Affairs established a small political office to assist in the raising of international funds and to act as liaison between the international community and the new Liberian government. ECOMOG also withdrew the majority of its forces from Liberia but continues to play a role in defusing tension in Monrovia. Such U.N. agencies as the High Commissioner for Refugees, UNICEF, and the Special Representative for Children in Armed Conflict have taken a lead role in repatriating the estimated half-million Liberian refugees and in demobilizing and reintegrating into society the former combatants in Liberia's civil war, many of them child soldiers.

Throughout early 1999 the Security Council "expressed grave concern at reports that both arms and mercenaries were being supplied to the Sierra Leonean rebels from Liberian territory" [S/PRST/1999/1; S/Res/1231, 3/11/99], and asked the Secretary-General to consider the practicality and effectiveness of deploying U.N. monitors, along with those of ECOMOG, at the Liberia/Sierra Leone border.

Guinea-Bissau

In June 1998 the army of Guinea-Bissau mutinied, largely in protest over the sacking of General Ansumane Mane. The action set off months of fighting between the government, supported by Senegal, and members of the armed forces loyal to the Army commander. After numerous truces, and a cease-fire signed in Nigeria's new capital of Abuja in November 1998, **the two sides signed a peace agreement on February 3, 1999,** brokered by France and Togo. About a third of the nation's total population was displaced during the conflict [*Washington Post*, 11/3/98].

Over 3,000 ECOMOG troops from Guinea and Senegal—and later Niger, Togo, Benin, Gambia, and Mali—participated in a **regional peace-keeping operation** that lasted long enough to oversee the installation of a government of national unity on February 20, 1999 [IRIN-West Africa Update, 4/14/99]. But early May 1999 saw the **resumption of fighting** in Guinea-Bissau, the ouster of President João Bernardo Vieira after 19 years of rule, and the surrender of his forces. A U.N. spokesman commented that the Secretary-General was "deeply dismayed about the resumption of fighting" [Reuters, 5/7/99].

Throughout the year-long crisis, **the United Nations has played a supporting and advisory role in the peace process,** allowing ECOWAS to deal directly with the situation. The Security Council passed two resolutions [S/Res/1216, 12/21/98, and S/Res/1233, 4/6/99] in support of the peace process, and authorized the establishment of a Peace-building Support Office in the capital city of Bissau (UNOGBIS) "to help create an enabling environment for restoring and consolidating peace, democracy and the rule of law" [S/1999/232, 3/3/99].

Nigeria

Africa's most populous nation saw the most promising year in its post-colonial history. Dictator Sani Abacha, who had assumed power by military coup in 1993, died of a heart attack in June 1998 and was succeeded by General Abdulsalami Abubakar. General Abubakar, breaking the mold of Nigerian strongmen, not only promised to hold democratic elections but actually supported the electoral exercise, which received a technical hand-up from the U.N. Electoral Assistance Division. In late February 1999, Nigerians went to the polls and elected **former General Olusegun Obasanjo—the nation's first non-military ruler in a generation.** Local and international observers reported blatant cheating—on both sides—but noted that, for the most part, "the cheating had not affected the final outcome of the election" [Reuters, 4/6/99].

Obasanjo, scheduled to take office on May 29, embarked on a public relations campaign to increase foreign investment in Nigeria, one of Africa's most resource-rich nations but, like much of the continent, **burdened with debt** after decades of military rule and a dramatic fall in oil prices. The President, and foreign investors as well, must also confront **Nigeria's human rights record**—one of the worst in Africa (the U.N. Special Rapporteur for Nigeria commented in 1998 that "the rule of law does not prevail in Nigeria" [Human Rights Watch, World Report 1999]). The international community has adopted a "wait and see" attitude in dealing with the new leader, but Nigeria's copious petroleum and mineral deposits have already begun to lure foreign investors back to Abuja and Lagos.

Western Sahara

Western Sahara has been in dispute since 1975, when colonial power Spain withdrew its forces from (then) Spanish Sahara. The area was immediately claimed by Morocco, which oversaw the transfer ("the green march") of some 350,000 of its own citizens, civilian and military, to the northern two-thirds of the colony. Neighboring Mauritania took the other third, driving the indigenous Sahraoui into Algeria. The guerrilla forces of the Sahraoui's Polisario Front forced the Mauritanians out in 1979 and fought the Moroccans to a stalemate, ending in a U.N.-brokered truce in 1991 [*Los Angeles Times*, 3/4/99].

The U.N. Settlement Plan was predicated on the assumption that the international community would organize a **referendum on whether Western Sahara would become independent or part of Morocco.** It was proposed that ballots be cast only by those (and the descendants of those) who had lived in the area before 1975. Morocco, fearing defeat under these terms, has stymied the preparation process at every turn. Other interested parties often appeared to doubt the actual value of a referendum: Mauritania believes that a political settlement between the parties should precede any referendum; Algeria chose not to support the U.N. peace plan until recently; and the Polisario points to statements from the

Moroccan government that it will not accept "a result that goes against incorporation of the territory into Morocco" [*Financial Times*, 12/4/98].

The major stumbling block to the holding of a referendum has been the identification and registration of those entitled to vote. The **United Nations Mission for the Referendum in Western Sahara (MINURSO),** established in 1991 in accordance with the Settlement Plan of August 30, 1988, was charged not only with monitoring the cease-fire, verifying reduction of Moroccan troops in Western Sahara, and ensuring the restriction of Moroccan and Polisario troops to agreed-on locations, but also with identifying and registering qualified voters for the referendum [S/Res/ 1228, 2/11/99]. That process, which sputtered briefly to life in 1994, began again in earnest in 1997, thanks largely to the mediation efforts of an American, James Baker, serving as Personal Envoy of the Secretary-General. Since then, the reenergized voter identification initiative has succeeded in identifying and registering 147,000 applicants. But **the status of three specific tribes**—involving some 65,000 voters—remains unresolved. Morocco considers them Sahraoui while the Polisario consider them Moroccan. A package of measures to implement **the Settlement Plan,** which includes a proposal to hold the referendum in December 1999, was presented to the parties in October 1998 and agreed to immediately by the Polisario. The Moroccan government "agreed in principle" on March 22, 1999, and registration is scheduled to continue during the summer of 1999 [S/1999/307, 3/22/99].

U.N. Secretary-General Kofi Annan has been personally involved in resolving seemingly intractable differences. In December 1998 he traveled to the region, securing a number of pledges from the actors, including a commitment from the Moroccan government to sign an important status-of-forces agreement (this was signed on February 11) and another to formalize the status of the U.N. High Commissioner for Refugees in the territory [S/1999/88, 1/28/99].

The Security Council renewed MINURSO's mandate eight times between September 1998 [S/Res/1198] and June 1999 [S/Res/1245], extending the mission through December 13. But clearly the patience of the international community is at an end, and the Secretary-General himself suggests a **reassessment of "the viability of the mandate of MINURSO** should the prospects for putting the package of measures into effect remain elusive" [S/Res/1228, 2/11/99]. Charles Dunbar, the American who has served as Special Representative of the Secretary-General for Western Sahara for the last two years, resigned effective March 31 [U.N. Daily Highlights, 3/19/99].

Western Sahara represents a significant commitment of blood and treasure for the Moroccan government, and a huge investment of personal credibility for the Moroccan King. Because of this, as well as the region's potentially lucrative phosphate mines and offshore commercial fishing, many observers feel that Morocco will simply not allow to go forward any referendum with a questionable outcome. Morocco's "moderate pro-Western" role in the region has kept some of the Security Council's permanent members from applying pressure to resolve the issue.

Eastern Africa

Eastern Africa teeters on the brink of absolute disaster. The all-out war between Eritrea and Ethiopia seems impervious to all the international community's best efforts at mediation. The bloody civil war in Sudan places a large percentage of the population at risk on a daily basis. Six years after the start of an ambitious U.N. mission, Somalia remains a failed state, divided among feuding clans and provincial warlords. As in the case of Central Africa, the conflicts and refugee flows these conflicts generate threaten to undermine comparatively stable nations, such as Uganda and Kenya, and to fracture already fragile regional coalitions. The international community, with the OAU acting as lead organization, remains involved—sporadically—in promoting a number of peace initiatives. But these have failed to drum up much enthusiasm among the parties to the conflict, who seem not yet ready for peace.

Sudan

Sudan's 16-year-old civil war and accompanying miseries—disease and famine—continue, and the country nears collapse. "Conducted in total disregard to [*sic*] human rights and humanitarian law principles . . . by all parties involved in the conflict," in the words of the Special Rapporteur for Sudan of the U.N. Human Rights Commission [Reuters, 4/6/99], the war has claimed between 1.6 and 1.9 million lives. Broadly stated, the conflict pits the **National Islamic Front (NIF) Muslim fundamentalist government** against the Christian and animist south dominated by the **Sudan People's Liberation Movement/Army (SPLM/A) and the National Democratic Alliance (NDA)**, a wide-ranging coalition of opposition movements based in Eritrea. There are 19 major ethnic groups in Sudan, Africa's largest country.

Although all parties have contributed to Sudan's present misery, international observers point out that the government has "deliberately bombed civilian structures in rebel territory, such as hospitals and relief sites, and its militias abducted women and children to use as slave labor, as a form of war booty" [Human Rights Watch, World Report 1999]. The government also has a policy of coercing conversions to Islam [Human Rights Watch, World Report 1998] and of forced recruitment and conscription of child soldiers [BBC "World News," 4/7/99]. Owing to shortages of food and medicine, often caused or encouraged by armed elements on all sides, famine directly threatens large segments of the population.

Taking its lead from the United States, the United Nations has generally pursued a policy of isolating the fundamentalist Khartoum regime by providing financial and humanitarian aid primarily to groups fighting the government without addressing the conflict as such. Most of the humanitarian aid from the United States (over $700 million in the last decade) also goes to areas controlled by the southern rebels. Yet as desperate as the situation is for the citizens of Sudan, the only time the country appeared on the Western media's radar screens this past year was when the United States launched a cruise missile strike against the factory in Khartoum suspected of producing a component of VX nerve gas.

U.N. participation in peacemaking efforts has been largely limited to providing overall assessments of the situation and assisting in the process of national reconciliation by attempting to mediate a north-south power-sharing arrangement. International mediation efforts have been spearheaded by the **Inter-Governmental Authority on Development,** chaired by Kenyan President Daniel arap Moi. Both the SPLM/A and the Sudanese government have agreed to a **Declaration of Principles,** but the situation on the ground remains hostile and nothing much has changed [off-the-record interview for *A Global Agenda: Issues/54*].

The Sudanese government's abysmal **human rights record** has served to distance both international actors and potential donors, as witness the U.N. Security Council's unanimous refusal to discuss Sudan's request—backed by the Arab League and the Organization of the Islamic Conference—for an investigation of **the U.S. attack against the factory in Khartoum** [*Financial Times*, 8/25/98].

The General Assembly, for its part, has condemned human rights violations on both sides every year since 1993. U.N. Special Rapporteur on Sudan Leonardo Franco is an outspoken critic of rebel groups as well as of the Khartoum regime, and has been particularly forceful in decrying—along with UNICEF—the government's support and perpetuation of a **domestic slave trade.** He has called on Khartoum to accept "a multilateral investigation into the causes of slavery and ways and means to obtain its eradication in Sudan" [U.N. press release HR/CN/896, 4/6/99].

The international community's humanitarian efforts in Sudan are simply massive. **Operation Lifeline Sudan (OLS)** deploys enormous resources through various agencies, feeding over a million people in the south [*New York Times*, 10/10/98], and also serves the country's 4 million or more internally displaced persons, both at the cost of about $1 million a day (totaling over $2 billion since 1989) [ibid.]. Two major U.N. agencies, UNICEF and the World Food Programme, are leading the international effort to overcome famine conditions in southern Sudan.

One troubling aspect of the relief has been the widespread problem of **"food leakages."** Aid earmarked for starving refugees has been systematically diverted to whatever military units control a given area, presenting the international community with a difficult choice: cut off aid and risk greater starvation or support the very groups responsible for perpetuating the famine.

Eritrea/Ethiopia

In May 1998 a minor border dispute between Eritrea and Ethiopia exploded into open conflict, killing 1,000 people before ending in a tense standoff [*Washington Post*, 2/10/99]. At issue was the ownership of the **Badme plain,** a sparsely populated, dusty hill region whose boundary was not clearly drawn when Eritrea seceded from Ethiopia in 1993. Despite peace initiatives by the OAU, United Nations, United States, and Kenya during the standoff period, the fighting started up again in February 1999 and quickly heated up.

When Eritrea became an independent state, it was with the full support of the Ethiopian government. Both nations—viewed by the West as bulwarks against the fundamentalist government in Sudan—enjoyed a special relationship with the United States and other Western governments. Ethiopia was the World Bank's biggest client in Africa in 1998, and both states saw a marked increase in foreign business investment. But within nine months after the fighting began, the two previously amicable neighbors—among the poorest nations in the world—had spent some $300 million on weapons [*New York Times*, 2/7/99], including such high-tech ordnance as helicopter gunships, top-of-the-line fighter aircraft, main battle tanks, multiple launched rocket systems, and other modern weaponry never used before in an all-African conflict. U.N. Special Envoy to the region Mohammed Sahoun warned that, with two such heavily armed and well-organized forces squaring off, "we might be witnessing the first high-tech war in Africa" [*Washington Post*, 2/11/99].

The Ethiopian offensive that rekindled the conflict in early February 1999 has been characterized as a **"World War I style assault"** [*New York Times*, 3/1/99]. Despite a moratorium on air strikes brokered personally by U.S. President Bill Clinton, the Ethiopian and Eritrean air forces attacked both civilian and military targets.

Ethiopia's February offensive was reported to have dislodged the Eritreans from Badme, and Eritrea has since indicated its acceptance of the **December 1998 OAU Mechanism for Conflict Resolution-brokered framework for peace,** beginning with a cease-fire. The plan calls for both sides to withdraw from the contested region until an international team of military observers deployed by the OAU (with U.N. support) settles the boundary issue [U.N. press release SC/6652, 2/27/99].

Meanwhile, the war continues. **Half-a-million soldiers are dug in,** the fighting reminding observers of "the massive battles of the two world wars, updated with some modern weaponry" [AP, 4/1/99]. Both sides quickly claimed to have captured, killed, or wounded "tens of thousands" of enemy soldiers [*New York Times*, 3/1/99].

Ethiopia's claim to have expelled 30,000 Eritreans and Ethiopians of Eritrean descent is disputed by Amnesty International, which cites twice that number [editorial, *New York Times*, 2/7/99]. As for Eritrea, independent observers report that its government, creating a "climate of fear," forced 22,000 ethnic Ethiopians to leave the country [ibid.].

The United Nations and the OAU continue their diplomatic activities, and the Security Council and Secretary-General have issued numerous resolutions and statements calling on Eritrea and Ethiopia to stop the fighting and adhere to the OAU's cease-fire framework [see S/Res/1226, 1/29/99; U.N. press release SC/6652, 2/27/99; S/PRST/1999/9; and U.N. press releases SG/SM/6863, 1/15/99, and 6892, 2/10/99]. The Council also strongly urged all states to immediately end all sales of arms and munitions to both countries [S/Res/1227, 2/10/99].

While expressing "its willingness to consider all appropriate support to implement a peace agreement between the two parties" [U.N. press release SC/6652, 2/27/99], the United Nations has been content to allow the OAU to take the lead in the peace negotiations. In mid-April 1999 the Security Council asked that Special Envoy Sahoun return to the region and attempt to restart the stalled peace process [Reuters, 4/13/99].

3. Central America and the Caribbean
By Nick Birnback

A region whose recent history has been characterized by political turmoil and instability experienced a year of comparative quiescence, with the greatest obstacle to peace coming from the ravages of the century's most extreme hurricane season. The Chairperson of the Commission on Human Rights commented that there had been "significant progress in the promotion and protection of human rights by the Central American region's countries during the present decade, transforming it into a region of peace and democracy" [U.N. press release HR/CN/918, 4/16/99]. Democratic gains continued and were consolidated in once-perpetually unstable El Salvador; and in Colombia the government and the Revolutionary Armed Forces of Colombia (FARC) agreed to convene peace talks for the first time since President César Gaviria took office in 1992 [Bloomberg, 5/7/99]. However, Paraguay experienced a wave of political instability when popular Vice President Luis María Argaña, chief political rival of President Cubas Grau, was assassinated in the nation's capital of Asuncion [Reuters, 3/23/99]. As of spring 1999 the situation in Paraguay remained unstable.

In what has become an annual event, in October 1998 the U.N. General Assembly voted to end the **U.S. economic embargo of Cuba.** This time the nonbinding vote was passed 157-to-2, with the United States and Israel accounting for the only "no" votes [*New York Times*, 11/14/98].

Hurricane Mitch

In late October 1998, Hurricane Mitch tore through Latin and Central America, dumping over four feet of rain, causing an estimated $7–10 billion in damage [*New York Times*, 3/7/99], and killing at least 10,000 people [ibid., 1/24/99]. The storm ravaged the region's infrastructure, leaving huge segments of the population completely isolated. While **Honduras** and **Nicaragua** bore the brunt of the destruction, **Guatemala, El Salvador, Panama,** and **Belize** were also affected by the killer storm. The Director of the U.S. Agency for International Development—which along with other U.S. agencies pledged over $1 billion in emergency aid and reconstruction assistance—commented that Honduras and Nicaragua "have been wiped out," disclosing that Honduras had lost its annual crops "in their entirety" [*New York Times*, 11/7/98]. Honduran President Carlos Flores Facusse bluntly stated that the hurricane left his country "mortally wounded" [*Washington Post*, 11/2/98], and the Inter-American Development Bank estimates that it will take six years for Honduras to recover [*Wall Street Journal*, 11/6/98]. Oxfam regional director Michael Delaney said that the storm was "even worse than all the damage done in Central America during the decades of war" [*New York Times*, 11/7/98]; and the United Nations considers Hurricane Mitch to be "the worst natural disaster in the Americas in the whole of the twentieth century" [U.N. press release HR/CN/918, 4/16/99].

The international community and the entire U.N. system have pledged significant **resources to repair the region's shattered infrastructure.** In December 1998 the United Nations presented donors with a unified, transitional appeal for $153 million to cover six months. The aid will target the poorest elements of society, providing "clean water and food, shelter, emergency health services, education as well as urgently needed help in agriculture" [U.N. press release DEV/2196, 12/4/98]. The Group of Central American Countries (GRUCA) presented a $6 million program of technical cooperation to potential donor countries at a March 1999 meeting sponsored by the U.N. Conference on Trade and Development (UNCTAD). This would be UNCTAD's first large-scale technical cooperation program to address an entire region across the complete spectrum of UNCTAD's programmatic areas [U.N. "Note to Correspondents," 3/22/99]. Even UNESCO announced that it would "give an immediate $150,000 for urgent relief . . . to serve as seed money for further assistance, notably to repair destroyed or damaged schools" [UNESCO press release 98–242]. The European Union has proposed spending over $266 million over four years to help rebuild the region [Reuters, 4/28/99].

The United Nations has expressed its concern over the shifting of the region's limited resources away from institution building and social initiatives. In an April 1999 statement the U.N. Commission on Human Rights noted with concern the negative impact of Hurricane Mitch on "the development of Central America in all its forms," especially "the enjoyment of human rights, in particular economic, social and cultural rights" [U.N. press release HR/CN/918, 4/16/99].

Colombia

While the U.N. Commission on Human Rights praised the Colombian government for the introduction of an **integrated human rights strategy** [U.N. press release HR/CN/936, 4/27/99], U.N. High Commissioner for Human Rights Mary Robinson asserted in her report on the situation in Colombia that "the human rights situation continued to deteriorate" and that "attacks on peace communities inhabited mainly by internally displaced, attacks on indigenous communities, threats and attacks on entire populations, and the continuous kidnapping of populations had also persevered" [U.N. press release HR/CN/918 4/16/99]. Peace between the government and FARC appears attainable, but Colombia's other rebel group, the ELN, remains unreconciled with the Colombian authorities.

Guatemala

In December 1996 the government of Guatemala and the rebel Guatemalan National **Revolutionary Unit (GNRU)** signed a cease-fire in Oslo, Norway. The cease-fire, and the subsequent **U.N.-supervised Agreement on Constitutional Reform, and Agreement on a Basis for the Reintegration of the GNRU into Political Life,** ended decades of bloody civil war that left over 200,000 Guatemalans either dead or missing. As part of the peace agreements, a Commission for Historical Clarification (**"truth commission"**)—based on the South African model—was created to seek reconciliation between the two parties. In late February 1999 the Commission issued its final report, a document the United Nations referred to as "an impartial and authoritative record on one of the most cruel and long-lasting conflicts in Latin America" [U.N. press release SG/SM/6905, 2/5/99].

The report was fiercely critical of the U.S.-backed national army, which it deemed responsible for 93 percent of the war deaths [*New York Times,* 2/27/99]. Ironically, it was the Clinton administration's decision to release classified documents that provided much of the Commission's documentation [ibid., 3/7/99]. Based on the testimony of over 9,000 witnesses, the report determined that most of the war victims were civilians and Mayan Indians, asserting that "[the army] completely exterminated Mayan communities." The Head of the Commission went so far as to comment that the army's actions were "clearly genocide and a planned strategy against the civilian population" [AP, 2/27/99]. "The **United States Government,**" the Commission asserted, "through its constituent structures, including the Central Intelligence Agency, lent direct support to some illegal state operations [*New York Times*, 2/26/99]. The report was especially critical of the CIA role, pointing to American counterinsurgency training of the Guatemalan officer corps as a key factor "which had a significant bearing on human rights violations during the armed confrontation" [ibid., 2/27/99]. During a four-day tour of Central America in April 1999, President Clinton apologized for the U.S. role in the Guatemalan civil war, saying that "for the United States, it is important that I state clearly that support for military forces and intelligence units which engaged in violence and widespread repression was wrong, and the United States must not repeat that mistake" [ibid., 3/11/99]. The GNRU formally renounced violent insurrection when it registered as a political party in October 1998 [Reuters, 10/19/98]. In addition to the difficult process of perpetuating national reconciliation, like most of its Latin American neighbors Guatemala was devastated by Hurricane Mitch, which destroyed more than two-thirds of the nation's crops [*New York Times*, 11/8/98].

Guatemala stands out as one of the few examples of a successful U.N. intervention across the democratization spectrum: peace enforcement, peacekeeping, and post-conflict peace-building. In the words of the Secretary-General: "One of the strengths of the Guatemalan peace process is its development of a comprehensive concept of the requirements of national reconciliation" [U.N. press release SG/SM/6905, 2/25/99]. Following his visit to Guatemala in July of 1998, the Secretary-General commented that "he was encouraged to see the progress made in the implementation of the peace agreements" [SG/SM/6853, 12/28/98]. He called the **U.N. Verification Mission in Guatemala (MINUGUA)** "the largest and most successful peace-building operation, laying the foundations for durable peace and long-term conflict prevention." The Secretary-General met with members of the Historical Clarification Commission in New York, congratulating them on the completion of their work and pledging continued U.N. support for the democratization process [SG/SM/6910, 3/1/99]. The Secretary-General's representative, Assistant Secretary-General for Political Affairs Alvaro de Soto, accepted the report on behalf of the Secretary-General in Guatemala City. In his remarks, de Soto conceded that the report is "no substitute for justice," but heralded its publication as a "great achievement for people everywhere who still struggle to achieve peace with justice, knowing that any peace that turns away from the truth about the past is built on sand" [SG/SM/6905].

While noting the overall positive direction of the peace process, MINUGUA's annual report took note of a number of **disturbing developments,** most notably "the end of the trend towards diminishing human rights violations in Guatemala" [U.N. Daily Highlights, 3/19/99]. MINUGUA also warned that the Guatemalan government's "overly optimistic" estimates of tax revenue could undermine spending on public investment programs vital to the reconstruction of the nation's social infrastructure [*Financial Times*, 9/15/98]. As the report's final paragraph concludes, "The country's future depends in great part on the response of the state and society to the tragedies suffered in flesh and blood."

Continuing with the Organization's peace-building work, the U.N. Department of Disarmament Affairs facilitated a workshop in November 1998 on weapons collection and integration of former combatants into civil society. The three-day event drew participants from 20 countries and ten U.N. agencies as well as numerous regional organizations and citizens groups [U.N. press release DC/2619, 11/23/98].

Haiti

In July 1997, René Préval became Haiti's first modern-day President to take office in a nonviolent manner. The peaceable transfer of power was greeted with jubilation on the streets of Port-au-Prince, but political infighting and the **inability of President Préval to form a government** soon dimmed the mood of optimism. Two years later, the situation in Haiti remains frozen. Mired in a seemingly intractable political impasse, the poorest country in the Western Hemisphere remains without a government, and the disbursement of over $100 million in desperately needed financial aid remains blocked. Haiti also was hit hard by **Hurricane Georges** in November 1998, which caused 250 deaths and damage of around $500 million.

In January 1999, President Préval dismissed all but nine senators, asserting that their constitutionally mandated terms had expired. Préval then appointed **a new Premier and cabinet,** and has begun ruling by decree [BBC "World News," 3/26/99]. Numerous démarches by "the Friends of the Secretary-General for Haiti" (Argentina, Canada, Chile, France, the United States, and Venezuela) have "done nothing to persuade him to alter his chosen course of action" [S/1999/181, 2/19/99].

In March 1999 talks between supporters of President Préval and **Haiti's main opposition party, the Organisation of People in the Struggle (OPL),** broke down when a prominent OPL senator (and member of the rump parliament) was assassinated in front of his home in Port-au-Prince [*Financial Times*, 3/2/99]. In response, the OPL announced that "it is impossible to negotiate in such a climate and will break off all discussions with President Préval until everything has been cleared concerning the assassination" [Reuters, 3/1/99]. Despite an accord signed that same month between Préval and five opposition parties, a **wave of political unrest** followed, and by late March several politicians and political activists had been killed on both sides [AP, 3/14/99]. "The increase in crime," the U.N. Civilian Mission Chief, Colin Granderson, commented, "is part of the weakening social fabric, which is related to the long political crisis" [AP, 4/21/99]. The dismissal of parliament has also fueled an increasingly violent feud between the OPL and the Lavalas Family party, which has close links to President Préval. Accusations of police participation in the killings of political activists also served to undermine public confidence in the neutrality of law enforcement officials.

Exhausted by perpetual instability and the seeming lack of a sincere desire to form an acceptable coalition government, the international community has begun to search for a way out of Haiti. There has been an international presence in Haiti since the United States invaded the island in 1994 to restore the democratically elected government of then-President Jean-Bertrand Aristide to power. In mid-March 1999 the Commander of U.S. forces in Latin America and the Caribbean recommended in testimony before the Defense Subcommittee of the House Appropriations Committee that U.S. troops be withdrawn from Haiti. General Charles Wilhelm reportedly argued that the deployment of some 500 U.S. troops and personnel should be "terminated," as "increasing political turbulence is placing them in danger" [*New York Times*, 3/14/99]. Commenting that he was not pleased with what is going on in Haiti, the U.N. Secretary-General also sounded a rare note of pessimism, admitting that "unless the political forces and the leaders come together to work in the interest of the nation, rather than undermining each other regardless of the impact on society, I do not think we are going to make much progress" [press conference, 3/2/99].

Following a two-day meeting on Haiti at U.N. Headquarters in January 1999, the international community resolved to intensify its efforts to find a political solution to the Haitian crisis. Both the Council and the Secretary-General warned of "increasing polarization in the country, and new risks to the constitutional government and the consolidation of democracy" [S/1999/181, 2/19/99]. They **called for the creation of a credible Provisional Electoral Council** "as soon as possible," with the goal of organizing new elections before the end of 1999.

Although the Council expressed its "deep regret that this political stalemate has not yet made possible the transfer of the activities of the **United Nations Civilian Police Mission in Haiti (MIPONUH)** to other forms of international assistance," upon the recommendation of the Secretary-General and the President of Haiti [S/1998/1003, 10/22/98] the Security Council extended the mandate of MIPONUH until November 30, 1999 [S/Res/1212, 11/25/98]. MIPONUH, established by Council Resolution 1141 (1997), is the follow-on mission to UNTMIH, the U.N. Transitional Mission in Haiti. UNTMIH was itself the smaller successor to UNSMIH, the U.N. Support Mission in Haiti. MIPONUH focuses primarily on the training of the new Haitian police force according to democratic norms and standards [for background on MIPONUH, UNTMIH, and UNSMIH see *A Global Agenda: Issues/53*]. The Council, which extended MIPONUH over the abstentions of China and Russia, also indicated that it did not intend to extend MIPONUH's mandate beyond the November date, and requested that the Secretary-General recommend **suggestions for a successor to MIPONUH by mid-1999.** Several Security Council member states have also gone on record advocating the "gradual transfer of the responsibilities of the Mission to the General Assembly" [U.N. press release SC/6603, 11/25/98]. In refusing to support the extension on MIPONUH's mandate, both Russia and China commented that Haiti was no longer "a threat to international peace and security" and should thus no longer be the responsibility of the Security Council. In a tragic development, a U.N. helicopter assigned to MIPONUH crashed in mid-March 1999, killing all 13 people on board [U.N. "Daily Highlights," 3/16/99].

While the Secretary-General has asserted that **the Haitian police force** has "performed in an efficient and exemplary manner since 11 January 1999, and has remained politically neutral" [S/1999/181, 2/19/99], the General Assembly has commented that the police "still lack the experience, professional skills and cohesion that are the hallmarks of a well-established police force." The Haitian justice system, singled out as "ineffective" by the U.N. Independent Expert on Human Rights in Haiti, is also in dire need of international attention.

The U.N. component of the **International Civil Mission to Haiti (MICIVIH)** was also extended by the General Assembly until December 31, 1999 [U.N. press release GA/AB/3288, 3/19/99]. MICIVIH primarily works to "enhance respect for human rights through its monitoring of, and technical assistance to, the police, the prison administration, the justice system, the Office of the Ombudsman, as well as its human rights promotion programmes" [GA/9529, 12/8/98]. Recognizing the need to move past police reform, the General Assembly called on the Secretary-General to submit two reports: one articulating specific ways in which the international community could continue to assist the Haitian authorities, another calling for coordination of system-wide efforts in providing humanitarian aid and contributing to the development of Haiti [A/Res/53/222].

4. The Commonwealth of Independent States
By Nick Birnback

Russia

The territory of the former Soviet Union (now largely referred to as the Commonwealth of Independent States, or CIS) remains one of the world's most volatile regions. Since the dissolution of the Union, ethnically motivated conflicts in such places as Chechnya, Nagorno-Karabakh, and Tajikistan have claimed about 135,000 lives, driven a million people from their homes, and created instability from Novorossiysk to Kholmsk.

A long-simmering **financial crisis** in Russia finally erupted in August 1998. The Russian government defaulted on its short-term foreign debt and devalued the ruble, and the already beleaguered economy all but collapsed. Russian President Boris Yeltsin dismissed Prime Minister Sergei Kiriyenko; and after a month of political infighting, the Russian Duma approved former Foreign Minister Yevgeny Primakov as the new Prime Minister. While Primakov has attempted to undertake serious fiscal reform, his efforts have remained largely unsuccessful, stymied by ethnic rivalries, organized crime, and systemic corruption.

Russia's attempts at **democratic reforms** remain inconsistent and sporadic. The rulings of the Western-minded national Constitutional Court are frequently ignored, with outlying provinces and republics choosing instead to enforce Soviet-style authoritarianism as they see fit. Mayor Yuri Luzhkov of Moscow, front-runner in the presidential elections scheduled for December 1999, publicly announced in March 1998 that he would not enforce the Court's ruling that the restrictive "civilian registration system," long-used as an excuse for discriminatory and racist policies, was unconstitutional. As Russia continues to subsist largely on disbursements from a U.S.-backed **$22.6 billion IMF bailout** [*Christian Science Monitor*, 10/10/98], "corruption and abuse are the rule rather than the exception" [Human Rights Watch, World Report 1999], and Russia remains "an experiment in democracy gone wrong, spewing out criminality, weapons and unemployment in all directions" [Thomas Friedman in *New York Times*, 2/16/99].

Security Concerns

Russia's **relationship with the West,** personified by NATO, is at a post–Cold War low. Already irritated by NATO's decision to admit three former Soviet client states (Hungary, Poland, and the Czech Republic) in March 1999, Russia was infuriated when NATO ignored its objections and launched air strikes on Yugoslavia. Close religious, ethnic, and geopolitical ties between the Serbs and the Russians led Russia to view NATO's actions as a direct challenge to Russian national security. Tensions were further exacerbated by the decision of former Soviet states and satellite nations to attend the NATO 50th anniversary commemoration held in Washington, D.C., in April 1999.

Russia's hegemonic position within the **Commonwealth of Independent States (CIS)** is also increasingly being called into question. In a bid to distance itself even further from Moscow, Estonia is hoping to be admitted into the European Union, the World Trade Organization, and NATO. Georgia, Azerbaijan, and Ukraine are all pressing for closer relations with NATO, if not full membership in the organization. Perhaps most significantly, in February 1999, Azerbaijan, Georgia, and Uzbekistan opted out of the CIS's mutual defense pact. The three even held four days of joint military exercises in Georgia in April 1999, under the auspices of NATO's Partnership for Peace program. In 1992 nine states—Armenia, Azerbaijan, Belarus, Georgia, Kazakhstan, Kyrgyzstan, Russia, Tajikistan, and Uzbekistan—signed the treaty that constituted the basis for the CIS military-political union. However, the other three CIS members—Ukraine, Moldova, and Turkmenistan—never became official parties to the defense pact. Reportedly, Moldova and Ukraine are also considering leaving the CIS treaty regime [Agence-France Presse, 2/23/99].

The **Central Asian Economic Association** (Kazakhstan, Kyrgyzstan, Tajikistan, and Uzbekistan) has also adopted a vaguely anti-Russian stance. Under its physicist President Askar Akayev, in December 1998 Kyrgyzstan became the first former Soviet republic to join the World Trade Organization. Over the objections of Moscow, Chechen President Aslan Maskhadov signed a number of decrees in early February 1999 suspending the legislative functions of the Chechen Parliament, ordering an immediate transition to Islamic law, and forming a commission to draft a new Islamic constitution. In response, Russia has tightened its relations with its allies Belarus, Kazakhstan, Kyrgyzstan, and Tajikistan, signing an agreement in April 1999 to work together on economic, customs, and humanitarian issues [ibid., 4/16/99]. Russia has also tightened **control of its borders,** and even arrested the pro-Western Executive Secretary of the CIS, Boris Berezovsky, on charges of corruption. Prime Minister Primikov suggested that China, the CIS, and India form a "strategic triangle aimed at countering U.S. influence" [*New York Times*, 12/23/98]. The CIS, viewed by some critics as "a vehicle for reintegrating the former Soviet Union" [editorial, *Wall Street Journal*, 3/1/99], is clearly undergoing a metamorphosis.

For its part, the West seems content to provide support for the fundamentally nondemocratic regimes as bulwarks against both Russian influence and Islamic fundamentalism. The **United Nations** remains regionally engaged, leading the Georgia-Abkhaz peace process and supporting the Organization for Security and Cooperation in Europe (OSCE) in its role as the point organization for Georgia-Ossetia negotiations. The Secretary-General also appointed senior Russian diplomat Ambassador Yuliy Vorontsov to serve as a Special Envoy of the Secretary-General for issues relating to the Commonwealth of Independent States [U.N. "Daily Highlights," 2/16/99]. However, Russia's status as a permanent member of the Security Council has kept the United Nations primarily on the sidelines as the CIS struggles to find its post–Cold War identity.

The Pipeline

Nations bordering on the Caspian Sea—an area fought over successively by the Persian, Russian, Ottoman, British, and Soviet empires—is the scene of a new high-stakes game with potential global implications. Untapped oil reserves have provoked a modern-day "gold rush" by the West, with oil consortiums frenzied by the prospect of cheap oil from non-Islamic countries scrambling for contracts with impoverished former-Soviet republics themselves dazzled at the prospect of OPEC-style petrodollars.

Despite concerns over cost, **the U.S.-supported plan of exporting Caspian Sea oil,** which avoids both Russia and Iran, won out over the Russian-backed scheme, which would have carried oil to its Black Sea port of Novorossisk. Two pipes—one going from the Azerbaijani capital, Baku, to the Black Sea port of Supsa, in Georgia, and a larger one from Baku through Georgia and Armenia to the Turkish Mediterranean port of Ceyhan—have been constructed or are being built. On April 17, 1999, the Presidents of Azerbaijan, Georgia, and Ukraine attended the opening of the new Baku-Supsa oil pipeline. On this issue, Russia has been completely marginalized, as emerging nations capitalize on a resource left largely untapped during the half-century of Soviet domination [Reuters, 4/21/99].

Azerbaijan had initially shied away from the pipeline route over its high cost. However, Richard Morningstar, the U.S. Special Envoy for Caspian energy, announced that "We're getting closer in bridging commercial and political realities," asserting "substantial progress" and telling the U.S. Senate Foreign Relations Subcommittee on International Economic Policy that the Ceyhan pipeline is "economically feasible" [Radio Free Europe/Radio Liberty, 3/4/99]. The pipeline has become a centerpiece of Washington's policy in the region, which aims to secure multiple routes to the West for Caspian oil. In the words of Energy Secretary Bill Richardson, "We've made a substantial political investment in the Caspian, and it's very important to us that both the pipeline map and the politics come out right" [*New York Times,* 11/8/98].

Georgia

The situation in Georgia's security and restricted weapons zones remains "tense and unstable" [S/1999/60, 1/20/99]. Violations by both sides of the **Moscow Agreement on a Cease-fire and Separation of Forces,** signed May 14, 1994, continue to occur. Adding to an already precarious situation, Georgia has requested the departure of Russian army units guaranteeing a truce between Georgia and the breakaway region of Abkhazia. Georgia accuses Russia of siding with the Abkhaz separatists.

Despite numerous attempts on his life, Georgian **President Eduard Shevardnadze** has aggressively **attempted to maintain Georgian independence from Moscow,** asserting that "Russia is fighting very hard against the establishment of democracy here" [*New York Times,* 5/3/98]. He also suggested that the forces responsible for the assassination attempts "were the same ones who nurtured and still support separatism in Abkhazia" [ibid.], and he bluntly accused Moscow of continuing "an imperialist policy at variance with civilized world standards" [*Wall Street Journal*, 3/1/99]. In response, on February 22, 1999, Shevardnadze announced that his country will not extend its membership in the CIS Collective Security Treaty. Georgia, along with Azerbaijan, refused to sign a CIS statement condemning NATO air strikes in Yugoslavia. Tbilisi also continues to build up its relations with its "anti-Russian" neighbors, agreeing to establish a peacekeeping unit with Azerbaijan and Ukraine to protect the transportation infrastructure that carries oil from the Caspian region. Georgia further demonstrated its decidedly pro-Western stance by allowing the United States and Britain to remove a sizable cache of highly enriched uranium and spent nuclear fuel from Georgia without Russian support.

Reform in Georgia was dealt a serious blow when, irked by one of the worst tax collection rates in Eurasia, the IMF withdrew its support for Georgia's ambitious national currency program. Georgia also has a problem with bureaucratic corruption, which the President admits has cost the state "hundreds of millions of dollars." At least $15 million of the $82 million in foreign aid granted since 1994 to fix Georgia's long-standing power problem has disappeared [*New York Times*, 2/7/99].

Security Situation

Some 15,000 **Russian troops** are currently stationed in Georgia, most to enforce a **1994 cease-fire between Georgia and Abkahzia,** a region that first broke away from and then fought a war with Georgia in 1992–93. By 1994 some 10,000 people had been killed and almost 300,000 displaced. Large portions of Georgian territory remain under the control of Abkhazian or South Ossetian separatists.

In October 1998 a **rebel offensive** came just short of reaching Kutaisi, Georgia's second city [*New York Times*, 10/20/98]. Following the October violence, both sides in the Georgian-Abkhazian dispute met in Athens and agreed on several confidence-building measures, but failed to secure agreements on security, return of refugees, and economic reconstruction.

The situation in the conflict zone remains "tense and unstable" [S/1999/60, 1/20/99]. For the last six years the **United Nations Observer Mission in Georgia (UNOMIG)** has carried out limited patrols, usually with CIS peacekeeping troops. At the headquarters level, the working relationship between UNOMIG and the CIS peacekeeping force remains good. At the local level, U.N. officials suggest that working relations could be improved.

A number of incidents in the mission area have directly endangered the **safety and security of UNOMIG personnel.** These have included grenades thrown into the UNOMIG headquarters compound in Su-khumi on three occasions, two car hijackings, and the ambush of a clearly marked UNOMIG vehicle. Continuing instability and widespread vio-lence have forced many international aid agencies to curtail their activities in the region; and the humanitarian situation and prospects for refugee return in Georgia and throughout the Caucasus remain bleak.

Following a flare-up in hostilities and the attacks on U.N. personnel, the Secretary-General asserted that "Unless the parties take urgent mea-sures to improve the security environment for the United Nations, I shall be obliged to draw down the strength of the Mission and to consider relocating United Nations personnel and facilities to more secure loca-tions. Should UNOMIG be compelled to withdraw from Abkhazia, Georgia, the situation in the security and restricted weapons zones would almost certainly become more serious, and a return to open hostilities could not be excluded" [S/1998/1012, 10/29/98]. Both the Secretary-General and the Security Council also issued statements expressing "concern over ris-ing tensions" and called for both sides to "avoid any action which could lead to violence and undermine the peace-making efforts of the UN and the international community" [U.N. press release SG/SM/6846, 12/18/98; S/PRST/1998/ 34]. By early 1999 the situation had stabilized somewhat, and pursuant to the Secretary-General's Report of January 20 [S/1999/60], on January 28, 1999, the Security Council extended the mandate of UNOMIG until July of that year [S/Res/1225]. The Council demanded that the Georgian and Ab-khazian parties "expand their commitment to the U.N.-led peace proc-ess" and expressed their concern over the plight of those displaced by the fighting in mid-1998 [U.N. press release SC/6635, 1/28/99].

Armenia, Azerbaijan

Armenia remains **one of Russia's closest allies** in the region. While Russia has denied it is supplying arms directly to Armenia, it has deployed ad-vanced S-300 surface-to-air missiles and MiG-29 fighters to Russian units stationed in that country. Armenia welcomes the Russian military pres-ence to bolster its position in the shaky truce with Azerbaijan over the predominantly Armenian enclave of Nagorno-Karabakh. That conflict has left thousands dead and almost a million people homeless [Reuters, 4/20/ 99].

Azerbaijani President Heydar Aliyev is pursuing relations with NATO countries to **counterbalance the Russia-Armenia alliance** and to assure the free flow of oil to the West [New York Times, 2/5/99]. Azerbaijanis across the political spectrum have come out publicly in favor of NATO air strikes against Yugoslavia, and the government announced its intention to send 50 soldiers as part of a Turkish unit to participate in NATO peace-keeping operations [ibid.]. President Aliyev has also raised the **possibility**

of a NATO air base on Azeri soil [ibid., 11/8/98]. The Azerbaijanis have even gone so far as to interdict a shipment of Russian fighter planes allegedly bound for Yugoslavia [*New York Times*, 3/23/99].

Tajikistan

A brutal five-year civil war between the weak Tajikistan government and the United Tajikistan Opposition (UTO) left an estimated 50,000 dead and 20 percent of the 5.6 million population displaced [*Christian Science Monitor*, 4/14/99].

To date, large areas of Tajikistan remain contested. In September 1998 a crisis erupted when Otakhon Latifi, a prominent UTO member and the senior member of the Commission on National Reconciliation (CNR), was shot dead outside his Dushanbe apartment. In response, the government of Tajikistan issued a statement accusing UTO of violating the **General Agreement on the Establishment of Peace and National Accord in Tajikistan** and accused its members of being involved in criminal activities. The UTO leadership firmly denied those allegations, suspended activities in both CNR and the government, and conditioned their return on the arrest of Latifi's assassin and concrete measures by the government to improve the security of its members [S/1998/1029, 11/3/98]. Complicating matters, in early November 1998 a non-UTO rebel offensive (allegedly launched from Uzbekistan) in Leninabad Province—the largest and most prosperous region of the country—succeeded in taking control of the provincial capital of Khujand [U.N. press release SC/6595, 11/12/98]. The government counteroffensive, actually supported by the UTO, succeeded in retaking control of the city. Tajikistan issued a statement accusing the Uzbek authorities of having assisted in the attack, and relations between the two countries remain strained [S/1999/124, 2/8/99].

However, the **peace process** between the government and the opposition continues to make slow progress. The UTO has indicated that it has closed "all of its bases outside the country," but it also received wholesale condemnation from the United Nations for its unhelpful attitude in investigating the killing of international personnel. In public statements at the beginning of 1999, **Tajik President Emomali Rakhmonov** declared his government's intention to hold a referendum on amendments to the constitution, as well as parliamentary and presidential elections in 1999, and called on the international community to provide financial assistance in this regard.

The **situation on the Tajik-Afghani border** also remains tense. Of the approximately 20,000 Russian troops in Tajikistan, more than half are deployed along the southern border with Afghanistan [Reuters, 4/9/99]. A Russian-Tajik agreement to create a large Russian military base provoked an angry response from Kabul, which urged the United Nations to block what it called "Russian interference" in the war-torn country. "The presence of this military base, in addition to damaging the UN peace process in Afghanistan, is also not in conformity with UN regulations, as well as other international conventions, and would cause a serious threat to peace and stability in the region" [ibid., 4/11/99].

The **United Nations Mission of Observers in Tajikistan (UNMOT)** was established in 1994 [S/Res/968] to monitor a cease-fire agreement between the Tajik government and the UTO, to advise the Commission on National Reconciliation on electoral issues, and to help reintegrate UTO soldiers into the community. The **United Nations recalled almost all of its foreign staff** from Tajikistan after three U.N. military observers (from Poland, Uruguay, and Japan) and their Tajik translator were ambushed and killed in July 1998 [AP, 4/9/99]. In early 1999 the United Nations announced its intention to return its staff following the conviction of three men charged with the murders. The Security Council "took note with appreciation the effort of the Government" in this regard, and called on the UTO "to contribute more effectively" to the investigations [S/PRST/ 1999/8]. The Council also reminded all parties that the international community's ability to mobilize and continue assistance for Tajikistan was linked to the security of UNMOT personnel [U.N. press release SC/6647, 2/23/99].

Following Security Council Resolution 1206 [11/12/98], the Council issued a Presidential Statement articulating the need to "speed up on the implementation . . . of the General Agreement on the Establishment of Peace and National Accord in Tajikistan" [S/1997/510], and calling for "a constitutional referendum and presidential elections, as well as the timely holding of parliamentary elections" in 1999 [S/PRST/1999/8]. The Secretary-General warned that while the international community applauded the adoption of a law on political parties and approved the cabinet appointments of the representatives of the UTO, "progress in the peace process has been slow and a great deal remains to be done." He added that a "precarious security situation" remains throughout large parts of the country, and expressed concern over "growing restlessness among groups not directly party to the peace agreement and its power-sharing arrangement and among Opposition fighters awaiting reintegration into the Tajik army or demobilization" [S/1999/124, 2/8/99].

In response to a dire **humanitarian situation** in Tajikistan, in December 1998 the U.N. Office for Coordination of Humanitarian Affairs issued a consolidated appeal for over $24 million to help populations at risk within the country [IHA/674, 12/4/98]. As of early April 1999, only $600,000 had been pledged by donors [U.N. "Daily Highlights," 3/26/99]. Approximately 80 percent of all Tajiks live below the poverty line.

Uzbekistan, Kazakhstan

Regional instability finally caught up with Uzbekistan, previously considered to be "an island of stability in post-Soviet Central Asia" [*New York*

Times, 2/18/99]. Eight car bombs went off around the capital of Tashkent in what officials claim was an attempt to kill **the pro-Western President, Islam Karimov.** Some Uzbek officials blame Islamic fundamentalists trained in Tajikistan for the attacks. President Karimov enjoys wide-ranging Western support because of his anti-fundamentalist/anti-Moscow stance, but like most of his fellow Central Asian leaders, his **commitment to democratization** remains dubious. In a speech to parliament in May 1998, Karimov said of fundamentalists: "Such people must be shot in the head. If necessary, I'll shoot them myself if you lack the resolve" [*Christian Science Monitor*, 11/20/98]. To the relief of his Western supporters, Karimov has recently been sounding considerably more democratic, telling the Uzbek parliament that "we have to work out a programme of reforming political institutions which would protect human rights." Karimov also expressed his desire to join "international treaties on human rights protection," "re-consider the whole system of the organization of foreign trade," "liberal-ize the foreign exchange market," and "cut governmental controls over the private sector of the economy" [Reuters, 4/14/99].

Despite a miserable record on democratization, and a "pattern of harassment" against his few political opponents, **Kazakh President Nur-sultan Nazarbayev** was recently elected overwhelmingly to another seven-year term [*New York Times*, 12/6/98]. Given his seemingly bottomless oil reserves and a decidedly pro-Western/anti-Russian stance, Western lead-ers have been reluctant to pressure Nazarbayev to implement **promised democratic reforms.** Systemic graft remains a major problem, with a third to half of more than $1 billion in foreign "privatization bonuses" having simply disappeared over the last two years [ibid., 1/3/99]. In the words of one observer, "[the Kazakhs] have handed over their crown jewels— their oil fields. So they want to know why Washington makes a fuss when they cheat in their elections, rule as autocrats and appoint relatives . . . to senior government posts" [ibid.].

Kazakhstan is also beginning to deal with an **environmental disaster** that could affect a large part of its population. During the Cold War the Soviet Union conducted over 500 nuclear tests in Kazakhstan, many of them without safeguards. The United Nations is appealing for $40 million to deal with the aftermath of the tests [*Christian Science Monitor*, 2/5/99].

5. Cyprus
By Nick Birnback

The situation in Cyprus has not changed much over the past year, or the year before, or even the year before that. The Greek and Turkish Cypriots remain polarized, the border between the northern Turkish enclave and the rest of the island is still heavily militarized, and the latest round of

U.N.-sponsored negotiations—some involving such high-level Western diplomats as Cyrus Vance and Richard Holbrooke—have been stalled since summer 1997 [see *A Global Agenda: Issues* 153, pp. 32–33].

Ethnic Greeks and Turkish Cypriots have remained geographically and politically divided since Turkish military forces invaded the northern third of the island in 1974 following a short-lived Greek Cypriot coup supported by the military junta then in power in Athens. The Turkish side has yet to back off officially from its 1983 demand for recognition of a "Turkish Republic of Northern Cyprus," and over 35,000 Turkish troops are stationed in that area.

During 1998–99, the decades' old game of provocation and tit-for-tat "one-upmanship" continued unabated. A crisis was narrowly averted when the country's President, Greek Cypriot Glafcos Clerides, **cancelled plans to deploy a battery of Russian-made S-300 antiaircraft missiles**—a move the Turkish authorities indicated they would have resisted with force [*New York Times,* 2/19/99]. U.N. Secretary-General Kofi Annan commented that he was "very glad" over the decision not to station the weapons system on the island, calling this a "tangible, positive response" to international pressure [U.N. press release SG/SM/6854, 12/30/98]. The missiles are now being installed on the Greek island of Crete, and Greece is in the process of modernizing its air force [Reuters, 4/30/99]. The Turkish authorities have called these moves provocative as well [BBC "World News," 12/29/98 and 2/10/99]. In early May 1999, **Turkey claimed that Greek military aircraft had attempted to land in Cyprus**—an act, the Turks asserted, that showed "the Greek-Greek Cypriot front is determined to increase tension on the island" [Reuters, 5/6/99]. The Greek side rejected the claim, commenting that "tensions in Cyprus are caused by the continued occupation and the presence of 36,000 Turkish occupation forces and the continued violations of human rights by Turkey" [ibid., 5/7/99].

The **capture of Kurdish rebel leader Abdullah Ocalan** also served to ratchet up the level of political hostility between the sides. Ankara accused Athens of backing and training Ocalan's Kurdistan Workers party. "Greek politicians with their incredible heartlessness, pitilessness and irresponsibility have made Greece into a terrorist country," said the Turkish Foreign Minister, announcing that "Turkey will not talk with Greece about the Aegean, Cyprus or any other important problem" [ibid., 3/5/99]. Said the Greek Foreign Minister: "In the Ocalan issue Turkish propaganda is finding the opportunity it seeks to justify its wholly negative attitude and its hostile intent to Cyprus and Greece. Turkey knows well that Cyprus had not been involved in any way in the issue of the Kurd people" [ibid., 2/28/99].

Fulbright Program-sponsored workshops for Cypriot citizens in the summer and winter of 1998 offered a small ray of hope: They yielded a peace framework that was agreed to—at least on an unofficial level—by both sides [*Christian Science Monitor*, 2/19/99]. Follow-up meetings reportedly are being scheduled.

The **United Nations Peacekeeping Force in Cyprus (UNFICYP)**, 1,270 strong and now in its 35th year, continues to monitor the tenuous cease-fire and monitor the demilitarized "buffer zone" between the two parties.

In response to the Nicosia government's plan to deploy antiaircraft missiles, the U.N. Secretary-General had called on both parties "to avoid any actions which might increase tension, including by further expansion of military forces and armament" [U.N. press release SG/SM/6854, 12/30/98]. The Security Council addressed the matter in two resolutions [S/Res/1217, 12/22/98, and S/Res/1218, 12/22/98] stressing the importance of "the eventual demilitarization of the Republic of Cyprus." The first of these resolutions also extended the mandate of UNFICYP until June 30, 1999. That mandate has since been extended to December 15 [S/Res/1251, 6/21/99].

In the hope that there might be an opportunity to break the political impasse after Turkey held its elections in April 1999, European Union negotiators traveled to Cyprus for a new round of talks. In September 1998 the U.N. Secretary-General asked his Deputy Special Representative, Dame Ann Hercus of New Zealand, to begin **a series of on-island talks** with both sides—this with a view toward "reducing tension and promoting progress towards a just and lasting settlement" [S/1998/1166, 12/14/98]. (She is reportedly to be "named shortly" as the new Special Representative [Reuters, 5/10/99], replacing former Ecuadorean Foreign Minister Diego Cordovez, who resigned in April after two years in the post [U.N. press release SG/SM/6963, 4/22/99].) As part of this latest initiative, Dame Ann met with British Foreign Secretary Robin Cook and the Secretary-General to jump-start the stalled peace process [BBC "World News," 1/14/99]. U.S. Special Envoy to Cyprus Thomas Miller has also been involved in this latest initiative.

In early March 1999 the **United Nations closed its aid office for Turkish Cypriots** located in the southern coastal city of Limassol, where hundreds of Turkish Cypriots live among the mainly Greek Cypriot population. Despite a significant public relations campaign, only 11 visits had been made to the office since it opened in December 1996 [Reuters, 3/1/99].

6. Cambodia
By Frederick Z. Brown

Three issues dominated politics in Cambodia over the past year. One was decided on July 26, 1998, when, after a brief but bitter campaign, national parliamentary elections returned the CPP (Cambodian People's Party) to effective power, albeit through coalition with its rival, FUNCINPEC

(National Unified Front for an Independent, Neutral, Peaceful, and Co-operative Cambodia). Second was the nagging question of accountability for the crimes of the Khmer Rouge era, 1975–78, and the related issue of the continued impunity of the country's current political and military leaders with regard to widespread lawlessness and disregard of human rights. The third issue—the principal concern for the 90 percent of the Cambodian people trapped in abject poverty—was finding some way out of Cambodia's economic misery. Although the international financial institutions and bilateral donor countries were resuming their lending and development programs, the fundamental problems of Cambodia's social and economic reconstruction remained largely unaddressed, let alone resolved.

National Elections

On July 28, 1998, 90 percent of Cambodia's 5.4 million registered voters went to the polls. Thirty-one political parties offered candidates for 122 seats in the National Assembly, but in reality the election was a contest between Hun Sen's powerful CPP and two feuding opposition parties: Norodom Ranariddh's FUNCINPEC and the party of Sam Rainsy, a former cabinet officer in the pre-July 1997 coalition government. When the results were tallied, the CPP had won 64 seats with 41 percent of the popular vote; FUNCINPEC, 43 seats (31.7 percent of the vote); and the Sam Rainsy party, 15 seats (14.3 percent) [*Phnom Penh Post* and *Far Eastern Economic Review* for the period 7/30–8/15/98]. Five hundred foreign observers (in-country for only a few days) and 20,000 Cambodian election monitors watched the polling stations and agreed generally that election day was satisfactorily free of violations. The previous months' campaigning, however, was anything but fair, free, and open. The CPP's domination of government administrative posts in rural areas, virtual monopoly of the electronic media, and vastly greater financial resources gave it a clear advantage. Voter intimidation, including murders of opposition candidates and staff, was frequent. That the CPP, with all its advantages, won only 41 percent of the vote, was itself remarkable. The inability of FUNCINPEC and the Sam Rainsy party to unite in opposition to the CPP was a sad reminder of Cambodian politics' heritage of divisiveness.

Complaints by Ranariddh and Rainsy of vote-counting fraud and other electoral abuses continued in September and October. Street demonstrations were put down harshly as CPP police fired into the crowds of protesters. Rainsy was forced to take refuge in the U.N. Special Representative's office in Phnom Penh [*New York Times*, 9/8/98, and *Far Eastern Economic Review*, 9/10/98] and then fled to Thailand. Ranariddh and his parliamentary colleagues, fearing for their safety, also absented themselves from the country, leaving the National Assembly unable to act; and because the

CPP did not have a two-thirds majority in the Assembly, there was an **impasse over formation of a new government** throughout the fall.

Ranariddh, no doubt recalling his unhappy experience as co-Prime Minister with Hun Sen in the period 1993–97, refused for a time to join in a coalition with the CPP. In November, however, he flew back to Phnom Penh after receiving guarantees of safety. A compromise—including amnesty for key opposition civilian and military leaders—was signed on November 23. In early December the National Assembly approved (vote: 99–13) **a CPP-FUNCINPEC coalition, with Hun Sen as Prime Minister and Ranariddh as President of the Assembly** [*Far Eastern Economic Review*, 12/10/98].

The CPP received the most significant economic and military posts in the cabinet. The deal not only gave Hun Sen almost unchallenged domestic power but also earned him the international prestige of an elected, hence legitimate, ruler of Cambodia—an endorsement he had sought since his days as leader of the People's Republic of Kampuchea. Yet to be established was the role of the newly created Senate, how it would relate to the Assembly, and who would lead it [*Phnom Penh Post*, 11/27–12/11/98 and 3/5–18/99].

Accountability

As of the new year, concern over the election and its violent aftermath were overshadowed by **the death or surrender of the top leaders of the Khmer Rouge** and the consequent disintegration of their movement as an organized force. Pol Pot died, an apparent suicide, in April 1998, not long after he had ordered the execution of Khmer Rouge Defense Minister Son Senn and his family. Ieng Sary, considered one of Pol Pot's closest colleagues, had already defected to the Phnom Penh regime and was living tranquilly in Pailin along the Thai border. On December 25, 1998 (the 20th anniversary of Vietnam's invasion of Cambodia), two of the three remaining senior Khmer Rouge leaders, ideologist Nuon Chea and former Democratic Kampuchea Foreign Minister Khieu Samphan, surrendered—and for their pains were treated to vacations on a Sihanoukville beach and a grand tour of Siem Reap's glorious Angkorean complex [*New York Times*, 1/5/99, and *Washington Post*, 1/4/99]. The formal surrender of the Khmer Rouge took place on December 4, when Chief of Staff Khem Nguon handed over to the government the remaining military units and their families [*Phnom Penh Post*, 12/11–24/98]. With the March 1999 capture of Ta Mok, the last Khmer Rouge military commander, the entire senior leadership of the organization was either dead or in the hands of the Phnom Penh regime they had fought for 20 years.

And that was the rub. Accountability for the **crimes of the Khmer Rouge during their 45 months in power**—April 17, 1975, through January 7, 1979—raised **complex personal, temporal, and jurisdictional issues.** Should accountability be confined to top leadership already dead or in custody, or should mid-level officials or even lower-level cadres be placed in the dock to answer for their deeds? With the civilian and military ranks of the government of Prime Minister Hun Sen staffed in large part by former Khmer Rouge, this was an explosive political question. So was the question of whether accountability should be limited to the period of actual rule or expanded to include the 1980s, when the Khmer Rouge were the military cutting edge of the joint ASEAN, Chinese, and American effort to force a compromise political settlement of the Cambodia conflict. That, too, would obviously rake up some disturbing history for U.N. Security Council members during the civil war period.

What *is* the responsibility of the United Nations, indeed of the international community more broadly construed, in bringing to account those responsible for the horrendous events in Cambodia of that period? Should legal proceedings take place in the country or outside it? Should the composition of the tribunal be uniquely Cambodian or include international jurists to ensure objectivity?

A consensus within the international community favored limiting accountability to 1975–79, but both in Cambodia and within the international community there were conflicting views on a U.N. war crimes tribunal. In some quarters there were fears that putting Khmer Rouge leaders on trial would revive the anguish of the past and might even rekindle a civil war. Prime Minister **Hun Sen's views** on this question oscillated over the year, but some statements indicated that his government would not agree to a tribunal in which an international presence would be dominant [*New York Times*, 1/22/99]. Others, including the United States, have argued strongly that the crimes of the Khmer Rouge constitute genocide and merit legal adjudication by an international tribunal under the United Nations.

In response to a resolution of the General Assembly noting the Cambodian government's desire "for assistance in responding to past serious violations of Cambodian and international law by the Khmer Rouge" [A/Res/53/145], the U.N. Secretary-General appointed a three-member **Group of Experts.** After visiting Cambodia in November 1998, it concluded that

> [T]he evidence gathered to date testifies to the commission of serious crimes under international and Cambodian law, and that sufficient physical and witness evidence exists to justify legal proceedings against the Khmer Rouge leaders for those crimes, . . . [including] crimes against humanity, genocide, war crimes, forced labor, torture and crimes against internationally protected persons, as well as crimes under Cambodia law. [A/53/850]

The Group's report analyzed **legal options for bringing Khmer Rouge leaders to justice:**

- a tribunal established under Cambodian law
- an ad hoc international tribunal established by the U.N. Security Council or General Assembly
- a Cambodian tribunal under U.N. administration
- an international tribunal established by a multilateral treaty
- trials by and in a state other than Cambodia [ibid.]

In its **Summary of Principal Recommendations,** the Group came down in favor of an ad hoc U.N. international tribunal whose independent prosecutor would limit his/her investigations to "those persons most responsible for the most serious violations of international human rights law," and it advised that the investigations, indictments, and trials "should take into account the twin goals of individual accountability and national reconciliation in Cambodia" [ibid.; and *Phnom Penh Post* for 3/5–18, 3/19–4/1, 4/2–12, and 4/30–5/13/99].

Secretary-General Annan supported the idea of an international tribunal but said that the success of such a body would depend on cooperation of the Cambodian government [Reuters in *New York Times*, 3/18/99]. The European Parliament, in a resolution passed May 17, 1999, condemned "all attempts by the Cambodian government to prevent the constitution of an international ad hoc tribune by the UN" [Camnews, 5/17/99].

By mid-July 1999 the Cambodian government had modified its position and agreed to the presence of foreign prosecutors and foreign judges on a mixed tribunal to try the former Khmer Rouge leadership. It also agreed to include foreign legal advisors in the process of drawing up procedures for the trial. Although China remained opposed in principle to a non-Cambodian element in the tribunal, Cambodian Foreign Minister Hor Namhong, during an official visit to Beijing, said that China considered the matter an internal Cambodian affair and would therefore respect Cambodia's decision to invite foreign judges and prosecutors [Reuters Phnom Penh, 7/12/99]. Still undecided was the basic question of how, when, and under whose auspices the tribunal would be constituted.

International Development Assistance; ASEAN Membership

At the opening of the 54th U.N. General Assembly, Cambodia remained **one of the globe's poorest countries** and had some of the worst human-development indicators in all of Asia [*Far Eastern Economic Review Asia 1999 Yearbook*]. With the formation of a coalition government, the international community was inclined to resume multilateral and bilateral economic assistance programs. On February 25, 1999, the Consultative Group of Donors, chaired by the World Bank, met in Tokyo and pledged $470 million in aid over the next year on condition that the government follow through on promised reforms—specifically, greater financial transparency and accountability, steps toward military demobilization, better forestry management, and respect for the rule of law. The government agreed to a process of quarterly aid review meetings with Consultative Group members to ensure it met these conditions [*Phnom Penh Post*, 2/19–3/4, 3/5–19/99].

In May an International Monetary Fund team visited the capital to review budget and fiscal discipline and forestry management and to discuss resumption of lending. Back in July 1997, the IMF had suspended its $120 million three-year support programs to Cambodia—with only half of the loans disbursed—because of the coup that ousted then-First Prime Minister Ranariddh [Reuters, 5/16/99].

In another positive development, **Cambodia was officially admitted to the Association of Southeast Asian Nations,** making good on ASEAN's pledge to incorporate all ten countries of Southeast Asia into one regional organization [*New York Times*, 4/30/99; and *Phnom Penh Post*, 4/30–5/13/99]. This move was in recognition of the CPP's decision to allow an opposition political party (FUNCINPEC but not the Sam Rainsy party) back into the government, and it strengthened the perception of Prime Minister Hun Sen as the legitimate leader of Cambodia.

7. The Middle East
By Gordon Goldstein

Rolf Ekeus—the deft, tenacious, and highly effective past Chairman of the **U.N. Special Commission** (UNSCOM)—stepped down from his post in June 1997. Upon leaving the United Nations to serve as Sweden's Ambassador to the United States, he reflected on the increasing difficulty of conducting disarmament inspections in Iraq, his mission since the beginning of the decade. Addressing the annual international gathering of nonproliferation experts sponsored by the Carnegie Endowment in Washington, D.C., Ekeus allowed himself a candid moment of regret before a group of colleagues. "We are nothing in Baghdad," he said. "We are at their complete mercy. They can just stop our work at any time." With his parting remarks Ekeus had foreshadowed the demise of a unique experiment in multilateral arms control.

In its seven-and-a-half years of operation, UNSCOM was an aggressive instrument for realizing the Security Council's mandate to **verify that Iraq no longer possessed weapons of mass destruction.** Indeed, it proved too aggressive an extension of the Council's will, and in the end it was blown apart by disparate centrifugal forces. The most powerful threat to the Special Commission was a systematic pattern of obfuscation and noncompliance by Iraq, but Baghdad's intransigence alone does not explain UNSCOM's decline.

One of the other factors was the widening split in the Security Council between permanent members. The United States and Britain insisted on strict adherence to all Council resolutions; indeed, the American President and the Secretary of State openly called for the overthrow of Saddam Hussein. Russia, France, and China each favored a lifting of sanctions and a clean bill of health for Iraqi weapons programs. Their attacks on UNSCOM became increasingly personal, focusing on the hard-nosed leadership style of its Australian Chairman, Ambassador Richard Butler, the successor to Ambassador Ekeus.

Compounding the disunity that was paralyzing the Council, and seeming to preclude the possibility that UNSCOM inspectors would resume their work, were the American and British air strikes against Iraq in December 1998—an act more of punishment than of coercion. But what sealed the fate of the Special Commission, and perhaps rendered it impossible to attempt anything so ambitious again in the future, was the charge that UNSCOM had engaged in inappropriate intelligence-sharing with the United States to accomplish its mission. Like all worthy spy stories, this one ultimately involved a deception within a deception. But by the time of its surprise revelation, UNSCOM was effectively dead, and the final twist in the plot was more like a coda than a climax to a remarkable chapter in U.N. history.

Flashback

In February 1998 the U.N. Secretary-General narrowly averted an American military strike on Iraq through an 11th-hour diplomatic initiative. Kofi Annan's efforts resulted in a putatively solemn Iraqi promise to cooperate with UNSCOM. That pledge, like so many previous Iraqi promises, was worth less than the paper on which the signature of Saddam Hussein's government appeared. On August 5, 1998, Iraq suspended all intrusive arms inspections. Diplomats from the permanent member states, weary of another showdown with Baghdad, mulled over their options, and the Security Council settled into another period of suspended animation until a common denominator of collective agreement could be found.

In early September the Council voted unanimously to deny Iraq a lifting of sanctions until President Hussein complied completely with UNSCOM's inspections and monitoring. Resolution 1194 called Iraq's decision not to cooperate with UNSCOM and the International Atomic Energy Agency (IAEA) a "totally unacceptable contravention of its obligations." It *did* call for a complete review of Iraqi relations with the United Nations—one of Baghdad's key aims—but not until UNSCOM and the IAEA were allowed to continue their work. China was the last holdout but eventually joined the Council's consensus [*New York Times*, 9/9/98].

As the United States tried to create a unified front in the Council, both the Secretary of State and the Chairman of the U.N. Special Commission deflected attacks from an unlikely source—**Scott Ritter, a former Marine Intelligence officer and UNSCOM weapons specialist**—who accused the two of conspiring to scuttle intrusive and potentially controversial UNSCOM inspections. In testimony on Capitol Hill, Ritter charged that on at least seven different occasions since November 1997, UNSCOM was the target of "interference and manipulation, usually coming from the highest levels of the Administration's national security team."

Secretary of State Madeleine Albright dismissed Ritter's accusations. "The critics are sincere," she said. "But they are sincerely wrong when they blame America for the world's failure to uncover the full truth about Iraq's weapons of mass destruction." Albright called the United States "by far the strongest international backer of UNSCOM" and the Security Council member most committed to "break through the smoke screen of lies and deceptions put out by the Iraqi regime." The UNSCOM Chairman, for his part, disputed Ritter's claim that the agency canceled investigations as a direct result of pressure from the Secretary of State. "Unfortunately," said Butler, "Scott Ritter's chronology of events is not accurate" [ibid.].

Butler's predecessor, Rolf Ekeus, praised Ritter's record as an inspector but cautioned that his charges were based on incomplete information. "I don't want to denigrate him at all," said Ekeus. "But he's not in a position to know all of the considerations that go into decision-making on the commission." In respect to Albright, Ekeus explained, "I had always found her to be a strong supporter of UNSCOM" [ibid., 9/10/98].

Putting aside the political trouble Ritter may have stirred up, his substantive claims about Iraqi weapons development were extremely serious. At a closed-door meeting of the Washington Institute for Near East Policy he said that Baghdad was hiding three "technologically complete" nuclear bombs that lacked only the fissile material to make them operational. Ritter was quoted as saying that the U.N. inspectors knew where the three nuclear devices were hidden and had information on how they were concealed and which officers were guarding them, but had not received orders to inspect the site [ibid.].

Some in Congress applauded Ritter's disclosures. "I have to tell you, I think he's an American hero," said Senator Sam Brownback, Republican of Kansas and Chairman of the Senate subcommittee on Near East policy. "Here's a stand-up guy that's out doing his job." Assistant Secretary of State Martin Indyk acknowledged **the truth of at least a portion of Ritter's testimony.** "If the allegation is that we sought to influence the pace of UNSCOM inspections, we did," said Indyk. "If the allegation is that we have undermined the effectiveness and independence of UNSCOM, the answer is, we have not" [*Washington Post*, 9/10/98].

In late October 1998 the spotlight was trained again on the question of Iraq's compliance with UNSCOM. An international panel of experts concluded that tests on missile fragments did not support **Iraq's denials that it loaded deadly VX nerve gas** into warheads prior to the 1991 Persian Gulf War. The test results indicated that Iraq was continuing to develop weapons of mass destruction despite sanctions and the continuing regime of UNSCOM inspections. The experts' report to the Security Council reviewed the results provided by a U.S. Army laboratory and confirmed the presence of VX on some fragments. The report was prepared by 17 scientists from seven countries who met at the request of the U.N. Special Commission to independently verify the results of the American tests [ibid., 10/27/98].

The results of those tests came at an inopportune moment for Russia and France, the permanent members of the Council most determined to offer favorable terms for the "comprehensive review" of Iraqi compliance with U.N. demands. On October 31 the Council presented its guidelines for that review in a letter to the Secretary-General. Washington, turning back an effort favorable to Iraq that would have included a promise to lift sanctions once it could be certified that Iraq no longer possessed weapons of mass destruction, had managed to insert language that tied the lifting of the sanctions not only to Iraq's disarmament but also to the return of Kuwaiti prisoners and property and the end of mistreatment of Kurdish and Shiite populations [ibid., 10/31/98].

The United States, supported by Britain, its ally in the Council, had crafted a **hard-line standard of compliance for Iraq,** which promptly rejected it. Iraq now banned UNSCOM from visiting sites that had already been inspected and were being monitored. After the Baghdad government stated that it would not back down on its ban of U.N. weapons inspections, the Council condemned the decision as a "flagrant violation" of Council resolutions and of the agreement reached the previous February with the Secretary-General [*Financial Times*, 11/2/98]. In Resolution 1205, passed on November 5, 1998, the Council demanded that "Iraq rescind immediately and unconditionally" its decisions in October and August to suspend cooperation with the Special Commission.

The Council's repeated expressions of diplomatic outrage did not prompt a quick resumption of Iraqi cooperation with UNSCOM. As more **American soldiers and warplanes were deployed to the Persian Gulf,** supplementing a force of 23,500 already there, President Bill Clinton warned that the United States was "prepared to act" militarily if Saddam Hussein did not resume cooperation with UNSCOM. Sergei Lavrov, the Russian envoy to the United Nations, warned that "the use of force is fraught with very serious consequences, not only for the UN's ability to continue to work inside Iraq but also for the stability of the region and for the Middle East in general." **The United Nations hastily withdrew**

practically all its staff, including weapons inspectors, from Baghdad [*Baltimore Sun*, 11/12/98].

In a letter delivered to the Secretary-General on November 14, Iraq tried to explain its refusal to cooperate: "The goal sought by Iraq from its decisions of August 5 and October 31 was not to sever the relationship with UNSCOM and the IAEA and to cease the implementation of its obligations. . . . The objective of Iraq is to end the suffering of its embargoed people."

In an apparent effort to forestall U.S. air strikes, **Iraq announced on November 17 that it would resume cooperation with the Special Commission.** The first order of business for U.N. weapons inspectors returning to Baghdad was to pry off the metal plates they had sealed onto their office doors a week earlier before withdrawing in anticipation of American reprisal attacks. Among the items still on the agenda for UNSCOM as it resumed its work were the remnants of seven indigenously produced missiles and 30 warheads Iraq claimed to have destroyed; more than 500 mustard gas shells; an adequate accounting of Iraq's biological weapons program, including the status of growth media; and what Scott Ritter claimed were three implosion-type nuclear devices lacking only the fissionable core of highly enriched uranium [*Christian Science Monitor*, 11/18/98].

Iraq's promise of cooperation collapsed almost immediately. Less than a week after Iraq averted American air strikes with its pledge of compliance, the government in Baghdad defied a request for documents relating to its prohibited weapons programs. The Iraqi foreign ministry issued a statement calling the request "provocative rather than professional" [*Washington Post*, 11/21/98].

The prompt but predictable **decision by Iraq to refuse further inspections** reinforced an already gloomy prognosis for UNSCOM's future. "The whole range of UNSCOM's authority has been eroded," said a long-serving member of the panel's leadership. "There is nothing we can do to return to the effectiveness we had in 1995 and 1996." Another inspector observed: "Prudent and smart Iraqi planners, and they have plenty of those, will have taken every precaution. Wherever we go, we'll find an empty room, and they'll hold the door open for us" [ibid., 11/22/98]. "For all we know," said another UNSCOM official, "there are refrigerated trucks traveling the country full of anthrax, to evade the inspectors. We know they are hiding things" [*Independent*, 11/22/98].

Richard Butler briefed the Security Council about Iraq's refusal to turn over documents, but the Council took no action other than to release a statement reiterating its "full support" for the inspectors. Reflecting the Council's disunity on the question of Iraq and UNSCOM, British Ambassador Jeremy Greenstock said, "This is a continuing matter and we reached no definite conclusions this evening" [*Washington Post*, 11/25/98].

In early December 1998, Chairman Butler announced that his teams would conduct **surprise inspections** within hours at Iraqi sites that might contain prohibited weapons, and that UNSCOM had completed testing of Iraqi compliance in four of five areas that the Commission was examining: access to documents, monitoring of former weapons sites, interviews with persons knowledgeable about the programs, and visits to sites of potential military use [ibid., 12/8/98]. Iraq blocked the inspectors, denying the U.N. team access to the headquarters of the ruling Baath party in Baghdad [ibid., 12/10/98].

The consistency of American threats, coupled with a string of broken Iraqi promises, now seemed to make a military strike inevitable. On December 16, **President Clinton ordered air attacks on Baghdad** in conjunction with Britain. "Their purpose is to protect the national interest of the United States and indeed the interests of people throughout the Middle East and around the world," Clinton said. "Saddam Hussein must not be allowed to threaten his neighbors or the world with nuclear arms, poison gas or biological weapons" [*New York Times*, 12/17/98].

The U.S. decision to launch air strikes was preceded by Chairman Butler's submission of a **report cataloguing the myriad instances of Iraq's failure to cooperate** with the Special Commission. That report was derided by the Russian and Chinese U.N. ambassadors, who characterized it as a trigger for American air strikes. Ambassador Lavrov charged that the crisis with Iraq had been "created artificially by the irresponsible acts of Richard Butler." Qin Huasun, the Chinese envoy, said Butler had played a "dishonorable role" in the confrontation with Iraq. Chairman Butler was defended, however, by British Foreign Secretary Robin Cook. "Baghdad pumps out propaganda against Mr. Butler all the time," he said. "In truth the only real criticism they have is that he tried to do his job only too well" [*Guardian*, 12/18/98].

President Clinton announced **a halt to the bombing after four nights of furious air strikes.** "I am confident," he said, "that we have achieved our mission." The joint U.S.-British effort had "significantly damaged Iraq's military capabilities and its ability to produce weapons of mass destruction" [*Washington Post*, 12/20/98]. The first casualty of the attacks, however, seemed to be the political future of the U.N. Special Commission. "UNSCOM as we've known it for seven and a half years is history," said David Kay, a former inspector. Russia, inclined to shoot the proverbial messenger of bad news, called for the resignation of Chairman Butler [*USA Today*, 12/21/98]. Iraq's Deputy Prime Minister announced that four days of bombing had left 62 soldiers dead and 180 wounded. UNSCOM inspectors, promised Aziz, would never be allowed to return to Iraq. "The moment the United States and Britain sent missiles at Iraq they killed UNSCOM," he said. "It is their casualty" [*Toronto Star*, 12/22/98].

As 1998 drew to a close, Secretary-General Annan was reported to have formed a **high-level task force to study ways of supplanting the**

U.N. weapons inspection unit in Iraq with a less aggressive arms control entity. The committee, composed of Annan's principal advisors and U.N. arms control expert Jayantha Dhanapala, was instructed to plan for the exit of Chairman Butler. According to the *Boston Globe*'s account [12/22/98], "Annan, who appointed Butler to his job but does not have the authority to fire him, will not be sad to see him go."

Foreign Intelligence

The coup de grace for both UNSCOM and its chairman was delivered early in 1999. An article in the *Washington Post* [1/6/99], relying on information leaked by unnamed "confidants" of Kofi Annan, charged the Special Commission with inappropriate **intelligence-sharing with the United States.** "While acknowledging that the eavesdropping aimed in part to help the inspectors hunt down forbidden weapons, or the means to conceal them," wrote the *Post*, "the Secretary General's confidants said Annan is convinced that Washington used the operation to penetrate the security apparatus protecting Iraqi President Saddam Hussein." What use was the Secretary-General expected to make of this information? Said the article:

> By widening the circle in which he makes known his concerns about UNSCOM's past, Annan is trying, some advisers acknowledged, to place pressure on executive chairman Richard Butler to resign in favor of a successor who might win the consent of Iraq and its defenders on the Security Council. His expressions of concern could also be aimed at protecting him against any future charges that he condoned eavesdropping conducted at least nominally under his authority.

Other news accounts provided additional details about UNSCOM and U.S. intelligence collaboration. The Special Commission had been dependent on intelligence from member states since 1992, when it sought help for tracking Saddam's chemical and biological weapons activities. The United States Air Force offered the use of a U-2 spy plane and crew and highly detailed photos from its KH-12 spy satellites orbiting above Iraq. **More than 40 other nations contributed information,** including France, Britain, and Russia, which sent a senior KGB officer who had previously served in New York City.

The need for foreign intelligence to support UNSCOM's mission was underscored in 1995, when, in a surprising turn of events, Saddam's brother-in-law, Lieutenant General Hussein Kamel al-Majid, defected to Jordan and described for his debriefers **Saddam's elaborate concealment system.** It was operated, Kamel told the CIA, by the Special Republican Guard and the Special Security Organization, the same contingents that serve as Saddam's personal and palace guards.

The inspectors decided they needed scanners and recorders that would let them listen in on the security forces as they shuttled weaponry, components, documents, technical manuals, and chemical and biological materials around Iraq. Scott Ritter, the former Marine and UNSCOM inspector, reportedly persuaded the Mossad, the Israeli intelligence agency, to provide devices to tap into the radio and cell-phone frequencies used by the Iraqi security agents.

At first the inspectors carried the scanners around the country in backpacks. By the end of 1997, however, Butler and his colleagues were worried that a surprise search of UNSCOM inspectors would reveal the listening equipment. The solution was for agents of the Defense Intelligence Agency to slip into Iraq as UNSCOM operatives and install miniaturized monitors in everyday objects, such as lamps, phones, signposts, building gutters, and commercial electric equipment. The devices were fueled by micro-batteries, some as small as fingernail clippings [*Time*, 1/18/99].

Editorial opinion in the most influential U.S. newspapers was supportive of Butler's efforts to penetrate the Iraqi system for concealing his arsenal of chemical, biological, and nuclear weapons. "U.N. Secretary General Kofi Annan and his team have turned on Ambassador Richard Butler . . . with pernicious tactics," declared the *Washington Post* [1/7/99], adding:

> The principal beneficiary of their gutless ploy will be Saddam Hussein. . . . It's long been known that U.N. arms inspectors cooperated with, and depended on, intelligence from the United States and other member countries. Given Saddam Hussein's determination to hide his proscribed nuclear, biological and chemical weapons capabilities UNSCOM had no choice. But both Ambassador Butler, an Australian, and his predecessor, Swedish diplomat Rolf Ekeus, have flatly denied collecting intelligence aimed at undermining or pinpointing the location of Saddam Hussein himself. If Mr. Annan or his inner circle nonetheless had reason to suspect the cooperation had crossed some line of propriety, they could have raised their concerns in private. Instead they chose to provide public support for Saddam Hussein's long-standing harangues against the U.N. inspectors as "Zionist" or American agents.

According to the *New York Times* [1/10/99]:

> The most sensitive American operation began last March, when an American spy serving as a U.N. inspector traveled to Baghdad to install especially advanced listening equipment. If this operation was authorized by the U.N. team, and employed for its benefit, as American officials say it was, the effort was a perfectly reasonable response to Iraq's attempts to thwart the inspectors. . . . Richard Butler, who has done a commendable job as the chief U.N. inspector, should not be sacrificed nor should his team be dismantled. Kofi Annan, the Secretary General,

must resist the notion that Washington and Mr. Butler somehow conspired to wrong Iraq.

The *Christian Science Monitor* [1/13/99] observed:

The cooperation between UNSCOM and US intelligence was not surprising, given their convergent goals. The US, clearly, could give weapons inspectors capabilities they couldn't get elsewhere. Other countries, too, contributed personnel and intelligence know-how. . . . UN inspectors had to use every resource available to counter Saddam's determination to thwart their work.

As the UNSCOM spy story imploded, destabilizing and dismantling a variety of diplomatic relationships, the Security Council scrambled to find some agreement on the **future of the sanctions and inspection regime imposed upon Iraq.** France proposed ending the embargo on Iraqi oil sales and replacing inspections with a new system that would abandon the search for existing weapons of mass destruction and focus instead on preventing the acquisition of such weapons in the future. Russia presented a plan similar to the French proposal. China soon joined the two other permanent Security Council members in calling both for an end to the oil embargo and for the replacement of UNSCOM with a less intrusive monitoring body.

According to one news account,

While silent in public, UNSCOM's leaders are fuming in conversations with supporters and friends at the widespread tolerance they perceive for Iraq's declaration that disarmament is complete and that UNSCOM may never return. "What are these guys doing?" one of them asked recently, referring to the Security Council. "Don't they understand that the authority of the Security Council is at stake? . . . Where is there a comparable case in which a member state so flagrantly" defied the Council? [*Washington Post,* 1/16/99]

The Secretary-General's relationship with the Clinton administration was also complicated by the disclosures to the news media. "This has done the Secretary-General an enormous amount of damage," said a senior official in Washington [ibid., 1/28/99].

After calculating that few other viable options existed, the United States threw its support behind a Canadian plan to convene **three expert panels to review all aspects of Iraq's relations with the United Nations.** The exercise appeared to be a variation on the comprehensive review first proposed in 1998—and resisted by the United States—as a reward to Iraq for cooperating with UNSCOM inspectors. Now it was the minimal course of action the Council could agree on following the December air strikes [*New York Times,* 1/28/99].

Just as the United States indicated its support for the three-part comprehensive review of the Iraq case—breaking the Security Council's prolonged internal stalemate—Secretary of State Albright conducted a swing through Arab capitals to promote a new Clinton administration policy dubbed "containment plus regime change." Albright sought to assure American friends and allies in the region that the United States was in fact serious in its determination to overthrow Saddam Hussein [*Washington Post*, 1/28/98].

Albright's zeal for **stimulating a coup in Iraq** was not shared by General Anthony Zinni, the commander of American forces in the Persian Gulf. Testifying before the Senate Armed Services Committee, the Marine Corps commander predicted that an overthrow "would be very difficult, and I think if not done properly, could be very dangerous" [*New York Times*, 1/28/99]. These reservations were reinforced in discussions between U.S. Assistant Secretary of State Martin Indyk and officials from Bahrain, Kuwait, Oman, Qatar, and the United Arab Emirates. Foreign officials told the U.S. envoy that, while most Arab governments would welcome Hussein's overthrow, there was trepidation about any regime change resulting from the active intervention of the United States, which had designated seven Iraqi opposition groups as eligible to receive some of the $97 million in military assistance authorized under the 1998 Iraq Liberation Act [*Financial Times*, 2/4/99].

In January 1999, **Iraqi planes and missiles began targeting U.S. and British planes,** and the two allies responded with attacks of their own against Iraqi aircraft and antiaircraft sites on the ground. "Saddam's reason for continuing this deadly game is simple," concluded one report. "He's hoping to down an American plane and capture an American pilot he can parade on television for propaganda purposes, and as leverage in getting economic sanctions lifted" [*Wall Street Journal*, 2/17/99]. The skirmishes continued well into February. In three separate incidents, U.S. and British warplanes struck targets in southern and northern Iraq, hitting communications centers, missile sites, and weapons depots in a wide swath of territory within the no-flight zones [*New York Times*, 2/23/99].

Back in New York, the long-delayed **Security Council review of the U.N.'s effort to disarm Iraq** got under way. Celso Amorim, a former Brazilian foreign minister who assembled and chaired the panel, excluded Richard Butler, the UNSCOM Chairman, but allowed the participation of Charles Duelfer, Butler's American deputy [*Financial Times*, 2/24/99].

The review panel was furnished with a **controversial 279-page report** that UNSCOM had delivered to the Security Council in January detailing large amounts of unaccounted-for Iraqi chemical, biological, and weapons components. The report, which French and Russian diplomats attempted unsuccessfully to restrict, described in explicit detail **Iraqi efforts to conceal proscribed weapons,** and estimated the number and type of weapons and material for which Iraq has not provided sufficient proof of destruction and might be concealing. Iraqi declarations about the destruction of 15 biological weapons warheads, it noted, "conflicted with physical evidence collected at the declared location of their unilateral destruction" [*Janes Defence Weekly*, 3/10/99].

On March 2, 1999, another media bombshell detonated, this one adding a new twist to the tale of UNSCOM espionage. In the latest revelation, the *Washington Post* described a deception within a deception, claiming that **U.S. intelligence services had penetrated elements of the UNSCOM operation** without the knowledge of its two chairmen, Rolf Ekeus and Richard Butler, and that UNSCOM did not authorize or benefit from the channel of U.S. surveillance. The unauthorized rigging by the United States of UNSCOM equipment and office space, the *Post* reported, was for the purpose of intercepting a high volume of ordinary Iraqi military communications. Those communications, carried between microwave towers and linking Iraqi commanders and infantry and armed forces in the field, were of considerable value to American military planners but generally unrelated to UNSCOM's special weapons mandate.

Pioneered in May 1993, **UNSCOM's remote monitoring system** grew over the years to encompass more than 300 arms installations and research facilities in Iraq. For the first three years of operation the video images and logs of electrical power use were recorded on magnetic tape at the remote sites. Inspectors based in Baghdad drove out periodically to collect the tapes.

In March 1996, with Iraq's consent, UNSCOM began transmitting images from the cameras back to Baghdad using radio signals. The signals were boosted by relays, known as repeater stations, arrayed along the paths from the camera sites to Baghdad. The new system gave UNSCOM inspectors a view of distant facilities in "near real time"—a significant improvement. But unknown to UNSCOM, the U.S. signals and sensor technicians who installed and maintained the system were intelligence operatives, and the repeater stations they built had a covert capability. Hidden in their structure were antennas capable of intercepting microwave transmissions.

The first intelligence system was known to UNSCOM. That channel, code-named "Shake the Tree," used commercial scanners to intercept low-powered VHF radio transmissions used by Iraq in its concealment efforts. The second system, however, was not disclosed to UNSCOM's leaders, whether to Ekeus or Butler. But it *was* disclosed to their American deputy, reported the *Washington Post* [3/2/99]. "The CIA notified Charles Duelfer," the *Post* said, "to help ensure that UNSCOM's headquarters staff did not interfere with the operation."

According to this account, Butler was distressed to learn of the allegations, and privately expressed his frustrations to colleagues. "If this stuff turns out to be true, then Rolf Ekeus and I have been played for suckers, haven't we?" he was quoted as saying. Butler, an arms control expert who wrote his postgraduate dissertation on nonproliferation, is also reported as saying: "I've spent a lifetime of helping build and defend the nonproliferation regimes. Piggybacking in this manner can only serve the interests of those who reject meaningful efforts at arms control." Asked what he knew about the allegations, Butler told reporters: "My answer couldn't be simpler: nothing" [ibid.].

In the spring of 1999, when UNSCOM—and the Security Council consensus that once supported its efforts—were in tatters, there was little that the paramount U.N. body could agree upon in respect to Iraq's future. On May 21 the Security Council voted to extend the **"oil for food"** **program** for a 180-day period to produce up to $5.26 billion worth of petroleum products [S/Res/1242, 5/21/99]. The sanctions regime against Iraq continues today—but UNSCOM monitoring does not.

The future of sanctions and monitoring in Iraq may be unclear, but some of the consequences of a divided Security Council are obvious. Over the past year, for example, both factions of permanent members have failed to realize key objectives. France, Russia, and China may have seen the collapse of UNSCOM and the departure of its Chairman (who indicated his intention to step down in June 1999), but the sanctions regime still stands, and there are no signs that Saddam Hussein will enjoy the benefits of its ending any time soon. The United States and Britain, for their part, have maintained the embargo, and that pressure is significant. So is the effect of sanctions on the size and equipment of Iraq's armed forces: The strict controls on Iraqi oil sales, by some estimates, have cost Iraq $120 billion in lost revenue; to restore and sustain its military at pre–Gulf War levels, Baghdad would have had to spend $48 billion [*Washington Post*, 11/15/98]. But even with Saddam Hussein's inability to reconstitute his conventional forces, the end of UNSCOM means that unless and until a new system of effective monitoring is implemented, he has a free hand to accelerate his development of nuclear, chemical, and biological weapons. No nation's interest is advanced by this outcome. Indeed, it is the very danger UNSCOM was designed to prevent.

Additional Developments

The General Assembly, taking up the enduring **Arab-Israeli conflict,** reiterated its determination that Israeli rule in "the Holy City of Jerusalem" is "illegal and therefore null and void and has no validity whatsoever" [A/Res/53/37], similarly dismissed Israeli claims to the Golan Heights [A/Res/53/38], and "demand[ed] complete cessation of . . . all Israeli settlement activities in the occupied Palestinian territory, including Jerusalem, and in the occupied Syrian Golan" [A/Res/53/55]. It went on to address the work of the Committee on the Exercise of the Inalienable Rights of the Palestinian People [A/Res/53/39], the Division for Palestinian Rights of the

Secretariat [A/Res/53/40], the Special Information Programme on the question of Palestine of the Department of Public Information [A/Res/53/41], the Special Committee to Investigate Israeli Practices Affecting the Human Rights of the Palestinian People [A/Res/53/53 and 53/54], and other bodies. Noting with satisfaction "the successful holding of the first Palestinian general elections," the Assembly spoke of the necessity for "commitment to the principle of land for peace and the implementation of Security Council resolutions 242 (1967) and 338 (1973)" as the basis of the Middle East peace process. Another resolution reaffirmed the right of anyone displaced by hostilities since June 1967 to return to their homes in territories occupied by Israel [A/Res/53/48]; yet another reaffirmed "that Palestine Arab refugees are entitled to their property and to the income derived therefrom" [A/Res/53/51]; and a third called for the establishment of the University of Jerusalem "Al-Quds" for the refugees [A/Res/53/52]. A subsequent resolution supported the right of the Palestinian people to self-determination [A/Res/53/136]. Additional resolutions dealt with assistance to Palestine refugees. The General Assembly also passed measures calling for the respect of human rights in **Iraq** [A/Res/53/157] and in **Iran** [A/Res/53/158].

In January 1999 the Security Council extended until July 31 the mandate of the **United Nations Interim Force in Lebanon** (UNIFIL; established 1978) [S/Res/1223]. The mandate of the **United Nations Disengagement Observer Force** (UNDOF; established after the Arab-Israeli war of 1973) was renewed in November 1998 [S/Res/1211] and given another six-month lease in May 1999 [S/Res/1243].

8. The Former Yugoslavia
By Gordon Goldstein

In the spring of 1998, roughly a year before Kosovo became the epicenter of perhaps the most convulsive global crisis since the Gulf War, a newspaper dispatch from the capital city of Pristina captured the ominous sense of inevitability that would plunge the Yugoslav province into a maelstrom of violence. "At noon a convoy of a dozen cars, carrying men with faces painted black and red, wound its way through the streets of this city. The automatic assault rifles cradled in their arms poked through the windows as stunned onlookers gawked. 'This is a warning that if we continue to ask for independence, we will die,' said a 37-year-old woman who watched the cars pass and asked to remain unidentified. 'The only things the Serbs offer us now is terror.'" A European diplomat similarly anticipated disaster. "The situation, as we saw in Bosnia at the start of the war, has deteriorated so rapidly that there is little, short of outside intervention, that will stop a war. Kosovo is lost" [*New York Times*, 4/29/98].

By the spring of 1999, Kosovo was indeed lost to the horror of war.

Ultimately, however, it was reclaimed—no longer as a Serbian territory but as a quasi-protectorate of NATO's military machine and the civilian administration of the United Nations. The trajectory of that narrative was fairly remarkable, revealing varied outcomes not necessarily consistent with conventional wisdom at century's end: NATO's surprising cohesion in its first sustained conflict; the leadership of the United States in prosecuting and prevailing in an immaculate war of zero NATO combat casualties; Russia's reluctant acquiescence to a strategy of coercive diplomacy directed at a nominal Slavic ally; the continued erosion of the classical norm of state sovereignty as a defense against barbarism; and, finally, the marginalization of the U.N. Security Council in respect to one of the decade's major questions of war and peace. In time, historians will no doubt ponder the peculiarity of such significant consequences evolving from the contest over a swath of land the size of Connecticut, inhabited by fewer than 2 million people.

In June 1998 the battle for Kosovo was heating up. The ethnic Albanian population, making up 90 percent of the province, was increasingly the target of vicious attacks by Serbian security forces and shadowy paramilitary groups. Ibrahim Rugova, a leader of the Albanian opposition, met with U.N. Secretary-General Kofi Annan and said the Serbs were conducting "massacres and massive ethnic cleansing." He asked for U.N. intervention to stop the bloodshed [Christian Science Monitor, 6/4/98]. Underscoring the scope of the turmoil, Albania's Foreign Minister said 20,000 ethnic Albanian refugees—double the U.N.'s estimate—had fled fighting in Kosovo and entered his country [Financial Times, 6/10/98]. The United States, once again confronting the familiar nemesis of Yugoslav President Slobodan Milosevic, indicated it would support a Security Council resolution authorizing "all necessary measures," including the use of force, to halt the Serbian attacks. The United States also announced it would "accelerate contingency planning" for possible NATO military action in Kosovo [Wall Street Journal, 6/9/98].

To reinforce that threat, more than 80 NATO warplanes lifted off from European bases and coursed across the skies over the Adriatic Sea and Albania and Macedonia. The exercise was timed to take place the day before Milosevic met with Russian President Boris Yeltsin in Moscow to discuss the growing crisis [New York Times, 6/16/98]. In his meeting with the Russian President, Milosevic promised access to relief groups and international monitors, arrangements to ensure the return of refugees, and the resumption of peace talks. But Milosevic failed to address the central demand required by the alliance: the withdrawal of Serbian security forces from Kosovo.

By August the situation in Kosovo was grave and unresolved. There was no progress on the political front, but NATO had not yet agreed to the use of force. After a flurry of shuttle diplomacy, the American Balkan envoy Richard Holbrooke was unable to stimulate a meaningful diplomatic dialogue between ethnic Albanian political leaders and the Yugoslav government [ibid., 8/11/98]. The Secretary-General described his growing concern in a report circulated to the Security Council. "The international community risks once again being placed in a position where it is only dealing with the symptoms of a conflict through its humanitarian agencies," Mr. Annan warned. "The continuation of further escalation of this conflict has dangerous implications for the stability of the region. Given the responsibilities of the United Nations in the wider region and the ethnic make-up in neighboring countries, I cannot but express my alarm at this prospect" [*Washington Post*, 8/12/98]. The Security Council issued a statement insisting that the "issue of Kosovo can have no military solution, and all violence and acts of terrorism from whatever quarter are unacceptable." It condemned the "ongoing offensive by Belgrade's security forces" responsible for "an appalling humanitarian situation" [*New York Times*, 8/31/98].

The Council's statement at the end of August reflected a weak lowest common denominator of diplomatic consensus. It was followed three weeks later by a more forceful and formal resolution, the first on the question of Kosovo to fall under the aegis of Chapter VII of the United Nations Charter, which contains the legal provisions authorizing the use of force. **Security Council Resolution 1199**, passed on September 23, **1998, called on Yugoslavia "to order the withdrawal of security units used for civilian repression."** The Albanian opposition leadership was also required to "condemn all terrorist actions." Both the Yugoslav forces and the Kosovo Liberation Army were called upon to implement a ceasefire and initiate political negotiations. The resolution made no reference to the use of force if Yugoslavia did not comply. The deliberate ambiguity of the Council's action allowed Russia to vote in favor of it, as did all other Council members except China, which abstained, making the familiar claim that the plight of Kosovo was an internal question to be resolved according to the "legitimate rights" of the Belgrade government.

In recent years Security Council resolutions have come to have little power of coercion and even less effect on actual enforcement. It was not surprising, therefore, that **one week after the Council issued its demand, 34 ethnic Albanian civilians were massacred,** including the 95-year-old patriarch of a Kosovar family. Monitors from the United States and Europe inspected the bodies of the victims and provided graphic details [ibid., 9/30/98]. Evidence of the massacre—apparently designed as a brutal message to intimidate ethnic Albanian Kosovars—wiped away any lingering resistance within the NATO alliance for military action against Serbia. Javier Solana, the NATO Secretary-General, said that the recently passed Security Council resolution provided **authorization for the alliance to use** force. "We have the legitimacy to act to stop a humanitarian catastrophe," he said [*Financial Times*, 10/8/98].

Seeking to exploit the leverage of the **renewed NATO military threat**, U.S. envoy Richard Holbrooke resumed his shuttle diplomacy and engaged in intense negotiations with both Albanian opposition leaders and Slobodan Milosevic. On October 13, **Milosevic agreed to allow 2,000 international monitors into Kosovo to verify the withdrawal of Yugoslav troops and police.** Holbrooke also announced that the Yugoslav President had committed himself to local elections and to amnesty for those accused of fighting on behalf of the ethnic Albanian resistance [*New York Times*, 10/14/98]. There was immediate skepticism, however, about the significance of the agreement, given Milosevic's record of broken promises. "The Clinton administration claims that it has made progress toward bringing peace to Kosovo," wrote John Mearsheimer, a leading scholar of international relations. "Don't believe it. The deal arranged by Richard Holbrooke is likely to fail sooner rather than later" [ibid., 10/19/98]. And as *The New Republic* observed: "While we hope, as does everyone, that this is the prelude to a permanent peace in Kosovo, we fear it is not. The problem is the peace plan doesn't really address the causes of the war: the Serbs' insistence on sovereignty over a province that is 90 percent Albanian and the Albanians' opposition to it" [11/2/98].

As the critics predicted, Kosovo was soon the scene of another spectacular spasm of violence. **In mid-January, 45 bodies were found** scattered on a hillside and in ravines close to the village of Racak. The victims, all ethnic Albanian Kosovars, included a 12-year-old boy. Some were found with their eyes gouged out, decapitated, or with their skulls smashed. William Walker, the American chief of the monitoring mission run by the Organization for Security and Cooperation in Europe, said the killings were the work of Yugoslav security forces. "I don't have words," said Walker, "to express my revulsion to what can only be described as an unspeakable atrocity" [*New York Times*, 1/17/99]. A defiant Milosevic ordered Walker's expulsion from Kosovo, calling the former Ambassador to El Salvador an "undesirable person." Louise Arbour, **the chief prosecutor of the U.N. war crimes tribunal,** was also refused entry to Serbia to investigate the killings [ibid., 1/18/99]. The Security Council issued a statement condemning the massacre at Racak and attributing responsibility for it to Yugoslav security forces [U.N. press release SC/6628, 1/19/99].

Despite Milosevic's effort to evade a formal inquiry into the killings, monitors from the **Kosovo Verification Mission** did compile a detailed report, which concluded that the attack in Racak was an act of revenge by Serbian forces for the killing of four of their men. The report graphically described the slayings, listing each body found at the scene. For instance, "One adult male killed outside his house. The top of his head had been removed and was found approximately 15 feet away from his place of death. The wound appeared to have been caused by an ax, but may have been from a bullet" [*New York Times*, 1/22/99].

The Racak killings confirmed the conviction that there would be no security in Kosovo if it depended on the word of the Serbian leader. "A lot of self-congratulatory White House spin followed last October's U.S.-brokered cease-fire in Kosovo," observed the *Wall Street Journal*. "But by now it should be glaringly clear that Yugoslav President Slobodan Milosevic never intended to fulfill the agreement" [1/19/99]. Milosevic soon withdrew his expulsion order for Ambassador Walker after mulling over renewed U.S. and British threats for military action. NATO's Supreme Commander, General Wesley Clark, said that by freezing the expulsion order Milosevic had "made a half-compromise." Noting that Yugoslav forces remained in Kosovo, Clark said Yugoslavia was "still defying the will of the international community." Just days later, five more unarmed Albanian Kosovars—two men, a woman, and two boys—were shot at close range with large-caliber machine guns and assault rifles as they rode in a tractor on a country road [*New York Times*, 1/23/99].

With its October agreement clearly in tatters, on January 27, 1999, the United States announced a far-reaching plan to end the fighting in Kosovo. The **new American approach** abandoned the diplomatic framework crafted by Richard Holbrooke three months earlier and instead **emphasized an immediate NATO threat to launch air strikes against Serbia, if the government in Belgrade did not agree to the imposition of a political settlement providing autonomy and self-rule for Kosovo** [ibid., 1/27/99]. According to Clinton administration officials, the American and allied ultimatum was to be implemented "within weeks" [*Washington Post*, 1/28/99]. The threat, formulated in a ten-point plan announced by NATO's Secretary-General, demanded a cease-fire from both sides. Secretary-General Annan visited the allies at their headquarters in Brussels, where he praised past U.N.-NATO cooperation and endorsed the proposal for Kosovo's autonomy. "We must build on the remarkable cooperation between the United Nations and the Stabilization Force in Bosnia," said Annan, "to further refine the combination of force and diplomacy that is the key to peace in the Balkans, as elsewhere. The success of the NATO-led mission operating under a United Nations mandate is surely a model for future endeavors." The Secretary-General added that the world community should be committed to "providing the people of Kosovo with the degree of autonomy that is consistent with their need to live lives free from terror and violence. What form such autonomy will take will depend not only on the wishes of the Kosovars, but also on the actions of the Yugoslav authorities. We can only hope that they, too, have learned the lessons of Bosnia." The Secretary-General indicated that collective action to halt the violence in Kosovo might be required. "The bloody wars of the last decade have left us with no illusions about the difficulty of halting internal conflicts—by reason or by force—particularly against the wishes of the government of a sovereign state," Mr. Annan said. "But nor have they left us with any illusions about the need to use force, when all other means have failed. We may be reaching that limit, once again, in the former Yugoslavia" [U.N. press release SG/SM/6878, 1/28/99].

A French castle in **Rambouillet** was chosen as the site to hammer out an autonomy agreement. The **peace talks,** held in early February, were a diplomatic debacle, compromised by a variety of flaws. As the negotiations progressed, the powers that convened the peace conference— the so-called Contact Group of the United States, Britain, France, Germany, Italy, and Russia—failed to agree on the command structure for any peacekeeping force that might be deployed to Kosovo. France wanted NATO to report to the Contact Group in an arrangement similar to the "dual key" structure of shared authority between the United Nations and NATO during the Bosnian war. The replication of such an unwieldy system was anathema to the United States. A further difficulty was that, unlike the Dayton accords that ended the Bosnian conflict, the Serbian delegation at Rambouillet did not include Milosevic, the one power with the authority to approve or scuttle an agreement on behalf of Yugoslavia.

As the talks continued, the United States and its allies were surprised that the Albanian Kosovar delegation—the weaker party, presumed to be more pliant than the Serbs—did not play the role it was assigned in the diplomatic script. The Albanian representatives insisted on a provision calling for a referendum on independence within three years of an autonomy agreement. None of the powers convening the conference, including the United States, supported Kosovo's formal secession from Yugoslavia—a precedent that might stimulate comparable ambitions among other ethnic groups scattered throughout the Balkans. On the other side of the negotiating table the Serbian delegation, backed by the vocal opposition of Boris Yeltsin, refused to allow NATO troops to serve as peacekeepers in Kosovo. The outcome of the talks fell even further into doubt when after 19 days of negotiation the 29-year-old guerrilla fighter at the helm of the Albanian delegation wrangled a three-week extension for his delegation to consult with members of its political party in Kosovo. The consultation period seemed to invite a stiffening of the Serb position as well [*Wall Street Journal,* 2/24/99]. The **ambiguous conclusion to the talks** was played in Serb media as a considerable success for Belgrade, an inference few in the diplomatic community contested [*New York Times,* 2/24/99].

In early March, following intense discussions with Christopher Hill, the U.S. Ambassador to Macedonia, **Kosovo Albanian rebel leaders finally offered their unconditional agreement to the Rambouillet formula—limited autonomy within Serbia, but not independence.** The agreement of the rebel leadership left Milosevic as once again the focal point for clinching a deal. Armed with the **renewed threat of NATO air**

strikes, Holbrooke was again dispatched to Belgrade to coerce the Yugoslav leader. After two days of fruitless talks, during which Holbrooke warned that Serbia was on a "collision course" with the NATO alliance, he returned to Washington empty-handed. In yet another gesture of defiance, the Belgrade government not only rejected Holbrooke's diplomatic overture but announced arrest warrants for eight Kosovo rebel leaders, including three taking part in the peace talks scheduled to resume in France [ibid., 3/10/99]. Even as Holbrooke was leaving Belgrade, fighting was spreading across southern Kosovo [ibid., 3/11/99].

As the **second round of peace talks** commenced in Rambouillet, U.S. Secretary of State Madeleine Albright did not even bother to attend. Having invested substantial personal and political capital in the failed first round of negotiations—and with the prospect of a breakthrough now increasingly remote—Albright determined that a return to Paris would be pointless. At a low-key ceremony on March 18, boycotted by the Yugoslav government, negotiators representing Kosovo's ethnic Albanian majority signed the autonomy plan for the Serbian province. The document, of course, would have no impact on Serbia, and thus it resolved nothing [*Washington Post*, 3/19/99]. The following day Kosovo was convulsed with violence. Hundreds of foreign monitors were ordered to withdraw to neighboring Macedonia, and Serbian security forces took advantage of their absence to press an offensive against the ethnic Albanian rebels. Thousands of panicked refugees fled on foot, by tractor, or by horse and cart [*New York Times*, 3/21/99]. The **withdrawal of the OSCE observers** brought the Western powers one step closer to air strikes, which were again threatened by General Wesley Clark, the NATO supreme commander. "This is likely to be as long and as difficult as President Milosevic makes it," Clark warned [ibid., 3/20/99]. While NATO repeated its now familiar threat, Yugoslav special forces searched door to door through Kosovo for KLA supporters. Ten men were detained and executed, including a father and his four sons [*Washington Post*, 3/22/99]. In a final encounter with Holbrooke, the Yugoslav President refused to relent from his military offensive in Kosovo. The American envoy reiterated that air strikes were inevitable if Yugoslav forces did not withdraw.

As the first NATO cruise missiles and high-altitude bombs rained down over Serbia on March 24, 1999, **the Secretary-General implicitly approved of the strike.** "I deeply regret that, in spite of all of the efforts made by the international community, the Yugoslav authorities have persisted in their rejection of a political settlement, which would have halted the bloodshed in Kosovo and secured an equitable peace for the population there," Mr. Annan said. "It is indeed tragic that diplomacy has failed, but there are times when the use of force may be legitimate in the pursuit of peace." The Secretary-General also noted—but with less emphasis— **his regret that NATO acted without explicit Security Council autho-**

rization. Russia and China condemned the air attacks as illegal and argued that the Western alliance was undermining international security. The U.S. Representative to the United Nations, A. Peter Burleigh, asserted that force was needed to prevent "a humanitarian catastrophe of immense proportions" [*New York Times*, 3/25/99].

The humanitarian disaster described by the U.S. Ambassador very quickly became an accomplished fact. Within one week, nearly a third of the 1.8 million ethnic Albanians in Kosovo were forced from their homes by Serbian troops. Hundreds of thousands of those refugees poured into Albania, Macedonia, and Montenegro. As reports of the **massive forced exodus** filtered back to the United Nations, the Secretary-General spoke in unusually blunt language. "I am profoundly outraged by reports of a vicious and systematic campaign of 'ethnic cleansing' conducted by Serbian military and paramilitary forces in the province of Kosovo," said Annan. "Concern about what is happening there can only be heightened by the fact that all independent international observers, including even the International Committee of the Red Cross, have now been obliged to withdraw" [U.N. press release SG/SM/6942, 3/30/99].

The **conflict in Kosovo raged for 78 days** before NATO air power finally coerced Milosevic to withdraw his forces. During the first month of air strikes, poor weather and NATO timidity conspired to undercut the strength of the air campaign. In the second month, however, NATO launched some 350 attack sorties every 24 hours and expanded its target list to hit heavy industry, the energy sector, power grids, and other vital targets throughout Serbia [*Time*, 6/14/99]. Roughly 20,000 bombs and missiles were launched in the course of the air war, including three missiles that struck the Chinese embassy in Belgrade. Hundreds of civilians were killed by accident and imprecision; the so-called "**collateral damage**" claimed the lives of Serbs and Albanian Kosovars alike. Remarkably, not a single NATO soldier was lost in the fighting (though a few lives were lost due to accident and, following the cease-fire, by mines and booby traps). The idea of fighting a war exclusively from the air was hotly debated throughout the entire military operation, and the outcome remained in doubt until the very end. As one account observed, "Bill Clinton proves—again—to be the luckiest President alive. At nearly the exact moment that Clinton gathered the Joint Chiefs to confront the unpalatable implications of a ground war to salvage the stalemated air campaign, Milosevic handed him a victory" [ibid.].

Diplomacy to engineer a Serbian withdrawal from Kosovo had a curious but ultimately effective triangular geometry. Neither the United States nor its NATO partners negotiated directly with Milosevic, but through two intermediaries: former Russian Prime Minister Viktor Chernomyrdin and Finnish President Martti Ahtisaari. The agreement first forged between NATO and Russia ultimately paved the way for Milosevic's pullout and the **U.N. Security Council resolution** that followed, which in essence **ratified the outcome of the war and made Kosovo a U.N. and NATO protectorate without ever calling it that.** On the eve of the U.N. vote, Karl Bildt and Eduard Kukan—the two Kosovo envoys appointed by the Secretary-General—briefed the Security Council on preparations for the refugees' return and plans for the post-conflict civilian administration of the province, including elections and the establishment of autonomy from Yugoslavia. The Council authorized the deployment of a force of up to 50,000 troops as well as an unspecified number of aid workers and reconstruction experts. The NATO character of the force was obscured in the official language of the resolution, which China unsuccessfully tried to dilute even further, fearful of a precedent that would qualify or limit the principle of state sovereignty [*New York Times*, 6/10/99]. Finally, **on June 20, the last of some 40,000 Serbian troops pulled out of Kosovo,** and another tragic chapter in the history of the former Yugoslavia came to a close [ibid., 6/21/99].

II
Arms Control and Disarmament
By Derek Boothby

It has been said that optimists are those who think they are living in the best of all possible worlds, and pessimists are those who fear they may be right. So it often appears with arms control and disarmament. There are those who point to the vast and positive steps that have been achieved in the past decade. No longer does the sword of a nuclear Damocles hang over humanity with an ever-present threat of global nuclear war. Nuclear weapon stockpiles have been considerably reduced, intercontinental missiles are no longer actively aimed at Russian and American targets, the Chemical Weapons Convention has been accepted broadly and its implementing organization has made a good start, efforts to improve the Biological Weapons Convention are making slow but steady progress, and annual global expenditure on arms and armed forces is significantly lower than it was ten years ago.

There are others who, while acknowledging the gains of the 1990s, look around the international scene and feel that many of the portents for the future are not good. Progress in nuclear arms negotiations seems to have ground almost to a halt, the United States and Russia still have far too many nuclear weapons, India and Pakistan have openly declared their own nuclear weapon status, disturbing reports appear about "loose nukes" in the former Soviet Union, there is talk about abrogating the Anti-Ballistic Missile Treaty, weapons inspections in Iraq have been halted, the possibility of terrorist use of chemical or biological weapons is growing, more countries are developing their ballistic missile capabilities, and wars—whether using basic conventional weapons, as in Eritrea and Ethiopia, or highly sophisticated ones, as in Serbia and in the no-fly zones of Iraq—continue to kill people and cause immense destruction.

Most of these issues are raised, in one form or another, in the halls of the United Nations. Some of them, such as weapons inspections in Iraq and the future of the U.N. Special Commission (UNSCOM), are addressed by the Security Council and are therefore not on the agenda of the 54th Session of the General Assembly. Others, such as the bilateral strategic arms negotiations between Russia and the United States, are of great importance to the international community but are dealt with only peripherally by the deliberative body. But it is the U.N. General Assembly, with its almost universal membership, that provides the global sounding board for national interests and international concerns, and through which the international community expresses its diverse views and struggles to find common positions. Protracted and often frustrating though it may be, there is no other forum for truly global consideration of the issues of arms control and disarmament.

1. The First Committee

At the 53rd Session of the General Assembly, the First Committee adopted 48 resolutions and one decision. In early December 1998, the General Assembly met in plenary to consider the reports of the First Committee. The highlights of the General Assembly consideration are described in the following paragraphs.

As always, the greatest importance was attached to **nuclear issues.** Among the resolutions adopted, the General Assembly expressed its grave concern over the nuclear tests carried out by India and Pakistan [A/Res/53/ 77 G, vote: 118 in favor, 9 against, with 33 abstentions], called for a review of nuclear doctrines and immediate and urgent steps to reduce the risks of unintentional and accidental use of nuclear weapons [A/Res/53/77 F, vote: 108–45–17], reaffirmed the importance of achieving the universality of the Treaty on the Non-Proliferation of Nuclear Weapons and called upon all States party to the Treaty to make their best efforts for the success of the Review Conference in 2000 [A/Res/53/77 U, vote: 160–0–11], urged early ratification of START II and the commencement of negotiations between Russia and the U.S. on START III [A/Res/53/77 Z, vote: 166–0–8], and recognized the continuing importance of nuclear weapon-free zones in various parts of the world [A/Res/53/ 74, adopted without a vote; A/Res/53/77 A, adopted without a vote; A/Res/53/77 D, adopted without a vote; A/Res/53/77 Q, vote: 154–3–10; and A/Res/53/83, adopted without a vote].

The draft resolution strongly deploring the nuclear tests in South Asia led to lengthy discussion and procedural debate. Non-aligned states criticized the tests but sought to place the criticism in the wider context of nuclear testing as a whole. The final vote on the resolution [A/Res/53/ 77 G] reflected the wide differences of position, even within the membership of regional groups.

The General Assembly adopted a resolution under the title "Towards a nuclear-weapon-free world: the need for a new agenda" [A/Res/53/77 Y, vote: 114–18–38]. This resolution, which is described in more detail below in the section on nuclear matters, aroused strong objections from the United States, the United Kingdom, and France. The three considered the concept unrealistic and felt it failed to recognize the progress that had been made in this area over the past few years. They, together with Russia, Israel, India, and Pakistan, voted against the resolution, and China abstained.

The topics of **chemical weapons and biological weapons** did not have a high profile at the 53rd Session. Resolutions on both items were adopted without a vote [A/Res/53/77 R and A/Res/53/84, respectively]. Both items will be on the agenda of the 54th Session too.

In the area of **conventional weapons,** there were a number of resolutions. Of particular interest was an initiative by South Africa on illicit traffic in small arms [A/Res/53/77 T, adopted without a vote], requesting the Secretary-General to hold broad-based consultations on the magnitude and scope of the phenomenon; on possible measures to combat illicit traffic; and on the role of the United Nations in collecting, collating, sharing, and disseminating information. The Secretary-General was asked to report to the General Assembly at its 54th Session.

In a resolution on small arms initiated by Japan [A/Res/53/77 E, vote: 169–0–1] the General Assembly welcomed the decision of the Secretary-General to establish the mechanism for Coordinating Action on Small Arms, and decided to convene an international conference on the illicit arms trade not later than 2001. Switzerland has offered to host the conference in Geneva. The Secretary-General was requested to report to the 54th Session his recommendations on the objective, scope, agenda, dates, venue, and preparatory committee of the conference. The Secretary-General was also asked to initiate a study, as soon as possible, on the possibility of restricting the manufacture and trade of such weapons to the manufacturers and dealers authorized by states.

A separate but related resolution was adopted on the topic of **practical disarmament measures** [A/Res/53/77 M, adopted without a vote]. By this resolution, the General Assembly encouraged the Disarmament Commission to continue its efforts to adopt guidelines on conventional arms control and limitation of armaments.

On the issue of **transparency in armaments,** the General Assembly adopted a resolution [A/Res/53/77 S, vote: 104–46–17] taking note of the report of the Secretary-General [A/53/334 and Add.1]. This resolution addressed the matter of the **U.N. Register of Conventional Arms,** which has encountered a number of difficulties in recent years. Among these problems, China objects strongly to transfers of U.S. arms to Taiwan and to recent reports of the possibility of the United States providing Taiwan with anti-missile defenses. Separately, some non-aligned states have made efforts to increase the scope of the Register to include transparency regarding weapons of mass destruction, in particular nuclear weapons, and to transfers of equipment and technology directly related to the development and manufacture of such weapons. By operative paragraph 3(b) of the resolution, member states are urged to submit their views to the Secretary-General with a view to their consideration by the group of Governmental Experts. This led to a large number of negative votes, predominantly from North America and Europe.

The Assembly also adopted a less contentious resolution on transparency in armaments [A/Res/53/77 V, vote: 159–0–12] in which it reaffirmed its determination to ensure the effective operation of the Register of Conventional Arms. Member states were asked to give their views to the Secretary-General on the continuing operation of the Register and its further development and on transparency measures related to weapons of mass destruction. The Secretary-General was also asked to convene a group of governmental experts in 2000 to prepare a report on the operation and development of the Register. The issue will be on the agenda of the 54th Session.

At the initiative of Russia, the General Assembly adopted a resolution entitled "Developments in the field of information and telecommunication in the context of international security" [A/Res/53/70, adopted without a vote]. Expressing concern that **information technologies** and means could potentially be used for purposes inconsistent with the objectives of maintaining international stability and security and may adversely affect the security of states, the General Assembly invited all member states to give to the Secretary-General their views and assessments on certain questions related to information security. The Secretary-General was requested to submit a report to the 54th Session.

Also adopted without a vote was a resolution [A/Res/53/77 AA] by which the General Assembly decided, subject to the emergence of a consensus on its objectives and agenda, to convene the **fourth special session of the General Assembly devoted to disarmament.** The three previous special sessions took place in 1978, 1982, and 1988. At the first, a Final Document was adopted by consensus that set out a Declaration, Programme of Action, and Machinery for disarmament. The second and third special sessions, however, failed to achieve agreement and proved to be highly contentious. The Disarmament Commission has for three years been trying without success to find a consensus on the objectives and agenda of a fourth special session. By this resolution the General Assembly recommended that the Disarmament Commission try again in 1999 and also decided to include the item in the provisional agenda of the 54th Session. Subject to the outcome of the Disarmament Commission's deliberations, the General Assembly would set an exact date and decide on organizational matters for the convening of the special session.

2. The Conference on Disarmament

The primary body for multilateral disarmament negotiations is the Conference on Disarmament (CD) in Geneva, with 61 members. It ended its first session in 1999 on March 26 **without agreement on an initial work program** and thereby failed to make any negotiating progress [*Arms Control Today*, 3/99]. The Group of 21 (G-21) non-aligned states has consistently pressed for inclusion of nuclear disarmament and preventing an arms race in outer space in the CD's work program, but the United States opposes formal negotiations on both issues. Without agreement on a work program, no talks on any subject can start.

The impasse over nuclear disarmament continues to be the principal stumbling block in the CD. Although the G-21 countries have displayed a readiness to consider options other than formal negotiations, provided that work on nuclear disarmament issues begins, the United States, supported by France, Russia, and the United Kingdom, remains steadfastly against the establishment of any formal group to negotiate nuclear disarmament.

On the issue of **fissile materials,** there continue to be deep divisions over the scope of the negotiations to be conducted in an ad hoc committee. Pakistan argued that the treaty should include existing fissile stocks but is opposed by the five nuclear weapon states plus India and Israel. The issue of fissile materials and the disagreements over the work of the ad hoc committee, which has yet to start its work, are described at greater length below.

On the matter of an **arms race in outer space,** the statement on January 20, 1999, by U.S. Secretary of Defense William Cohen regarding funding for a national missile defense system provoked strong calls by some members of the CD to take up the space issue. China wished to see the establishment of an ad hoc committee to prevent the "weaponization" of space, while Pakistan and others preferred the use of the term "militarization," which could include satellites used for military purposes [ibid.]. However, the United States continues to withhold its agreement to the establishment of any committee on the issue.

Negotiating on these issues is an esoteric business that, to outsiders, is akin to a black art. It does not require greater skills than in other parts of the U.N. agenda, but it often demands a unique combination of great political sensitivity and highly technical knowledge. It is also an environment in which the politics move very slowly but the technology moves very fast. Despite the fact that the Cold War is now ten years in the past, the Conference on Disarmament still divides itself more or less into the Western Group, the Eastern European Group, and the Non-Aligned—even though the first contains several members who do not always follow the same line, the second scarcely exists as a group, and the third has no one to be non-aligned against.

Commenting on this aspect, Robert T. Grey Jr., U.S. Ambassador to the CD, has said: "We should try to get chairmen, and friends of the chair, and coordinators, on the basis of their interests, and their merits, and their capabilities, not on the basis of what group they're from, especially when the groups no longer function as groups. It's a real frustration. Arms control is pretty rarefied stuff to begin with, especially multilateral arms control, with all the ideological baggage and yearnings and things people bring to it. It's even more unreal when you're dealing as if there were three blocs in a world where there are no blocs" [ibid., 10/98].

3. The Disarmament Commission

The 1999 session of the Disarmament Commission took place April 12– 30. Of the three substantive items on its agenda, texts on two were adopted without a vote: **principles and guidelines for the establishment of nuclear weapon-free zones** (see the relevant paragraphs below), and **principles and guidelines on conventional arms control and limitations**—in particular, practical measures for disarmament. The Commission was unable, however, to find consensus on the objectives and agenda for a fourth special session of the General Assembly devoted to disarmament (SSOD IV).

At the closing meeting of the session, several speakers noted that, when measured against the Commission's inability to reach consensus in past years, the successful conclusion of two disarmament items was remarkable [U.N. press release DC/2641, 4/30/99]. In the opinion of many of the 28 speakers, the two consensus texts reaffirmed their belief in the value of the Commission as a specialized deliberative forum capable of identifying disarmament and security-related principles and guidelines. The conventional arms control guidelines are aimed at consolidating peace in post-conflict situations. Their basic premise is that the excessive accumulation of small arms and light weapons can best be averted by a combination of reduction and prevention measures. They cover: practical disarmament measures in post-conflict situations; confidence-building in post-conflict situations; regional and international financial and technical assistance; other conventional arms control/limitation and disarmament measures; and the role of the United Nations [ibid. and A/CN.10/1999/CRP.6, 4/28/99].

The Commission's **inability to find consensus agreement on a text setting out the objectives and agenda for SSOD IV** was a setback. On December 4, 1998, the General Assembly had adopted a resolution [A/Res/ 53/77 AA, adopted without a vote] giving the Commission the opportunity of an additional yearly session to find agreement. In 1996 and 1997 it had been the United States that was against the convening of SSOD IV, but by 1998 this opposition had been withdrawn on the basis of a text on objectives and agenda put forward by the Chairman. However, this was a text that India and Mexico could not accept, and at the 1999 session they proposed various amendments.

Through protracted negotiations, Mexico and India continued to insist on the disarmament priorities set out in the Final Document of SSOD I, while the Western Group held the position that there was a need to look forward to the principles, guidelines, and priorities of the future. Two efforts by the Chairman of the Working Group to bring the differing views together were rejected by India, although India maintained that agreement had not been reached because some states refused to allow the critical issue of the retention of nuclear weapons to be brought to the table. The U.S. representative said that her country had accepted the notion of another special session because a forward-looking meeting to elaborate an agenda for multilateral disarmament and arms control in the post-Cold War world was useful, assuming that states displayed a willingness to compromise and limit their aspirations to the attainable. Unfortunately, she said, such a willingness had not emerged in spite of four years of painstaking work [U.N. press release DC/2641, 4/30/99].

Despite the lack of consensus agreement in the Commission, it remains for the 54th Session of the General Assembly to resolve the issue by a resolution adopted by majority vote. If, however, there is no decision on the issue, there is a risk that the proposal to convene SSOD IV may die altogether, further dampening the prospects for agreement in the CD and at the 2000 Review Conference of the Nuclear Non-Proliferation Treaty.

4. Nuclear Matters

START II

The pace of efforts to reduce nuclear weapons continued to be desultory in 1999. In late 1998 it appeared that the Russian Duma might at last be moving toward ratification of the long-delayed START II strategic arms accord. The treaty, which had been signed in January 1993 by Presidents Bush and Yeltsin, was ratified by the U.S. Senate in January 1996. Under START II, the number of nuclear warheads on each side would be reduced to no more than 3,500. Once ratified, according to a framework understanding reached by Presidents Clinton and Yeltsin in Helsinki in 1997, negotiations would begin on a START III accord. That accord would set a new floor of between 2,000 and 2,300 deployed strategic nuclear warheads to be achieved by December 31, 2007; include measures for the destruction of nuclear warheads; and provide transparency measures for dismantling non-deployed nuclear weapons in storage [*Jane's Intelligence Review*, 2/1/99].

In the Duma, the lower house of the Russian parliament, the START II treaty has long faced **opposition from the nationalists and commu-**

nists who command the majority of the 450-member chamber. But in October 1998, a report by Deputy Prime Minister Yuri Maslyukov had indicated that, because of obsolescence and other factors, Russia's strategic arms capability would suffer a serious decline in coming years and therefore Russia should ratify the treaty [Washington Post, 11/19/98]. By December 1998 it appeared that Prime Minister Yevgeny Primakov had persuaded a majority in the Duma to approve the treaty in view of the heavy costs to the faltering Russian economy of maintaining current nuclear weapon levels [ibid., 12/10/98]. However, hopes for progress in the Duma were dashed by the U.S./U.K. air attacks on Iraq in December, followed by the announcement on January 20, 1999, of the U.S. administration's decision to proceed with a national ballistic missile defense system. Secretary of Defense William Cohen announced the intention to spend $6.6 billion over five years to develop the system and to seek unspecified changes in the 1972 Anti-Ballistic Missile (ABM) Treaty with Russia [ibid., 1/22/99]. In mid-March, before a scheduled visit to Washington for talks with the Clinton administration and the International Monetary Fund, Prime Minister Primakov again urged the Duma to ratify START II. President Yeltsin submitted for the Duma's approval a ratification law with provisions that would give Russia the right to withdraw from the treaty in certain circumstances, such as the deployment of nuclear weapons on the territory of countries that may join NATO after the signing of the treaty [ibid., 3/17/99]. But the Kosovo crisis came to a head a few days later, and the prospect of progress on the treaty was made yet further remote by the NATO decision to launch air attacks on the Federal Republic of Yugoslavia.

Although the United Nations has no direct role in the strategic arms talks between the United States and Russia, the evidence or absence of progress in this vital area sets an important tone for much of the U.N. debate over arms limitations and disarmament. This is particularly the case as the next Review Conference of the Nuclear Non-Proliferation Treaty (NPT) approaches, in 2000.

The Nuclear Non-Proliferation Treaty (NPT)

At the 1995 Review Conference, the NPT was extended indefinitely. Many delegates went home with sighs of relief and feelings that common sense had triumphed; others perhaps felt that they had made a flawed but unavoidable compact with the nuclear devil. But probably all were of the view that they had contributed to an international agreement that would stand the test of time. Yet, only four years later, there are serious concerns and anxieties: No further progress has been made by the nuclear weapon states toward negotiating nuclear disarmament agreements; China, Russia, and the United States have yet to ratify the Comprehensive

Test-Ban Treaty; Russia has yet to ratify START II, and so no formal progress has been made toward START III; some voices in the United States challenge the ABM Treaty; India and Pakistan have openly declared themselves as possessing nuclear weapons; worries remain about Israel's nuclear capability; inspections in Iraq have halted; questions continue regarding the nuclear activities and intentions of the Democratic People's Republic of Korea, particularly since its missile test over Japan's territory in August 1998; and disturbing reports abound concerning access to "loose nukes" by either rogue states or terrorist groups.

Despite these concerns, the NPT regime has in many respects fared quite well [Janyantha Dhanapala, USG for Disarmament Affairs, Address to the Seventh Carnegie International Non-Proliferation Conference, Washington, 1/11/99]. There are now **187 parties**, the Treaty is close to full universal membership, and, in general, compliance has been commendable. But while there are certainly external challenges, such as the Indian and Pakistani tests, it is perhaps the challenges from within that should be given more attention.

In the run-up to the **2000 Review Conference,** to be held April 24–May 19 in New York, it was agreed that there would be three preparatory committee meetings, with the possibility of a fourth in the year of the Conference. The first two meetings, in April 1997 and April–May 1998, were inconclusive. That in itself was not remarkable, as the issues under consideration are acutely sensitive and difficult and therefore delegates did not feel under pressure to make concessions early in the process. But the formal and informal exchanges indicated sharp differences of opinion which, if not successfully resolved, could lead to an impasse at the Conference itself.

According to observers and commentators, the differences are several [*Rebecca Johnson in Bulletin of the Atomic Scientists,* 3/1/99, and other sources]. The **Western group** of about 40 countries wishes to see the NPT regime strengthened by India and Pakistan joining the CTBT and concluding a fissile material cutoff treaty, a stronger export control regime, increased powers for the International Atomic Energy Agency, and more effective arrangements for ensuring compliance with the nonproliferation provisions of the Treaty. **The Non-Aligned** wish the focus of attention to be on nuclear disarmament, on a nuclear weapon-free zone in the Middle East, and on improved negative security assurances.

The most contentious topic will continue to be **nuclear disarmament.** The Group of 21 in the CD have long pressed for a time-bound program of action [CD/1419, 8/7/96]. On June 9, 1998, a number of other states, while criticizing the attitude of the nuclear weapon states (NWS), which they see as complacent, self-serving, and in default of their commitment, presented a somewhat more centrist initiative [A/53/138, annex]. These critics, which include Brazil, Egypt, Ireland, Mexico, New Zealand, South Africa, and Sweden, forming a group known as the "New Agenda

Coalition," want to see more dynamic action by the NWS in discharging their commitment to nuclear disarmament but do not try to set any specific dates. Slovenia was also an original member but subsequently withdrew its sponsorship of the draft resolution submitted to the First Committee.

By the resolution [A/Res/53/77 Y, vote: 114–18–33], entitled "Towards a nuclear-weapon-free world: the need for a new agenda," the General Assembly called upon the NWS "to demonstrate an unequivocal commitment to the speedy and total elimination of their respective nuclear weapons and, without delay, to pursue in good faith and bring to a conclusion negotiations leading to the elimination of these weapons, thereby fulfilling their obligations under Article VI of the Treaty on the Non-Proliferation of Nuclear Weapons." At the end of 19 operative paragraphs calling for action, the Secretary-General was requested to compile a report on the implementation of the resolution for consideration at the 54th Session of the General Assembly.

There has also been criticism of NATO's nuclear policy; and **NATO's new Strategic Concept,** approved at the North Atlantic Council's meeting in Washington on April 23 and 24, seems likely to be given close attention. In carefully measured language [NATO press release NAC-S(99)65, 4/24/99], the document states that "the Alliance's conventional forces alone cannot ensure credible deterrence. Nuclear weapons make a unique contribution in rendering the risks of aggression against the Alliance incalculable and unacceptable. Thus, they remain essential to preserve peace." NATO's new Strategic Concept is silent on the policy of first-use, but declares that "the fundamental purpose of the nuclear forces of the Allies is political: to preserve peace and prevent coercion and any kind of war. They will continue to fulfil an essential role by ensuring uncertainty in the mind of any aggressor about the nature of the Allies' response to military aggression." The document makes clear the need for "widespread participation by European Allies involved in collective defence planning in nuclear roles, in peacetime basing of nuclear forces on their territory, and in command, control and consultation arrangements" and the maintenance of "adequate nuclear forces in Europe." Even with such assurances as "The circumstances in which any use of nuclear weapons might have to be contemplated by [the Allies] are therefore extremely remote," it seems unlikely that the language of the new Strategic Concept will placate members of the New Agenda Coalition.

The **third meeting of the Preparatory Committee** took place in New York from May 10 to 21, 1999. Of 187 states parties to the NPT, 157 participated in the work of one or more of the meetings, and representatives of over 60 nongovernmental organizations were present. The Committee endorsed unanimously the candidature of Ambassador Jacob Selebi of South Africa for the presidency of the Conference and agreed on the chairmanship of the various committees. It also agreed on a provisional agenda, the draft rules of procedure, the schedule of the division of costs, and the preparation of a number of background papers. But on substantive matters, the Preparatory Committee could find no agreement. As in the Disarmament Commission, the argument over backward-looking or forward-looking reemerged. Other substantive issues on which agreement has yet to be found include the universality of the Treaty (four U.N. member states—Cuba, Israel, India, and Pakistan—have yet to join the NPT), questions regarding compliance with articles I and II of the Treaty, the stationing of nuclear weapons on the territories of non-nuclear weapon states, the lack of progress in negotiated nuclear disarmament, and concerns over security assurances and the incompleteness of the safeguards regime [Programme for Promoting Nuclear Non-Proliferation, Issue Review No.15, 5/99, "Why the 1999 Preparatory Committee Session for the 2000 Review Conference Is So Crucial for the Strengthened Review Process," by Emily Bailey and John Simpson].

The 2000 Review Conference of the NPT will not be a priority on the agenda of the 54th Session of the General Assembly, but the current disagreements on nuclear issues are deep and long-standing. Inevitably, they will significantly color the debate in the First Committee at the Session.

CTBT and Nuclear Testing

On January 12, 1999, the Clinton administration announced that it would make the ratification of the Comprehensive Nuclear Test-Ban Treaty (CTBT) a priority for 1999. National Security Advisor Samuel Berger said, "This treaty is in America's national interest. If the Senate rejected or failed to act on the test ban treaty, we would throw open the door to regional nuclear arms races and a much more dangerous world" [*Los Angeles Times*, 1/13/99]. Notwithstanding U.S. public opinion polls showing wide support for the test ban, there is much **opposition to ratification among conservative Republicans in the Senate,** who believe that other nations will evade its restrictions, leaving the United States at a disadvantage. U.S. supporters of the CTBT are increasingly disturbed by Senate inaction. Spurgeon M. Keeny Jr., President of the Arms Control Association, wrote that "If the Senate's advice and consent on this critical treaty is delayed another six months, the future of the treaty will be in doubt and the United States will have seriously endangered its leadership role in the efforts to contain further nuclear proliferation" [*Arms Control Today*, 1–2/99].

Adopted by the General Assembly on September 10, 1996 [A/Res/50/245], the CTBT was opened for signature on September 24, 1996, at U.N. Headquarters in New York. For the Treaty to enter into force, all 44 states listed in annex 2 to the Treaty must deposit their instruments of ratification with the Secretary-General. The list comprises the states that formally participated in the 1996 session of the Conference on Disarmament, and that appear in table 1 of the December 1995 edition of "Nuclear Research Reactors in the World" and table 1 of the April 1996 edition of "Nuclear Power Reactors in the World," both compiled by the International Atomic Energy Agency [Article XIV of the CTBT]. Of these 44 states, as of May 25, 1999, 41 had signed and 18 had ratified the Treaty [www.ctbto.org/ctbto/sig_rat.shtml]. By the same date, a total of 152 states had signed and 35 had ratified it.

Article XIV of the Treaty also contains an interesting provision, added at the initiative of Canada and other friends of the CTBT. If the Treaty has not entered into force "three years after the date of the anniversary of its opening for signature," the Secretary-General could, at the request of a majority of states that had ratified it, convene a conference to examine the situation and to "decide by consensus what measures consistent with international law may be undertaken to accelerate the ratification process." It follows that those states that have not yet ratified the Treaty, such as China, Russia, and the United States, would not be able to participate fully in such a conference and express their voice in its outcome. Signatories may attend as observers, but not as full participants.

At the time of writing, it appears that a **three-day conference** will take place in early October 1999, probably in Vienna, and will be repeated annually. The prospects for this conference are complicated by the absence of a formal preparatory process. For a three-day meeting to be successful, it is almost essential to have an accepted draft agenda and a well-prepared draft text that has been seen beforehand by participants. Without any agreed preparatory process to pursue in such matters and a provisional chairman to steer the advance discussions, it will be difficult for the conference to achieve much of a meaningful outcome.

Following nuclear tests in May 1998, **India and Pakistan declared themselves as nuclear weapon states,** although they are not formally recognized as such by the five nuclear weapon states of the NPT. On June 6, 1998, the Security Council unanimously adopted a resolution [S/Res/1172] in which the Council condemned the nuclear tests conducted by the two countries and demanded that they refrain from further nuclear tests. On December 4, 1998, the General Assembly followed suit, although not in such strong terms and only after a procedural battle, by adopting a resolution [A/Res/53/77 G, vote: 118–9–33] expressing grave concern and strongly deploring the recent tests conducted in South Asia. Despite fears that relations between the two countries would worsen, both governments took steps in early 1999 to improve their bilateral relations. On January 1, India and Pakistan exchanged lists of the nuclear facilities that they have agreed to refrain from attacking. In February there was a much-publicized visit by Indian Prime Minister A. B. Vajpayee to Lahore for discussions with Prime Minister Nawaz Sharif of Pakistan.

Since June 1998, Washington has been conducting separate but parallel discussions with New Delhi and Islamabad aimed at heading off an escalation of nuclear and missile competition in the region [Strobe Talbott, *Foreign Affairs*, 3–4/99]. Both countries have committed themselves to voluntary moratoriums on further nuclear testing. In February 1999, Deputy Secretary of State Strobe Talbott visited the capitals of both countries to urge restraint and pursue an effective arms control dialogue, although his efforts were not successful in dissuading the two countries from carrying out missile tests, which they did in April. Both countries appear to embrace a concept of "minimum credible deterrence." Until the Indian government narrowly lost a confidence vote in April, there were indications that India would sign the CTBT before the September 1999 conference, and it was expected that Pakistan would follow suit. However, with a general election in India not until late September or early October, Prime Minister Vajpayee has been reported as saying that it would be improper to sign the treaty before the election unless he can build a consensus that includes the opposition, led by the Congress party [*New York Times*, 5/9/99]. This seems an unlikely development; and if India does not sign, neither will Pakistan.

While awaiting the entry into force of the CTBT, preparatory work has continued. The **Preparatory Commission for the Comprehensive Nuclear Test Ban Treaty Organization** is now over two years old. With headquarters in Vienna, at the end of April 1999 it had a staff of 184 persons from 58 states signatories and is making steady progress in setting up the verification regime to monitor compliance [CTBTO PrepCom Information Note PI/PTS/Ann. 2/1/Rev.1, available at www.ctbto.org/announcements]. The regime will consist of an International Monitoring System of 170 seismological, 60 infrasound, 11 hydroacoustic, and 80 radionuclide stations (supported by 16 radionuclide laboratories) to be upgraded or newly established in some 90 countries around the world. The budget of the CTBTO PrepCom for 1999 is $74.7 million, for 1998 it was $58.4 million, and for 1997 it was $27.7 million [ibid.].

Nuclear Weapon-Free Zones

Mongolia declared itself a nuclear weapon-free zone (NWFZ) in 1992, and on December 4, 1998, the General Assembly adopted without a vote a resolution [A/Res/53/77 D] welcoming Mongolia's NWFZ status. This is the first occasion on which a single state has been recognized as a NWFZ.

As it has done annually since 1974, in December 1998 the General Assembly adopted a resolution calling for the establishment of a NWFZ in the region of the **Middle East** [A/Res/53/74], and the issue will be pressed by its proponents again at the forthcoming session of the General Assembly.

Efforts to establish a NWFZ in **Central Asia** (Kazakhstan, Kyrgyz-stan, Tajikistan, Turkmenistan, and Uzbekistan) are continuing. They were commended by the General Assembly [A/Res/53/77 A], and the item will be on the agenda of the 54th Session.

Similarly, efforts are continuing to establish the southern hemisphere and adjacent areas as nuclear weapon-free space. The **Antarctic Treaty** and the **treaties of Tlatelolco, Rarotonga, Bangkok, and Pelindaba** cover extensive areas of the globe, and the aim of the proponents of this initiative is eventually to free all the relevant areas covered by those trea-ties from nuclear weapons. At its 53rd Session, the General Assembly adopted a resolution calling for the ratification of these four treaties by all regional states, and called upon all concerned states to continue to work together in order to facilitate adherence to the protocols to NWFZ treaties by all relevant states that have not yet done so [A/Res/53/77 Q, adopted without a vote]. This item will also be considered at the 54th Session.

Another item that is seeing progress and will be on the agenda of the 54th Session is the **consolidation of the NWFZ regime in Latin America and the Caribbean** under the terms of the Treaty of Tlatelolco, which is now in force for 32 sovereign states of the region. Cuba signed the Treaty in 1995 but has not yet ratified it. Until Cuba's ratification, the sea areas identified in Article 4.2 of the Treaty are not yet covered by the nuclear weapon-free provisions.

At the 1999 session of the Disarmament Commission, held in New York in April, agreement was achieved on **principles and guidelines for the establishment of NWFZs** [press release DC/2641, 4/30/99]. According to the report of the working group on this issue, 107 states had signed or become parties to treaties establishing existing NWFZs and, with the addition of demilitarized Antarctica, those zones cover more than 50 percent of the Earth's land mass. The principles and guidelines adopted by the Commis-sion should be regarded only as a nonexhaustive list of generally accepted observations at the current stage of the development of NWFZs. Accord-ingly, the initiative to establish a NWFZ should emanate exclusively from states within the region concerned and be pursued by all the states of that region. Any such proposal should be considered only after consensus on the objective had been achieved in broad consultations within the states of the region concerned. In addition, the nuclear weapon states, as well as any states with territory or internationally responsible for territories within that zone, should be consulted during the negotiations. Finally, a zone must conform to international law, and its status should be respected by all states parties to the treaty establishing it, including the nuclear weapon states.

Fissile Materials

"Fissile materials" is the term used to describe the key explosive compo-nents of nuclear weapons, namely plutonium and highly enriched uranium (HEU, i.e., uranium enriched to more than 20 percent U-235). It has been estimated that there are more than 3,000 tons in the world, of which some 1,900 tons were produced by Russia and the United States in various military and civil programs. According to one knowledgeable account [*The Challenges of Fissile Material Control*, edited by David Albright and Kevin O'Neill, Washington, D.C.: The Institute for Science and International Security, 1999] the estimated global inventories in tons at the end of 1997 were:

	HEU	*Plutonium*
Military	1,700	250
Civil	20	1,100*
Totals	1,720	1,350

*Mostly non-weapon grade

The military stocks of fissile materials are assessed as being held by Russia, the United States, the United Kingdom, France, and China, with much smaller quantities held by Israel, India, Pakistan, North Korea, and South Africa. The first four named have all announced a halt to the production of fissile materials for nuclear weapons and, unofficially, it is believed that China has followed suit.

In 1995 the Conference on Disarmament (CD) in Geneva adopted "the report of the Special Co-ordinator (CD/1299) and the mandate contained therein" for **negotiations on a Fissile Materials Cut-off Treaty (FMCT).** The importance of this formula lies in the fact that the report itself addressed concerns of some states regarding existing stocks that they wanted to see addressed during the negotiations. Since then there has been little progress.

Although the ad hoc committee on FMCT was established in 1995, it did not commence its work. There has continued to be disagreement in the CD over the scope of the negotiations. In addition, a number of non-nuclear weapon states belonging to the Group of 21 took the position that in exchange for their agreement to an ad hoc committee on FMCT, the nuclear weapon states should allow the establishment of an ad hoc committee on nuclear disarmament. The political impasse in the CD appeared to have been overcome in August 1998, when it was at last agreed to proceed with an ad hoc committee on FMCT. This decision was welcomed at the 53rd Session of the General Assembly [A/Res/53/77 I, adopted without a vote] on December 4, 1998.

The CD mandate was to negotiate a treaty that was "non-discriminatory, multilateral and internationally and effectively verifiable." A major division of views has arisen, however, over whether the treaty should relate to the cut-off of any further production of fissile materials (the view of nuclear weapon states and their friends) or whether it should also pertain to pre-existing stocks and thereby contribute to nuclear disarmament as well as nonproliferation (the view of the Group of 21 non-aligned countries and their friends at the CD). This dispute is reflected by some delegates in the CD referring to the acronym FMCT, while others prefer the acronym FMT to show that the treaty should be broader than simply a "cut-off."

By March 26, when the CD ended its first session of 1999, there was still no progress. As stated earlier in this chapter, the CD was unable to decide on its own work program due to a deadlock over linkage with work on other issues, such as nuclear disarmament and the prohibition of an arms race in outer space. Although fissile materials are not directly on the agenda of the 54th Session of the General Assembly, the stalemate seems likely to contribute a negative tone to the consideration of disarmament issues as a whole.

5. Chemical Weapons

As of July 6, 1999, there were 126 states parties to the **Chemical Weapon Convention (CWC)** [www.opcw.org]. The ratified membership has increased from 87 since April 29, 1997, when the CWC entered into force. The establishment of the **Organization for the Prohibition of Chemical Weapons (OPCW)** in the Netherlands and the commencement of its inspections, advisory, and training activities have done much to take the issue of chemical weapons out of the fevered atmosphere of political negotiation and into the calmer air of implementation. This has been reflected in less attention to chemical weapons issues in the General Assembly.

On October 19, 1998, Director-General José Maurício Bustani of the Organization for the Prohibition of Chemical Weapons (OPCW) addressed the First Committee in New York. He informed the Committee that in declarations received by that time from states parties, a total of 59 chemical weapon production facilities had been disclosed, 24 of them Russian, and all of them had been inspected pending their destruction or conversion. Inspections of declared industry facilities were proceeding at a steady pace, in an atmosphere of increasing mutual confidence, at a rate of two or three per week, and about 100 industrial facilities had been inspected in 25 states parties [*CBW Conventions Bulletin*, Issue 42, 12/98].

Director-General Bustani pointed to a number of **outstanding issues.** Several key countries in Southeast Asia, such as Indonesia, Malaysia, and Thailand, had not completed the ratification process, and no effective communication had been established with North Korea. In Africa, only 29 out of the 53 African states were members of the CWC. In the Middle

East, a number of key states had yet to ratify or accede to the Convention. He urged Egypt, Israel, Lebanon, Libya, Sudan, Syria, and Yemen to follow the example of Jordan, and he asked why Iraq should not also follow suit [ibid. and OPCW S/80/98]. He also expressed concern at the failure of the United States to submit declarations with respect to its chemical industry under Article VI of the Convention and to subject its chemical industry to inspections. The chemical industries of Europe and Japan were complying fully and were becoming increasingly concerned at what they saw as the unfair commercial advantage being given to the chemical industry of the United States.

On the same day, in the **U.S. Congress,** House-Senate conferees agreed on a conference report on an omnibus appropriations bill that included **legislation to implement the CWC.** It was signed into law by President Clinton on October 21 as PL 105-277. Under the CWC, nearly 2,000 commercial facilities in the United States making dual-use chemicals would be expected to file annual declarations, and about 200 of these facilities would be subject to routine, on-site inspections [*Chemical Market Reporter*, 10/26/98]. On May 18, 1999, Director-General Bustani, in an address at the Centennial of the First International Peace Conference in The Hague 1899–1999, said that since its inception the OPCW had carried out 475 inspections at both military and chemical industry facilities in almost 30 countries. By May 1, he reported, 2,500 tons of chemical agents and about 700,000 CW munitions and containers had been destroyed under OPCW supervision [www.opcw.org].

While these reports of steady progress are to be welcomed, the international community must not allow itself to be lulled into a false sense of security. **Russia,** with a stockpile of some 44,000 tons, is required to destroy its first 400 tons by 2000 but will have difficulty in meeting this deadline [*Foreign Report*, Jane's Information Group Limited, 11/19/98]. Over the next 10–15 years, Russia will need $6 billion to build plants to destroy chemicals, including mustard gas and nerve gas. As yet, Russia has still not appointed a federal agency to coordinate the work, and a special presidential committee lacks the needed executive authority. Separately, since December 1998 there have been no weapons inspections in **Iraq,** there continue to be major concerns over the CW capabilities of **Iran** and the **Federal Republic of Yugoslavia,** and there are rising anxieties about the dangers of terrorist use of chemical weapons.

At the 53rd Session, the General Assembly adopted a resolution noting with appreciation the ongoing work of the OPCW, urging all states parties to the Convention to meet in full and on time their obligations under the Convention, and deciding to consider the item again at its 54th Session [A/Res/53/77 R, adopted without a vote].

6. Biological Weapons

Under its full name—the Convention on the Prohibition of the Development, Production and Stockpiling of Bacteriological (Biological) and Toxin Weapons and on Their Destruction—the Biological Weapons Convention (BWC) entered into force in 1975. At present it has **141 states parties.** While it was the first multilateral treaty to ban an entire class of weapons of mass destruction, it has a major weakness in that it **lacks a verification mechanism** to ensure compliance.

From their September 2, 1998, summit meeting in Moscow, Presidents Clinton and Yeltsin issued a "Joint Statement on a Protocol to the Convention on the Prohibition of Biological Weapons." In the statement, the two leaders expressed their "strong support for the aims and tasks" of the **Biological Weapons Convention Ad Hoc Group (AHG).** They urged "the further intensification and successful conclusion of those negotiations to strengthen the Convention by the adoption of a legally binding Protocol at the earliest possible date" [*CBW Conventions Bulletin*, Issue 42, 12/ 98]. Later that month, at Australian initiative and in the margins of the ministerial sessions of the General Assembly, an informal ministerial meeting was held under the chairmanship of the Foreign Minister of New Zealand, Donald McKinnon. Subsequently, a Declaration was issued co-sponsored by 57 ministers, 25 of whom had attended the meeting ["Declaration of the Informal Ministerial Meeting on the Negotiation Towards Conclusion of the Protocol to Strengthen the Biological Weapons Convention," 9/23/98]. The ministers affirmed their strong support for the BWC and for strengthening its effectiveness and improving its implementation. They called for acceleration of the negotiations within the AHG and reaffirmed their high-level support, including through convening a high-level meeting at the most appropriate time during the negotiating process in 1999, open to all states parties to the Convention.

At its 53rd Session, the General Assembly adopted a resolution [A/ Res/53/84, adopted without a vote] welcoming the information and data provided to date and the progress of the AHG so far. The Assembly urged the conclusion of the negotiations in the AHG as soon as possible before the commencement of the Fifth Review Conference, and urged the AHG to submit its report, "which shall be adopted by consensus," to the states parties to be considered at a special conference. The item will be on the agenda of the 54th Session.

The difficulties of strengthening the BWC are considerable and negotiations are now in their fifth year. The Ad Hoc Group established in Geneva held its 12th, 13th, and 14th sessions in September-October 1998, January 1999, and June 1999, with over 60 states parties and several signatory states participating (the numbers vary slightly at each session). At the January 1999 meeting there was a widespread sense of progress with serious negotiations in the area of visits and consolidating previous work on confidentiality and legal issues [*CBW Conventions Bulletin,* Issue 43, 3/99]. The seventh version of the rolling text was produced, amounting to 312 pages. Significant portions of the text continue to have square brackets, indicating they remain under discussion; but each new version of the rolling text is composed of relatively small sections of new language surrounded by much larger sections of older text. Except, therefore, for those working closely on the text in the AHG, it is easy to become confused.

At the January 1999 session, the European Union issued a declaration that it would be imperative to have completed all the stages necessary to ensure that a protocol be opened for signature prior to the Fifth Review Conference of the BWC, due to be held no later than 2001. The aim is that the protocol should be adopted by a special conference of states parties in 2000 [ibid.]. Also at the January session, Switzerland offered Geneva as a candidate city to host the headquarters of the future BWC organization [ibid.].

The task of creating a reliable regime of verification is immense, and many experts consider it significantly more difficult than arrangements to monitor and control nuclear, chemical, or conventional weapons. The nature of biological weapons, where only small quantities may be manufactured and stored, lends itself to cheating. Moreover, many modern pharmaceutical facilities use clean-in-place technology and routinely maintain high standards of cleanliness. Such practices can quickly, in hours, remove all signs of prohibited manufacture and thereby render short-notice challenge inspections of very little value. More attention has to be given, therefore, to defining reliable measures of verification through industrial computer monitoring systems and documentation.

In the case of the CWC, the chemical industry has been of great assistance in offering ideas and methods for carrying out inspections, as its members have come to recognize the value of being seen to embrace the concept of meaningful measures to ensure the effectiveness of the Convention. It is also in the commercial interests of the industry to have inspections and other controls that are practicable, intrusive without giving away industrial secrets, and not too administratively burdensome. It is very much the hope of the AHG that the pharmaceutical industry, particularly in the United States, will view the control measures of the BWC in the same way.

7. Conventional Weapons

Small Arms and Light Weapons

Since 1995, when the former U.N. Centre for Disarmament Affairs and the U.N. Institute for Disarmament Research (UNIDIR) took the initiative to carry out research on small arms as the weapons of choice in intra-state conflicts, the subject has drawn increasing attention within the U.N. system. In December 1995, when the General Assembly overwhelmingly voted to establish the **Panel of Governmental Experts** to study the issue [A/Res/50/70 B], small arms were thought to be essentially a disarmament and security problem. In the Secretary-General's comprehensive **Report on Small Arms** of August 1997 [A/52/298], however, the Panel found that virtually every part of the U.N. system was dealing in one way or another with the consequences of the armed conflicts, insecurity, violence, crime, and displaced peoples that are directly or indirectly associated with the wide availability and use of small arms. The Report's far-reaching impact among member states, regional and sub-regional organizations, and NGOs acted as a catalyst to place the issue of small arms firmly on the international agenda, and the United Nations has taken a lead role in encouraging and supporting all efforts to address the wide-ranging humanitarian, security, and development challenges posed by small arms.

In operative paragraph 5 of General Assembly Resolution 52/38 J [9/12/97], the Secretary-General was requested to prepare a report for the 54th Session, with the assistance of a group of governmental experts, on the progress made in implementing the recommendations of the Panel's report and on further actions recommended to be taken. The 23-member **U.N. Group of Governmental Experts on Small Arms** was established in early 1998 to assist the Secretary-General in preparing the report. A separate study on the problems of ammunition and explosives, also requested in the resolution, will be submitted by the Secretary-General to the 54th Session by an eight-member **U.N. Study Group on Ammunition and Explosives in All Their Aspects.**

As a coherent strategy was required to address the wide-ranging challenges posed by the excessive accumulation, uncontrolled proliferation, and recurrent use of small arms and light weapons, a proposal for a coordinating mechanism in the U.N. system was submitted by the Department for Disarmament Affairs and approved by the Secretary-General's Senior Management Group in mid-1998. The objectives of the **"Coordinating Action on Small Arms" (CASA) mechanism** [see www.un.org/Depts/dda/CAB/casa.htm] are fivefold and mutually supportive:

- To retain the lead taken by the United Nations in putting the issue on the global agenda by projecting itself as a leader, a catalyst, and a clearinghouse for different initiatives;
- To channel the growing international concern into the realization of some realistic and attainable goals by assuming a coordinating role in determining priorities;
- To encourage widespread involvement of civil society, including

NGOs, in building societal resistance to the illegitimate use of small arms and light weapons;

- To strengthen the U.N.'s ability for responding speedily and effectively to requests for assistance by subregions and countries severely affected by the excessive accumulation, proliferation, and use of small arms, including their illicit traffic;
- To ensure that the above objectives are pursued within the framework of, and without prejudice to, the U.N.'s overall objectives in the field of disarmament.

With a view to promoting advocacy in the framework of CASA, tools have been identified and **specific projects** have already been assigned. The U.N. Department of Public Information is finalizing work on a U.N. television documentary on small arms (September/October 1999). In July 1999, UNICEF launched a mobile exhibit on small arms and children. Since January, the Department for Disarmament Affairs and the United Nations Development Programme have been implementing a pilot project on voluntary weapons surrender by the civilian population in Albania, for which labor-intensive and income-generating community development activities are offered as non-cash incentives. The Office for the Coordination of Humanitarian Affairs has taken a lead role in the creation of a Reference Group on Small Arms within the humanitarian aid community (Inter-Agency Standing Committee) to determine how baseline data can be collected at the country level on the use of small arms and how an overall humanitarian strategy on small arms can be devised.

The **involvement of civil society** has received priority attention in organizing events, such as the sub-regional workshop on the exchange of national experiences in weapons collection in Central America. The workshop, co-organized by the U.N. Department for Disarmament Affairs (DDA) and the Guatemalan Ministry of Foreign Affairs, was held in Guatemala City in November 1998. The DDA briefed CASA on the preliminary findings of the workshop and published an information paper on the meeting. In late May 1999 representatives of the International Action Network on Small Arms (IANSA), a collective of some 200 NGOs from around the world working to prevent the proliferation of small arms, briefed the members of CASA following its launching during the Hague Appeal for Peace. In General Assembly resolutions and documents, member states have called for increased cooperation and coordination between U.N. intergovernmental bodies and the Secretariat so that the United Nations will continue to play a leading role in addressing the issue of small arms.

Illicit Traffic in Small Arms

The illicit trafficking in small arms has been of growing concern to governments since the early 1990s. This has been a particular problem in

Africa, and Mali has been instrumental in pushing the matter of assistance to states in curbing the traffic to the forefront of the Assembly's attention in the consideration of conventional weapon issues. The Assembly regularly adopts a resolution under this heading and did so at the 53rd Session [A/Res/53/77 B, adopted without a vote], requesting the Secretary-General to continue to examine the issue and submit a report to the Assembly at its 54th Session.

At the initiative of South Africa, a new resolution was presented at the 53rd Session [A/Res/53/77 T, adopted without a vote], requesting the Secretary-General to hold broad-based consultations with all member states, interested regional and sub-regional organizations, international agencies, and experts on:

a. the magnitude and scope of illicit trafficking in small arms,
b. possible measures to combat illicit trafficking and illicit circulation of small arms,
c. the role of the United Nations in collecting, collating, sharing, and disseminating information on illicit trafficking.

In response to the resolution, workshops were arranged to take place June 23–25 at the U.N. Regional Centre for Peace, Disarmament and Development in Latin America and the Caribbean, located in Lima, and July 26–28 at the U.N. Regional Centre for Peace and Disarmament in Africa, in Lomé. The Secretary-General will report to the 54th Session on the outcome of those consultations.

Practical Disarmament Measures

A valuable practical mechanism has developed from General Assembly Resolution 52/38 G, entitled "Consolidation of Peace through Practical Disarmament Measures." Known as the **Group of Interested States,** it has met on seven occasions under the chairmanship of Germany. It has two main purposes: to examine and, wherever possible, give joint support to concrete projects of practical disarmament and its dissemination to interested countries, and to exchange information about relevant lessons learned in the field of practical disarmament. The Group meets on an open-ended basis and is attended by between 40 and 60 representatives, depending on the issues under discussion. To date, meetings have been held on such issues as "Training of Trainers" in disarmament measures (Yaounde, Cameroon, July 27–31, 1998) and "Weapons collection and reintegration of former combatants into civil society—the experiences of Guatemala, El Salvador, Honduras, Nicaragua, and Colombia" (Guatemala City, November 18–20, 1998) [www.un.org/Depts/dda/CAB/measure.htm].

The initial mission to Albania in June 1998, to consider the feasibility of and arrangements for **weapons collection in Albania,** was also financed by the Group. This effort is being implemented by a combination of U.N. departments, the government of Albania, and a small number of interested states. It is aimed at extending aid in the form of development assistance to the region of Gramsh, Albania, in exchange for the handing in of weapons taken by the population from government storage depots in 1997 [U.N. press release DC/2626, 1/29/99].

8. Landmines

Anti-Personnel Landmines and the Ottawa Convention

On September 16, 1998, Burkino Faso became the 40th state to ratify the **Ottawa Convention on the Prohibition of the Use, Stockpiling, Production and Transfer of Anti-Personnel Mines and Their Destruction.** The significance of this event was that six months later, on March 1, 1999, the Convention entered into force. As of May 3, 1999, 133 countries had signed the Convention and 81 had ratified it.

With its **entry into force,** the focus of attention shifts to its implementation. By September 1999 and every year thereafter, the 55 states that were parties to the Convention when it entered into force are expected to report to the Secretary-General on what they have done to implement the agreement and provide detailed data on anti-personnel mine types, characteristics, stockpiles, and destruction. An innovation of the Convention is that the reporting can be done electronically.

Following the adoption by the General Assembly at its 53rd Session of a resolution welcoming the generous offer by Mozambique to host the **first meeting of states parties** to the Convention [A/Res/53/77 N, adopted without a vote], that meeting took place in Maputo, Mozambique, from May 3 to 7, 1999, and all states—whether parties or not—were invited. Forty-three states parties participated in the meeting, which was also attended as observers by representatives of 64 states not parties to the Convention. The United States and Russia were not officially represented at the meeting, but this appeared to be because as non-parties they did not wish to assume significant shares of the costs of the meeting rather than for any deeper political reasons.

A program of intersessional work was agreed to, with meetings of Standing Committees of Experts scheduled to take place in Geneva on mine clearance (September 13–15, 1999); on victim assistance, socioeconomic integration, and mine awareness (September 15–17); stockpile destruction (December 9–10); technologies for mine action (December 13–14); and general status and operation of the Convention (January 10–11, 2000). It was also agreed that the next meeting of the states parties will take place in Geneva from September 11 to 15, 2000.

It is expected that at the 54th General Assembly there will be a resolution welcoming the entry into force of the Convention and the convening of the first meeting of the states parties. The swift pace of the Convention's ratification is unusual and is widely regarded as a noteworthy indication of the international community's commitment to this important initiative. Although the humanitarian aspects of mine clearance are not part of the disarmament debate, it should be noted that there is a separate item on the General Assembly agenda entitled **"Assistance in mine action."** At its 53rd Session, the General Assembly adopted Resolution 53/26 without a vote, and this item will be considered again at the 54th Session.

III
Development and Trade

1. The United Nations and Development
By Roger A. Coate

Even though only implicitly mentioned in the U.N. Charter, promoting and facilitating social and economic development have been central missions of the world organization throughout its history. Social and economic stability were viewed by the chief architects of the post-war liberal world order as key requisites for creating and maintaining stable democracies, which, in turn, were seen as essential for international peace and security. Yet, in practice, the U.N.'s development "mandate" has generally been treated as a discrete—if not separable—phenomenon from peace and security as well as from humanitarian assistance, human rights, and other economic and social affairs. And it has not always been clear how "development," an ever-ambiguous concept, actually relates to the U.N.'s core peace and security mission.

The North-South debate of the 1970s and the associated call for the establishment of a new international economic order can be seen as attempts to provide coherence and direction to the U.N.'s development work. But the global development agenda remained unfocused and out of control as member states—in the name of promoting social and economic development—piled more and more items on U.N. agencies' already overcrowded agendas.

The North-South Summit in Cancun in 1981 provided an indication of what was in store for the U.N.'s Third Development Decade, the 1980s. The developed countries, led by the United States, were unwilling to launch a renewed round of negotiations over restructuring global economic relations, and the developing-country majority in the General Assembly was not about to give up its struggle to have the United Nations play an even larger role in promoting and facilitating development.

It was during this period that a conservative administration came to power in the United States that was arrogantly belligerent toward the United Nations and its developing-country majority and toward multilateralism more generally. For a complex set of reasons the United States,

Table III-1. Developed economies: rates of growth of real GDP, 1991–1999 (Annual percentage change[a])

	1991	1992	1993	1994	1995	1996	1997	1998[b]	1999[c]
All developed economies	0.7	1.6	0.8	2.7	2.2	2.9	2.7	1.8	1.5
Major industrialized countries	0.7	1.7	0.9	2.7	2.1	2.9	2.6	1.6	1.5
Canada	-1.9	0.9	2.3	4.7	2.6	1.2	3.8	2.9	2.5
France	0.8	1.2	-1.3	2.8	2.1	1.6	2.3	3.0	2.5
Germany	1.2	2.2	-1.1	2.9	1.9	1.4	2.2	2.7	2.3
Italy	1.1	0.6	-1.2	2.2	2.9	0.7	1.5	1.7	2.0
Japan	3.8	1.0	0.3	0.7	1.4	4.1	0.8	-2.7	-1.0
United Kingdom	-2.0	-0.5	2.1	4.3	2.7	2.2	3.4	2.3	1.5
United States	-0.9	2.7	2.3	3.5	2.3	3.4	3.9	3.4	2.3
Other industrialized countries	0.9	1.1	0.5	3.0	2.9	2.6	3.3	3.3	2.7
Australia	-1.3	2.7	4.0	5.3	4.1	3.7	2.8	3.8	3.0
Austria	3.4	1.3	0.5	2.5	2.1	1.6	2.6	3.0	2.7
Belgium-Luxembourg	1.7	1.5	-1.1	2.5	2.2	1.6	3.1	2.9	2.5
Denmark	1.4	1.3	1.3	3.5	3.1	3.5	3.4	2.4	2.0
Finland	-7.1	-3.6	-1.2	4.6	5.1	3.6	6.0	4.9	3.5
Greece	3.5	0.4	-0.9	1.5	2.0	1.8	3.2	3.4	3.5
Iceland	1.1	-3.4	1.0	3.7	1.0	5.5	5.0	5.6	4.3
Ireland	2.0	4.2	3.1	7.3	11.1	7.4	9.8	9.1	6.7
Malta	6.3	4.7	4.5	3.4	7.3	3.6	2.9	3.8	4.5
Netherlands	2.3	2.1	0.3	2.6	2.3	3.5	3.7	3.6	2.7
New Zealand	-2.3	0.6	5.1	5.5	3.3	2.7	3.1	0.2	-1.0
Norway	3.1	3.3	2.7	5.5	3.9	5.5	3.4	2.3	2.3
Portugal	2.1	4.2	7.8	1.9	2.0	3.2	3.7	4.1	3.5
Spain	2.3	0.7	-1.2	2.1	2.8	2.2	3.6	3.7	3.5
Sweden	-1.1	-1.4	-2.2	3.3	3.6	1.3	1.8	3.0	2.3
Switzerland	-0.8	-0.1	-0.5	0.5	0.6	0.0	1.7	1.7	1.5
Western Europe of which:									
European Union (15)	0.7	1.1	-0.5	2.9	2.5	1.7	2.7	2.8	2.3
EUR11	1.2	1.4	-0.9	2.7	2.4	1.6	2.5	2.8	2.5

Source: UN/DESA; based on IMF, *International Financial Statistics*.
[a] Data for country groups are weighted averages, where weights for each year are the previous year's GDP valued at 1993 prices and exchange rates.
[b] Preliminary estimates.
[c] Forecast.

the U.N.'s wealthiest and largest contributing member state, fell further and further behind in meeting legal financial obligations, eventually becoming the Organization's largest financial deadbeat. When it came to development-assistance financing, the United States strengthened its preference for bilateralism or, if multilateral, toward channeling assistance through the Bretton Woods institutions.

By decade's end the world had begun to experience a major political-economic transformation that at once eclipsed and captured the global agenda: the ending of the Cold War. Now the developing world became even further marginalized as the countries of Eastern and Central Europe and Central Asia making the transition to democracy and to market economies took center stage. Statist economic models of all sorts had become discredited; the virtues and triumph of liberal capitalism were extolled.

A new U.S. president, George Bush, declared the beginning of a new world order in which the United Nations might finally play the role its founders had envisioned 50 years before. That role, of course, had to do with maintaining international peace, military security, and stability rather than with promoting what has come to be called *human* development.

In fact, the early 1990s were heady times for the United States at the United Nations. U.S. policy-makers found the world organization a useful tool for selected aspects of its foreign policy, especially when, as in the days leading to the Persian Gulf War, the United Nations could be used to maneuver around various domestic political hurdles. With strong U.S. engagement and support, the U.N.'s peacekeeping, peacemaking, and peace-enforcement plate was full. In time, it began to overflow.

Meanwhile, the other United States—the financial deadbeat United States—kept a stranglehold on the world organization, demanding that it do more and better with less. But with mounting U.S. arrearages, the U.N.'s financial and human-resource base was already seriously overtaxed, and U.S. policy-makers were finding that the multilateral organization had severe limitations as a foreign policy tool. Once again, the United States began to turn its attention elsewhere.

If the 1990s have not ushered in a new world order, they have provided irrefutable proof that this is an age of globalization and interdependence, and that there are numerous global problems that must be confronted multilaterally. Moreover, the perception has been growing in the developed and developing worlds alike that this multitude of global problems is inextricably linked to problems of development and underdevelopment.

Development by Any Other Name . . .

During the 1990s a series of reports, global conferences, and other important activities have helped to refocus and redirect the global development agenda:

- South Commission Report (1990)
- World Summit for Children (1990)
- *Human Development Report* (1990; annual)
- World Conference on Education for All (1990)
- U.N. Conference on Environment and Development (UNCED, or "Earth Summit," 1992)
- Eighth session of the United Nations Conference on Trade and Development (UNCTAD VIII, 1993)
- World Conference on Human Rights (1993)
- Commission on Sustainable Development (established 1993)
- International Conference on Population and Development (1994)
- *An Agenda for Development* (1995)
- World Summit on Social Development (1995)
- Fourth World Conference on Women (1995)
- Commission on Global Governance Report (1995)
- Second U.N. Conference on Human Settlements (HABITAT II, 1996)
- World Food Summit (1996)
- Ninth session of the United Nations Conference on Trade and Development (UNCTAD IX, 1996)
- Special Session of the General Assembly to Review and Appraise the Implementation of Agenda 21 ("Earth Summit + 5," 1997)
- General Assembly Special Session on the International Conference on Population and Development (1999)

One of the most striking outcomes of this collection of activities was **the merging in the development debate of two concepts, human development and sustainable development, to become "sustainable human development" (SHD).** This was further refined in the mid-1990s as the UNDP/UNFPA Executive Board [decision 94/14] adopted sustainable human development as a mission of the U.N. Development Programme (UNDP). Like other development concepts before it, SHD is viewed as a **key to creating and maintaining a secure and peaceful world order.** The debate over development in the 1990s indicates that most member states of the world organization expect the United Nations to play some meaningful role in achieving it.

When Kofi Annan assumed the post of Secretary-General in 1997, he inherited an organization that was less and less the large donor states' mechanism of choice for facilitating and promoting development. Despite the U.N.'s self-ascribed "comparative advantages" in the development field, major donors were turning to the Bretton Woods institutions as the venue for their multilateral development-assistance financing. Annan has moved to reverse that trend by attempting to **restore "unity of purpose" and coherence to the U.N.'s five core missions:** peace and security, economic and social affairs, development cooperation, humanitarian affairs, and human rights [Report of the Secretary-General, A/51/950].

On Secretary-General Annan's watch, **the U.N.'s primary raison d'être—promoting peace and security—has come to mean promoting "human security,"** and is now inextricably linked to sustainable human development. In the Secretary-General's words: "We are focusing on the importance of sustainability—on 'sustainable development'—in all aspects of our work, including peace and security" [Kofi Annan, "The Quiet Revolution," *Global Governance*, 4–6/98, p. 136].

Annan's predecessor, Boutros Boutros-Ghali, had laid some important conceptual groundwork for revitalizing the U.N.'s development role in his *An Agenda for Development* (1994) but had failed to provide clear guidelines for setting organizational priorities and strategies and for establishing a clear division of labor among U.N. bodies [see *A Global Agenda: Issues Before the 53rd General Assembly of the United Nations*, pp. 94–95]. The ensuing debates about the development agenda in the General Assembly and other deliberative bodies were similarly unfocused.

It is the **U.N. Development Programme** that has assumed an important intellectual role in facilitating the debate over the concept of human security and development, both theory and practice. UNDP's *Human Development Report 1993* provides a framework. It suggested that the U.N.'s work be based on at least **five "new pillars" that give unity of purpose to the world organization:** new concepts of human security; new models of sustainable human development; new partnerships among states, markets, and other elements of civil society; new patterns of national and global governance; and new forms of international cooperation [New York: Oxford University Press, 1993, p. 2]. The five pillars also provide a convenient framework for exploring the development issues that dominate the global agenda at the opening of the 54th Session of the General Assembly.

New Concepts of Human Security

Human security, a qualitative condition, is based on individual and collective perceptions of present and potential threats to physical and psychological well-being from all manner of agents and forces affecting lives, values, and property [Thomas Weiss et al., *The United Nations and Changing World Politics*, 2nd ed., Boulder, Colo.: Westview Press, 1997, p. 260]. Such a notion of security dispenses with the traditional division of international issues into matters of "war and peace" on one hand and "economic and social" affairs on the other. Here, security from direct violence is only one attribute of a humanly secure environment. The absence of structural violence, such as poverty and other forms of social, economic, and environmental degradation, is another.

Table III-2. Developing countries: Rates of Growth of GDP, 1991–1999 (Annual percentage change)

	1991	1992	1993	1994	1995	1996	1997	1998[a]	1999[b]
Developing countries[c]	3.2	5.0	5.2	5.6	4.6	5.7	5.7	1.6	3.0
of which:									
Africa	0.8	-0.4	-0.6	2.0	2.8	4.5	2.7	2.6	3.5
Eastern and Southern Asia	6.9	7.8	7.9	8.6	8.2	7.4	6.3	0.8	4.3
Region excluding China	6.2	5.6	5.9	7.0	7.3	6.5	5.2	-2.2	2.3
of which:									
East Asia	7.2	6.0	6.5	7.6	7.6	6.6	5.2	-4.2	1.5
South Asia	2.9	4.2	3.9	5.2	6.2	6.0	5.3	4.4	4.5
Western Asia	-5.0	5.5	4.3	-0.9	4.1	4.8	5.9	1.7	2.5
Latin America and the Caribbean	3.4	2.9	3.5	5.5	-0.1	3.7	5.4	2.6	1.3
Memo Items:									
Sub-Saharan Africa (excluding Nigeria and South Africa)	-0.3	-1.2	-2.9	1.8	4.2	4.9	4.2	2.7	4.0
Least developed countries	-0.5	0.5	-1.1	1.9	4.7	4.7	4.4	2.3	3.3
25 largest developing economies									
Algeria	0.1	1.4	-1.2	-1.1	3.9	3.8	1.3	3.7	4.0
Argentina	8.9	8.7	6.0	7.4	-4.6	4.4	8.4	4.5	2.0
Brazil	0.1	-1.1	4.1	5.8	4.1	3.0	3.0	0.5	-1.5
Chile	7.1	10.5	6.0	4.1	8.2	7.2	7.1	4.5	3.0
China	9.2	14.2	13.5	12.6	10.5	9.6	8.8	7.5	8.0

Colombia	1.6	4.0	5.1	6.3	5.7	2.1	3.0	2.5	2.0
Egypt	2.3	2.5	2.0	2.3	3.2	4.0	5.3	4.9	5.0
Hong Kong, China	5.1	6.3	6.1	5.3	4.7	4.8	5.3	-4.0	0.0
India	2.0	4.0	3.9	5.4	6.7	6.4	5.5	4.8	5.0
Indonesia	7.0	6.5	6.5	7.5	8.1	8.0	4.6	-15.0	-2.0
Iran (Islamic Republic of)	6.0	6.0	2.6	1.8	4.2	5.0	3.5	-2.5	0.5
Iraq	-45.0	3.0	1.5	-5.0	-1.0	0.0	25.0	15.0	8.0
Israel	6.2	6.6	3.4	6.6	7.1	4.5	2.1	1.1	2.0
Republic of Korea	9.1	5.1	5.8	8.6	8.9	7.1	5.5	-6.2	1.5
Malaysia	8.6	7.8	8.3	9.2	9.5	8.2	7.8	-6.0	1.0
Mexico	4.3	3.7	1.9	4.6	-6.2	5.1	7.0	4.3	3.0
Pakistan	6.7	5.1	3.1	4.2	4.9	5.2	4.2	3.0	2.0
Philippines	0.0	0.0	2.1	4.4	4.8	5.5	5.1	1.0	2.5
Saudi Arabia	6.0	3.0	1.6	-2.7	-0.2	4.0	3.0	-2.0	1.0
Singapore	6.7	6.0	9.9	10.1	8.9	7.0	7.8	0.0	0.5
South Africa	-1.0	-2.2	1.3	2.7	3.4	3.2	1.7	0.5	2.0
Taiwan Province of China	7.6	6.8	6.3	6.5	6.1	5.6	6.7	4.5	5.0
Thailand	8.5	7.8	8.3	8.7	8.6	6.7	-0.4	-7.0	-0.5
Turkey	0.8	5.0	8.1	-6.1	8.0	7.0	6.8	4.5	3.7
Venezuela	9.7	6.1	0.7	-2.5	2.2	-1.5	5.0	-1.5	0.0

Source: UN/DESA.
a Preliminary estimates.
b Forecast.
c Covering countries that account for 98 percent of the population of all developing countries.

Human security focuses attention directly on human beings and their circumstances. As noted in the *Human Development Report 1993*, human security stresses "the security of people, not only of nations. . . . The concept of security must change [the report argued]—from an exclusive stress on national security to a much greater stress on people's security, from security through armaments to security through human development, from territorial security to food, employment, and environmental security." To make people psychologically secure may, under some circumstances, be the antithesis of making the governments of states and their territorial boundaries physically secure, especially when state entities themselves are the perpetrators of individual insecurities, as is the case with human rights violations.

If the United Nations is to fulfill a mandate to promote *human security*, its programs have to be placed in this much broader perspective. This is especially true today, when the General Assembly is grappling with the implications and impacts of globalization and interdependence.

Growing Human Insecurity: The Impact of Global Economic Contagion

The impact of the global financial and economic crises of late 1997 and 1998, for example, has seriously undermined human security on a worldwide scale. What began as a currency crisis in Thailand in July 1997 had spread to Indonesia, Malaysia, Philippines, Republic of Korea, and other East Asian economies by the end of the year. Given the interdependence of international financial markets and the global trading order, the crisis contributed to economic decline and disorder elsewhere as well. Among other, associated problems, the largest single development-assistance donor, Japan, drew inward as the country's economy slumped into recession. As commodity prices fell and short-term investment and private lending declined, they made ripples around the world. Eventually, the global economic downturn affected developed economies as well.

The developing world and transitional economies were by far the hardest hit. In 1998 the rate of growth of GDP of the developing countries as a whole was the lowest since 1983. And while some improvement was forecast for 1999, that largely represented a tapering off of the huge contraction in a few East Asian economies rather than a resumption of the kind of growth that many developing economies had experienced during much of the 1990s [United Nations, *World Economic Situation and Prospects for 1999*, 1999]. In fact, the World Bank's *Global Development Report*, released in April 1999, substantially adjusted downward its forecast for economic growth in the developing world. Instead of the 2.7 percent growth previously predicted for 1999, the new forecast projects only a 1.5 percent growth rate. These revised figures reflect a continuing deterioration of international trade, especially non-petroleum commodity trade. The

World Bank report also indicated that the **net flow of financial aid to developing countries** had fallen significantly as well (by 6 percent in 1997), reaching its lowest level in real terms since 1981. **Net concessional assistance** to developing countries has fallen by a third during the last decade; in Japan, the United States, and Germany, the percentage of GDP set aside for aid has been cut significantly.

But what does all this mean from a human security perspective and the U.N.'s role in promoting human development? In **East Asia,** where the crisis began, there has been a dramatic rise in unemployment and a substantial decline in real income linked to increasing inflation. Domestic violence, criminal behavior, and suicides have increased. Of course, the poorest segments of the population have been the hardest hit. In Indonesia, for example, 48 percent of the population is estimated to exist below the poverty line as compared with 11 percent just two years ago. Moreover, the situation is getting worse, and the proportion living in poverty is projected to reach almost two-thirds by the end of 1999 [ibid., p. 20]. In **other developing regions** the direct impact of the global financial crisis has been less severe, but when linked to uneven weather patterns, declining commodity prices, dramatic declines in short-term investment and official development finance flows, political turmoil, civil strife, and many other factors the overall impact on human security has been quite substantial.

This most recent global economic crisis, however, represents only a small part of the human insecurity picture for the citizens of developing regions. Even in the period immediately preceding the Asian financial crisis, most of the developing world experienced only limited success at sustaining growth at the levels needed for poverty reduction. As noted by UNDP:

> Well over a billion people are deprived of basic consumption needs. Of the 4.4 billion people in developing countries, nearly three-fifths lack basic sanitation. Almost a third have no access to clean water. A quarter do not have adequate housing. A fifth have no access to modern health services. A fifth of children do not attend school to grade 5. About a fifth do not have enough dietary energy and protein. Micronutrient deficiencies are even more widespread. Worldwide, 2 billion people are anaemic, including 55 million in industrial countries. In developing countries only a privileged minority has motorized transport, telecommunications and modern energy. . . . In 70 countries with nearly a billion people consumption today is lower than it was 25 years ago.
> [*Human Development Report 1998*]

These conditions cry out for new solutions, which, if the past provides any lessons at all, must be based in new conceptualizations and models of development.

New Models of Sustainable Human Development

From the above it is clear that promoting human development involves much more than altering the economic and demographic profiles of particular countries. Human security emphasizes the psychological end state of development instead of the more mechanical aspects of development. Creating the foundation for sustainable human development entails empowering individuals, groups, and communities to become engaged constructively and effectively in satisfying their own needs, values, and interests, thereby providing them with a genuine sense of control over their own futures. As simply stated by UNDP,

> Human development is development *of* the people *for* the people *by* the people. Development *of* the people means investing in human capabilities, whether in education or health or skills, so that they can work productively and creatively. Development *for* the people means ensuring that the economic growth they generate is distributed widely and fairly. . . . [D]evelopment *by* the people [means] . . . giving everyone a chance to participate. [*Human Development Report 1993*]

The 1993 report went on to argue that "people's participation is becoming the central issue of our time" and that it is inextricably linked with—and is an inherent component, if not requisite, of—both sustainable human development and human security. Right now, however, the various bodies of the U.N. system do not take a uniform approach to **popular participation.** And even within individual agencies, the meaning and practice vary. In the World Bank, for example, "participation" has been used variously to mean empowering the poor and previously excluded groups to participate in development policy processes; enhancing the involvement of nongovernmental organizations (NGOs) in the making of World Bank policy; increasing the accountability of Bank programs and projects by domestic actors in recipient countries; and integrating local knowledge and oversight into project planning, implementation, and evaluation.

Participation and the empowerment of women and other marginalized groups in society have been two of the priority themes stressed by UNDP, the U.N.'s central operational development arm, throughout the 1990s in its annual *Human Development Report.* The way to eradicate poverty, the reports have argued, is to empower the poor and marginalized elements of society to provide for the satisfaction of their own basic needs and values. UNDP sees its role as "promot[ing] the empowerment of people through measures to build their coping and adapting capacities, to increase their productivity and income, and to participate more fully in decision-making" [*UNDP Today: Reform in Action,* 4/98].

UNDP has declared as its top priority the **eradication of poverty** and has adopted a multipronged strategy for accomplishing this goal. One cornerstone of that strategy is **good governance**. The belief is that well-functioning, effective, and accountable public and private institutions that are viewed as legitimate in the eyes of those being governed will help to mobilize the social capital required for sustaining development. UNDP programs provide support for holding free and fair elections, respecting fundamental human rights and the rule of law, building strong and vibrant civil societies, enhancing local institutional capacity for supporting decentralized policy-making processes, and increasing the accountability and transparency of government institutions and operations [ibid.].

Creating sustainable livelihoods is another dimension of the agency's strategy. This entails supporting local cooperatives and micro-enterprises, providing assistance and extending credit to disadvantaged and previously marginalized groups in society, increasing employment opportunities for displaced persons and refugees, and making technology available and spawning local productive enterprises. An important element of this strategy is to redefine economic growth so as to link it to family income and not solely to national account statistics. Closely linked to this strategic dimension is a strong commitment to "gender mainstreaming"—that is, assuring that men and women are accorded equal opportunities to develop their productive potentials and sustainable livelihoods. UNDP, says one of its promotional pieces, "works both 'upstream' to sensitize policy makers to gender issues and to create national capacity for gender analyses, and 'downstream' to extend women's access to education, training, credit and other assets" [ibid.].

While sustainable human development has remained a somewhat ambiguous concept in many respects, almost every definition shares at least one common element: **concern for environmental regeneration and sustainability of resources**. The UNDP development strategy is no exception, focusing on helping governments design and implement development programs and projects to protect the human environment and promote sustainable economic growth and the management of natural resources, all in the hope of benefiting and preserving development choices for future generations. Today, the agency's activities focus on the role of food security in building human security, on improving aid and debt coordination and management, and on reforming and modernizing financial institutions.

These activities are currently bundled together as "comprehensive development," in U.N. jargon. Comprehensive development, like sustainable human development, offers "two fundamental messages," says the U.N. Deputy Secretary-General:

> —The first is that development is not only, or even essentially, about economics. It is, or should be, about human beings: about satisfying their aspirations to live their lives in dignity, free from want and free from fear.

—And the second is that development comes about, when it does, as the result of a complex set of interactions between political, economic, social, environmental and cultural factors. [U.N. press release DSG/SM/56, 6/8/99]

In this context one thing seems clear: No matter what direction new models of development may take, the forces of globalization and the capitalist global economy have penetrated even the remotest areas of human settlement. The U.N. activities promoting human development must take these forces fully into account. This will require new forms of cooperation and partnerships among states, markets, the private sector, voluntary and civic organizations, and local communities.

New Partnerships among States, Markets, and Other Elements of Society

A central component of Secretary-General Annan's "Quiet Revolution" has been to build and expand constructive U.N. partnerships with civil society and the private sector. Underpinning this strategy is the belief that "people should guide both the state and the market, which need to work together in tandem, with people sufficiently empowered to exert a more effective influence over both" [*Human Development Report 1993*]. An important task for the U.N.'s development work is to help create the conditions that are necessary for such **people-centered development.**

Within the developing world the initiative to forge new partnerships has taken a variety of forms and complexions. In general there has been a move to strengthen the direct involvement of UNDP and other U.N. agencies with diverse elements of society, including NGOs, the private sector, and civil society organizations. Similar efforts have also been made by the Bretton Woods institutions. Although NGOs and U.N. development agencies have worked together for some time now, cooperation between U.N. agencies and private sector entities at the country level is relatively new. Because some governments see the U.N.'s excursions with such entities as an encroachment on state sovereignty, this development is not without controversy.

Examples of UNDP initiatives with private sector support are MicroStart, a $41 million program operating in 25 countries designed to strengthen the capacity of microfinance institutions to provide credit to individuals to assist them in starting or expanding small businesses; the African Project Development Facility, providing entrepreneurs in 29 African countries with investment funds; "Money Matters: Private Finance for Development," assisting emerging market economies to mobilize and attract private finance for sustainable human development; the Africa 2000 Network, providing small grants (up to $50,000) to villages for community-based sustainable human development activities; and the Sub-Regional South Asia Poverty Alleviation Programme, providing assistance for the training of community organization leaders and for organizing villagers into community-based organizations in Bangladesh, India, Nepal, Maldives, and Sri Lanka.

Concerted action has also been taken over the last several years to reform the way U.N. bodies relate to indigenous institutions as well as to each other at the country level. The **Resident Coordinator system** has been revitalized, with the Resident Coordinator serving as the designated representative of the Secretary-General for development operations in the field and as the designated leader of the U.N. country team. More rigorous selection criteria for Resident Coordinators, enhanced training, performance evaluations, and increased planning and reporting requirements have bolstered the system.

The **country-team** notion has been strengthened by a move to establish "**U.N. Houses**"—shared premises for all U.N. agencies, funds, and other bodies working at the country level—and by a move to provide common administrative services for those agencies. Beyond the obvious cost-cutting and efficiency-enhancing aspects of these moves, the goal is to create a more effective U.N. presence for building the necessary linkages and partnerships that can make sustainable human development a reality.

Building a more unified country approach has also been the objective of creating the **U.N. Development Assistance Frameworks (UNDAFs)** program. UNDAFs are basically collaborative planning, programming, and resource-coordinating frameworks designed to enhance the overall contribution by U.N. bodies to national development strategies and policies. The pilot phase, involving systematic experiments in 18 countries, has been completed and evaluated, and "the provisional UNDAF guidelines have been finalized." Twenty more countries were scheduled to begin the exercise in June 1999, with the rest to follow by 2002 [U.N. press release DSG/SM/56, 6/8/99].

Underlying all these initiatives is the assumption that "poverty eradication and good governance are inseparable"—inseparable, says UNDP, because "good governance brings about a proper balance among state action, the private sector, civil society, and the communities themselves" [*UNDP Today: Fighting Poverty*, 6/98].

New Patterns of Governance

So convinced is UNDP of the validity of this assumption that, today, good governance projects comprise **the single largest share—28 percent—of its budget.** Under the good governance program, UNDP gives priority to the following objectives:

- Democratization and political empowerment of the poor through participation and strengthening of civil society organizations

- Strengthening of judicial, electoral, and parliamentary systems
- Human rights and the rule of law, with special emphasis on women's legal rights
- Decentralization and strengthening of local governance
- Policies and frameworks for market-based economic transitions, private sector development, and globalization challenges
- Public administration reforms for accountable governance
- Crisis management and rebuilding government capacities in post-conflict situations [*UNDP Today: Introducing the Organization,* 9/98]

All these objectives feed into a commitment to building stable, open, well-functioning, and accountable political institutions that are perceived as legitimate in the eyes of those being governed. "[W]e must learn from past mistakes," former UNDP Administrator James Gustave Speth has argued, "and ensure that development cooperation supports the polity and not just the economy. . . . The challenges of growing poverty and widening inequity will not be met without democratization and good governance" ["Non-Benign Neglect: America and the Developing World in the Era of Globalization," speech delivered at the National Press Club, Washington, D.C., 10/14/98].

This focus on promoting good governance represents **a not-so-subtle challenge to the concept of sovereignty** that underpins the interstate legal order and the U.N. system itself. Consider, for example, two newly launched projects in the Philippines, one aimed at strengthening the skills of journalists assigned to investigate the behavior of public officials, the other establishing an electronic network [the "Good Governance Forum"] for policy-makers, NGOs, private enterprises, and civil society organizations to promote dialogue on governance policies [*UNDP Flash,* 4/12/99].

One or two decades ago most U.N. member states would have deemed such activities outrageous and totally unacceptable intrusions. In the global political climate of the late 1990s, however, they do not seem as troubled. The forces of globalization and interdependence have violated (from top-down and outside-in) much of the sanctity of this legal notion. Indigenous social, cultural, political, and economic forces have brought complementary pressures (from bottom-up and inside-out).

As reflected above, the issues of **people's participation and democratization** have become central themes in the debate over and practice of development and governance. Neither participation nor democratization, as a multilateral policy issue, is clear-cut or without its problems. Whose voices, claims, and interests are to be heard and acted upon? How do U.N. agencies decide between and manage competing and conflicting claims by domestic political groups and forces? For that matter, how does one create democratic institutions in the absence of democratic culture? If decentralizing government is one of the best means of promoting participation and increasing local decision-making, how do you do so in societies in which resources, political power, and wealth are highly concentrated at the central government level? And how do U.N. agencies respond to and resolve issues related to basic contradictions between democratic values and liberal capitalist values and practices?

Certainly there are no straightforward answers to these questions. They are thorny political issues with which the General Assembly and other multilateral institutional bodies must deal for years to come.

Good governance and creating new patterns of governance do not, of course, stop at the water's edge. There is the matter of **promoting effective governance in the U.N. itself and among the specialized agencies of the U.N. system.** And then there is the larger issue of promoting good governance more generally, by stressing such concepts as transparency, the rule of law, and fiscal responsibility.

In the Secretary-General's effort to bring unity of purpose to the diverse activities of the world organization and provide clear lines of responsibility for carrying them out, he has created a **cabinet structure, the Senior Management Group,** comprised of the Under-Secretaries-General, the heads of U.N. funds and programs, and the newly created Deputy Secretary-General (who, among other things, is responsible for overseeing the reform process and the coordination of development activities). Four new **thematic Executive Committees** (Peace and Security, Humanitarian Affairs, Economic and Social Affairs, and United Nations Development Group) oversee the coordination of policy development, management, and decision-making. The convenors of each of these committees sit on the Senior Management Group.

Two of these Executive Committees are of particular importance for development. The **Economic and Social Affairs Executive Committee,** convened by the Under-Secretary-General for Economic and Social Affairs, is comprised of representatives of 18 U.N. bodies, including UNDP, UNCTAD, and other development assistance units. The **United Nations Development Group Executive Committee,** convened by the Administrator of UNDP, includes the United Nations Population Fund (UNFPA), United Nations Children's Fund (UNICEF), and World Food Programme (WFP). This body also serves as the secretariat for the **United Nations Development Group (UNDG),** created in 1997 to provide better coordination among the numerous U.N. funds, programs, and other bodies that have proliferated over the years in the development area. UNDG's members include UNDP, UNFPA, UNICEF, WFP, United Nations Development Fund for Women (UNIFEM), United Nations Office for Project Services, Joint United Nations Programme on HIV/AIDS (UNAIDS), United Nations Centre for Human Settlements, United Nations International Drug Control Programme, United Nations Department of Economic and Social Affairs, International Fund for Agricultural

Development, Office of the High Commissioner for Human Rights, the Economic and Social Council's five regional commissions (for Africa, Europe, Western Asia, Asia and the Pacific, and Latin America and the Caribbean), and the Special Representative of the Secretary-General for Children in Armed Conflict.

In the context of this new cabinet system, **UNDP plays the central role in the development area.** In addition to its own operational activities, it administers several special-purpose funds and programs, including the U.N. Capital Development Fund, UNIFEM, United Nations Volunteers, and the Special Unit for Technical Cooperation among Developing Countries. And in cooperation with the World Bank and the United Nations Environment Programme (UNEP), UNDP serves as an implementing agency for the Global Environmental Facility, which provides concessional funding and grants for certain environmentally sound development projects.

Beyond the UNDG, UNDP works in conjunction with units in other thematic areas in a variety of ways. It assists the Department of Economic and Social Affairs in the U.N.'s normative work in developing countries and in providing integrated follow-up to the U.N.'s global conferences of the 1990s. In the normative area the United Nations is working in the field to promote such ideas as good governance, the importance of the role of the market as a "powerful motor of development," the importance of private capital flows, the importance of "unleashing creativity and entrepreneurial spirit . . . [to] produce better results than paternalistic, dependency-created strategies," the importance of operating in accord with universal norms as those expressed in the Universal Declaration of Human Rights, the International Labor Organization's Declaration on Fundamental Principles and Rights at Work, and the Rio Declaration on Environment and Development [U.N. press release DSG/SM/56, 6/8/99; and David Crane in *Toronto Star*, 2/1/99].

UNDP also works with bodies in the security realm to support elections, demobilization, and reconciliation initiatives; to support the protection of fundamental human rights; and to promote peace through development. Linkages with the U.N. High Commissioner for Refugees and other U.N. bodies in the humanitarian field find UNDP lending support for disaster prevention, mitigation, and preparedness; reintegration of refugees, former combatants, and internally displaced people; implementation of post-disaster national plans for reintegration, reconstruction, and recovery; and similar activities [UNDP Today: Introducing the Organization, 9/98].

A key to making these and other relationships work effectively is coordination. And, indeed, Kofi Annan's "Quiet Revolution" places a good deal of emphasis on **enhancing U.N. system-wide coordination,** especially in the development area. For example, he has appointed an Assistant Secretary-General for Policy Coordination and Inter-Agency Affairs and given that office responsibility for identifying ways to strengthen the role of the Economic and Social Council (ECOSOC) as a mechanism for facilitating inter-agency cooperation within the U.N. system. For two consecutive years (April 1998 and April 1999), ECOSOC has hosted a joint high-level meeting between its members and officials of the Bretton Woods institutions. At the behest of the General Assembly [A/Res/53/169] the 1999 meeting focused on the "functioning of international financial markets and stability in financing for development." The President of the World Bank, the Managing Director of the International Monetary Fund (IMF), the U.N. Deputy Secretary-General, the Chairman of the IMF's Interim Committee, the Chairman of the Development Committee of the World Bank, and the finance ministers who attend the IMF/World Bank's biannual meetings of the Interim and Development committees were among the participants. These meetings have been notable for a **spirit of cooperation between the U.N. and the Bretton Woods institutions** that was often lacking in the past. Better integration of the U.N. and the Bretton Woods institutions is needed to lay the foundation of a more stable global economic order, declared IMF Managing Director Michel Camdessus at the 1999 meeting [press release ECOSOC/5818, 4/29/99].

Notable too is the fact that the U.N. Secretary-General and the World Bank President held a retreat the previous year; and UNDP and the Bank have initiated a pilot program at the country level to explore the interface between UNDAF and the Bank's Country Assistance Strategy. Even stronger evidence of cooperation may come in the future as the **new UNDP Administrator, Mark Malloch Brown,** settles into the job. Before assuming office, Malloch Brown served for several years as Vice-President for External Affairs and Vice-President for United Nations Affairs at the World Bank.

Upon assuming office, Malloch Brown cautioned:

> It is now evident that the decline in [UNDP] core funding over the last few years has not been checked, that indeed it has worsened and that, as a result, UNDP faces a new crisis that challenges its capacity to remain relevant. Consider the facts: the programme has been slipping since 1996 when resources initially covering three years were stretched to include a fourth year, 2000. Last month [June 1999], the organization reduced programme resources for 2001 to 50 percent of the level forecast earlier because the $1.1 billion assumed for the current period is not forthcoming. . . . The momentum of a declining resource base has not been broken. Indeed, it is accelerating. . . . We are rapidly slipping beneath the point where we can remain a universal organization. [Inaugural speech, U.N. Trusteeship Council chamber, 7/1/99]

The financial facts speak for themselves. By now finance flows—both public and private—to developing countries have declined significantly. **Official overseas development assistance (ODA)** reached an all-time low

(0.22 percent of GDP) in 1997. But the development finance crunch began long before the global economic crisis. ODA and other development assistance have declined significantly over the past decade, with bilateral assistance flows accounting for most of it. Private finance flows also fell as international bank lending dropped dramatically [United Nations, *Development Update*, 3/99]. Creating stability for development financing is of particular concern for the least developed countries (LDCs), which rely heavily on ODA as the main source of their external resource flows and are extremely vulnerable to such shifts.

A final dimension of good governance relates to **governance of the global political economy as a whole.** In the wake of the Asian financial and global economic crises, questions are being raised about the wisdom of "letting the market rule." This was precisely the question that Secretary-General Annan was asking when he called on the Group of 8 "to adopt policies favouring more balanced patterns and higher levels of output growth, to consider additional steps to protect the international financial system against instability, to take quick action to reduce the debt of the poorest countries and to increase development aid." He challenged this group of influential member states to take the lead in creating a new financial architecture for the global economy for which the United Nations would provide the "soft infrastructure" [U.N. press release PI/1142, 5/26/99].

New Forms of International Cooperation

The Organization has been actively engaged in building innovative partnerships with other international organizations, local governments, NGOs, the private sector, and civil society. Each of the private sector initiatives discussed above involves **transnational partnerships linked to local sustainable human development projects.** UNDP's "Money Matters: Private Finance for Development" initiative, for example, has six global corporate co-sponsors, including Fidelity Investments, Banque Nationale de Paris, and State Street Bank. International banks have also been instrumental in supporting the agency's "MicroStart" program. At the initiative of UNDP and other U.N. agencies there is now a partnership—the World Alliance of Cities Against Poverty, enlisting members of civil society, the private sector, and local government—to carry out the goals of the 1995 "Social Summit."

With ODA on the downswing, UNDP and other U.N. agencies have stepped up their efforts to find other sources of development assistance transfers to LDCs. The **"Partners for Development" summit,** hosted by the U.N. Conference on Trade and Development (UNCTAD) in Lyons, France, in November 1998, is illustrative of the innovative approaches being taken. The summit brought together representatives of government, the private sector, NGOs, civil society, and international organizations and treated them as equals. Organized around two central tracks—one focusing on "global electronic trade U.N. partnerships" and the other on "profit and development"—the summit attempted to put theoretical ideas about building partnerships to "the test of a real-life meeting in which Governments and non-governmental actors would be given equal treatment" [UNCTAD, TD/B/EX(20)/2, 1/27/99]. To broaden the impact of the summit, several other events were held parallel to it: the annual meeting of the World Association of Investment Promotion Agencies, the fifth World Trade Point Meeting, and the sixth World Summit of Young Entrepreneurs.

UNDP has taken a slightly different approach to building partnerships. In March 1999, for example, UNDP officials announced that 16 major global corporations, headquartered in eight different countries, had joined discussions aimed at establishing **a Global Sustainable Development Facility (GSDF).** Each of the 16 companies had contributed $50,000 to cover the initiation phase of the project, which is designed to integrate the U.N.'s goal of promoting sustainable human development and the investment goals of corporations [UNDP press release, 3/12/99]. UNDP and UNCTAD, for another example, have launched a $4 million program on **"Globalization, Liberalization, and Sustainable Development"** that brings together experts from international organizations, the private sector, civil society, and academe to explore ways in which developing countries can better manage their integration into the world economy and to develop a strategy for achieving it [UNDP press release, 2/2/99].

In his inaugural speech, UNDP Administrator Malloch Brown outlined what he termed UNDP's "100-yard sprint" for renewed partnerships with five critical constituencies: program country governments, civil society, the Bretton Woods institutions, the private sector, and the rest of the U.N. family [Trusteeship Council Chamber, 7/1/99]. In this context he stressed the need for "partnerships on results, not process."

These attempts to create new forms of international cooperation have not been without their **critics.** Among them are the many **governments** that are tenacious in upholding the tenets of sovereignty and resent actions by multilateral agencies that do not respect the sanctity of that legal norm. **Various NGOs and civil society groups,** for their part, have expressed concern about U.N. agencies becoming too closely involved with private sector entities, especially large global corporate enterprises and international banks.

The response from U.N. agencies has been clear. To promote sustainable human development and meet its goals, we must find new ways—new mechanisms—to generate the needed resources.

In responding to criticism from NGOs about UNDP's private sector initiative, the agency's Administrator said:

We are exploring with banks ways in which they might make resources available to microfinancing initiatives—initiatives which have proven not only to contribute to poverty eradication but are also financially viable investments. . . . We are convinced that the innovation, technology and resources that corporations are known for can have a positive impact on SHD, and this is what we are exploring. If we can help bring new processes, products, technologies and partnerships to the poor, we will have contributed something important. The reality is that developing countries are increasingly seeking out investments by the transnational corporations. Similarly, these companies are continuously searching for new production bases and new markets. The question, therefore, is not whether global corporations will increase their investments in developing countries, but how can we, as the United Nations Development Programme and others committed to sustainable human development, seek to ensure that at least some of these investments occur in ways that are pro-poor, pro-environment, pro-jobs, and pro-women. [UNDP press release, 3/17/99]

What these examples illustrate is that, by focusing on human security and sustainable human development in the context of a comprehensive approach to development, the world organization is able to explore new forms of international cooperation—cooperation that holds out the promise of getting done, and done effectively, the tasks it has been mandated.

An important step was taken toward realizing this promise in July 1999, when the International Chamber of Commerce (ICC) signed on to the "global compact" with business that Secretary-General Annan had called for at the World Economic Forum in Davos, Switzerland, in January 1999. In a joint statement, the leadership of the ICC and the Secretary-General pledged that the two organizations would work together to create open markets, deal effectively with labor issues and human rights questions, and promote the protection of the human environment. Reflecting a major and historic shift in attitude toward the world organization, the ICC stressed that the United Nations, not the World Trade Organization and the rule-based trading system, should play the primary role in "setting the rules of the global economy for the benefit of workers and the environment" [transcript of press conference by Secretary-General Kofi Annan and the Leadership of the International Chamber of Commerce, Geneva, 7/5/99].

2. The World Trade Organization and Trade
By David Lynch

If all goes according to plan, trade ministers gathered in Seattle in December 1999 will launch the next round of global trade negotiations. To some it may seem a strange time to venture into the complex, uncertain, and contentious terrain of multilateral trade negotiations. The world is still digesting **the last agreement, the Uruguay Round of the General Agreement on Tariffs and Trade (GATT),** which took seven years to negotiate. (This was the round that created the World Trade Organization [WTO] and extended the multilateral trade regime to such important economic sectors as agriculture, textiles and apparel, and services.) The economies of many nations are struggling, which makes the lowering of trade barriers an even more politically sensitive issue. The global clamor for higher barriers to steel imports demonstrates this, as does President Clinton's continued inability to win fast-track negotiating authority from Congress. The WTO itself has displayed a conspicuous lack of consensus about who should lead the organization since Director-General Renato Ruggiero stepped down on April 30 at the end of his term [*Economist*, 5/8/99]. There are important questions to answer about which nations will gain admission to the WTO. The line is long and at the front stands China. Will this be the year in which China, with its rapidly growing exports and imports but less-than-transparent regulations and still inchoate steps toward economic liberalization, is covered by WTO rules? Can the United States and the European Union (EU) put behind them their acrimony over a number of import issues—bananas, hormone-treated beef, genetically altered agricultural products? Trade rows between the world's most powerful traders threaten the power and effectiveness of the WTO. Adding to the uncertainty about the future of trade negotiations is the fact that the major powers have yet to agree on the shape and direction of those negotiations. How comprehensive should they be? On what economic sectors should they focus? Although many developing nations doubt the wisdom of lowering trade barriers at this time, the trading powers—principally the United States, the EU, and Japan—are insistent that another round will begin just after the Seattle ministerial meeting.

The WTO: Leaderless and Divided

By the time the WTO's first Director-General stepped down on April 30, WTO members had been divided for months about who would follow him. They had, in fact, missed their self-imposed deadline for choosing a successor back in December 1998 [*Financial Times*, 2/23/99]. The **leading candidates,** after months of wrangling, are Supachai Panitchpakdi, Thailand's Deputy Prime Minister, and Mike Moore, New Zealand's former Premier. Moore was the front-runner in a May meeting of the WTO's General Council, but some 50 nations supported Supachai and the session ended in deadlock [Dow Jones International News Service, 5/6/99]. The General Council is supposed to be ruled by consensus and does not want simply to vote on the issue [*Financial Times*, 5/5/99]. Moore, backed by the United States, the EU, and many Latin American nations, is widely perceived as the developed nations' choice, while Supachai, backed by Japan and many Asian countries, is perceived as the developing-nations' candidate [Dow Jones International News Service, 5/5/99].

There was a battle over Ruggiero's nomination in 1994, and it was hoped that consensus would prevail the next time around. The deadlock has soured relations within the organization, and as Pakistan's WTO envoy put it: "There is so much bad blood among WTO members at the moment that it is going to be more difficult to agree on many issues." Some fear that this will harm the WTO's reputation [*Far Eastern Economic Review*, 5/13/99]. David Hartridge, head of the WTO's services division, is acting director [Dow Jones International News Service, 5/6/99].

State of the World Economy and Trade Levels

The world economy remained sluggish in 1998, with the United States one of the few bright spots. Some Asian economies are recovering from the **"Asian flu"** that struck in the summer of 1997, but it has spread elsewhere. Brazil stumbled and for a time looked into an economic abyss. It avoided the abyss but struggles still. This is particularly worrying in the rest of Latin America, for which Brazil's economy is very important.

The poor global economic performance carried over into trade levels. Growth in world trade slowed to 3.5 percent in 1998, down from 10 percent in 1997, and 1999's trade growth is not expected to differ significantly from 1998's [*Economist*, 5/8/99].

Given slow domestic markets, many nations had excess production, which they exported cheaply. Many countries therefore found themselves **awash in inexpensive imports** and are now hearing **louder cries for protectionism**. The United States had a record trade deficit of $168.8 billion in 1998 [Dow Jones News Service, 2/21/99]. The trend continues in 1999. Each of the first three months brought a record monthly trade deficit. March's was $19.7 billion [*Los Angeles Times*, 5/21/99].

China and the WTO: A Marriage Ceremony?

Among the most important issues facing the WTO is China's potential admission to the organization. The WTO's claim to be global in scope certainly seems hollow without China, a major and rapidly growing trading nation with over a billion in population. No one can accuse China and the WTO of a shotgun marriage: **They have been courting since 1986,** when China formally applied for membership in the WTO's forerunner, the General Agreement on Tariffs and Trade (GATT), but they continue to bicker about the wedding plans [*Wall Street Journal*, 3/5/99]. The problem is complex because it is not merely the betrothed that are making the final decision. For the WTO to agree to China's admission, the primary trading powers must agree. Nor is it a simple decision within China, where there are signs of disagreement among the Communist party leadership about whether the liberalization required by the WTO would be worth the pain.

Many of these disagreements between China and the West stem from **different economic philosophies.** The WTO and its more powerful nations are followers of laissez-faire economics, or something approaching it. They generally support low barriers to trade, minimal state subsidies to industries, the rule of law, and transparent regulations and law-making. In practice, of course, they are not so pure, but compared to China the difference is striking. China's economic philosophy is still influenced by communism, even though it is no longer truly a socialist nation. By Western standards, the Chinese government has a significant role in the economy. Massive and inefficient state-owned industries are still common in China, for instance, and these would be severely threatened by further economic reforms. Moreover, the Chinese economy is not known for its transparency or for the rule of law. Both practical and philosophical considerations are behind the dispute about how wide China must open its markets to gain WTO admission.

In fact, many of the details over which China and WTO members differ were settled but are being questioned anew. In April 1999, Chinese Premier Zhu Rongji went to Washington prepared to make **significant concessions to close a deal on WTO membership,** and he put them on the table: China would agree to allow majority foreign ownership in its telecommunications companies, a longstanding demand by the United States and EU; to allow the United States to export 40 films per year instead of the current ten [*Wall Street Journal*, 4/9/99; and Dow Jones News Service, 5/6/99]; and to lower tariffs on a host of goods and services. But these concessions were not quite enough for the Clinton administration, which kept a wary eye on Congress, whose members are skeptical of China and of the administration's China policies. The United States pressed for more open Chinese markets but at times resisted further opening of its own—for example, by seeking continued protection of the U.S. textile and steel industries. The Uruguay Round is phasing out textile quotas, and China has the potential for massive textile exports. Washington wanted China to accept quotas for five years longer than other WTO members. But China was not convinced, nor did it agree to the limits on Chinese steel exports to the United States that Washington had sought as well.

U.S. resistance to China's offering was seen as an affront by Chinese leaders, especially after the additional concessions Beijing had made—and will stick to, even though it came away from Washington empty-handed. Independent of a final agreement on WTO membership, China agreed to allow greater citrus imports from the United States and more flights between the United States and China, lifted a ban on grain from the Pacific Northwest, and cut some agricultural tariffs [*Wall Street Journal*, 4/9/99]. Wu Jichuan, the head of the Ministry of Information Industries, offered his resignation to protest Zhu's concessions to the United States [Dow Jones News Service, 5/2/99].

China believed itself jilted, and a parade of officials from various WTO nations made their way to Beijing to soothe it and nudge it into further reforms. Then came NATO's accidental bombing of the Chinese embassy in Belgrade [*Asian Wall Street Journal*, 5/17/99], word of which brought furious protests outside the U.S. embassy in Beijing. The factions in the Chinese leadership skeptical of WTO-required market reforms found themselves in a stronger position after the Washington visit, and China is no longer offering many of the concessions that it had put on the negotiating table in Washington, such as majority foreign ownership in Chinese telecommunications companies [Dow Jones News Service, 5/10/99]. Charges of Chinese nuclear espionage have further cooled U.S.-Chinese relations.

Despite the sound and fury, it is likely that China will soon become a WTO member. Beijing and its trading partners have much to gain from more regularized trade relations. Many politically powerful multinational corporations would also benefit from China's admission to the WTO— and, over time, these corporations tend to get their way in trade policy.

Taiwan, a significant world trader, wants admission to the WTO too. Its primary stumbling block in achieving admission has been China. Taiwan has been told by the WTO that it will gain entry, but only after China joins [Dow Jones International News Service, 5/16/99].

Bananas and Beef: The EU versus the United States with the WTO in the Middle

While the European Union and the United States seemed the closest of allies as they prosecuted the air war in Yugoslavia under the NATO banner, on numerous trade issues they have been hurling bombs at one another. The two most contentious issues are the EU's banana-importing policies and restrictions on hormone-treated beef. Both issues have been straining the WTO.

The banana battle can be traced to the EU's banana-importing policies established in 1993. The European Union gave favored access to bananas grown in Caribbean and North African nations, most of which are former European colonies. Various Central American nations and the United States filed a dispute resolution case with the WTO. Upon first glance, U.S. involvement might seem odd, but U.S. companies own banana plantations in nations that are harmed by EU banana restrictions. Moreover, the chairman of Chiquita bananas is a significant contributor to both the Democratic and Republican parties [*Los Angeles Times*, 2/4/99]. In a

1997 case, the WTO ruled against the EU and gave it until January 1, 1999, to open its banana market [U.S. ITC, *International Economic Review*, 11–12/98]. When the EU made only marginal changes to its banana-importation policies, the United States readied a list of EU products worth $520 million in annual imports that would face punitive duties of 100 percent [*New York Times*, 1/30/99; and Dow Jones News Service, 1/31/99]. The United States made this decision unilaterally, however, and the European Union complained that Washington was thumbing its nose at WTO procedures. Other WTO nations agreed that the United States should use punitive duties only when allowed by the WTO. The EU hinted at retaliatory sanctions if the U.S. sanctions were put into place but said later that it would not engage in tit-for-tat duties and would seek a **WTO dispute-resolution panel** to determine if U.S. sanctions were warranted [*Los Angeles Times*, 2/4/99; and Dow Jones News Service, 3/9/99 and 4/19/99]. The Europeans, although stubbornly holding on to their banana protectionism, adhered to WTO procedures as the United States rode roughshod over the international organization it was central in creating.

Said one newspaper: "The United States and Western Europe are tangled up in a smoldering feud over a fruit they barely grow, that provides them with next-to-no jobs, that matters to only a few companies in each region and that nobody even pretends has a lot of strategic importance" [*Los Angeles Times*, 2/4/99]. Despite such barely concealed amusement at these "banana wars," the dispute does have great importance for the WTO and for banana-exporting countries of the Caribbean, Latin America, and North Africa. Caribbean nations went so far as to suspend a treaty that pledges cooperation with U.S. anti-drug trafficking efforts [Dow Jones International News Service, 3/7/99].

The **WTO ruled against the European Union.** It authorized the United States to apply the punitive tariffs on $191.4 million of imports from the EU—**the WTO's first authorization of retaliatory duties** and only the second authorization since the organization of the world trading system under GATT [Dow Jones News Service, 4/19/99]. The EU did not challenge the panel ruling, but announced that further changes in its banana-importing regulations might not be realized until January 2000 [*Financial Times*, 4/20/99; and Dow Jones News Service 4/21/99]. Washington went ahead and placed tariffs on some EU goods [Dow Jones International News Service, 4/9/99]. With the WTO ruling and punitive tariffs, the EU seems more likely to negotiate a settlement with the United States and with the Latin American banana-growing nations.

As the banana dispute was unfolding, another contentious issue was also giving rise to cross-Atlantic salvos: hormone-treated beef. For 11 years the **EU has banned beef treated with growth hormones** [Dow Jones News Service, 6/2/99]. The Europeans view such beef as unsafe; the United States and Canada view the Europeans' health concerns as unfounded and protectionist. The WTO agrees with the latter and ruled that the EU must lift the ban on hormone-treated beef by May 13 [Dow Jones News Service, 1/26/99; and *Economist*, 5/8/99]. The EU missed the deadline, arguing that future scientific studies will vindicate its position. It has no intention of allowing importation of hormone-treated beef. The United States and Canada have turned to the WTO for authorization of retaliatory tariffs on $202 million and C$75 million worth of imports, respectively. The EU has not challenged whether the United States and Canada can retaliate but does argue that the amount sought is too much. **The WTO panel ruled that the United States and Canada are authorized to retaliate;** there will be a ruling on the amount by July 13 [Dow Jones News Service, 5/18/99; and Dow Jones International News Service, 6/3/99]. The EU hopes that the United States will accept tariff concessions on other products as compensation for the beef ban, but the United States has resisted this idea [Dow Jones International News Service, 5/18/99]. Will the EU heed the WTO's ruling? Will the United States act within the WTO as it attempts to open EU beef markets? As with bananas, the process and outcome will have an effect on the WTO itself.

The European Union and the United States have numerous other arguments as well. These range from genetically altered crops to subsidies for European airplane manufacturer Airbus and for farm exporters. This sort of acrimony used to be reserved for U.S.-Japanese trade relations. To free traders, this is all the more worrying because the United States and the EU are among the most important nations pushing for the 2000 millennium round trade negotiations.

Steel Trade: Bent Out of Shape

With much of the global economy struggling, demand for steel is down in many nations. Many steel-producing countries have seen their currencies weaken, with the effect of making their exports more affordable to stronger currency nations. As a result of these two factors, cheap steel is being shipped across borders and domestic competitors and politicians are voicing concern about steel industry jobs. In many countries, this has led to **complaints about dumping**—selling a product in a foreign market at unfair prices—**and about Byzantine anti-dumping procedures.** Such procedures have been used to restrict steel imports into many countries, including Argentina, Canada, the members of the European Union, and the United States [*Economist*, 11/7/98; Dow Jones International News Service, 5/11/99; and Dow Jones News Service, 5/19/99 and 5/25/99].

The **anti-dumping process in the United States** is complex, involving primarily the Commerce Department and the U.S. International Trade Commission (U.S. ITC). These organizations determine whether dumping has occurred, if the dumping harmed U.S. companies, and if anti-dumping duties should be prescribed. Complaints are specific as to types of steel and nation of origin.

U.S. steel producers filed complaints, for instance, that Brazil, Japan, and Russia were dumping hot rolled steel in the U.S. market. The U.S. Commerce Department found that Brazil and Japan were dumping steel and imposed a provisional tariff of over 25 percent [*Minneapolis Star Tribune*, 2/23/99; Dow Jones Capital Markets Report, 3/23/99; Japan Economic Newswire, 5/13/99; and *Latin Trade*, 5/99]. Russia, feeling the pressure, agreed to reduce its steel exports to the United States by 70 percent [Dow Jones News Service, 1/31/99 and 2/25/99; and *Minneapolis Star Tribune*, 2/23/99]. Brazil has sought a similar arrangement [Dow Jones Capital Markets Report, 3/23/99].

Other anti-dumping cases have brought mixed results. The U.S. ITC found that cut-to-length steel imports to the United States were dumped by France, India, Indonesia, Italy, Japan, and South Korea [Dow Jones News Service, 4/4/99]. Not long after, however, the U.S. ITC rejected anti-dumping duties on stainless steel round wire imports from Japan, Canada, India, South Korea, Spain, and Taiwan [Japan Economic Newswire, 5/11/99 and 5/13/99]. Many nations contend that anti-dumping procedures like these are protectionist even when the anti-dumping duties are *not* levied because steel imports are subject to so much legal maneuvering. Steelworkers, on the other hand, consider anti-dumping procedures too timid.

Meanwhile, **anti-steel-import sentiment builds in the U.S. Congress.** The House of Representatives voted to limit steel imports, but the bill failed in the Senate.

2000 Negotiations: The Millennium Round

Some free trade proponents adhere to the bicycle theory of trade: Free trade needs to move forward, else it might fall over. It seems the world's economic powers agree and have called for **a new round of trade negotiations to begin in January 2000,** just after the Seattle WTO ministerial meeting. Simply opening the talks would be something of an achievement. Leon Brittan, the EU's trade commissioner, called for such talks for three years before getting the United States to call for them publicly, as President Clinton did in his January 1999 State of the Union address [Dow Jones News Service, 1/20/99; and *Economist*, 2/6/99]. Congress, however, strongly rejected extending **fast-track negotiating authority** to Clinton, by which terms any trade agreement negotiated by the Executive Branch can be voted up or down by Congress but cannot be amended. The result is that the partners to the agreement would not have to worry about Congress renegotiating the agreement [*Congressional Quarterly*, 9/26/98]. Negotiations could start without fast-track authority, but at some point in the negotiations, any significant WTO round will need U.S. fast-track.

There is certainly no shortage of issues in the world trading system to be addressed. Some are **traditional trade issues,** such as lowering tariffs in various economic sectors. Textile and agriculture trade rules were excluded from GATT. They were brought into the WTO with the Uruguay Round but have much higher levels of protection than other economic sectors. The EU, for instance, has its Common Agricultural Program (CAP) through which farm prices are held artificially high and excess production receives export subsidies. According to U.S. Agriculture Secretary Dan Glickman, the EU budgeted $6.1 billion for agricultural export subsidies in 1997 [Dow Jones News Service, 4/20/99]. All told, the CAP takes up more than half of the entire EU budget [*Economist*, 5/8/99]. While the EU is perhaps the leader in agriculture protectionism, other nations also protect their farmers—Japan, for instance, its rice farmers and the United States its sugar and peanut farmers. Developing nations find high barriers to trade in agriculture and textiles particularly galling because they often have a competitive advantage in these sectors. These sectors are ripe for further negotiations. Trade in services has risen quickly, and trade rules for services are not as liberal as for goods. It too is ripe for further negotiation.

There are many issues that need to be addressed that are **not traditional to trade negotiations.** The fact is that, when such traditional trade barriers as tariffs and quotas are reduced, other governmental policies can have a significant, if unintended, impact on trade patterns. Rules about foreign investment are one example. **The Multilateral Agreement on Investment (MAI) negotiations** conducted under the auspices of the Organization for Economic Cooperation and Development (OECD) have not produced an agreement on investment regulation, and the issue may therefore be the subject of the millennium round talks. The MAI talks proved contentious even among the industrialized and usually likeminded members of the OECD. Nations are disinclined to give up control over foreign investment in their domestic market. Some governments fear that foreign investment will lead to unwanted social change. Environmental and labor activists fear that rules protecting foreign investment might override domestic environmental or worker safety regulations.

Competition policy, or industrial policy—defined as government support of an industry through subsidies, research and development aid, or government contracts—is another potential issue for the next round of WTO negotiations. The United States has already launched a complaint with the WTO over the **subsidies for Airbus** [*Economist*, 5/8/99], a European consortium that has received money from the various national governments for a long time and now rivals Boeing in airplane production. Airbus and the EU argue that Boeing receives subsidies in the form of U.S. military contracts. Negotiations on competition policy would attempt to regulate such policies. Still, many nations are hesitant to have their domestic policies scrutinized and influenced so much by an international organization.

While these are some of the issues that appear ripe for negotiation, there is **no agreement about lumping them together in comprehensive talks,** Uruguay Round style, or leaving some issues for other WTO-sponsored negotiations. Japan and the EU have pushed for the comprehensive talks; the U.S. has hesitated. All three call for the talks to be completed in approximately three years, well down from the Uruguay Round's seven [Dow Jones International News Service, 5/10/99]. Among other WTO members a consensus is emerging around this three-year plan.

Many developing nations are skeptical of the WTO and of further WTO talks as envisioned by the major trade powers. India, long a leader among developing nations, stands against comprehensive talks until the Uruguay Round changes are more fully digested. Indian Commerce Minister Ramakrishna Hegde explained that "The very concept of a new round frightens many of us. We are yet to recover from the hangover of the Uruguay Round" [Dow Jones International News Service, 5/10/99; and *Financial Times*, 3/3/99]. Indonesia, Malaysia, and Pakistan are also opposed to the new round of talks as presently conceived [*Far Eastern Economic Review*, 5/13/99]. It is a widely held belief in the developing world that the world trading system is tilted to favor developed nations and that new talks should focus on remedying this imbalance [*Financial Times*, 3/3/99]. Other developing nations, "while taking a softer line, have yet to be convinced of the benefits of discussing such new issues" as investment and competition policy, notes the *Financial Times* [3/3/99].

The Environment, Safety, and Trade: Concerns about a Brave New World

Those **fears of environmental and labor activists** that rules protecting foreign investment will roll back environmental regulations are not unwarranted. One U.S.-based company, for instance, successfully sued Canada into reversing an environmental regulation. This was Ethyl, which makes a controversial gasoline additive whose importation Canada moved to ban. Because Ethyl is the only maker of this additive in North America, it used investment-protection provisions of the North American Free Trade Agreement (NAFTA) to argue that the ban discriminated against its investment. Canada subsequently removed the ban and paid Ethyl to settle the case [*Los Angeles Times*, 2/8/99].

In attempting to ban the additive, Canada had acted out of genuine environmental concern. Many question the motivation behind other such regulations. Is the EU ban on hormone-treated beef unfairly protecting EU beef producers or is the EU acting prudently, out of concern for the safety of its citizens? Are restrictions on genetically modified agricultural products protectionist or a real effort to promote consumer safety and protect the environment?

Concerns regarding genetically modified crops are the latest chapter in the trade versus environment conundrum. These concerns are based on fears that the crops could escape into the wider environment. Once there, a crop with a gene to make it more resistant to herbicides, for instance, might make other species herbicide resistant as well [Dow Jones News Service, 5/10/99]. One recent study, although preliminary, breathes life into such fears. Here, milkweed sprinkled with pollen from genetically altered corn proved harmful to monarch butterflies. Milkweed is the monarchs' only food at the larval stage and most that ate the milkweed with Bt corn pollen died or were stunted. Bt corn has been approved for use only since 1996 but accounts for up to 25 percent of the U.S. corn crop [*Time*, 5/31/99].

What can the WTO do to foster cooperation on such issues? One step that the WTO took was to sponsor **negotiations on a "Biosafety Protocol" to regulate the trade in genetically modified organisms (GMOs).** The talks, which drew representatives of some 130 nations to Cartagena, Colombia, ended without an agreement because a handful of major agricultural exporters, led by the United States, felt that the limits on GMOs went too far. For the United States, Canada, Australia, Chile, Argentina, and Uruguay, which refused to sign the protocol, there were **two main sticking points.** One had to do with receiving advance approval from the importing nation. The dissenters had no objection to obtaining such approval in the case of genetically modified seeds but took exception to the majority's wish to include commodities meant for eating and processing as well. Argued the dissenters: These goods do not enter the environment and thus pose no threat to it. Sticking point number two was the power to be wielded by the Biosafety Protocol. Most nations at the Cartagena negotiations wanted the protocol to be the winner in any conflict with WTO rules. The United States rooted for the WTO [*New York Times*, 2/25/99; and *Economist*, 2/20/99].

These are issues of growing importance, given the rapid expansion of GMOs. Twenty-five percent to 45 percent of U.S. corn, soybean, and cotton crops are genetically modified [*New York Times*, 2/25/99]. There are no studies indicating that the genetically modified agricultural products cause human health problems, but many consumers fear that they are yet to be discovered—a concern shared by Europe, Australia, Japan, and New Zealand but apparently less so by the United States, whether government leaders or consumers.

Some developing nations actively resent biotechnology companies. U.S.-based Monsanto, for instance, is developing a gene that would prevent farmers from keeping some of their harvest for next year's seeds. The seeds would self-destruct, ensuring that farmers will buy more next year.

Activists in India went so far as to destroy some Monsanto cotton fields
[Dow Jones News Service, 5/10/99].
Whether motivated by science or by politics, most of the world was
angry at the six dissenting nations, and especially the United States. Washington, said one delegate, "is holding the world at ransom" [*New York Times*,
2/25/99]. Among those that want the strictest standards for GMOs are many
African nations, Malaysia, and some Latin American nations [*Economist*, 2/20/
99]. The participants did agree to continue the talks, no later than May
2000. Look for this debate to continue.

Developing Nations

If developing nations often have a different perspective on world trade
than do developed nations, it must also be said that developing nations
are a varied lot, and some are quite well integrated into the global economy. Only a few short years ago the Asian economies were developing at
an amazing pace and giving hope to other developing nations. Then came
the summer of 1997 and the Asian financial crisis, which has since spread,
hitting Russia and Brazil, among other nations. This was proof, if any
were needed, that globalization, with its openness to capital and lower
trade barriers, can cause painful economic changes as well as positive ones.
The World Bank predicts that the economic growth rate of developing
nations will decline to 1.5 percent in 1999. From 1991 to 1997 the average
for developing nations (excluding the former Soviet Union) was 5.3 percent [*Minneapolis Star Tribune*, 4/27/99]. What do developing nations and development professionals think is necessary to **help the developing nations
break out of tough times?** There are a number of possibilities.

Many developing nations feel constrained by the economic openness
required of them by the Uruguay Round, and they are seeking time to
adjust to changes wrought by economic liberalization. (One of the big
changes, of course, is that domestic producers now face greater competition from large multinational corporations with more capital and better
technology. Many of the developing nations' domestic producers simply
will not survive.)

The WTO, like GATT before it, allows preferential treatment for
certain exports from some developing nations through the **Generalized
System of Preferences (GSP).** The General Assembly has called for the
renewal and improvement of the GSP. The General Assembly also calls
for continued progress toward duty-free imports from least developed
countries [A/53/606/Add.1].

Another possible means of helping many developing nations is to
expedite their admission into the WTO. The challenge for many of these
countries is adjusting to the economic openness that admission brings and
shouldering the administrative burden of changing so many policies over

relatively short periods of time. Some nations simply cannot afford to make the effort without external help. Laos, for instance, is receiving aid from Australia and from the United Nations Development Programme (UNDP) to help it meet WTO admissions criteria [Dow Jones International News Service, 5/13/99]. EU trade commissioner Brittan and others have called for simplified admission procedures and easier entry terms [*Financial Times*, 2/16/ 99]. Estonia will become the 135th member of the WTO, having gained the organization's approval in May [Dow Jones News Service, 5/21/99]. More than 30 nations, most of them in the developing category, are waiting to join the WTO.

Agricultural reform in the global trading system is also of the utmost importance to developing nations. As United Nations Conference on Trade and Development (UNCTAD) Secretary-General Rubens Ricupero points out, while agricultural trade accounts for approximately 11 percent of world merchandise trade, it is vastly more important for many developing nations. In the low-income nations, agriculture accounts for an average of 30 percent of Gross Domestic Product and over 70 percent of employment, as compared to only 1.5 percent and 5 percent, respectively, in high-income OECD nations [UNCTAD press release 2802, 4/26/99]. Ricupero argues that, owing to the greater economic and social importance of agriculture in developing nations, the latter should receive "special and different" treatment in the upcoming WTO talks [UNCTAD Press Release 2804, 4/29/99].

Agriculture remains among the most protected economic sectors, and Brazilian President Fernando Henrique Cardoso is among those calling for greater agricultural market access in developed nations. "The developing nations' goodwill to lower their own tariffs for industrial products cannot be taken for granted indefinitely while barriers to products they want to export are kept high," he noted recently [Dow Jones International News Service, 2/21/99]. Developing nations also need assistance in meeting agricultural safety regulations in order to take full advantage of any gains in agricultural market access.

Full access to developed-nation markets in trade sectors important to developing nations, while likely to help, is not enough to pull many developing nations out of poverty. Said former WTO Director-General Ruggiero:

> Trade alone cannot solve all their problems. Very little can be done without an integrated strategy which takes into account the great number of issues these countries face—from health and education, to technical assistance, capacity building and, very importantly, debt relief. This is the area where we are beginning to move—collaboration with the ITC, the IMF, the World Bank, UNDP, UNCTAD. [WTO press release, 2/19/99]

UNCTAD, which has long directed attention to developing-country needs in the area of trade, will be holding its next quadrennial conference—UNCTAD X—in February 2000. Bangkok is the venue. This should be an ideal forum to push ahead on those issues. Look for the issues to surface at the WTO gathering in Seattle and subsequent WTO negotiations.

Regionalism

One of the most notable trends in the world trading system during the 1990s has been the **proliferation of regional trade accords.** During the first 50 years of GATT and the WTO, 153 regional trade accords were registered by the organization. Almost half of these have been developed during the 1990s (although some are revivals of older agreements). Only three WTO members—Japan, Hong Kong, and South Korea—are not members of any regional trade agreement [*Economist*, 10/3/98].

Over the past year or so, **regionalism has slowed somewhat.** With the global economic downturn and the accompanying flood of cheap imports, domestic producers and workers have soured on regional integration. (A notable exception to the slowdown was the launching of a common currency, the euro, by 11 of the EU's 15 nations on January 1, 1999.)

Mercosur, the trade agreement between Latin American nations Argentina, Brazil, Paraguay, and Uruguay (with separate accords with Bolivia and Chile), offers one example of the potential difficulties of regionalism. When the Brazilian currency, the real, fell dramatically, it made exports to Mercosur partners cheaper. Argentina, whose currency is tied to the stronger U.S. dollar, slapped anti-dumping duties on Brazilian steel and has also called for the end of Brazilian industrial subsidies [*Economist*, 2/13/99; and Dow Jones International News Service, 5/11/99]. Nonetheless, Mercosur and the EU are still considering a free trade agreement, but EU agricultural protection is a major hurdle [Dow Jones International News Service, 3/23/99].

The 21-member **Asia-Pacific Economic Cooperation forum** (APEC) has been divided by the Asian crisis. Malaysia was hit hard by the crisis, and its controversial Prime Minister, Mahathir Mohamad, blamed his nation's troubles on Western currency speculators. He has been highly critical of developed nations and has taken steps to insulate the Malaysian economy from globalization by placing controls on foreign exchange. Despite this, he hosted the November 1998 APEC forum. APEC members could not agree upon further lowering of trade barriers, and U.S. Vice President Al Gore publicly called for greater democratic reforms in Malaysia, further cooling the meeting. A May 1999 APEC meeting went more smoothly, but APEC will not be heading toward economic integration anytime soon [*Economist*, 11/21/98; and *Wall Street Journal*, 5/17/99].

When observers express concern about marginalization of developing nations, the image conjured is probably of **Africa,** and in particular sub-Saharan Africa—the region least connected to the global economy. President Clinton has repeatedly called for closer economic ties to Africa. His African trade initiative would lower tariffs on some goods for 48 sub-Saharan nations, eliminate quotas on textiles and apparel, and clear the way for a U.S.-Africa free trade agreement. The plan has met with resistance in Congress, so its future is in question [*Congressional Quarterly*, 2/6/99 and 2/13/99].

Africa's efforts to integrate internally have not been progressing well either. A May meeting of the 21-member **Common Market for Eastern and Southern Africa** (Comesa) ended in acrimony. This should not be surprising, given the strife in the region: war in the Democratic Republic of Congo, involving many of its neighbors; the resumption of the Angolan civil war, leading to the withdrawal of U.N. peacekeepers; and a major border war between Ethiopia and Eritrea [Dow Jones International News Service, 5/25/99].

Pacific Island nations are calling for a free trade area among the 14 members of the South Pacific Forum. The proposed free trade area would be phased in over eight to ten years beginning in 2001. The South Pacific Forum consists of some of the world's smallest nations, and they hope that a free trade agreement would help increase their clout in international trade [Dow Jones International News Service, 6/1/99].

Mexico, hoping to draw investment and increase exports, has been aggressively courting a wide array of nations for bilateral free trade agreements. The aim is to become a trading hub with many spokes. It has reached agreements with Bolivia and Chile and is currently negotiating one with the EU. (The EU seeks treatment for its Mexican trade and investment similar to that which Canada and the United States receive under NAFTA [*Wall Street Journal*, 1/18/99; and Dow Jones International News Service, 5/21/99].) Mexico is also negotiating with Panama and separately with Guatemala, Honduras, and El Salvador [Dow Jones International News Service, 4/14/99]. It is said that Japan and Mexico are also considering free trade negotiations [ibid., 4/8/99].

IV
Global Resource Management

1. Environment and Sustainable Development
By Gail V. Karlsson

Focus Sharpens on the Role of Free Trade in Sustainable Development

Trade liberalization has been promoted widely as the key to global economic prosperity. Yet many questions are being raised about the relationship between open markets and sustainable development. In some cases free trade pressures may actually conflict with environmental protection measures or with social welfare.

At the **1999 World Economic Forum** in Davos, Switzerland, U.N. Secretary-General Kofi Annan warned that markets are spreading beyond the ability of societies and political systems to adjust to them or to control them. He challenged business leaders to embrace voluntarily and support a core set of values on human rights, labor standards, and environmental protection, or else face increasing threats to the multilateral trading regime. "There is enormous pressure from various interest groups to load the trade regime and investment agreements with restrictions aimed at reaching adequate standards in the three areas I have just mentioned. These are legitimate concerns. But restrictions on trade and impediments to investment flows are not the means to use when tackling them" [U.N. press release SG/SM/6881/Rev. 1, 2/1/99].

Secretary-General Annan explained that he focused on human rights, labor standards, and environmental protection because these are areas in which universal values have already been defined by international agreements—notably, the Universal Declaration on Human Rights, the International Labour Organization's Declaration on Worker Rights, and the Rio Declaration adopted at the U.N. Conference on Environment and Development. He called on business leaders to encourage states to give the United Nations the resources and authority it needs to promote these values, and to uphold these values in their own global operations. "What we have to do is find a way of embedding the global market in a network of shared values. . . . We have to choose between a global market driven only by calculations of short-term profit, and one which has a human face. Between a world which condemns a quarter of the human race to starvation and squalor, and one which offers everyone at least a chance of prosperity, in a healthy environment" [ibid.].

Biological Diversity

Consensus on values within the global marketplace is not easily accomplished. Within weeks of the Davos meeting, disputes over trade restrictions derailed the adoption of a new **Biosafety Protocol** by the parties to the **Convention on Biological Diversity.** The protocol is meant to be a legally binding agreement setting international standards for trade and transport of **genetically modified products.** It would require that trade in living modified organisms be approved in advance by recipient countries. Countries exporting genetically modified products would have to make sure that importing countries had the opportunity and ability to assess the effects of introducing these products.

"Biotechnology can contribute enormously to human well-being, but it poses potential risks," noted Klaus Töpfer, Executive Director of the United Nations Environment Programme (UNEP) [UNEP News Release 1999/17, 2/24/99]. Through new bio-engineering processes, genes from one organism can be spliced into another, transferring desirable characteristics like higher productivity and nutritional value and resistance to disease or insects. These processes could potentially produce significant benefits in terms of world food supplies. But many countries are worried about **possible adverse effects on human health and the environment.** Some consumers are afraid that genetically modified foods could spread toxins, induce allergies, or spread resistance to antibiotics. Others are more generally concerned about the unknown effects of tinkering with basic genetic material. Still another fear is that genetically altered seeds and plants will spread in the natural environment, displacing or altering native species and reducing the variety of the existing gene pool. This could have long-term negative consequences for preservation of biological diversity.

One of the major disputes concerning the Biosafety Protocol is whether the rules on advance notification should apply to agricultural products as well as to living plants, animals, and seeds. The United States, as the leading producer of genetically engineered agricultural products, joined with other exporting countries to oppose measures that would apply the **"advance informed agreement" requirement** to marketing of genetically modified commodities like corn, soybeans, and cotton. Some importing countries, however, want the rules to apply not only to agricultural commodities but to products made from these crops, like cornstarch or baked goods made from genetically altered grains. The United States proposed that concerned countries use domestic laws rather than trade restrictions to protect their natural biodiversity, but many developing countries do not have adequate regulatory systems in place and are looking to the protocol to provide risk assessment procedures.

Despite nonstop negotiations from February 14 to 23 at a special session held in Cartagena, Colombia, the parties to the Convention on Biological Diversity were not able to agree on the protocol. The session was suspended, but negotiations are expected to resume no later than May 2000.

The World Trade Organization

The general debate about the ecological impact of trade continued in March at the World Trade Organization's **High-Level Symposium on Trade and the Environment,** held in Geneva. In a message read to the symposium, President Bill Clinton stressed the need to ensure that trade rules support national policies providing for high levels of environmental protection, and he pledged that the United States would conduct an environmental review of the next round of trade negotiations [*Earth Negotiations Bulletin*, 3/22/99]. Renato Ruggiero, then Director-General of the WTO, emphasized that the trade and environment communities have common objectives in a strong rule-based trading regime and strong, effective environmental protection policies, and that these could be attained through consensus and negotiations [ibid.]. Klaus Töpfer of UNEP noted that there can be environmental benefits from economic liberalization, such as full cost internalization and the removal of subsidies that distort prices and promote environmental damage [ibid.].

Other participants in the symposium, especially representatives of nongovernmental organizations, were less positive about **synergies between international trade and environmental regimes.** Vandana Shiva, from the India-based Research Foundation for Science and Technology and Ecology, charged that free trade rules have a negative impact on biodiversity and encourage nonsustainable use of natural resources. Since biodiversity is the basis for most livelihoods in developing countries, destruction of biodiversity eliminates options for the poor [ibid.]. A representative of Environnement et Développement du Tiers-Monde stated that the failure of the negotiators to agree to the Biosafety Protocol illustrated the need for trade rules to encompass the culture of precaution and risk management [ibid.].

A number of developing countries expressed concern about limited economic benefits to them from recent trade liberalization measures. A participant from Mexico observed that the future of the international trading system is dependent on integrating developing countries and that unless developing countries have access to global markets to generate economic growth, they will not have the financial ability to protect either their domestic environments or the global resources under their control [ibid.].

The Commission on Sustainable Development

Discussions at the annual meeting of the Commission on Sustainable Development (CSD) in April 1999 echoed many of the same themes about the effects of the international trading system. As part of its work, the CSD acted as a preparatory committee for a **General Assembly Special Session in September 1999 to review progress on the Barbados Plan of Action for Sustainable Development of Small Island Developing States** in the five years since it was adopted. One of the major items of contention unresolved at the CSD meeting related to requests by the small island states for special treatment under the international trading rules.

Speaking for the Alliance of Small Island States (AOSIS), Minister Tuala Sale Tagaloa from Samoa explained **the need for international cooperation:** "In large measure, the problems we face, and their origins, call for global responses. Moreover, since the Barbados Conference, the challenges of globalization and trade liberalization, in particular the erosion of trade preferences, have seriously undermined our ability to compete effectively within the international trading system. The threat of marginalization, compounded by vulnerabilities, including fragile environments and susceptibility to natural disasters, have hampered our efforts to achieve sustainable development" [4/23/99].

Under the Lomé Convention, European countries established trade preferences for imports from their former colonies. One of the primary effects of this agreement has been support for small banana producers in the Caribbean. The United States, responding to pressures from large American fruit companies operating in Latin America, challenged European trade preferences for Caribbean bananas in proceedings before the World Trade Organization. The WTO ruled in favor of the United States, and a number of small islands heavily dependent on banana exports are worried about economic and political destabilization should they lose special access to the European markets.

In general, it is difficult for small islands to compete effectively in global markets. Constraints on their development include: narrow resource bases, which limit economies of scale; small domestic markets; long distances from export markets and import sources; high costs for transportation, energy, and infrastructure; lack of technological sophistication; and vulnerability to natural disasters. The Report of the Secretary-General on progress in implementing the Barbados Plan of Action, prepared for the CSD, concluded: "While in the long run small island developing States will benefit from a stronger and more integrated global economy, in the short and medium term they need support to enhance the viability of their export sector through appropriate restructuring and diversification" [E/CN.17/1999/6, 2/1/99].

The CSD was unable to agree on measures to assist the small islands in becoming better integrated into the world economy, and the issue was referred to the General Assembly for consideration there. However, many others matters were agreed upon. **Areas of concern identified for priority action** were climate change (including climate variability and sea level rise), natural disasters, freshwater resources, coastal and marine resources, energy, and tourism. Tourism, a major source of income for many islands, often overloads fragile ecosystems as well as island facilities for providing electricity and fresh water and for handling sewage and garbage. Recommendations for sustainable tourism emphasized integrated land-use planning and coastal zone management to protect vulnerable ecosystems, partnerships with local and indigenous communities, and voluntary eco-efficiency initiatives by the tourist industry. To educate consumers about sustainable tourism practices, the CSD also encouraged airlines to show destination-specific educational in-flight videos on sustainable tourist practices.

Small islands hold a critical position in global environmental protection efforts in part because they are **custodians of large amounts of the world's oceans and marine life.** Coral reefs are often called the rainforests of the sea because they provide homes for a great variety of marine plants and animals. But coral reefs, and other marine ecosystems, are being threatened by pressures from human activities, including coastal development, destructive fishing practices, pollution, and erosion. Overall, there is increasing international concern about the deterioration of the marine environment. Major problems have intensified in recent years—including spills of oil and hazardous materials, dumping of shipboard wastes, transport of nuclear materials, and watershed destabilization. These problems have serious consequences for human health and the future availability of ocean resources as well as for the protection of precious plants and animals.

Reviewing the condition of oceans and seas, the CSD recommended that the General Assembly establish an open-ended informal consultative process to intensify its consideration of marine protection and management. There is currently no single intergovernmental body responsible for overseeing the myriad agencies and treaties involved with oceans. Some governments have suggested that a **new forum on oceans** is needed to coordinate political negotiations and research, but this was not agreed to at the CSD, and the oversight function was referred to the General Assembly. Overfishing and wasteful fishing practices are continuing threats to the health of marine ecosystems, and to the continuing availability of ocean resources. The Food and Agriculture Organization

(FAO) estimates that 60 percent of all major world fisheries are either fully exploited or overfished ["Oceans and Seas: Report of the Secretary-General," E/CN.17/1999/4, 2/8/99]. Prior CSD recommendations for urgent action to rebuild depleted fish stocks have not been sufficient to prevent overfishing. One of the critical issues is **government subsidization of fishing fleets,** which promotes fishing overcapacity. Too many ships are chasing too few fish. There are about 4 million fishing vessels in the world, and the FAO reported that as of several years ago the fishing industry worldwide was spending $54 billion more than it earned annually [*New York Times,* 3/9/99]. Despite the fact that many fleets would be operating at a loss without government subsidies, the CSD was still not able to reach consensus on eliminating subsidies for fishing fleets. The CSD did urge countries to voluntarily adopt international plans formulated by the FAO on sustainable fisheries management and environmental conservation. In February 1999 the **FAO Committee on Fisheries** adopted a Plan of Action for the Management of Fishing Capacity that calls on states and regional fisheries organizations to work toward efficient and equitable management of fishing capacity, and to progressively eliminate subsidies that promote overcapitalization of fishing industries.

Chemicals

Perhaps the most pervasive threats to humans, ecosystems, and wildlife come from a group of synthetic chemicals known as **persistent organic pollutants (POPS).** These chemicals are extremely toxic, bio-accumulate in fatty tissues, and are transported throughout the world in the air and water without decomposing. They are primarily pesticides, chemicals used in industrial production, and unintended byproducts of industrial processes. Scientific evidence indicates that even very low exposure to these contaminants can cause cancer, immune system disorders, reproductive malfunction, and interference with normal child development. They are found everywhere in the world, even where synthetic chemicals have never been used.

Because of growing global awareness concerning the serious hazards presented by these chemicals, an International Negotiating Committee is preparing a **legally binding treaty on persistent organic chemicals.** Meeting in Nairobi, Kenya, in January 1999, the negotiating committee discussed prohibiting the production and use of POPS, and debated whether the prohibition should also include the import and export of such products [*Earth Negotiations Bulletin,* 2/1/99]. Because it is so very difficult to contain or control these substances once they have been released, the key objective is to prevent their release in the first place. Destruction of existing stockpiles of chemicals was also considered.

Although most industrialized countries seemed to support an agreement to eliminate the production and use of POPS, some argued that the elimination of POPS as byproducts of production processes is unrealistic, although significant reductions would be manageable and appropriate. For example, some developing countries are concerned about eliminating the use of DDT because of its major role in combating malaria and other diseases carried by insects. Malaria contributes to approximately 3 million deaths per year, mostly among young children, and cost-effective alternatives are not readily available [*Linkages Journal*, 2/1/99]. Discussions on these matters will continue at the third session of the International Negotiating Committee, scheduled for the fall of 1999.

Climate Change

In November 1998 the parties to the **U.N. Framework Convention on Climate Change** met in Buenos Aires to consider the agreements put together in the **Kyoto Protocol,** adopted in December 1997. The Kyoto Protocol set greenhouse reduction targets for industrialized countries to be met during the years 2008–12, but the agreement was put together hastily at the end of a very long and contentious negotiating session, and there were many unanswered questions about how it would actually work. Many of the questions have to do with market-based measures for achieving the promised emission-reduction levels, and how to create frameworks and structures for implementing them.

Under the Climate Convention, adopted in 1992 at the Earth Summit in Rio de Janeiro, governments agreed to take remedial action after an international panel of scientists warned that increased levels of carbon dioxide and other greenhouse gases (primarily produced by power plants, factories, and motor vehicles in industrialized countries) could have dangerous and irreversible effects on the Earth's atmosphere. The ultimate objective of the Convention is to stabilize greenhouse gas concentrations in the atmosphere at a level that does not pose a danger to the planet's climate system. From the beginning, the Convention called on all countries to take voluntary steps to reduce greenhouse gas emissions. It set specific goals for industrialized countries, however, given their greater contribution to the problem and their greater resources for addressing the problem. Developing countries currently have much lower per capita emissions levels, while at the same time they have growing populations that lack basic power for electricity and transportation.

When it became apparent that voluntary commitments would generally not be met, the parties to the Convention began negotiating the Kyoto Protocol, which would include **legally binding targets for industrialized countries.** Under the Protocol, industrialized countries agreed to reduce their emissions an average of about 5 percent below 1990 baseline levels during the 2008–12 period. Individual countries have different targets, and some will actually be able to increase their emissions. The United States agreed to a 7 percent reduction, Japan agreed to 6 percent, and the European Union as a whole agreed to an 8 percent reduction. Since greenhouse emissions are projected to increase substantially during the next decade, reductions below 1990 emissions levels could require significant changes in industrial production processes and transportation technologies.

The Kyoto Protocol introduced a number of **"flexible mechanisms" to reduce the potential costs of complying** with the emission reduction commitments, notably "emissions trading," joint implementation activities, and the Clean Development Mechanism. Emissions trading is a market-based system patterned after the U.S. experience with permitting trading in sulfur dioxide allowances. Countries with emissions below their established target level would be able to sell their excess to countries exceeding their target levels. Theoretically, it should make no difference where the emission reductions are effected, since the impact on the atmosphere would be the same. But there is concern that in some cases, like Russia, the allowance was set so high (because of the post-1990 economic recession) that the trades might make it possible for one country to buy another's emission allowance without any real reductions by either party.

The **Clean Development Mechanism** is meant to encourage early cooperation between developing countries and industrialized countries in adopting climate change mitigation measures. Industrialized countries, or companies within them, could get credit for investments in developing countries that create new emission reductions. Joint implementation is a similar concept, but limited to cooperation between industrialized countries that are both subject to emission reduction requirements. These mechanisms have been heavily promoted by the United States but viewed with skepticism by developing countries and the European Union because they seem to diminish the likelihood of real changes in domestic greenhouse gas emission levels. Since the United States is the biggest producer of emissions worldwide, it is looking for cost-effective ways to meet its targets.

There are many outstanding questions about how these flexible mechanisms will work, and the Buenos Aires meeting set up a timetable for working out the details. The Clean Development Mechanism is meant to come into effect in 2000, well before any emissions trading would start, so there is particular pressure to develop rules and guidelines for that process. However, many countries want the framework for all the flexible mechanisms to be established at the same time, so the **Buenos Aires plan** calls for all the procedures to be negotiated by the end of 2000, at the sixth meeting of the Conference of the Parties to the Climate Convention. The European Union wants to limit the portion of reduction targets that can be met through flexible mechanisms rather than domestic reductions, but that is not acceptable to the United States at this time.

Another controversial aspect of the Kyoto Protocol is the provision that allows increases in carbon dioxide absorption to be applied against emission reduction targets. This is known as the "sinks" provision. It means that a country could get credit for planting new forests or increasing carbon dioxide absorption in soils through agricultural innovations. There will need to be agreement on how to define "sinks" and how to determine what were 1990 levels of forestation, since there have been significant reductions in forest cover since then.

The parties to the Climate Convention meet again in Bonn in the fall of 1999 to see what progress can be made in answering some of these questions. Meanwhile, technical experts are meeting on a regular basis to work out as many details as possible and to present possible scenarios for these very complicated mechanisms.

The Ozone Layer

Shortly after the climate meeting, the parties to the Montreal Protocol on Substances that Deplete the Ozone Layer met in Cairo. For the first time, they considered how to make policies to protect the ozone layer consistent with measures designed to reduce greenhouse gas emissions. The Montreal Protocol limits the release of certain substances used for refrigeration and industrial processes that destroy ozone in the upper levels of the Earth's atmosphere, allowing more ultraviolet radiation to reach the Earth's surface. Certain gases now being used as safe alternatives with respect to the ozone layer have been identified under the Kyoto Protocol as significant greenhouse gases.

Efforts are being made to coordinate the work of scientific and technical panels on the ozone layer with similar groups working on climate change. In the fall of 1998, scientists reported that the ozone hole over Antarctica was the largest ever recorded. Although atmospheric levels of some ozone-depleting substances are declining because of controls under the Montreal Protocol, scientists now think that global warming may slow the healing of the ozone layer [U.N. Non-Governmental Liaison Service, *Go Between*, 2–3/99].

Forests

Sustainable management of forests is closely linked with implementation of the climate convention and the biodiversity convention. The role of forests as sinks for carbon dioxide was one of the topics discussed at the May 1999 meeting of the International Forum on Forests held in Geneva. In the long run, credits earned under the Kyoto Protocol for planting trees and restoring forests could provide powerful incentives for improved forest management practices. In the meantime, however, international funding for forest preservation is declining. Delegates at the forest forum considered **innovative financial mechanisms,** including compensation to forest owners for such environmental services as carbon sequestration, preservation of biological diversity, and watershed functions; eco-tourism schemes; and debt-for-nature swaps.

The **role of trade** in environmental degradation came up again at this forum, since forest deterioration is often triggered by unsustainable logging and trade in forest products. Voluntary certification procedures and product labeling that identifies items as coming from sustainably managed forests can provide consumers with information to support conservation efforts. But such labeling might also unfairly limit market access for small forest-related enterprises in developing countries that would have difficulty obtaining certification. Although some countries are concerned that eco-labeling schemes will create barriers for their exports, conservationists are worried that unrestrained trade will lead to the elimination of most remaining tropical forests in a very short time. Since rainforests contain a high percentage of the Earth's species, the consequences in terms of biodiversity loss, as well as adverse climate impact, could be devastating.

There is **still no general global agreement on forest management,** despite several years of international discussions on whether such an agreement is needed. Existing international instruments relating to forests include a complex mix of legally binding conventions, non-binding agreements, and an internationally accepted statement of principles. Some countries are pressing for a general comprehensive convention on forests, but others would prefer to focus on implementation of existing, legally binding international agreements relating to forests, particularly the biodiversity convention [*Go Between*, 10–11/98].

Desertification

Forest management also plays a key role in combating desertification and land degradation. Dry land can be rehabilitated through tree planting, and forest restoration can provide the basis for soil and water conservation, improving agriculture and food security. Rehabilitation of degraded lands is of critical importance for poverty alleviation and preservation of indigenous communities in some of the poorest nations.

The parties to the **Convention to Combat Desertification** met in December 1998 in Dakar, Senegal, to discuss plans and progress. Increasing drought and desertification threatens the survival of millions of people in the least-developed countries, particularly in sub-Saharan Africa. Because desertification is caused by a complex interaction of physical, political, and socioeconomic factors, including international trade and economic relations, implementation of the convention requires coordinated action on many levels. The primary focus is on **national action plans** that engage local communities in formulating anti-desertification strategies. At the Dakar meeting, Iran, for example, reported that its national plan emphasizes population controls, use of new technologies, public participation in decision-making, and better use of indigenous knowledge [ibid., 2–3/99]. Recognizing that those closest to the land often have the most insight into what is needed to preserve it, the convention's Committee on Science and Technology established an ad hoc panel to follow up on its discussions about links between tradition and modern technology.

The desertification convention also encourages cooperation through **regional and sub-regional action programs** to support poverty alleviation, food security, and adoption of energy-efficient technologies. Although desertification affects areas in Asia and Latin America as well, most of the emphasis so far has been on Africa. Since some critics question whether this really qualifies as a global convention, efforts to find synergies and collaboration points with other conventions—notably on climate change and biodiversity—could lend needed international support to implementation efforts, especially in terms of financial assistance and technology transfer.

Debt Relief

For many of the least-developed countries, especially in Africa, one of the greatest barriers to sustainable development is an overwhelming burden of debt and interest payments that drains economic resources away from domestic investments. In many cases the original loans were made years ago and the proceeds squandered by prior rulers, while the debt burden rests on poor communities that received no benefits from the borrowings. There are 41 countries defined as "heavily indebted poor countries" that are eligible for a debt-reduction initiative begun in 1996 by the World Bank and International Monetary Fund. Thirty-two of these countries are in Africa, and some pay as much as 60 percent of their annual budgets for debt service, severely limiting their government's ability to provide basic education, health care, and poverty alleviation programs [*New York Times*, 4/30/99].

The **World Bank/IMF initiative** is very slow in allowing real debt relief. Countries must meet IMF-mandated economic reform requirements for six years before getting relief, and even then there is no substantial debt forgiveness. In March 1999, Bill Clinton joined the growing campaign for debt relief led by nongovernmental groups and aid workers and already supported by several European countries, stating that "We should provide extraordinary relief for countries making extraordinary efforts to build working economies" [*Economist*, 3/20/99]. He proposed forgiveness of an additional $70 billion of the debts of the poorest countries, much of it owed bilaterally to richer countries. He also asked for expansion of the World Bank/IMF program, and amendments to allow for quicker debt relief under its provisions, to be considered at the Group of 8 meeting in June 1999.

At that meeting, the seven leading industrial nations did agree to a debt-relief plan that would cancel about $15 billion of debt owed to them by some of the world's poorest countries. Additional debt relief contingent on the countries' future economic reforms could bring the total relief to $65 billion, and more if other industrial nations participate. However, even the eligible countries would continue to owe tens of billions of dollars to the world's richest countries, which did not want to set a precedent by canceling all of the borrowers' debt [*New York Times*, 6/19/99].

Another of President Clinton's suggestions was that new aid offered by donor countries to the heavily indebted least-developed countries take the form of grants rather than new loans. Before providing new assistance, however, many donors are likely to impose requirements for good governance and for the allocation of freed-up resources to education and health care programs, as opposed to increased military expenditures.

Financing for Development

In 1998 the General Assembly established an ad hoc working group to make recommendations concerning a summit, international conference, special session, or other appropriate **high-level intergovernmental forum on financing for development** to be convened no later than the year 2001 [A/Res/52/179]. Some developing countries hope the session, whatever its form, will provide an opportunity for general restructuring of the international financial institutions. The G-8 are not as enthusiastic about **an enhanced U.N. role in economic policy**, preferring to deal with financial issues in the World Bank and IMF, with their more limited membership and less democratic decision-making procedures. In December 1998, the U.S. Ambassador to the General Assembly's Second Committee, Betty King, stated that her country does not believe "international macroeconomic policy-making, globalization and debt relief are proper subjects for discussion in this forum" [*U.N. Development Update*, 1–2/99].

In recent years, as overall levels of international development assistance have declined, greater emphasis has been placed on private financial flows into developing countries. Faith in this route, however, has been seriously eroded by the recent financial crisis in Asia. At a **General Assembly Dialogue on Globalization** in September 1998, the Indonesian Minister of Foreign Affairs, Ali Alatas, pointed out that "Even the more dynamic developing economies, those that have managed to integrate themselves with the global economy through judicious macro-economic policies and painstaking structural adjustments, have seen the development gains that they earned over the decades crumble in the span of a few weeks. The fact that the Asian crisis has been particularly harsh on those economies that have been liberalizing financial flows and investment for a good number of years should therefore teach a valuable lesson to all of us in the developing world" [*Go Between*, 10–11/98]. At the dialogue session, other government representatives and U.N. agencies described situations of massive unemployment, diminishing health care, children forced to give up their education, and families sinking into poverty [ibid.].

The G-8 countries have acknowledged failures of the IMF in dealing with the Asian financial crisis; and in a major policy declaration issued at the end of 1998 they stated that "more attention must be paid in times of crisis to the effect of economic adjustment on the most vulnerable groups in society" [*U.N. Development Update*, 1–2/99]. Because of the far-reaching consequences of decisions on international economic policy, developing countries are seeking a greater say in the policies of the World Bank and IMF. Their concerns are now finding some support within those institutions. Joseph Stiglitz, a senior economic advisor at the World Bank, has called for a "new paradigm" that favors full consideration of social well-being and technical capacities as well as greater ownership of development strategies by developing countries themselves [ibid.].

In light of widespread questioning about the effects of globalization and trade liberalization, and ongoing efforts to redefine an appropriate architecture for the international financial system, the United Nations may be able to play a crucial role in formulating broad-based financial policies that are more responsive to development needs. In his 1998 year-end review, Secretary-General Annan pointed out that economic and political security are closely linked, and warned that "unless we tackle the underlying distortions and imbalances in the global economy, we must expect more [political and military] conflicts and even more intractable ones" [ibid.].

2. Food and Population Issues
By Peggy Polk

The 18th-century English economist and mathematician Thomas Malthus gained enduring fame with his deeply pessimistic theory that the Earth eventually would prove unable to sustain its ever-growing population. Written in 1798, his "Essay on the Principle of Population as It Affects the Future Improvement of Society" warned that if population is not controlled, the world would face increasing poverty, hunger, and general misery. His reasoning was simple: While population grows geometrically, food supplies increase arithmetically at a much slower rate.

Two centuries later, Malthus's theory remains as current—and as controversial—as it was on publication. He can be proved both right and wrong. The U.N. Food and Agriculture Organization (FAO), for one, contends that food production *is* keeping up with population growth. It is the lack of access to food, mainly due to poverty, that is the problem. Others are far less sanguine. The Worldwatch Institute, in a study of "the population challenge" aptly entitled *Beyond Malthus* [New York: Norton, 1999], warns that in many countries with growing populations, the demand for food, water, and forest products already is outrunning the capacity of local support systems.

Arguments converge, however, on the view that action to protect the environment and curb the consumption of nonrenewable resources is crucial to the well-being of future generations. FAO makes "sustainability" its watchword and has created a Sustainable Development Department. Both sides agree that the environment is under attack, whether from the desperate fight for survival of sustenance farmers or from the demands of affluent consumers. Clearly, deforestation and air and water pollution have crucial effects on food production, leading to climate change, the threat of rising sea levels, disappearing habitats, and species extinction.

At a 1998 symposium of the American Anthropological Society, participants addressed the question Was Malthus Right? [*New York Times*, 12/8/98]. Some panelists disagreed with details, but none quarreled with his assessment of the consequences of overpopulation. "[I]t is fair to say that Malthus was mostly right," Dr. Kenneth Wise of Pennsylvania State University said. "He took the prospect of technological innovation into account but still foresaw social inequities and growing misery as inevitable."

Revised Population Growth Estimates

World population has more than doubled over the past three decades, the largest population growth in the history of mankind. As of June 1998 the estimated number of men, women, and children inhabiting the Earth stood at 6 billion. Nevertheless, the United Nations sees progress in population control. Analyzing data from 228 countries and areas—ranging from Pitcairn Island in the South Pacific (pop. 46) to China (pop. 1.3 billion)—the United Nations Population Division reported that **the world's population growth rate is dropping,** and there will be 458 million fewer people on Earth in 2050 than it had projected two years earlier. It now foresees a world population of 8.9 billion in 2050, down from an estimated 9.4 billion [*Christian Science Monitor*, 10/28/98].

This still means that almost as many people will be added to the total population over the next half-century as were alive in 1960. And it appears that virtually all of the increased population (some 97 percent) will be in the developing world, where many countries already are struggling with population density. Europe had three times the population of Africa in 1900; but by 2050, Africa will have three times the population of all of Europe, including Russia. India is projected to overtake China as the world's most populous country, followed by the United States, Pakistan, Indonesia, Nigeria, Brazil, Bangladesh, Ethiopia, and Congo [ibid.].

The drop in population projections reflects both good and bad news. The good news is that there has been a **faster than expected fall in the average number of children that a woman will bear**—particularly in developing nations, but in developed countries as well. In the United States, for example, the National Center for Health Statistics reported in April 1999 that the birthrate among American teenagers dropped 16 percent over six years, from a peak of 62.1 births for every 1,000 women in the 15-to-19 age group in 1991 to 52.3 in 1997. Experts attributed the decline to decreased sexual activity among teenagers and improved contraception practices [*Washington Post/International Herald Tribune*, 4/30/99].

The bad news is **the ravages of AIDS**, especially in sub-Saharan Africa, Cambodia, India, Thailand, Brazil, and Haiti. The United Nations expects that in Botswana, the hardest hit country, the population will be 25 percent smaller in 2050 than it would have been without the epidemic. Life expectancy dropped from 61 years in 1993 to 47 in 1998 and is expected to fall to 41 between 2000 and 2005. Even so, Botswana's population is expected to nearly double. In Zimbabwe, where AIDS infects one of every five adults, the population growth rate has gone from 3.3 percent a year between 1980 and 1985 to 1.4 percent in 1998 and is projected to fall below 1 percent in 2000 [*Christian Science Monitor*, 10/28/98; *New York Times*, 10/28/98].

Lester Brown, President of the Worldwatch Institute, says the effect of AIDS on population trends in Africa, where up to 25 percent of the population is HIV positive, is of historic importance. Notes Brown, "In looking at global epidemics, one has to go back to the 16th century and the introduction of smallpox in the Aztec population of what is now Mexico to find anything on that scale, and before that, to the bubonic plague in Europe in the 14th century" [*New York Times*, 10/28/98].

The **U.N. Conference on Population and Development**, held in Cairo in 1994, called for spending $17 billion a year worldwide on **family planning, maternity care, and reproductive health** by 2000 and $22 billion by 2015. A third of the funds were to come from developed countries and two-thirds from developing countries, but 1998 funding fell far short, mainly because developed countries failed to meet their commitment [*Beyond Malthus*].

The U.S. appropriation got caught up in a larger battle over abortion. Although the United Nations maintains that it provides no funds for abortion, Congress refused to include any funding for the United Nations Population Fund, the main source of international family planning assistance, in the $520 billion spending package for fiscal 1999. But the House International Relations Committee moved in April to renew funding at the level of $25 million a year for the fiscal years 2000 and 2001 with the proviso that none of the U.S. contribution could be used in China, which abortion foes contend practices forced abortion [Religion News Service, 4/15/99].

Another important voice in the population debate is that of the Roman Catholic Church, whose members number a billion worldwide. In May 1999 the Vatican reiterated its opposition to abortion and all forms of artificial birth control at a meeting at U.N. Headquarters to review the implementation of the Cairo recommendations and determine priorities for future action. "The Holy See recalled with insistence that the human person must be placed at the center of every development program. This requires that the solution to problems relating to population must respect the dignity of every human being and at the same time promote his or her fundamental rights, first of all the right to life," Pope John Paul II told his weekly general audience [*Bollettino della Sala Stampa della Santa Sede*, 5/5/99].

That May 1999 meeting anticipated a Special Session of the General Assembly to assess world progress on the Cairo agenda. At "Cairo+5" (as the June 30–July 2 event was dubbed), member states rejected moves to weaken agreements made at the Population and Development conference five years earlier and recommended further actions to promote the Cairo Programme of Action—among them measures to ensure reproductive rights and sexual health. The final document does, however, set boundaries on one thorny issue: Abortion should not be promoted as a means of family planning [U.N. press release GA/9577, 7/2/99]. It also spoke of "an urgent need" for funds to implement the action agenda.

Food for All (Who Can Afford It)

Although living standards are rising worldwide, more than a billion people cannot meet their most basic needs. According to the United Nations Development Programme (UNDP), the richest 20 percent of the world's population in the highest income countries account for 86 percent of total private consumption expenditures, the poorest 20 percent only 1.3 percent. The wealthiest consume 45 percent of all available meat and fish; the poorest, 5 percent [Ninth Annual Human Development Report, UNDP; *Financial Times*, 9/10/98]. Said UNDP Administrator James Gustave Speth, "Despite the fact that there has been this enormous surge in consumption, not everybody has been invited to the party."

There is no doubt that access to food is as basic a concern as is increasing the production of food. Both UNDP and FAO consider the alleviation of poverty through development the best route to a fairer distribution of food stocks. FAO grappled with both problems—**production and access**—in the light of population growth at the 1996 **World Food Summit,** held at FAO headquarters in Rome. At that time it warned that Africa faced the most serious problems.

"In the decades leading to 2050, by which time most of the increase before stabilization will have taken place, world population growth will dominate over other demographic factors as the primary cause of increasing global food demand," FAO said in a technical background paper [Food Requirements and Population Growth, 1996]. "Food production is expected to increase broadly in line with this rise in demand, but not without further stress on agricultural, economic and environmental resources. **The situation in parts of Africa is of particular concern.**"

"Where land and water become scarce, increases in yields will be achieved mostly through an increase in productivity sustained by the development of human capacities. In light of the level of education already achieved, many countries in Asia seem well prepared for the change in the nature of development. On the other hand, Africa's lower level of development of economic infrastructures and of human resources will constitute a serious handicap for this region." FAO noted further that for Africa to solve its long-term food security problem, it would have to overcome "the challenge of simultaneously improving its human resources and infrastructure while facing a very difficult food situation."

The FAO's forecast, based on the earlier estimate of a world population of 9.4 billion in 2050, was that in order to adequately nourish their growing populations, developing countries would have to increase harvests by 174 percent. "This means that, while the countries of Latin America and Asia would roughly have to double their plant-derived energy, Africa would have to multiply it by five."

Biotechnology promises increases in food production comparable to what Dr. Norman Borlaug achieved in India in the 1950s and '60s by introducing high-yield strains of rice and wheat. But, just as the Green Revolution was attacked for its effects on biodiversity and the amount of fertilization and irrigation it required, **critics of bio-engineered crops** fear they may create pesticide-resistant weeds and pests and have a negative effect on the environment. The Worldwatch Institute warns that population pressure is already leading to the **depletion of aquifers and shrinking cropland,** with serious effects on food production.

In *Beyond Malthus,* part of an "environment alert series," the Institute contends that if rapid population growth continues indefinitely, the demand for water will eventually exceed the sustainable yield of aquifers so that water tables will fall. Because 40 percent of the world's food comes from irrigated land, water shortages will mean food shortages. In India, it says, water withdrawals already are estimated to be double the rate of aquifer recharge, and water tables are falling by 1 to 3 meters a year.

The study also points out that shrinking cropland threatens to make countries with growing populations dependent on imported food, which may not be available or may be too expensive. It notes that Japan, South Korea, and Taiwan import some 70 percent of their grain because grainland per person has shrunk to 0.03 hectares. But even under their present economic constraints, they can afford the imports far better than the countries of sub-Saharan Africa.

3.   Law of the Sea, Ocean Affairs, and Antarctica
By Lee A. Kimball

The Oceans

The **1982 U.N. Convention on the Law of the Sea (LOS)**, which entered into force in 1994, is the global framework convention governing all ocean uses. As of May 1999, 129 states and the European Community had become party to the Convention, and there were 94 parties to its **1994 implementing agreement on deep seabed mining.** The **1995 implementing agreement on straddling fish stocks and highly migratory fish stocks** (Fish Stocks Agreement or FSA) was nine short of the 30 ratifications required for it to enter into force.

The comprehensive scope of the LOS Convention touches on the mandates of nearly every major U.N. organ and establishes parameters and principles for a large number of specialized conventions governing fisheries, international shipping and navigation rights, overflight rights, marine pollution and waste disposal at sea, offshore oil development, maritime boundaries, conservation of marine species and biodiversity, maritime terrorism, illegal drug trafficking by sea, and other matters. Many members of the international community have expressed the need for more in-depth discussion by ocean specialists in order to tackle emerging and interconnected issues and improve coordination among the various international instruments and programs in the field [see *A Global Agenda: Issues Before the 53rd General Assembly of the United Nations* and *Issues Before the 51st General Assembly of the United Nations*]. This topic received a good deal of attention during the many events of the **1998 International Year of the Oceans,** including recommendations by the Independent World Commission on the Oceans. As a result, the U.N. Commission on Sustainable Development (CSD) at its April 1999 session recognized that oceans and seas present a special case for international coordination and cooperation, and recommended a more integrated approach at both intergovernmental and interagency levels. Building on existing arrangements for the annual debate in the General Assembly, it suggested that the General Assembly establish an **annual, open-ended, informal, one-week consultative process** or other processes under its auspices to enhance its regular consideration of ocean matters. The 54th General Assembly will debate the modalities for doing so, bearing in mind the need for more time, better preparations, working within existing budgetary resources, and expert participation, including participation by representatives of intergovernmental agencies and major groups. There are differing views on whether the one-week session should coincide with the General Assembly, the meetings of states parties to the LOS Convention, the CSD, or another event. A related issue, on how to provide for input from major groups, is linked to broader debates on observer status for NGOs in the General Assembly.

The 54th General Assembly will also consider how its annual oceans debate can complement the various specialized forums dealing with ocean issues and best address needs and characteristics that vary from region to region. The CSD has recommended that the General Assembly review whatever process it establishes within four years, setting the stage for a "sunset" provision if it is not working out. Regarding interagency arrangements, the CSD suggested that the Secretary-General work with the heads of U.N. bodies to improve the effectiveness, transparency, and responsiveness to member states of the Administrative Committee on Coordination subcommittee on oceans and coastal areas. It reiterated earlier urgings that the U.N. sponsoring agencies for the **Joint Group of Experts on the Scientific Aspects of Marine Environmental Protection** enhance its effectiveness and explore means to interact with scientific representatives of governments and major groups.

Meeting of States Parties to the LOS Convention (SPLOS)

The SPLOS met in New York from May 19 to 28, 1999. Among other business, seven judges were elected to the LOS Tribunal and its budget was adopted, while decisions on the Tribunal's financial regulations and a trust fund for the Commission on the Limits of the Continental Shelf were deferred (see below).

The 53rd General Assembly highlighted the institutional aspects of ocean governance as well as concern over piracy and unsustainable fishing practices. Several countries referred to the need for consistency with the LOS Convention in UNESCO's work on a new draft convention for protection of the underwater cultural heritage, and one or two expressed similar views regarding initiatives on illegal transport of migrants (International Maritime Organization [IMO]) and the transport of radioactive materials (International Atomic Energy Agency). Another matter cited in the debate was the innovative use of ocean space for launching spacecraft. A commercial project supported by both private and public sectors in Russia, Ukraine, Norway, and the United States envisages a moored platform for launching space rockets or satellites near the equator [U.N. press release GA/9514, 11/24/98]. As usual, the Secretary-General's comprehensive oceans report [A/53/456] was well received, and member states praised the efforts of the **Division for Ocean Affairs and the LOS (DOALOS)** in the Office of Legal Affairs for its support of the Convention, including maintenance of a Web site [www.un.org/Depts/los] and advice and assistance to states on implementation. DOALOS is working on a study aimed at helping states prepare for and negotiate maritime boundaries, draft delimitation agreements, and handle possible dispute settlement proceedings. The publication will draw on an experts workshop held in April 1999 [U.N. press release SEA/1613, 4/22/99].

The **omnibus oceans resolution** [A/Res/53/32] urges all states to prevent piracy and armed robbery at sea and cooperate with the IMO in this respect. To ensure safe navigation, it invites states to promote hydrographic surveys and the widespread availability of nautical information. Concerns with the financial situation of the International Seabed Authority and the International Tribunal on the Law of the Sea are noted, and states are encouraged once again to deposit charts and geographical coordinates as called for in the Convention to identify their offshore zones and to indicate which means of compulsory, binding dispute settlement they will accept. The resolution notes the importance of ensuring that the underwater cultural heritage convention conforms fully with the LOS Convention.

In keeping with an earlier **decision to rotate consideration of fisheries issues,** the 53rd General Assembly considered drift-nets, unauthorized fishing, and fisheries by-catch and discards while the 54th will concentrate on implementation of the **Fish Stocks Agreement (FSA).** The Secretary-General's report [A/53/473] and General Assembly Resolution 53/33 draw attention to re-flagging of vessels as a means to avoid complying with high seas fishing rules. States are encouraged to ratify relevant agreements like the FSA and a 1993 **Food and Agriculture Organization Compliance Agreement,** to observe the global moratorium on large-scale pelagic drift-net fishing [A/Res/46/215], and to take measures to deter re-flagging and ensure that their vessels do not engage in unauthorized fishing in the offshore zones of other states. Donor countries and organizations are encouraged to assist developing states to promote sustainable fisheries and improve related monitoring, control, and enforcement. The resolution endorses FAO's progress on three global action plans to reduce incidental catch of seabirds, conserve shark populations, and control excess fishing capacity. These plans were subsequently adopted by the **FAO**

Committee on Fisheries in February 1999 and were expected to be formally adopted by the FAO assembly in the fall.

The Seventh Meeting of the **Commission on Sustainable Development** (CSD7), held in April 1999, concentrated on four major challenges in its review of chapter 17 of *Agenda 21* and the Rio + 5 Programme adopted at the 1997 Special Session of the General Assembly. In addition to international coordination and cooperation, considered above, it emphasized threats to the ocean from pollution and the overexploitation of marine living resources, and the need for better scientific understanding of these issues and of ocean interactions with the world climate system. Singled out for particular attention were illegal, unregulated, and unreported fishing (see also CCAMLR, below) and destructive fishing practices, for which FAO is called upon to develop global action plans; the role of distant water fishing; and slow progress with implementation of the **1995 Global Programme of Action for Protection of the Marine Environment from Land-Based Activities (GPA)**, for which UNEP serves as secretariat. Relatedly, the UNEP Governing Council at its meeting in January 1999 agreed to explore the feasibility of convening a global conference in 2000 to address sewage in the context of the GPA and continued to support the preparation of a convention to control persistent organic pollutants (POPs). On **three controversial issues,** CSD7 was unable to agree on recommendations: subsidies related to fisheries, schemes for improving consumer information on fish products (e.g., certification or "green" labeling schemes), and the disputed right of states to prohibit the transboundary movement of hazardous and radioactive wastes and materials in marine areas subject to their jurisdiction.

The International Seabed Authority (ISBA)

The August 1998 meeting of the Authority at its Kingston, Jamaica, headquarters was followed by a brief meeting in New York in October to agree on a scale of assessments for the 1999 budget. In view of the precarious financial situation of the Authority [see *A Global Agenda: Issues/52*], it was decided to hold a single, three-week session in 1999. The ISBA's relationship agreement with the United Nations, adopted in November 1997, was followed by a protocol on privileges and immunities in March 1998. A **draft relationship agreement between the ISBA and the Tribunal** will be considered at the ISBA's August 1999 session, as will the draft headquarters agreement with the government of Jamaica and the financial and staff rules of the Authority. The 2000 budget will also be on the agenda.

The ISBA continued work in 1999 on the **draft mining code.** Its Council has been reviewing the document completed by the Legal and Technical Commission. It covers the prospecting and exploration stages of manganese nodule development, leaving rules and regulations for the exploitation stage to a later date when prospects for commercial operations improve. The draft rules on environmental protection have engendered quite a bit of discussion, with concerns expressed about the rules covering prospecting and how to provide for liability and repair of environmental damage. As interest in other types of seabed minerals grows, additional rules governing their development will have to be elaborated. At the August 1998 meeting, the Russian Federation formally requested that the ISBA adopt rules on exploration for deposits like cobalt-rich crusts and polymetallic sulphides found at or near hydrothermal vents where the sea floor is spreading apart. The Convention provides that rules and regulations for any seabed mineral resource other than manganese nodules must be adopted within three years of a request by any state [U.N. press release SEA/1608, 8/31/98]. The ISBA's Legal and Technical Commission will take up in August the guidelines on data collection and assessing the environmental impacts of exploration activities developed at a workshop in China in June 1998.

The International Tribunal on the Law of the Sea (ITLOS)

The Tribunal was expected to deliver its first judgment in June 1999—this concerning the same vessel-seizure dispute between Guinea and St. Vincent and the Grenadines that was the subject of prompt release proceedings in 1997 [see *A Global Agenda: Issues/52*].

On organizational matters, at the ninth meeting of the parties to the Convention (SPLOS9) seven judges were elected to the Tribunal. The 21 members serve nine-year terms, but the three classes initially elected in 1996 received three-, six-, and nine-year terms so that a third of the members would be reelected every three years. SPLOS9 also adopted the Tribunal's 2000 budget, but deferred adopting its financial regulations until its next meeting, in May 2000. The Tribunal plans to move to its new premises in Hamburg in late 1999 or early 2000 and is expected to complete an occupancy and use agreement and a headquarters agreement with the government of Germany in 1999.

The Commission on the Limits of the Continental Shelf (CLCS)

The CLCS is charged with guiding states as they establish the outer limits of their continental shelf where the limits extend beyond 200 nautical miles. At its August/September 1998 meeting it completed adjustments and formally adopted its rules of procedure [ibid.]. Scientific and technical guidelines were formally adopted at the May 1999 meeting. Their purpose is to clarify for states the nature, scope, and depth of scientific and technical evidence to be submitted to the CLCS. The Commission was to meet again from August 30 to September 3, 1999, at which time it would consider a proposal on training to help states apply the guidelines and on supplemental annexes illustrating how to do so [CLCS/12]. In response to the CLCS request for a decision regarding the creation of a trust fund to help finance participation in the Commission by developing-country members, SPLOS9 recommended that the Commission provide a written assessment of actual needs and financial estimates [U.N. press release SEA/1617, 5/28/99].

Antarctica

The General Assembly last took up the question of Antarctica in 1996. Developments at the annual meetings of the parties to the 1959 Antarctic Treaty (Atps) and the 1980 Convention on the Conservation of Antarctic Marine Living Resources (CCAMLR) may be found in *A Global Agenda: Issues/52* and *Issues/53* and in the summaries below.

XXIII Antarctic Treaty Consultative Meeting (ATCM)

All 27 consultative (decision-making) parties to the Antarctic Treaty attended the 23rd ATCM meeting, held in Lima, Peru, May 24 to June 4, 1999, together with 12 non-consultative parties—including new member Venezuela. There was a major push to overcome several years of stalemate and agree next year at XXIV ATCM on the **location of a secretariat.** Argentina's offer is still on the table and widely supported. Last year Australia offered Hobart (the seat of CCAMLR) as an alternative, hoping to find consensus. This issue is increasingly linked with strengthening support for treaty meetings and institutional memory, and with proposals for cost-sharing among the parties as it becomes more burdensome for individual governments to host ATCMs. Suggestions that the ATCM revert to meeting every other year and convene for only one week may also be considered. In a departure from normal practice, there was no decision about the host for the next meeting; and the United States, as depository, has been requested to coordinate consultations on this matter. The final annex to the **1991 Environmental Protocol on protected areas** is expected to enter into force by the next meeting.

Little progress was made on the issue of **liability for environmental damage,** although delegations reaffirmed their commitment to developing a regime on prevention, response, and liability. They agreed in general on strict liability and that coverage should include public and private legal entities or individuals engaged in activities in Antarctica, in addition to states. On a related matter, the meeting endorsed further work by the Council of Managers of National Antarctic Programs (COMNAP) and the Scientific Committee on Antarctic Research (SCAR) to assist the liability deliberations. They will outline practical aspects of planning and response for environmental emergencies arising from scientific and logistical support and help clarify several definitional questions.

In light of the work of the IMO on a **polar shipping code,** the ATCM set up an experts group to draft non-binding guidelines for Antarctic shipping. It will seek their subsequent adoption by the IMO in order to extend applicability to members of the IMO that are not bound by ATCM decisions.

The parties continue to improve and rationalize Antarctic information. Several aspects of the Antarctic Treaty System information exchange will be carefully analyzed by XXIV ATCM to promote more timely and efficient exchanges based on standard reporting formats. SCAR will prepare a feasibility study on a state of the Antarctic environment report in collaboration with CCAMLR, the World Meteorological Organization, and COMNAP. COMNAP expects to produce a technical manual on environmental monitoring by March 2000.

The work of the Committee on Environment Protection (CEP), established by the Protocol, led to several ATCM decisions, including the adoption of **guidelines for environmental impact assessment (EIA)** in Antarctica. These are expected to improve understanding of the EIA process and lead to more uniform practice among parties. Concern was expressed about tourism activities by non-consultative states that have yet to become party to the 1991 Environmental Protocol and are thus not subject to EIA requirements. In another initiative, SCAR has been asked to review the list of specially protected species in Antarctica, assisted by the World Conservation Union and its Red Lists, and to advise the CEP regarding species that should remain on the list or be designated as specially protected.

CCAMLR XVII

The CCAMLR Commission continues to address a number of fishery issues common to other regional fishery organizations. Its efforts to develop measures to address illegal, unreported, and unregulated (IUU) fishing inform, and benefit from, broader global discussions; and they are likely to be influential in FAO's initiatives in this field, as noted above. The same is true of CCAMLR initiatives on marine debris and on the reduction of incidental mortality of seabirds [see *A Global Agenda: Issues/53*]. CCAMLR also continues to elaborate its precautionary approach to fisheries management.

It is estimated that IUU fisheries take two to three times the legal catch of Antarctic fisheries, although IUU fishing has decreased over the last year. **Conservation measures adopted at CCAMLR XVII** in October/November 1998 include a requirement for satellite-based vessel monitoring systems by the end of the year 2000 on all vessels fishing finfish (excluding krill fishing vessels); agreement on strengthened port state inspections regarding the vessels of non-CCAMLR parties sighted fishing in the Convention area; agreement that each CCAMLR party will inspect its own flag vessels in port and ensure compliance with the fishing authorization it is required to issue, and that other parties may also undertake port state inspections; and improved marking of fishing vessels and gear for purposes of identification. Two states implicated in unregulated fisheries in the CCAMLR area, Mauritius and Namibia, accepted invitations to attend CCAMLR XVII. The meeting noted their interest in cooperating with CCAMLR and agreed to share information on contracting parties' vessels so that IUU fishing would be easier to identify. A vessel register scheme will be considered further at the Commission's next meeting during the fall of 1999.

V
Social and Humanitarian Issues

1. Human Rights
By Felice D. Gaer

Human rights issues are among the most contentious and time-consuming items on the General Assembly's agenda, addressing as they do basic issues of governance and, often, the abusive behavior of specific states. How individual states treat their own citizens is a central concern of the U.N.'s human rights bodies, and so is the effort to apportion responsibility for upholding universal standards of behavior. Given their involvement in setting these standards *and* in recommending actions to correct particular abusive situations, the General Assembly's Third (Social, Humanitarian, and Cultural) Committee and the Human Rights Commission, which meets in Geneva, are among the liveliest spots in the U.N. system.

Nineteen ninety-eight—the 50th anniversary of the landmark Universal Declaration on Human Rights (UDHR) and of the Convention against Genocide, the first human rights treaty adopted by the United Nations—saw a series of key developments for the human rights movement. One was the adoption of the statute to create an international criminal court (see "Legal Issues," Chapter VI of the present volume)—a step toward realizing the Genocide Treaty's vision of a permanent court to try those charged with committing the heinous crimes that constitute genocide. A second development was the decision of a British court that Chile's former dictator Augusto Pinochet could be extradited to Spain, where he had been charged with torture and crimes against humanity when he was head of state (see "Legal Issues")—another signal that gross violations of human rights cannot be committed with impunity. This was also the year in which the General Assembly formally reviewed the progress that governments and the United Nations itself have made since the Vienna World Conference on Human Rights in 1993, and encouraged further efforts to mainstream human rights in all areas of U.N. activity.

The U.N. Role in Human Rights

The U.N. Charter identifies human rights as one of the four purposes of the Organization and calls specifically for the establishment of a commission on human rights. Moreover, member states and the Organization itself are obliged to promote "universal respect for, and observance of, human rights and fundamental freedoms" [Art. 55 (c)], and the members are exhorted to take "joint and separate action . . . for the achievement of the purposes."

The first priority of the Commission on Human Rights in the 1940s was to prepare a draft Universal Declaration of Human Rights and to follow up with binding treaties. Today, there are six core treaties and numerous other instruments addressing human rights standards.

Since taking office as Secretary-General, **Kofi Annan has put his rhetorical skills and institutional support behind the centrality of human rights in U.N. programming**—calling for human rights to be mainstreamed throughout all U.N. programs; appointing Mary Robinson, former President of Ireland and a human rights attorney, as High Commissioner for Human Rights; and asking her to serve on the various executive and coordinating committees for core U.N. programs. He has addressed the Commission on Human Rights several times, and in 1999 explained why, in his words, he has "made human rights a priority in every program the United Nations launches and every mission we embark upon." Said Annan: "I have done so because promotion and defense of human rights is at the heart of every aspect of our work and every article of our Charter. Above all, I believe human rights are at the core of our sacred bond with the peoples of the United Nations." No other Secretary-General has spoken so boldly on these issues, nor dared to speak so frankly about the relevance of human rights to security as well as development.

Annan speaks not only about defending human rights but of punishing those who abuse them:

> We should leave no one in doubt that for the mass murderers, the "ethnic cleansers," those guilty of gross and shocking violations of human rights, impunity is not acceptable. The United Nations will never be their refuge, its Charter never the source of comfort or justification. They are our enemies, regardless of race, religion, or nation, and only in their defeat can we redeem the promise of this great Organization.
> [U.N. press release SG/SM/99/91, 4/7/99]

At the annual meetings of the Commission on Human Rights, 53 states, elected for four-year terms, examine, discuss, set priorities on, and approve the creation of mechanisms to address human rights issues. The annual six-week spring session of the Commission, like the General Assembly session that follows in the fall, addresses scores of issues. The latest Commission, in spring 1999, adopted a total of 93 texts, including 82 resolutions, 7 decisions, and 4 Chairperson's statements (agreed statements that are not formal resolutions).

Thirty-seven government ministers and top officials spoke at the Commission in 1999—only half of the number who arrived for the 1998 commemorative session on the 50th anniversary of UDHR, but an impressive showing of political support for the U.N. body that the members transferred to Geneva from New York in the early 1970s in an effort to remove it from the political and public limelight. Officials of numerous U.N. agencies and programs, from UNICEF to UNHCR to the ILO, UNCTAD, and UNIFEM, also attended the Commission session—a visible sign that mainstreaming human rights had taken hold since Vienna.

The High Commissioner for Human Rights

Under the newly reformed agenda of the Commission on Human Rights, the U.N. High Commissioner for Human Rights now delivers a report at the opening of the Commission session, and in March 1999, Mary Robinson posed a series of challenges to its members. Acknowledging that **"the greatest threat to human rights is war,"** she argued that the challenge today is "to prevent the tragic violations committed in the course of conflict and reconstruct the societies which conflict has destroyed." Knowing how to prevent it, she stated candidly, is not easy or obvious: "Modern media technology has ensured that we can witness the atrocities as we go about our ordinary lives, but it has not given us the tools to halt them. I face this dilemma daily—of knowing but lacking the means to take effective action" [statement at the opening of the Commission, 3/22/99; available at www.unhchr.ch].

The good news, she said, is that the special procedures and mechanisms of the Commission can help address these matters, step by step. The Commission's reporting mandates, for example, give it a unique role in the U.N. system, by providing early warning. But to be effective, Robinson pointed out, the reports have to be noted elsewhere in the system, acted on "without delay" and implemented by other parts of the United Nations as well. And the job does not stop with U.N. agencies. Robinson went on to note the importance of regional human rights bodies; and even as the Commission was meeting, she traveled to Mauritius for the first Ministerial Meeting of the Organization of African Unity devoted to human rights, to encourage the development of regional and sub-regional strategies to protect rights. Expressing her intention to develop regional efforts even further, Robinson advised that her office has already "deployed regional human rights advisors on the ground in some regions."

At another point in her report to the Commission, the High Commissioner drew attention to the **situation of all human rights advocates**

working under difficult, often threatening circumstances. "I think the most tangible way . . . [to] demonstrate our support . . . would be to assure our non-governmental colleagues who have come here to bring issues to our attention that they will be able to return to their places of residence and continue their work in safety," said Robinson—words intended to remind member states of the year-old Declaration on Human Rights Defenders. That Declaration, which spent 13 years in committee, was finally adopted during the 50th Anniversary of the Universal Declaration on Human Rights in 1998.

Those pressing for creation of the post of High Commissioner had long conceived of this office as that of a human rights champion—someone able to speak out clearly and take actions to protect human rights worldwide, responding to serious violations of human rights. Although the mandate adopted in 1993 was not as strong as those defenders hoped for, there was ample room in it for the High Commissioner to change the way the United Nations acts to prevent and protect against human rights violations. The first High Commissioner, José Ayala Lasso of Ecuador, established new field offices for monitoring human rights in trouble spots. Many observers felt Ayala Lasso did not serve as a strong voice for human rights within the U.N. system, and he was widely criticized for allowing his country visits to pass without much to show for them. Others point out that the previous Secretary-General, Boutros Boutros-Ghali, publicly opposed creation of the post and never supported its development, limiting results in the early years.

The second High Commissioner, Mary Robinson, took office in September 1997. She cited her "duty to ensure leadership on human rights issues and to emphasize the importance of human rights on the international and national agendas," her obligation to anticipate or react to serious violations of human rights, and her intention to be "a strong moral voice for the defense of the victims."

During 1999, as the discussion below under "Country Situations" makes clear, Robinson seems to consider country visits one of her most important activities. It is certainly the one most visible to the press.

The Human Rights Machinery

Many human rights standards and structures have been established by the United Nations and other international organizations, legal norms being a core tool in establishing the legitimacy and global reach of human rights. Today there are **six major human rights treaties**—they address civil and political rights, economic and social rights, racial discrimination, discrimination against women, torture, and the rights of the child—and numerous other instruments. (Signing and ratifying these treaties is voluntary, and each signatory pledges to implement the treaty norms at home.) Three of the treaties—the Civil and Political Covenant and the Torture and Race conventions—have been ratified by the United States. Many countries have ratified all six treaties, and the Convention on the Rights of the Child is in the lead with 191 ratifications—every country but Somalia and the United States. Individuals can bring complaints through "optional protocols" to three international treaty monitoring bodies that oversee compliance with treaty norms. The treaties on racial discrimination and torture and the civil and political rights convention are the instruments involved. As described in "The Advancement of Women," section 2 of the present chapter, another such protocol comes before the 54th General Assembly for approval.

The challenge to human rights today, however, is not drafting more standards but implementing those that already exist. Each of the treaties establishes a process for reviewing compliance with its provisions. In each case, states parties are required to submit periodic reports on compliance, and the experts elected to that treaty body ask questions of the state's representatives for anywhere from a few hours to two days (depending on the treaty, whether the report is the first or a repeat performance, and whether the human rights situation is known to be grave). In this process, the experts rely heavily upon information, usually delivered informally, from diverse sources, including NGOs. Several recent expert meetings have explored the consolidation and effectiveness of the six treaty bodies; and the Human Rights Commission and General Assembly have already received numerous reports and updates recommending changes in the way these bodies function.

In 1979–80, the Commission on Human Rights began to establish "special procedures" to look into individual violations on an urgent basis, conduct country investigations, and report publicly on their findings. These procedures are staffed by experts, who are appointed in their individual capacity and, thus, are independent of their governments. Some of the appointees are called "special rapporteurs" while others are known as "independent experts." One type of special procedure takes action on certain "thematic" human rights violations and examines the situation in particular countries. The subjects covered are as diverse as torture, forced "disappearances," summary executions, arbitrary detention, violence against women, freedom of expression, racial discrimination, religious intolerance, the sale of children, independence of judges and lawyers, use of mercenaries, the effects of dumping toxic wastes, the right to education, and (new this year) human rights of migrants—and this is only a partial list. Many "thematic" mechanisms address incidents in as many as 50 countries annually.

The special rapporteurs and thematic working groups are the leading edge of the U.N. human rights system, mandated to look into specific cases and allegations of human rights abuses on an emergency basis. Their status as independent experts gives them a freedom of action that governmental and intergovernmental employees do not have. They are particularly important to the Office of the High Commissioner, whose work they often assist.

Some 15 "thematic rapporteurs" and "working groups" now look into egregious human rights violations on a real-time basis, in all countries of the world. These thematic mechanisms capitalize on the U.N.'s strength: its legitimacy as the premier global international institution, able to reach out to or into virtually every society, and to establish norms applicable universally. So it is that they are able to look into human rights violations affecting individuals, to contact governments on an emergency basis, and to report their findings and recommendations publicly.

Another type of special procedure investigates and reports publicly and in depth on human rights conditions in a particular country. "Country rapporteurs" today cover numerous situations, including Afghanistan, Burundi, Haiti, Israel, Rwanda, Somalia, Iran, Iraq, Myanmar (Burma), Sudan, Bosnia, Croatia, and Serbia. The findings are often the basis for U.N. action that ranges from censuring a country to providing it with targeted technical assistance to improve human rights conditions. But both thematic and country-specific procedures are poorly financed and thinly staffed, limiting their effectiveness.

Repairing and Reforming the Human Rights Machinery

The issue of reforming and strengthening the human rights machinery of the United Nations moved to center stage in 1999. At the previous Commission on Human Rights, Chairman Jacob Selebi of South Africa initiated a comprehensive review of the special procedures and mechanisms of the Commission—the thematic and country special rapporteurs, working groups, the Sub-Commission on Prevention of Discrimination and Protection of Minorities, and the "1503" confidential procedure—by that body's own officers.

As the human rights mechanisms outlined above have grown in recent years, so has a strong backlash to them. Countries that had been subjected to unwanted scrutiny, or that opposed so close a review, had begun to propose ways of "rationalizing" or reining in the burgeoning human rights machinery at the United Nations. The 1993 Vienna World Conference on Human Rights may have called for a High Commissioner, but the opponents of this post also made certain it called for and created a working group to examine "adaptation" of the U.N.'s human rights machinery to improve its "coordination, efficiency, and effectiveness." To the uninitiated, this was a mere managerial call for reform to make things work better; to the rejectionist states, it was a way to cut back the investigatory and public reporting functions of the independent experts and special procedures of the Commission.

The reform process started by Ambassador Selebi would put the issue more clearly on the table of the Commission on Human Rights. And it would either strengthen the system or weaken it. He left the recommendation to be decided by the "Bureau"—the officers of the 1998 Commission, drawn from each regional group.

As it turned out, **the report by the Bureau** did not hold sway with all the 1999 Commission members. Almost immediately after the report was released, the Asian Group—which had spearheaded the attack on the Commission's investigative machinery in 1993 and on every occasion since—distanced itself from the Bureau's report, which contained both modest and sweeping proposals for reviewing the human rights machinery. The Asian Group now offered a paper containing numerous counterproposals. As the Commission considered these issues at special evening sessions, the report encountered intense criticism from a small but extremely active group that included Algeria, Bhutan, China, Cuba, Egypt, India, Iran, Malaysia, Mexico, Myanmar, Nepal, Pakistan, Sri Lanka, and Vietnam, with Cuba, India, and Pakistan acting as spokesmen.

A broad-based group headed by Argentina and enlisting more than 50 co-sponsors (including 27 members of the Commission—a majority) sought to forge support for the Bureau's report and its machinery-strengthening proposals—a move thwarted at the 11th hour when the 1999 Commission Chair, Ambassador Anne Anderson of Ireland, inexplicably introduced a proposed chair's text—requiring consensus of all Commission members. In the end, her **"chair's statement,"** rather than a resolution, was agreed upon. It calls for establishing a working group in Geneva during the course of the year to review the Bureau's review and sort out aspects of the reform proposals. It also calls for some specific changes, including term limits of three years on special rapporteurs; executive summaries on all reports of the special rapporteur reports, something completely new; and the renaming of the Sub-Commission. Several of its points overlap or are similar to the Argentine text, but the Commission's momentum in creating a pro-monitoring, pro-mechanisms leadership group appears to have been lost.

In what human rights advocates saw as an ominous signal, delivered only after the chair's statement was agreed to, those opposing the Bureau's report indicated that they not only wanted to look at the review produced by the Bureau but also wanted to use the new working group in Geneva to review the scope of concerns and means of decision-making of the Commission on Human Rights itself. Among the proposals of this group of states is that the Commission must reach a consensus before adopting a resolution (with the potential for putting an end to votes on any and all country-specific resolutions) and that special rapporteurs will have to gain the Commission's political approval before reports of the expert investigators and special rapporteurs become public (signaling the end of candor and public criticism of human rights abuses). Although the negotiations will take place out of sight in Geneva, the reverberations will be felt at the General Assembly in New York.

Country Situations

Kosovo

The U.N.'s role and response to the crisis in Kosovo will be analyzed and debated by scholars and policy-makers for years to come, and there will be no overlooking the human rights dimensions of that crisis. Kosovo "exploded" after years of discrimination and human rights violations directed against the ethnic Albanian population, who were forced by Serbian leaders from jobs, education, health care, and other services—and many of whom were arrested, or tortured, or abused. In 1998 and 1999, the human rights abuses grew; now violence, massacres, summary executions, torture, rape, and the ominous separation of men from their families were reported. "Ethnic cleansing" aptly described these acts. The escalation of the crisis, from discriminatory abuses to violent, wholesale physical abuses, raises questions about the efficacy of U.N. action in the field of human rights: What difference does it make? When is it most effective? And what kind of action is, in fact, needed to protect vulnerable populations?

Since 1992 the U.N. Special Rapporteur on Former Yugoslavia has been reporting on the discriminatory treatment of ethnic Albanians in Kosovo. Some of the Commission's resolutions addressed this mistreatment, but since the early years of the conflict in the Balkans, the United Nations has been unable to focus its or anyone else's attention on changing the behavior of the government of the Federal Republic of Yugoslavia (FRY). To establish its presence, the United Nations tried, unsuccessfully, to reopen offices in the FRY. (No other entity, governmental or private, was able to resolve the problems posed in Kosovo either.) In 1998, following attacks by Serbian special police units and similar acts in the Drenica region of Kosovo, the Commission on Human Rights turned its attention to Kosovo as a more urgent matter. Within a week of its opening session, the 1998 Commission adopted a chairman's statement on Kosovo. Shortly afterwards the new Special Rapporteur on former Yugoslavia, Jiri Dienstbier, made a "flash" visit to the region and reported back before the end of the six-week Commission session.

Although the Commission later adopted an omnibus resolution on former Yugoslavia, those with real potential for effecting change were members of the so-called "Contact Group," the United States, the United

Kingdom, France, Germany, Russia, and Italy. The group had agreed, with difficulty, on a Security Council resolution that established an arms embargo on the FRY [S/Res/1160, 3/3/98] and had refused to supply equipment to the Serbian authorities that could be used for internal repression of Kosovars or, for that matter, for terrorism. As attacks by Serbian special police forces increased and ethnic Albanians fled their homes, the number of internally displaced persons in the region quickly grew to well over 100,000. **In June 1998, High Commissioner Mary Robinson asked Yugoslav authorities for permission to open an office in Pristina.** U.N. Special Representative to Former Yugoslavia Elizabeth Rehn (herself a former Special Rapporteur on human rights) warned that "the eleventh hour is approaching" and that it would take urgent action by the international community to prevent a massacre or worse. It was at this point that FRY President Slobodan Milosevic, in a highly publicized June meeting with President Boris Yeltsin of Russia, agreed that Serbian forces would not carry out repressive actions against the civilian population, that refugees would be permitted to return, and that humanitarian organizations, such as the U.N. High Commissioner for Refugees (UNHCR) and the International Committee of the Red Cross, would have full access to the region—all promises honored in the breach.

The Kosovo Liberation Army (KLA), an armed resistance group that had become visible in 1996, claiming responsibility for various violent acts, now found itself in a stronger position. It had been growing in legitimacy in the eyes of Kosovar Albanians and in public support as the Serbian armed attacks grew. In July 1998 the KLA launched a major offensive of its own against the town of Obrahovac. Conflict in the region escalated, as did reports of atrocities and the number of internally displaced. The **U.N. Security Council** came back into the picture shortly after the opening of the 53rd General Assembly in September 1998. On September 23 it **adopted Resolution 1199, which condemned acts of violence committed in Kosovo,** called on all parties to denounce terrorism, and, under Chapter VII of the Charter, demanded an immediate end to the fighting. It also called on Milosevic to implement the June agreement with Yeltsin and warned that, "should the measures demanded in this resolution . . . not be taken . . . , additional measures to maintain or restore peace and stability will be considered."

The situation continued to deteriorate. In October, U.S. envoy Richard Holbrooke was sent to broker an agreement with Milosevic calling for a withdrawal of Serbian special forces and reduction of their numbers. Part of the deal was a **2,000-person Kosovo Verification Mission (KVM), to be established by the Organization for Security and Cooperation in Europe (OSCE)** for deployment in Kosovo.

Shortly after the October agreement, **U.N. Special Rapporteur on Former Yugoslavia Jiri Dienstbier made his third visit to the FRY,** focusing for these eight days on "rapidly evolving developments in Kosovo and the situation of the media in Serbia" [E/CN.4/1999/42, par. 79]. (A visit in April and an 11-day visit in September had preceded it.) In each case, said Dienstbier, accurate information was the hardest to come by. He noted that the Serbian police, the Kosovo Liberation Army, and local militias were responsible for the violence. Although repeatedly blaming both sides for it, he did identify the government forces as "us[ing] excessive force . . . leading to extensive civilian casualties" [par. 86].

In November 1998, **High Commissioner Mary Robinson signed a Memorandum of Understanding with Yugoslav authorities**— succeeding, at long last, in her goal of establishing an office of the High Commissioner for Human Rights in the FRY. The office made represen- tations on various human rights problems encountered by ethnic Serbs, Albanians, and others [E/CN.4/1999/SR.14, par. 66.]. In the weeks and months that followed, the KVM deployed its personnel, **the Rambouillet negoti- ations came and went,** the KVM withdrew its personnel, and the violent clashes continued.

Days after the Commission on Human Rights convened on **March 22, NATO forces began bombing Serbia** (and only later, Kosovo) in an effort to bring about agreement to the Rambouillet accords, a withdrawal of Serb forces, and related acts central to a political settlement. The Com- mission took little note of these developments at first. None of the open- ing speeches, and very few of the speeches by the foreign ministers who took the podium at the outset of the Commission, even mentioned Ko- sovo. At the end of the second week of the six-week session, reportedly responding to the desire of the Commission's chairperson, Ambassador Anne Anderson of Ireland, to pause and focus on the Kosovo events— this, after all, was a conflict generated by long-standing human rights abuses—the Commission held a two-hour debate on the subject. The High Commissioner for Human Rights, for her part, made a point of providing updates to the Commission on the situation in Kosovo every Friday and in person. A representative of the High Commissioner for Refugees presented data at the same time; and the Special Representative of the Secretary-General on children in armed conflict, Olara Otunnu, presented a "special agenda" to respond to the need of Kosovo child refu- gees.

Three draft resolutions were offered and two adopted: One, pre- sented by the Organization of the Islamic Conference (Russia offered the only negative vote and there were six abstentions), on April 13; the other—an omnibus resolution on former Yugoslavia that included a sec- tion on what had to be done in Kosovo to restore respect for human rights—later in the session. The third resolution, introduced by the Rus- sian Federation, was defeated overwhelmingly.

The Kosovo briefings by the High Commissioner for Human

Rights were unprecedented: She explained later that because the Commission was meeting as the reports of massacres and ethnic cleansing were unfolding, she felt it especially important to present information on the atrocities in person. She also dispatched a mission consisting of the Special Rapporteur and a personal representative to the FRY for the purpose of establishing a "human rights presence," of consulting and liaising with "institutional partners," and of gathering information about human rights violations to provide to the Commission [U.N. press release HR/CN/99/29, 4/9/99]. At a press briefing on April 12, she explained the importance of ongoing reporting of the situation and noted her attempts to make sure "that the Commission be aware, while it was in session, of the extent of the human tragedy unfolding and which had human rights violations at its heart." All of this attention to Kosovo brought into focus the problem Robinson had raised at the outset of the Commission: "How does the Commission deal with situations of conflict and of gross violations of human rights?"

On April 30, Robinson turned from reporting on the atrocities affecting Kosovar Albanians to a broader picture. After providing the details of ongoing reports of ethnic cleansing, destruction of property, and looting by Serb forces, she questioned the actions of NATO as "the sole judge of what is or is not acceptable to bomb" and the proportionality of the damage inflicted by the NATO bombing, particularly the collateral damage to civilians [U.N. press release HR/99/34, 4/30/99]. These comments were widely covered by the press, unlike the remarks and assessments Robinson had been offering at the Commission for weeks on the atrocities against Kosovar Albanians.

Not many days later **Robinson left for a week-long visit to Serbia** (including Kosovo) and neighboring states. The more she traveled and the more people with whom she spoke, the more she expressed her shock, horror, and outrage at the atrocities perpetrated by Serb forces and militias. It was these acts, she said, and not the NATO bombing, that had caused the flight of so many Kosovars. Those who perpetrated the ethnic cleansing and related acts could not go unpunished, Robinson pointed out, and the war crimes tribunal must be brought in to investigate and hold accountable those responsible for it. "It is too late to prevent the current catastrophe," she said after visiting Albania, "but we owe it to the survivors and the victims to make sure that the ethnic cleansers of today have no impunity tomorrow." After all, "this is a wake-up call to the international community. . . . The signs of this tragedy were there for all to see for a long time. We must move away from crisis management to crisis prevention" [HR/99/39, 5/6/99]. Robinson had announced to the press her intention of meeting with Slobodan Milosevic, but the FRY President refused to meet with her [*New York Times*, 5/14/99]. (He was publicly indicted by the War Crimes Tribunal for Former Yugoslavia shortly after this.)

The United Nations is being given responsibility for civilian implementation and oversight of the peace agreement on Kosovo that was brokered with the Russians' help—a major undertaking for the world body—and prominent among its duties will be monitoring and reporting on human rights. How well equipped it is to do this remains to be seen: There is no certainty that the U.N. staff provided will be appropriately trained or have the proper expertise to take on the reconstruction of respect for human rights in Kosovo, much less hold perpetrators of war crimes accountable for their actions or even restore public order through police oversight.

The activities of the U.N. human rights bodies prior to and during the Kosovo conflict had little effect on the lives of individuals in the region—other than to offer them the hope that awareness of massive abuses might generate political pressure to bring them to a halt. U.N. monitoring and reporting may have offered hope, but it contributed little to devising strategies for preventing or putting a stop to the systematic brutalization of Kosovar Albanian civilians, providing no protection to those caught in the waves of ethnic cleansing, killing, and other abuses.

The Special Rapporteur helped to ensure monitoring and reporting on conditions in the region, and from time to time helped to free or to better the conditions of specific detainees. But his efforts did little to deter human rights abuses. The High Commissioner, once she had opened the office in Kosovo that had been her goal for so long, helped focus the attention of diplomats at the Commission and, more significantly, the media that government capitals may pay attention to, on some of the human rights concerns in the region. However, so many reporters and NGOs were already interviewing refugees and reporting details of ethnic cleansing that the High Commissioner's role in rallying and informing the conscience of the world was marginal at best.

The years of repression in Kosovo, unchecked and unpunished, were reported on by the Commission's Special Rapporteurs, but little action was taken to mobilize genuine preventive or protective responses. Even as the Security Council became involved in the issue, demanding withdrawal of Serbian police units, it was not ready to propose action to end the years of divisive repression, or to accept responsibility for stopping it. The Commission and the General Assembly can shine a spotlight on a problem, as they did with Kosovo, but whether they can propose—and carry out—effective protection strategies is still open to doubt.

China

U.N. human rights bodies have grappled with the status of human rights in China in a variety of ways since the government's suppression of the democracy movement, which reached its height in the massive demonstrations in Tiananmen Square in 1989. The most visible of the U.N.'s diplomatic efforts has been **the move to introduce and adopt a resolution critical of human rights violations in China at the annual sessions of the Commission on Human Rights.**

Though introduced in 1990, and every year from 1992 through 1997, no such resolution was ever adopted, but the exercise served an important purpose: It was a gathering point for information on the human rights situation in China and a rallying point for advocates of change in China's human rights practices. Human rights leaders argued that public debate over the China resolution at the Commission helped to make some changes that the Chinese government would not have made otherwise. Indeed, just before the opening of the 1998 Commission, China announced it would sign two human rights treaties and would invite for a visit the U.N. High Commissioner for Human Rights and the Working Group on Arbitrary Detention. For China, the result was just what it had hoped: The European Union, which had employed diplomatic pressure to encourage these actions (and had launched its own dialogue as an alternative course of action to Commission resolutions, as proposed by China), promptly declared that none of its members would co-sponsor or introduce a resolution on China at the United Nations. The United States, which had stated for years that it would support a resolution if introduced by the European Union, soon announced it would follow their lead, declaring that the treaties offered "a new and promising approach" to holding China to high standards on human rights. U.S. officials, pointing to the release of several prominent political prisoners, made clear their expectation that more improvements would follow from bilateral dialogue and contacts.

High Commissioner Mary Robinson was duly invited to China and scheduled her visit for the beginning of September 1998. After some lobbying, she was permitted to travel to Tibet—described as a "breakthrough" [*Irish Times*, 9/1/98]. Once in China she promptly signed an overarching agreement on cooperation with China to help implement international human rights commitments [ibid., 9/8/98]. Later that month she told the press at a briefing at U.N. Headquarters that she "had discussed 'tough issues' at the highest level of government and had been struck by the commitment of the government to the concept of the universality of human rights" [briefing, 9/23/99; available at www.un.org/news/briefings/docs/1998/19980923.hrights2.html]. She noted that she had raised individual cases as well as the subject of law reform and of criticisms by the human rights mechanisms and treaty bodies.

In response to press questions, Robinson acknowledged that some "issues concerning the harsh treatment of dissidents had not been addressed." She tried, she said, "to ensure that issues brought to her attention would be passed on to the relevant [U.N. body]" and had raised "tough issues, including issues related to Tiananmen . . . and the Dalai Lama," adding that "China had made a commitment to review the cases . . . she had presented" [ibid.].

Some human rights activists expressed disappointment that Robinson had not met with dissidents or their relatives in the course of her trip [*New York Times*, 9/16/98]—a visit that had enormous symbolism for China—and noted that the most memorable press story arising out of the trip had to do with the arrest of the wife of an imprisoned dissident as she tried to deliver a letter to Robinson's hotel lobby [*Irish Times*, 9/9–10/98]. Robinson stated that she had raised with officials the case of the detention by Chinese authorities of the young boy designated the Panchen Lama by the Dalai Lama. Activists questioned why she, as High Commissioner, had not made such an appeal in public.

In response to the criticisms of her visit, Robinson insisted that the main goal of her trip was "to start a process of cooperation," later commenting to the press that "The psychological barrier is broken" and that China had accepted the idea that the Commission on Human Rights has a role in the country [ibid., 9/16/98]. More specific activities to promote human rights would follow, she seemed to say.

Chinese authorities were clearly pleased with the visit. China's representative to the Commission on Human Rights stated in March that China appreciated the High Commissioner's appeal for "cooperation . . . rather than unnecessary political confrontation." It was "gratifying," he said, "that she was attaching greater importance to economic, social and cultural rights and improving the effectiveness of the interior coordination of her Office." In short, "The High Commissioner's visit to China . . . had been a success and Chinese officials had participated in a training course in human rights. The first steps had been taken in the direction of cooperation on the basis of equality" [E/CN.4/1999/SR.3, par. 57–58]. (A follow-up assessment mission was sent to China by the High Commissioner's office in spring 1999, just prior to the Commission on Human Rights, in an effort to establish a firm agreement on ongoing cooperative activities.)

The year that followed the European Union/U.S. decision not to introduce a resolution on China at the Commission failed to fulfill China's promise that "dialogues" would be more productive than "confrontation." On the contrary, notes Amnesty International (AI), those months brought "one of the most disturbing crackdowns seen in China in the past decade" [Open Letter from AI to European Union (EU) governments on the eve of EU-China human rights dialogue, AI Index: ASA 17/01/99, 2/5/99].

A month after the High Commissioner's visit, the Chinese government signed (but has yet to ratify) the International Covenant on Civil and Political Rights, yet within a few weeks it had adopted two laws that put further constraints on the freedom of association and on free expression, and launched a campaign of arrests against human rights and political dissidents. Tightened restrictions on religious groups, and ongoing abuses against Tibetans and Uighars in Xinjiang province, were reported. Challenging the European Union to reconsider its approach, Amnesty characterized these developments: "They are not simply abuses of human rights, but strike at the heart of the EU and other human rights dialogues. They call into question China's sincerity in signing key human rights conventions in 1997 and 1998 and represent a serious setback on many of the core issues the EU and others have claimed to be pursuing" [ibid.].

Pressure to introduce a resolution at the Commission grew. In March the European Parliament adopted a resolution calling on the EU to "make China a priority at the forthcoming session" [FIDH/HRIC press release, 3/11/99], and both houses of the U.S. Congress adopted resolutions calling for such action.

Nonetheless, on March 22—opening day for the Commission on Human Rights—the EU foreign ministers confirmed that they would not introduce a specific motion on China. The very next day, German Foreign Minister Joschka Fischer, addressing the Commission [E/CN.4/1999/SR.2, par. 12], did state publicly that the EU saw the sentencing of activists as "unacceptable" and expressed concern over the imposition of the death penalty, administrative detention, and the situation of "minorities, particularly in Tibet" and urged China "to ensure . . . concrete improvements in respect for human rights, democracy, and rule of law." The EU, he added, "was ready . . . to engage in a more focused dialogue on human rights and to continue its cooperation programme in support of that process." There was, however, no reference to a resolution at the Commission.

Three days later, stating that China's human rights record had "deteriorated sharply over the past year," State Department spokesman James P. Rubin announced that **"The United States will introduce a resolution on China's human rights practices"** at the Commission [press statement, 3/26/99]. Assistant Secretary of State for Human Rights Harold Koh later explained that "Bilateral efforts to engage with the Chinese have produced dialogue, but that has not produced real human rights improvements on the ground. We reject the notion that dialogue, which we intend to continue with the Chinese, is in some way inconsistent with engagement on the question of human rights before this, the most prominent Human Rights Commission in the world" [press conference in Geneva, 3/30/99; available on USIS Internet page for Geneva].

Intense lobbying ensued. When the director of Human Rights in China (HRIC), an influential nongovernmental group, took the floor for a five-minute speech on behalf of the Robert F. Kennedy Memorial Foundation, a Chinese representative twice interrupted the speaker, questioning his credentials to speak [HRIC press release, 4/7/99]. The speech "welcomed the principled step taken by the . . . [United States] at a time when dialogue behind closed doors has become a convenient substitute for effective action" [ibid.].

Introducing the resolution on April 23, U.S. Ambassador Nancy Rubin pointed out that "It was not 'confrontation' or 'interference in internal affairs' to ask a Member State to respect the right of democratic dissent, as protected by international law" [E/CN.4/1999/SR.51].

When the resolution came to a vote, China once again employed the procedural tactic it had used to prevent action on a substantive vote: calling for a motion not to take action—which, if adopted, prevents further consideration. No-action motions have been utilized every year since 1990, except 1991 and 1998 when no resolution on China was introduced, and only once, in 1995, was this procedural motion defeated.

China's no-action motion was successful in 1999, when it was adopted by a vote of 22–17, with 14 abstentions. The United States pointed out that this had narrowed the 1997 margin by half. In the end, only Poland had stepped forward to co-sponsor the resolution with the United States. European Union members voted in favor but provided little active encouragement. Commenting on this, the Human Rights Watch's U.N. representative, Joanna Weschler, stated: "This vote undermines the Commission. . . . If all members had joined forces to sponsor the resolution or defeat the no-action resolution, the danger of China playing one off against another would be eliminated" [press release, 4/23/99].

U.S. Secretary of State Madeleine Albright, however, reflecting on this vote afterwards, offered a more upbeat comment: "We sponsored this resolution as part of our principled, purposeful policy of engagement with China. Our goal was to focus international attention on the sharp deterioration in the human rights situation in China. . . . We have accomplished that goal, even though the Commission chose not to take action on our resolution" ["Statement on Key Votes at the United Nations," 4/24/99].

CEDAW: Women's Rights in China

In January 1999, China's representatives presented the country's report to CEDAW, the Committee on the Elimination of All Forms of Discrimination against Women, one of four human rights treaties to which it is a party. A thorough review of China's treatment of women ensued, led by CEDAW member Carmel Shalev of Israel, who was appointed "rapporteur" on the country by CEDAW. The Chinese representatives answered many questions—on drug trafficking, domestic violence, rural poverty, health care, and the one-child policy, among others—but when the experts raised human rights issues—women's freedom of expression and right to association, including the right to form independent groups, such as women's groups—China's Ambassador stepped in to challenge the questioners. These human rights issues are too often used for "confrontation," he declared, and it would be better for CEDAW to leave such issues to others [U.N. press release WOM/1094, 2/2/99]. **Never before had a government representative challenged the right of CEDAW to raise such issues**—and certainly none had ever suggested, as did this speaker, that the treaty committee and its members did not rank with the other human rights treaty bodies and could not handle such issues. In reply, Germany's CEDAW member pointed out that these issues fell squarely within the provisions of the treaty, reminding the representative that "women's rights *are* human rights" and that the phrase was incorporated into the Beijing Declaration at the Fourth World Conference on Women in 1995.

In concluding comments, CEDAW members pointed out that the Convention recognizes all rights—civil, political, economic, social, and cultural—and expressed concern that China's women's law contains neither a definition of discrimination nor effective remedies in case of violations of the law. Further, CEDAW characterized the Chinese approach to women as focused on protection rather than empowerment, encouraged China to invite the Special Rapporteur on Violence against Women to the country (noting inter alia its concern about coercive measures employed by family planning officials in the country). They went on to urge a mass campaign to promote awareness of "legal literacy" so that all Chinese women would know their rights and be able to act on them [www.un.org/womenwatch].

Sierra Leone

In May 1998, Médecins sans Frontières (MSF, Doctors without Borders) reported **"an alarming increase in the number of patients suffering from severe mutilations"** in Sierra Leone, where troops (acronym ECO-MOG) of the Economic Community of West African States had recently restored to power the country's first democratically elected president but where the ousted ACRF/RUF rebels had embarked on a war of terror directed at civilians. A MSF report revealed the kinds of amputations and described the perpetrators as instructing their victims to go and tell "President Kabbah" what happened ["Atrocities Against Civilians in Sierra Leone," 5/98]. Human Rights Watch noted that "Between February and June 1998 alone, [members of the rebel forces] raped, deliberately mutilated, or killed outright thousands of . . . civilians" [Human Rights Watch World Report 1999]. Further, they abducted men, women, and children "for use as combatants, forced laborers, or sexual slaves." Children were targeted, both as victims of atrocities and as child soldiers. Hundreds of thousands of Sierra Leoneons fled, becoming refugees or internally displaced persons.

On July 13, the U.N. Security Council established the **U.N. Ob-**

server Mission to Sierra Leone (UNOMSIL) [S/Res/1181]. Among UN-OMSIL's responsibilities was reporting on violations of international human rights and humanitarian law and, in consultation with relevant U.N. agencies, helping the government rebuild institutions of justice and meet other human rights needs. **A civilian human rights advisor to the Special Representative** monitored the situation and began to set up technical assistance programs.

Curiously, the only scrutiny of Sierra Leone by regular U.N. human rights bodies came about through the confidential "1503" procedure, which allows individuals to send communications documenting gross abuses of human rights. After a working group and the Sub-Commission on Prevention of Discrimination and Protection of Minorities review these communications, they may be passed to the Commission on Human Rights for consideration by a working group and examined in a closed session of the entire Commission. Under this procedure, then, it takes close to a year of confidential review before the country's actions can be evaluated by the Commission.

When Sierra Leone reached the 1999 Commission on Human Rights at the end of March, it took the **rare action of discontinuing confidential scrutiny and making Sierra Leone the subject of the very first public resolution adopted by the Commission this year.** (In 1998 the Commission's very first action was a statement on Kosovo—which, as described above—would return as a major concern of the 1999 Commission.) The "1503" procedure, it explained, "does not provide an appropriate forum to address the dramatic circumstances facing [Sierra Leone]."

The 1999 Commission on Human Rights appealed to all factions and forces in Sierra Leone to respect human rights and abide by applicable international humanitarian law; and it reminded all sides that, in any armed conflict, the taking of hostages and willful killing and torture or inhuman treatment of persons taking no active part in the hostilities constituted grave breaches of international humanitarian law [res. 1999/1]. The same resolution requested the High Commissioner for Human Rights to apprise the Commission about violations of human rights and international humanitarian law in Sierra Leone. High Commissioner Mary Robinson has two sources to draw from: the Secretary-General's quarterly reports on UNOMSIL to the Security Council; and her own experience.

The **quarterly reports** are quite revealing. The March report, for example, stated that the members of the assessment team had "witnessed violations during their visit." It "found that the ultimate responsibility for the fighting, for most of the civilian casualties, and for the related humanitarian emergency . . . rested with the rebel forces. . . . Much of the killing [it went on to say] seems to have been arbitrary and to have been carried out by child fighters or rebel fighters under the influence of drugs or alcohol. However, there is also evidence that some of the rebel murders were targeted, including, reportedly, the murder of 200 police personnel" [S/1999/237, 3/4/99, par. 21–23]. Amputations, rape, sexual abuse, and forced recruitment are noted. So, too, are some reports of "summary executions" of rebels by ECOMOG soldiers.

In a subsequent report [S/1999/645, 6/4/99] the Secretary-General indicates that the rebel forces have agreed to investigate the allegations of rights violations and have "requested support from the international community" to do so [par. 33]. He states that ECOMOG, for its part, has already begun to take "positive steps" to curb any abuses by its forces.

Some weeks earlier, **High Commissioner Robinson** announced that she had "been following with deep distress successive reports" of atrocities in Sierra Leone, particularly by the rebel forces, and condemned these "in the strongest possible terms." On this occasion she also announced her acceptance of an invitation to visit Sierra Leone in June, which she made, accompanied by the former President of Botswana, the chair (a Tunisian) of the African Group at the Commission, the chair (a Swede) of the Working Group on children in armed conflict, and the American member of the Committee on the Elimination of Racial Discrimination.

Human rights groups, prominently Amnesty International, Human Rights Watch, and the International League for Human Rights, continued to urge greater attention to human rights in that country:

- Amnesty International, concerned about peace talks and reports of amnesty for perpetrators of the atrocities, suggested that the High Commissioner's visit would provide "an excellent opportunity to encourage the inclusion of human rights at every stage of efforts to meet the political, humanitarian, peace-keeping and reconstruction needs of Sierra Leone" [AI Index: AFR 51/06/99, 6/23/99].
- Human Rights Watch issued a new report, which found that the "rebel forces . . . systematically murdered, mutilated and raped civilians during their January offensive" [HRW, "War Crimes in Sierra Leone," 6/24/99]. HRW urged Mary Robinson "to mobilize international support for the investigation and punishment of Sierra Leone's war criminals" and "cautioned against granting amnesty to human rights violators as a condition for peace," citing a "cycle of impunity" as responsible for the viciousness of the conflict.
- The International League for Human Rights called for discussion of a U.N. role in providing specific protections for civilians, through "safe corridors" or "safe zones." Inability to protect its citizens had led the government to hire mercenaries, who seemed to "gain legitimacy by default." Freedom of the press also needed attention, since many journalists had themselves been targets of

human rights abuses [letter to Mary Robinson from Kakuna Kerina, International League for Human Rights, 6/23/99].

Upon completing her two-day visit to Sierra Leone, the High Commissioner declared herself "deeply shocked" and would seek international assistance to document the violations as a step toward establishing accountability, to increase the number of human rights monitors in the country, and to work within the country to create a "human rights infrastructure" [U.N. press release HR/99/60, 6/25/99]. During her visit a **"Human Rights Manifesto"** was issued, affirming the government's commitment to human rights and providing for the establishment of a national "Truth and Reconciliation Commission."

In early July came reports of a successful conclusion to the peace talks. **The peace pact included an amnesty provision for most of the rebels,** and Human Rights Watch immediately issued a statement calling upon U.N. Secretary-General Kofi Annan to reject the peace accord because of the amnesty provision. A U.N. spokesman advised that the United Nations had played a major role in brokering the accords and would "witness" them but would note on the agreement that it did not recognize the amnesty for gross violations of human rights. Pointing out that the notation would not be binding on the warring parties, HRW "condemned the UN for acting as a moral guarantor" of this agreement with such a blanket amnesty in it. "The UN should know that any peace built on impunity is unlikely to last—and may well serve as an invitation to more atrocities in the future," the human rights organization stated [HRW press release, 7/8/99].

Iran

Iran's human rights record has been under scrutiny by the United Nations since 1984. A Special Representative surveys conditions in the country and reports annually to the Commission on Human Rights and the General Assembly. In 1998 the High Commissioner for Human Rights made **several gestures to develop a relationship between her office and the government of Iran**—attending a regional seminar in Iran on technical cooperation in human rights and hosting a seminar in Geneva on Islamic perspectives on the Universal Declaration of Human Rights, as suggested during her visit to Iran.

Iran, for its part, has launched a campaign to end U.N. scrutiny by defeating the annual resolutions criticizing its human rights practices that are presented at the Commission on Human Rights and the General Assembly. There have been assurances by the government—at least rhetorically—that it will change some of the practices for which it has been criticized. The lifting of the *fatwa* against Salman Rushdie is one; a pledge to review problematic legal measures is another.

Mohammad Khatami was elected President of Iran in May 1997. According to Canada's **Maurice Copithorne, Special Representative on Iran,** the President's "plans for a tolerant, diverse and law-abiding society continue to unfold" [E/CN.4/1999/32]. Copithorne reported that "full implementation" of those plans could have a major impact but that, while he has noted the beginnings of progress, there is still great concern over the lack of rule of law; public executions and the practice of stoning the accused to death after brief, often summary, trials; torture and censorship; and discrimination against religious minorities (in particular the Baha'i); and the status of women. Despite pockets of progress, many in the area of freedom of expression, there were still many ongoing problems, he said, noting intimidation of journalists, closing of publications, strict rules prohibiting women from being treated by male physicians or in mixed-sex hospitals, and "a rash of unexplained disappearances, and suspicious deaths of intellectual and political activists" [ibid., especially par. 7].

The past several years have seen a **narrowing of the margin by which the resolution on Iran is adopted,** and one of the major but unpublicized crises at the 1999 Commission session was, in fact, the near-defeat of the annual resolution criticizing Iran's human rights practices. After a frenzy of last-minute lobbying, notably by the United States, the resolution passed by a vote of 23–16 with 14 abstentions.

Some of those abstentions were surprising, among them that of Argentina, which stated before the vote that it wished "to encourage the development of a more tolerant society" in Iran and cited the "considerable progress" of the Iranian government toward that goal. On Argentina's list of positive items, said the country's representative, Mrs. Lorenzo Alcala, were the February 1999 state and local elections—the first since 1979—legal changes, progress toward free expression and association, and (in a reference to Iran's relationship to terrorism abroad) "the government's determination to continue the struggle against terrorism, including state terrorism." This last was surprising, given the widely suspected Iranian involvement in the 1994 bombing of Jewish community offices in Buenos Aires. Argentina had a list of negative developments too, citing Iran's control of the press, capital punishment, treatment of women, and "the situation of the Baha'is."

Among **those who spoke for the resolution** during what turned out to be an unusually lengthy preliminary debate were Germany, on behalf of the European Union, the sponsors of the text; Chile and Ecuador, both of which called their support contingent on the inclusion of a reference to "positive changes"; and Guatemala, citing the benefits it had received from Commission scrutiny. Among those speaking against were Pakistan, on behalf of the Organization of the Islamic Conference, which Iran currently chairs; Sudan; Russia, claiming that the draft did not send the right "signal" to "a Government that was pursuing a course of improving human rights"; Venezuela, arguing that the resolution might help hardliners opposed to human rights changes; and Bangladesh, China, Cuba, Philippines, Qatar, and Sudan—all citing "positive developments" in Iran.

Germany (on behalf of the EU) expressed regret that the Iranians had refused to negotiate with the European Union on the resolution's provisions and, instead, had set "preconditions" to any substantive discussion: a "termination clause" in this year's text that would set the stage for ending scrutiny next year and an acknowledgment of improvements. The EU representative noted that the final text was intended "to reflect the complex and evolving human rights situation" in Iran, "based on the findings of the Special Representative"—who had not even been permitted a visit—and that the "EU has taken great care to acknowledge . . . all noticeable improvements" [EU press release, 4/23/99].

The **Iranian Ambassador,** calling the resolution "politically motivated" and "an unwarranted and counterproductive exercise," said that it discredited those sponsoring it—and warned them that they might find themselves the subject of future resolutions. He then **launched an attack on the very concept of country-specific human rights resolutions,** which, he stated, are "flawed" and can easily be exploited for political purposes. Furthermore, he said, there are no specific criteria for such resolutions "except the obscure concept of 'gross and systematic violations of human rights.'" His comments were reinforced by the Pakistani delegate, who complained about "the politicization of human rights," the Commission's "selective targeting for political purposes," and more: This resolution, he said, "was yet another example of the targeting of Islamic countries in the Commission."

Cuba

The 1998 visit of Pope John Paul II to Cuba inaugurated a series of events that, coupled with anger over American laws providing for sanctions against Europeans and others doing business with Cuba, led to **the defeat in 1998 of a perennial resolution critical of Cuba's human rights record** that had renewed the appointment of a special rapporteur to document developments on the island. The 1999 Commission on Human Rights returned to the question of human rights in Cuba, but it was two new members of NATO, the Czech Republic and Poland, and not the United States, that took the initiative in sponsoring a resolution.

At the beginning of the **1999 Commission session** Cuba's Carlos Lage Dávila, Vice President of the Council of State, criticized the United States for having raised issues of human rights in Cuba. "That super-

Power had assumed," he said—and "apparently for life"—"the role of prosecutor in the public trial of Cuba and supreme judge of human rights at the global level." But could the United States be allowed to judge others when drugs, homelessness, poor health care, and poverty are endemic to its own society [E/CN.4/1999/SR.4, par. 62], he asked. Fascist groups, tolerance of discrimination and violence, and discriminatory application of the death penalty riddle American life, he noted, and so does the fact that Washington contributes so little to development aid overseas and owes so much in U.N. dues. He warned that "If the world were to convene as a court, the United States would be constantly in the dock." Further: In the Czechs, the United States "found a traitor prepared to accuse Cuba of numerous vile deeds." Cuba itself has "no racial discrimination, torture, forced disappearance, death squads or summary executions," asserted Dávila in conclusion.

In dramatic public addresses to the Commission as well as in private meetings with national delegations, Czech Deputy Foreign Minister Martin Palous offered some reasons why two former Communist countries of Eastern Europe were now sponsoring a resolution critical of Cuba. He pointed out, for example, the parallels between the recent trial of four dissident leaders in Cuba and the show trials staged in the Czech Republic and elsewhere in Eastern Europe when it was dominated by the Soviets.

Weeks later, another Cuban representative said that the Czech Republic and Poland were being used as "puppets" by the United States and reiterated that the United States was trying to destroy Cuba.

Mexico, for its part, declared that the resolution "lacked balance," and China remarked that human rights issues should be resolved by negotiations, not by interference and confrontation. Colombia complained that the text "ignored unilateral actions against [Cuba]."

Chile disagreed with its Latin colleagues: In 1988 the Chilean representative pointed out, his delegation had abstained on the draft resolution about human rights in Cuba to encourage the Cuban government to take further steps toward ensuring the fulfillment of human rights. The Pope had asked Cuba to open up to the world when he visited that country. Chile was still concerned about the lack of observance of fundamental freedoms in Cuba. The draft resolution recognized progress in Cuba and did not call for a Special Rapporteur, yet the resolution took cognizance of the fact that Cuba had moved backward by curtailing individual freedoms. It offered a good picture of the situation of human rights in Cuba, said Chile; it was a picture of "highlights and dark spots" [U.N. press release, HR/CN/930, 4/23/99].

The **Commission's resolution on Cuba, adopted by a hairline margin of 21–20 with 12 abstentions,** called upon Havana to ensure respect for human rights and fundamental freedoms, including freedom of religion, and "to provide the appropriate framework to guarantee the rule of law through democratic institutions and the independence of the judicial system." It reiterated its concern about the continued repression of members of the political opposition and about the detention of dissidents, most recently, four members of the "Grupo de Trabajo de la Disidencia Interna," and called upon the government "to release all persons detained or imprisoned for peacefully expressing their political, religious and social views and for exercising their rights to full and equal participation in public affairs." Finally, it invited the Cuban government "to afford the country full and open contact with the democratic world" and "to cooperate with other mechanisms of the Commission" by allowing them to visit and report.

What the resolution did *not* call for was the appointment of a special rapporteur, but it did direct that Cuba's human rights record be considered again at the next Commission, in the year 2000. The word was being spread at the Commission that Cuba had extended an invitation to visit to the Special Rapporteur on Violence against Women, and, indeed, she traveled to Cuba shortly after the Commission session and before the Economic and Social Council held its annual meeting, where it reviews decisions of the Commission. A report on that visit will be presented before the Commission on Human Rights session in 2000.

Reflecting on the outcome, Cuba called the vote "shameful," but U.S. Assistant Secretary of State for Human Rights Harold Koh called it "a wake-up call to begin protecting human rights and preparing for a transition to democracy" [Reuters, 4/24/99].

Israeli-Occupied Territories

Over 30 years of effort have left nearly every U.N. body with a special resolution, procedure, or agenda item dealing with Israel. The 53rd General Assembly adopted 21 resolutions addressing Israel-related issues; the 1999 Commission on Human Rights itself passed five. Despite American efforts in 1997, a general reform of the agenda at the Commission on Human Rights did not succeed in eliminating the separate agenda item on Israel by combining it with the agenda item addressing violations in all other parts of the world. Israel thus remains the only country in the world with its own agenda item at the Commission. The consideration of Israeli actions is no longer the first item on the Commission agenda, however, but comes later in the session, just before the Commission considers human rights violations in country situations around the world. Earlier, oral assurances that the separate item would be eliminated came to naught in 1999.

Special Rapporteur Hannu Halinen of Finland has previously criticized the mandate given by the Commission in 1993 when it created this mechanism to "investigate Israel's violations" in the occupied territories and "to report . . . to the Commission . . . until the end of the Israeli occupation of those territories" [res. 1993/2 A]. "It puts Israel in a different position compared to other countries subject to the scrutiny of a special rapporteur," he pointed out, and "prejudges the outcome of the investigation." Moreover, he stated, it is "limited only to Israel" and "unlike all other mandates . . . is not reviewed periodically" [E/CN.4/1998/17, par. 5]. Halinen is asking for equal treatment for himself, not for Israel—that is, a mandate parallel to that given all other special rapporteurs: to investigate all violations in the territory in question.

In 1999, Halinen concluded that "the human rights situation in the occupied territories is hostage to political considerations and expediences [*sic*]" and urged that human rights be "integrated into the political and economic discussions" on the conflict. The human rights situation is "worrying," Halinen said. He had identified a "certain positive development . . . on the Israeli side—such as the decrease in administrative detentions and discontinuation of the most flagrant torture methods"—but advised that "such violations are increasing on the Palestinian side." (Noting that Israeli "pressure" on the Palestinian Authority is often cited as the reason for abuses by the P.A., he remarked that "explaining . . . violations does not justify them.") "Of utmost importance," said Halinen, is an "early and well-prepared convening of a conference" of the parties to the Fourth Geneva Convention. Such a conference—unprecedented in the 50-year history of the Geneva Conventions—was demanded in resolutions adopted at the resumed Emergency Sessions of the General Assembly convened since 1997 because of Israeli building in East Jerusalem. Halinen concluded his report by stating that "almost all provisions of the [Universal Declaration of Human Rights] are being violated in the occupied territories" [ibid., par. 66].

Commending Palestinians for their cooperation with him, Halinen regretted Israel's refusal to work with him and included, in full, **a letter from Ambassador David Peleg detailing Israel's criticism of the Rapporteur's mandate.** It added to the Special Rapporteur's bill of particulars the fact that the mandate "predetermines the Rapporteur's role, resolving . . . that Israel is ignoring international law," that "there are two sides to the Middle East conflict," and that, despite Palestinian human rights abuses and deaths in custody, the Rapporteur is "not authorized to investigate" the latter [E/CN.4/1999/24, par. 56]. Then, turning to the work of Halinen himself, the Ambassador took issue with the assertion that Israel has refused to work with him, noting its informal cooperation, and stated that "your reports have been consistently inaccurate and misleading, containing unsubstantiated or simply false facts, and repeatedly disregarding Israel's position."

Halinen replied to these points, recalling his oral comments the year before, to wit: "The attempt to discredit the report of the Special Rapporteur by the Government is not new. . . . [T]he mandate is not and need not be the obstacle to the cooperation. . . . [M]y voice seems to be among those very few who are asking amendments to the mandate—although in my case from the point of view of overall consistency" [ibid., par. 58]. Halinen adds that "human rights concerns in the occupied territories cannot be held hostage to the political processes and discussions. . . . [The debate] . . . should not be used to attack either party for political purposes only" [par. 63].

Considerable acrimony surrounded the discussion of these and other points at the Commission on Human Rights. There were commentaries by representatives of both Middle Eastern member states and observer delegations, and there were criticisms by NGOs concerned about the region, many complaining that the Rapporteur's report was too weak. (One pointed out, for example, that Halinen never stated that the "reports" of violations he presented were substantiated.) Palestinian observer Nabil Ramlawi, for his part, contributed a letter complaining that Halinen "has exceeded his mandate when he talked about matters related to the peace process. . . . [H]e also exceeded his mandate when he talked about allegations concerning Palestinian justice" [E/CN.4/1999/152]. Ramlawi stated that the Commission can decide what to do by itself and without prompting from the Special Rapporteur. Thus, Halinen's request to change the mandate "is aimed at keeping out of sight the practices of Israel. . . . It is also aimed at creating the impression that the Commission . . . is wrong." Ramlawi "definitely rejects" the request by Israel and the Special Rapporteur to change it [ibid.].

When the Israeli Ambassador mentioned alleged abuses by the Palestinian Authority, the Palestinian observer raised a point of order to object that this was beyond the scope of the discussion. The Chair became embroiled in a procedural wrangle over who can participate in Commission debates. She ended up ruling that a General Assembly resolution a year before upgrading the rights and privileges of the Palestinian observer delegation at the United Nations applied to the Commission in Geneva. Although the Commission had never permitted any observer delegation to raise points of order, the Chair ruled (after lengthy consultations with the U.N. Legal Office, and in contrast to prior opinions and overruling the long-standing procedures of the Commission itself) that all observers—including the Palestinian observer—may raise points of order. This also meant that Israel—or any other government not a member of the Commission—could raise such points.

As an unexpected result, prior to the voting on each of the five resolutions on Israel adopted by the Commission, the Israeli Ambassador outlined his country's perspective on the text. The lengthiest of these discussions focused on a perennial resolution on "occupied Palestine," which has long justified and called for self-determination of the Palestinian people. Ambassador Peleg complained that the resolution made no mention of the **Oslo peace process** or of **Security Council Resolutions 242 or 338,** which were the basis for it. Instead, he said, they cited **General Assembly Resolution 181,** the 1947 partition plan, long ago rejected by the Arab states, but which had been resurrected in recent international debates because, among other things, it would change the terms of the debate over final status talks and territorial issues, such as the status of Jerusalem. Only the United States spoke up in favor of the Israeli position in the debate. As in past years, the resolution was adopted by a lopsided majority.

Subsequent press and NGO criticism of the Commission on Human Rights characterized these references to Resolution 181 as something recent and politically pernicious, allegedly revealing a new bias of the international community. The reporters did not do their homework: In fact, the Commission's resolution on occupied Palestine has referred to Resolution 181 since 1983, and has not referenced the Security Council resolutions or the peace process. The real difference at the 1999 Commission was that, for the first time, the member states of the European Union voted in favor of this resolution rather than abstaining, as they had for years.

Somalia

The Commission's special procedure on Somalia, called an **"Independent Expert,"** is mandated under the agenda item on technical assistance yet functions along the lines of the country special rapporteurs. Mona Rishmawi, the Expert, reminded member states at the 1999 Commission that **the "complex emergency situation" continues in Somalia,** where there is no central government, just warring factions. Noting that political initiatives in the country "have yet to make a real difference on the human rights situation on the ground," she called for human rights issues to be "integrated in the peace negotiations" sponsored by the United Nations or its members. Because many of those human rights abuses take the form of "systematic attacks against life, pillage, hostage-taking, rape and sexual violence, as well as displacement," and attacks against humanitarian relief workers committed by the warring factions—all war crimes and/or crimes against humanity—the Expert suggested the creation of an international tribunal to try the perpetrators. She expressed special concern about the situation of minorities, especially the Bantus, and about women, who are "systematically discriminated against."

Rishmawi's recommendation last year for a human rights officer, to be based in the UNDP Somalia office in Nairobi, was endorsed by the High Commissioner for Human Rights and then by the Commission but is yet to be realized. She reminded Commission members that **forensic** experts had confirmed existence of mass graves in the northwest of Somalia—the result of a 1988 massacre, she concluded—and that the experts made recommendations after their December 1997 investigation. Endorsing their recommendations, she expressed the hope that the United Nations would act on them after releasing the expert report to the public in 1999. Rishmawi spoke again of her hope for inquiries into the reported abuses by foreign (presumably referring to Canadian, Belgian, Italian, and U.S.) soldiers in Somalia in 1992–93, so that "impunity is not granted to the perpetrators of unlawful behavior."

Efforts are already being made to integrate human rights into the work of international agencies in the country, reported the Independent Expert, who indicated that three other key areas also demand attention: raising awareness of women's rights; law enforcement; and supporting Somali human rights defenders [U.N. press release OHCHR/99/04/22, 4/22/99, "Oral statement, Human Rights in Somalia, by Mona Rishmawi, Independent Expert"].

Iraq

Former Dutch Foreign Minister **Max van der Stoel has been the U.N.'s Special Rapporteur on Iraq since the post was created in 1991.** In his most recent oral presentation and written report to the Commission, he reflected back to 1991 and recalled that the data he had amassed prior to his visit to Iraq in 1992 were consistent with his findings based on meetings and direct testimony during that visit: All "revealed a pattern of systematic gross violations of human rights." When he reported this to the Commission, he recounted, the government of Iraq "denied everything, refused me a return visit, and cut off contacts with me." Though he has continued his efforts to collect information, the Iraqi government "has continued simply to deny everything or to offer limpid excuses even for its own laws which blatantly sanction arbitrary killing for anyone who insults the President or institutions . . . and laws which prescribe tortures for criminal acts like petty theft." The government "finds comfort in attacking my personal integrity," he added.

The violations continue "without the slightest indication of any change in Government policy," the Special Rapporteur explained, and went on to detail those violations, naming "systematic arbitrary executions; interference with the independent religious practice of the Shi'ite community; continuing internal deportations of ethnic Kurds; violations of the rights to food and health; violations of the rights of the child; and the Government's continuing failure to cooperate in efforts to resolve the hundreds of cases of missing Kuwaitis." As for the humanitarian situation in the country, van der Stoel states: **"the Government is not only the cause of great suffering but it has on a number of occasions interfered with efforts to improve the situation."** The fact that the government has failed to comply with its obligations under the International Covenant on Economic, Social, and Cultural Rights, particularly with regard to the Oil for Food program, is explored and explained at length [see E/CN.4/1999/17, par. 29–43]. He also notes that landmines placed by the government between 1992 and 1997 "have caused more than 15,000 casualties, of which 30% of the victims were children."

Van der Stoel concluded that the human rights situation shows no sign of improving and will continue "so long as there remains the same politico-legal order in Iraq. I believe it is up to the Government of Iraq . . . to change the situation" [statement of Mr. Max van der Stoel, Special Rapporteur . . . on the Situation of Human Rights in Iraq, 3/31/99].

Iraq's government spokesman charged that the Special Rapporteur "invented lies and fabrications and issued judgements that are not objective and not honest"and urged the world community to replace van der Stoel [Reuters Baghdad, 3/24/99]. The EU statement at the Commission revealed continuing strong support for van der Stoel, notes that his report does not "indicate any improvements in the human rights situation in Iraq over the last year," and "deplores" the Iraqi failure to permit a visit from the Rapporteur since 1991 [EU press release, 4/23/99].

Other Country Situations

The Commission on Human Rights also approved resolutions on conditions in Nigeria, Myanmar, Burundi, Afghanistan (see "The Advancement of Women" in this chapter), Democratic Republic of Congo (it agreed to send a joint mission of rapporteurs, along the lines decided a few years back but blocked by the Kabila government [see *A Global Agenda: Issues Before the 53rd General Assembly*]), the former Yugoslavia, Sudan, Equatorial Guinea (the Special Rapporteur has been renamed a Special Representative), Haiti, and Cambodia. Some, but not all, of these country situations will be taken up by the General Assembly, depending on whether the mandate specifies a report to the Assembly. The Commission also agreed to end scrutiny of Nigeria, following the change in government.

The Commission's confidential "1503" procedure discontinued review of Gambia, Nepal, Saudi Arabia, and Yemen. Chad will now be considered under the item on technical assistance and advisory services—a public procedure. Sierra Leone, as noted earlier, was taken public too and will be considered next year under the Commission's public agenda item on country situations.

World Conference against Racism

The U.N. General Assembly has agreed to convene a World Conference against Racism, Racial Discrimination, Xenophobia and Related Intolerance in Geneva in 2001. The 1999 session of the Commission on Human Rights convened a working group to serve as the first preparatory conference. Section V of resolution 1999/78 outlines the provisions for the conference. The High Commissioner for Human Rights will serve as Secretary-General for the event and will conduct a series of preparatory consultations, including a number at the expert level. Further details may be available by the time the 54th General Assembly takes up the subject.

Both **logistical and substantive ideas for the conference** were considered by the 1999 Commission. Participants recommended that the conference be held in Geneva, where meeting facilities are readily available, unless another government offers to serve as host by the end of the calendar year and pay for all added costs. Developing-country advocates of the conference consider Geneva an appropriate venue, since they want to highlight the problems of the developed world in dealing with racial discrimination—one of the issues many see the developed countries as particularly vulnerable on—thus turning a spotlight on those countries instead of their own. Western governments stress that the conference is about racism and xenophobia, both of them worldwide phenomena.

Several governments and NGOs expressed concern at the Commission debate about the apparent lack of importance the United Nations has accorded to the conference thus far. **The Commission, as the preparatory committee,** has requested the Office of the High Commissioner to launch a global public information campaign on the world conference and to enlist the participation of both member states and civil society. But a great deal more would have to be done for these critics to view U.N. preparations and resources as adequate.

Issues suggested for the agenda include prevention and early-warning measures to combat racism; racism and economic status; implications of multiple identities (color, ethnic origin, etc.); treatment of migrants, refugees, and indigenous peoples; combating hate speech and the use of the Internet to propagate racism; and remedies and means of redress. Although **the agenda does not mention anti-semitism or other specific forms of racism,** it is expected that anti-semitism and similar topics will be included, since they fall within the mandate of specialized U.N. bodies on racial discrimination, which is defined in the treaty on this topic as including discrimination against ethnic as well as racial groupings. The 53rd General Assembly referred specifically to anti-semitism—for the very first time in U.N. history—in its 1999 resolution on the mandate of the Special Rapporteur on Contemporary Forms of Racial Discrimination. Whether it will do so again, or whether it will mention anti-semitism by name in the context of the World Conference, remains to be seen.

Implementing "All" Rights

The 1993 Vienna World Conference on Human Rights affirmed, and the General Assembly and the Commission have acknowledged every year since, that all human rights are universal, interdependent, interrelated, and indivisible. With this all-encompassing phraseology the conference tried to end the quarrel over which "set" of rights—civil and political or economic, social, and cultural—gets priority. This sort of argument over priorities characterized the Cold War years, infecting the debates on human rights in the United Nations. By stating that all rights are interrelated and indivisible, many felt, it would become possible to focus attention on the fulfillment of rights rather than engage in sterile ideological debates. The Vienna World Conference also affirmed that democracy, development, and respect for human rights are interdependent and mutually reinforcing, and that a country's level of development is no excuse for failing to uphold rights.

Those who thought Vienna would end the battle over sets of rights have been proven wrong. U.N. High Commissioner for Human Rights Mary Robinson—a former President of Ireland—noted early in her tenure that one of her priority concerns is to correct what she terms the "imbalance" in human rights, by emphasizing economic, social, and cultural rights and the right to development more than has been done in the past. Efforts to address this issue have brought considerable interaction between her office and the U.N.'s many development agencies, from the U.N. Development Programme to UNICEF to the World Bank. The term "rights-based approach" has become quite common in the programming and the activities undertaken by such agencies over the past two years. Prominent representatives of the development agencies were present at the 1998 anniversary session of the Commission on Human Rights and at the ECOSOC review of "Vienna + 5" in July 1998. U.N. Secretary-General Kofi Annan came to the Commission on Human Rights in April 1999 to announce that he has made human rights a part of every activity of the United Nations—whether development, peacekeeping, political analysis, or humanitarian affairs. "Mainstreaming" is the U.N.'s word to describe the process.

One of the major problems with addressing economic and social rights has been the lack of effective criteria for distinguishing and monitoring those rights. Too often, complaints about a need to address economic and social rights seem to reflect the desire for resource transfers from wealthy countries to underdeveloped ones. Complainants often lack a clear concept of how to measure, monitor, or implement a successful rights-based approach to economic and social rights aimed at the empowerment of the individual.

Are there ways to identify "violations" of these rights and hold those responsible to account? The fact that economic and social rights are to be "realized progressively" adds layers of complexity to the monitoring process. And there is no avoiding the fact that, sometimes, government efforts to emphasize economic and social rights are aimed at diverting attention from a country's poor performance on civil and political rights or on respect for the individual. Unfortunately, genuine concern about the individual's ability to exercise his or her economic and social rights is often eclipsed by the politics that surround the subject.

A number of **new special procedures of the Commission on Human Rights** are now addressing aspects of economic and social rights as well as the relationship of various macro-economic factors (structural adjustment policies, debt, extreme poverty) on the enjoyment of human rights. In 1999, the first reports were presented by three new human rights special procedures created the year before: an Independent Expert on Structural Adjustment Policies and Human Rights, an Independent Expert on Extreme Poverty and Human Rights, and a Special Rapporteur on the Right to Education. Their reports to the Commission grapple with the issue of violations, obligations of governments, and the issue of empowerment of the individual.

Fantu Cheru of Ethiopia, **the Independent Expert on Structural Adjustment Policies and Human Rights,** examines the links between underdevelopment and debt, and between structural adjustment programs and the realization of economic, social, and cultural rights. Mr. Cheru points out that the ultimate responsibility for managing national economies and promoting human development rests with national governments. Citing many reasons for the Third World debt crisis, he concludes that it would be wrong to place all the blame on either the debtor governments or the creditor institutions. He recommends canceling the debt of the poorest countries; instituting human rights conditionality in future lending; establishing international mechanisms to retrieve money stolen by corrupt leaders; reforming the international economic, financial, and trade systems; and preserving natural resources [see U.N. press release HR/CN/99/ 25, 4/8/99].

Anne-Marie Lizin of Belgium, **the Independent Expert on Extreme Poverty and its effect on human rights,** observes that 1.3 billion people are affected by extreme poverty worldwide, most of them women. She concludes that "Poverty is therefore the most massive cause of human rights violations in the world" and goes on to argue that "Extreme poverty is thus a violation of all human rights." The reason: It challenges human dignity and the principle of nondiscrimination [E/CN.4/1999/48, par. 115]. Greater resources, sufficient political will, and better channeling of resources to health, social, and educational programs are necessary to overcome extreme poverty. And more: Poverty eradication should be made "an absolute priority" throughout the U.N. system ("the Government's political will" is the key at the national level) [ibid., par. 124]. Legislation should be enacted to guarantee all persons a "minimum guaranteed income"; official policies should facilitate access to individual rights, such as food, housing, employment, and education; all nations should devote

0.7 percent of their national budget to official development assistance; and human rights education should be provided for persons living in extreme poverty.

The Commission welcomed her observations and invited her to report to several other U.N. bodies, including the preparatory committee for "Copenhagen + 5" (to review developments since the World Summit on Social Development of 1995), the Commission on Social Development, and the Commission on the Status of Women.

The first report of the **Special Rapporteur on the Right to Education,** Katerina Tomasevski of Croatia, reviews the current work of the U.N. system and outlines an analytical scheme for identifying governmental obligations to fulfill this right, consisting of (1) availability of primary schools; (2) accessibility of primary schools, without discrimination; (3) acceptability of the idea that the state is the facilitator and regulator of education rather than the sole funder and provider of it; and (4) adaptability as to what is taught and how the learning process is organized, so as to be responsive to the reality facing children in their own communities. The Special Rapporteur argues that rights-based development and human rights criteria should be applied to education. Moreover, she points out that the right to education is in every major human rights instrument, and every government's obligation should be clear. For example, governments are obliged to provide primary education free of charge [see E/CN.4/1999/49]. Ms. Tomasevski promises to outline in future reports a means of assessing when the right to primary education is fully realized.

In this inaugural report, the Special Rapporteur gives considerable attention to the denial of primary school education to girls and to gender-specific aspects of the right to education. "It may well be that women's rights shall lead the way for the mainstreaming of human rights in development, and education may represent the catalyst," she stated to the Commission [4/8/99]. Her analysis, along with the report of the Independent Expert on Extreme Poverty, presents striking evidence of the particular ways in which both these issues affect women and girls, and how denial of the right to education helps maintain women in poverty and without power.

Tomasevski's care in addressing the issues of what constitutes the right to education and what could be considered violations of it use the criteria common to mainstream human rights analysis: identifying what obligations are, what constitute violations, and who is responsible. The Expert on Extreme Poverty, on the other hand, while characterizing extreme poverty as a "violation" of human rights, fails to clarify who is responsible for "violations" of that right and how to measure them. Expect these matters to become the subject of future reports.

Addressing yet another economic and social right—**the right to food,** explored at the World Food Summit in Rome in 1996—the office of the High Commissioner for Human Rights itself provided a report reviewing the conclusions of a seminar on progress in defining the right to adequate food. It draws on a variety of sources in international law, and examines the role of international organizations in implementing rights related to food and nutrition [E/CN.4/1999/45].

The 54th General Assembly is sure to see a lively debate on these reports on economic and social rights as the Third (Social, Humanitarian, and Cultural) Committee focuses in on the effects of macroeconomic policies on its core concerns. It is unclear how—or even if—the Second (Economic and Financial) Committee will respond to the injection of "rights-based" language of the rapporteurs and experts into its deliberations and programs. In the past, many Third World government representatives on the Second Committee and on the oversight bodies of the specialized agencies with operational development programs have strongly resisted the use of rights language and even more determinedly resisted the concept itself—fearing that development aid would then become conditioned on rights performance.

At the 1999 Commission on Human Rights, a representative of UNDP explained that its **new rights-based approach to poverty eradication** was beginning to strengthen and energize its work. To those who worried that some conditionalities might be applied to receiving UNDP assistance as a result of human rights concerns, UNDP replied that it was not its role to monitor a country's human rights record or denounce violations publicly; it would, nonetheless, continue to take a strong stand on social justice [U.N. press release HR/99/26, 4/8/99]. It remains to be seen how these issues interact and whether a rights-based approach to development takes hold alongside a new development-oriented approach to human rights, which is gaining strength with the High Commissioner's new emphasis on "the right to development."

The United States, which had long resisted the idea that economic and social rights are, in fact, rights, embraced this idea in Vienna but seemed to back away from it at Habitat II and the World Food Summit, and at sessions of the Commission of Human Rights during the years that followed. However, at the 1998 session of ECOSOC, the United States made pointed references to the **Four Freedoms of Franklin Roosevelt, and particularly "freedom from want."** U.S. Ambassador Betty King stated that

> Economic rights and the pursuit of happiness are fundamental rights that must be recognized and realized progressively. Their realization remains a joint endeavor between the individual and the state. . . . Economic, social and cultural rights have direct and immediate relevance for the process of economic development and must also infuse our approach to discussion on the right to development. [speech, 8/17/98]

Stating that civil and political rights, while central, "must be complemented by the realization of economic, social and cultural rights," Ambassador King described these rights as being **concerned with the empowerment of the individual** and with his or her freedom to participate fully in decision-making about government and its social policies. In her words:

> Protecting and advancing economic, social, and cultural rights requires policies and laws that encourage entrepreneurial risk-taking; that generate new jobs; that guarantee labor rights and non-discrimination in the workplace; that promote gender equality, the advancement of women, and the protection of the child; that provide access to education and medical care; that protect the environment; that offer a safety net and a path to advancement for the poorest segments of the population; and that ensure the rule of law for everyone. [ibid.]

At the 1999 Commission on Human Rights, the Ambassador of Bangladesh seemed to echo these sentiments, explaining that **human rights is about "freedom from both fear and want"** and that the responsibility for enforcement of rights lies in national governments—with the clear implication that the demand for resource transfers must not be used to shift responsibility for development policies from the national government to the international community [UN press release HR/CN/99/26, 4/8.99]. And at the 1999 session of ECOSOC, where poverty eradication and capacity-building were a main focus, the United States continued its emphasis on the individual in economic development programs, stating that "The passive psychology of victimhood is simply not a part of an enabling environment for poverty alleviation. . . . Empowerment and investment in people is the key to poverty alleviation" [speech by Ambassador Betty King, 7/8/99].

Gender Integration

The newly reformed agenda of the Commission on Human Rights includes, for the first time, **an agenda item on "Integration of Gender and the Human Rights of Women."** It reflects years of effort—buoyed by the successes of the Vienna World Conference on Human Rights and the Beijing World Conference on Women, where there was considerable pressure from women's human rights NGOs—to recognize "women's rights are human rights." For this approach to be meaningful, however, women's rights cannot be addressed only under a single "separate" item but must enter into the thinking, planning, monitoring, and implementation of all human rights matters.

This is beginning to happen, in part because of the prodigious efforts of women's human rights experts to make clear to U.N. human rights specialists why certain abuses of human rights are specific to women and how women are affected by them—while also making clear that these are abuses of traditional human rights. It therefore represented something of a breakthrough when the **Special Rapporteur on Extrajudicial, Sum-**

mary and Arbitrary Executions, Mrs. Asma Jahangir of Pakistan, drew attention to "honor killings" by the male relatives of women alleged to have committed adultery or who may be seeking divorce. The Special Rapporteur states that such killings cannot be explained away by tradition or culture or dismissed as private matters; they are nothing less than murder. The Rapporteur goes on to demonstrate that impunity for so-called "honor killings" ignores the rule of law and due process, and undermines individual human rights protections. As such, these killings are the legitimate concern of the human rights community.

The new **Special Rapporteur on the Right to Education** and the **Independent Expert on Extreme Poverty,** as noted above, also brought a gender-perspective to their studies. And so did the **Special Rapporteur on Freedom of Expression,** who addressed the right of women to seek, receive, and impart information, and the link between freedom of opinion and expression and the elimination of discrimination and violence against women. These are but a few examples of what gender integration really means: breaking the silence, ensuring the visibility of abuses against women, and pressing for accountability of those who perpetrate those abuses.

The **Special Rapporteur on Religious Intolerance** has proposed undertaking "a series of studies on discrimination" against women. And several country-specific special rapporteurs have reported about the treatment of women in, among other countries, Iran, Nigeria, and the former Yugoslavia. The **Special Representative on Iran,** for example, concluded that, despite well-meaning declarations, the government has so far achieved little improvement in the condition of Iranian women. The **Special Rapporteur on Nigeria,** for his part, criticized the slow pace of eradicating harmful traditional practices, such as female genital mutilation and early marriages. The **Special Rapporteur on the former Yugoslavia** addressed gender concerns in his discussion of Croatia (although not in the other countries that fall within his mandate). The Special Rapporteur on Religious Intolerance concluded that the Taliban has introduced "what is in point of fact a system of apartheid" with respect to women [for more on Afghanistan, see "The Advancement of Women" in the next section].

The Right to Democracy

The United States introduced, and the 1999 Commission on Human Rights adopted, a **resolution proclaiming the "right to democracy."** The final vote—51–0 with 2 abstentions (China and Cuba)—speaks volumes about both the importance of the subject matter and the politics of the United Nations.

The new U.S. Assistant Secretary of State for Human Rights, Harold

Koh, formerly of Yale Law School, promoted this issue in speeches and press conferences in Geneva. His argument was simple:

> [It is time for the Commission] to acknowledge the link between human rights and democracy. . . . Democracy is not just an experiment, it is a right in itself. Democracy is not just an end that we try to achieve, it is also a means of greater improvement of human rights. In many countries around the world, human rights violations are the symptom, and the cause is a lack of open political discussion. [press briefing, Geneva, 3/30/99]

In support, Koh and the U.S. delegation cited various provisions of the Universal Declaration of Human Rights, such as Article 21: "The will of the people shall be the basis of the authority of the government and this will shall be expressed in genuine and periodic elections which shall be held on the basis of universal and equal suffrage." Unlike the Reagan and Bush administrations, which emphasized elections and election-monitoring as measures of democracy, Koh laid out for Commission members and Commission-watchers the wide range of human rights guarantees needed to ensure genuine democratic governance:

> Promoting democracy means much more than just elections. It means that we support the development of civil society, the independent media, the equal protection of women, ethnic and religious minorities and the political process as well as the free labor movement. All of these are crucial to promotion of democratic discussion.
>
> When democracy is absent, human rights suffer. We think this is the primary lesson of the former Yugoslavia where not only is there violence and atrocities in Kosovo but a broader deprivation of human rights in Serbia and Montenegro where the free press has been muzzled and the universities have been stifled. We also see this problem in countries such as Sierra Leone and the DRC [Democratic Republic of Congo], which are facing intense conflicts and human rights abuses. [press briefing, 3/30/99]

The sponsors, representing all regions of the world, pointed out that the resolution itself builds not only on the clear provisions of the Universal Declaration and the International Covenant on Civil and Political Rights, but also on previous resolutions of the Commission on Human Rights, such as "Free and fair elections" of 1989 and annual resolutions on the rule of law and on good governance. It also builds upon the annual General Assembly resolution "Support by the UN system of the efforts of Governments to promote and consolidate new or restored democracies," not to mention the work of UNDP to build good governance and democratic rule, of the U.N.'s Election Unit to monitor free and fair elections, and of the High Commissioner to promote democracy-building efforts and the rule of law.

Nonetheless, the Commission had not previously addressed the central matter of democracy as a right. And even though the 1999 Commission considered the "right to potable water," the "right to food," and "the right to development," its members seemed uncomfortable in affirming it now. The draft painstakingly set out the elements of the "right of everyone to democratic governance," including freedom of expression, freedom of thought, conscience and religion, rule of law (providing for independence of the judiciary), the right to universal and equal suffrage, the right of political participation, the right to transparent and accountable governmental institutions, the right of citizens to choose their governmental system, and the right of equal access to public service. Even more significant was the fact that **the resolution asks the High Commissioner to give priority to technical assistance for democracy-promoting projects,** and urges all human rights treaty bodies, special procedures, and the High Commissioner's office to pay due attention to the elements of democratic governance in their mandates.

It can be expected that the 54th General Assembly will also be asked to affirm the "right to democracy"—a right that today is honored more in practice than in the breach, but which is constantly in peril and needs bolstering where it is still taking hold. In the 1970s, Koh has pointed out, there were only 40 democracies; today there are 110.

2. The Advancement of Women
By Felice D. Gaer

A Century of Progress

The 54th General Assembly will commemorate the 20th anniversary of the adoption of the Convention on the Elimination of All Forms of Discrimination against Women (CEDAW), the landmark treaty that affirms the human rights of women.

In a dramatic development coinciding not only with the CEDAW anniversary but also with the close of a century that has meant so much for the advancement of women, the General Assembly of the United Nations will be asked to adopt an **Optional Protocol to CEDAW** that would permit individual women to send in complaints about the abridgement of rights that are protected by that treaty. This would be the first petition procedure covering many of CEDAW's broad rights guarantees for women—guarantees that span economic and social rights as well as civil and political rights. And it would include not only a complaint procedure but also an inquiry procedure (as in the case of the Convention against Torture) permitting members of the treaty body to conduct an on-site investigation when appropriate. Approval of the Optional Protocol would put CEDAW on a par with the other major human rights treaties that have individual complaint procedures: the International Covenant on Civil and Political Rights, the International Convention on the Elimination of All Forms of Racial Discrimination, and the Torture Convention. The protocol has been a high priority of the women's human rights movement since the beginning of the decade but has been in the formal drafting process only since March 1996. The chair of the Working Group that drafted the Optional Protocol, Aloisia Worgetter of Austria, predicted that once the Assembly acts, "women will have an effective instrument in their hands to fight discrimination." Patricia Flor of Germany, current chair of the Commission on the Status of Women (CSW), characterized the adoption of the protocol as "a supreme moment for gender equality." Because the Commission adopted the text by consensus—an achievement that required a significant number of compromises—the General Assembly is expected to adopt it without reopening the text for debate or voting upon it. The Optional Protocol would enter into force after only ten ratifications.

As if the adoption of such a protocol were not enough of an event, it is scheduled to take place at a time when the United Nations is preparing for its **five-year review of the World Conference on Women (the Beijing Conference)**. The review, June 5–9, 2000, will be conducted at a Special Session of the 54th General Assembly entitled "Women 2000: Gender equality, development and peace for the twenty-first century." Preparatory meetings, regional conferences, and related activities are already under way around the world. The issues to be sorted out by the 54th General Assembly before the review session range from protecting the **1995 Beijing Platform for Action** (that is, keeping the Platform for Action from being reopened and its commitments from being rolled back), to appraising progress and setbacks in implementing it, to developing the means of expanding on the commitments that governments made at Beijing.

The United Nations has begun a series of five-year updates/reviews of the agenda-setting world conferences of the early 1990s and, rather than convene new world conference-type events throughout the world, has decided to conduct these reviews at special sessions of the General Assembly in New York. Special sessions on the environment ("Rio + 5") and population ("Cairo + 5") were the first in the series. (Although the World Conference on Human Rights was not allotted a special session— its fifth anniversary in 1998 was marked by only a modest review at the ECOSOC annual meeting and the regular General Assembly fall session—human rights received major play that year. This was the year that marked the 50th anniversary of the Universal Declaration of Human Rights, culminating in a wide range of special activities in December 1998.) The upcoming "Beijing + 5" Special Session, like the 1995 conference itself, will consider a wide array of issues related to women and development. And it will feel the effect of some of the troublesome divisions that dogged the Cairo + 5 Special Session (June 30–July 2, 1999) on issues related to population policy and the empowerment of women.

Every year since the 1995 Fourth World Conference on Women in Beijing, the **Commission on the Status of Women**—a 45-member functional commission of the U.N.'s Economic and Social Council—has conducted a review of clusters of the 12 critical areas of concern identified in the Platform for Action adopted in Beijing (PFA), reaching "agreed conclusions" (action-oriented recommendations) on each. The aim is to encourage implementation of the Platform, and some of these conclusions do serve the intended purpose. But human rights activists complain that the agreed conclusions are often selective, ignore or minimize key language and elements that were negotiated with much difficulty at the original conference, and may even try to roll back understandings reached at that time.

The 1999 CSW session focused on two issue clusters: women's health, which includes issues of sexual and reproductive health—the PFA's most controversial topic—and the national and international mechanisms it will take to implement the 11 other topics in the PFA.

Among the increasingly professional preparations for the CSW reviews by the Division for the Advancement of Women (DAW, in the Department of Economic and Social Affairs) were two conferences of experts in the areas under review. One of the 1998 gatherings, on "Mainstreaming the Gender Perspective into the Health Sector," explored elements of a gender-sensitive framework for designing national health policies. Held in Tunisia, it addressed not only sexual and reproductive health but also areas not well covered by the PFA, such as women's mental, environmental, and occupational health and the health problems of older women. A second expert session, this one organized in Chile by DAW and the Economic Commission for Latin America and the Caribbean, examined nearly 100 diverse national mechanisms focused on gender mainstreaming and went on to identify the three major roles they play: as catalyst, as partner of civil society, and as monitor, holding governments accountable for making progress on their commitments.

At the **March 1999 CSW session,** panels of experts offered insights into both topics and gave representatives of member governments, NGOs, and international institutions an opportunity to question them. The recommendations of the conferences and the panels set the stage for the **adoption of so-called "agreed conclusions"** by CSW.

Commission members identified the ways in which women's health needs often differ from men's and called for the recognition—and elimination—of gender-based inequities in medical research so that funds can be directed at the different needs of women. Women's lack of equal access to health care and information was noted time and again in this session, as was the need for policy-makers and planners to develop programs to ensure (in the words of the agreed conclusions) "universal access, on a basis of equality, to quality, comprehensive, and affordable health care, health services, and information." Regarding sexual and reproductive health, the agreed conclusions called for measures to reduce maternal and child mortality and to promote female-controlled methods of family planning and male contraceptive methods too. The conclusions also pressed for an end to female genital mutilation and other "harmful traditional practices," including early and/or forced marriage. Focusing on HIV/AIDS and other sexually transmitted and infectious diseases, the CSW urged an expansion of preventive measures; and recommended gender and age-sensitive mental health services and counseling as well as prevention programs aimed at, among other things, reducing tobacco and drug use, and equitable sharing of household and family responsibilities. Still other "agreed conclusions" on women's health called for an array of measures relating to occupational and environmental health, policy development and research, reform of the health sector, and international cooperation for development and for mobilizing both domestic and international financial resources.

The "agreed conclusions" regarding institutional mechanisms emphasized the need for political support for gender mainstreaming, for ensuring that national machineries are invested with sufficient authority to institutionalize and implement that goal, and for transparency and accountability at both the national and the international level. The conclusions also spoke of acknowledging the value of involving nongovernmental organizations (NGOs)—including coordinating and consulting with them—in national and international activities aimed at publicizing and implementing the PFA. At the international level the emphasis is on implementing the ECOSOC conclusions on gender mainstreaming throughout the U.N. system and holding U.N. managers accountable for meeting PFA goals relevant to improving the status of women in the U.N. Secretariat itself [U.N. press release WOM/1124, 4/1/99; and International Women's Tribune Center (IWTC) Women's Globalnet #122, 3/24/99].

The CSW also adopted an **"enabling" resolution for Beijing + 5**— setting out the framework of the June 2000 Special Session, including the substance of the review and the rules of participation—and this will be presented to the 54th General Assembly for approval. The single most important provision of this resolution is contained in the statement that "the Special Session will be undertaken on the basis of and with full respect for the Platform for Action and that there will be no renegotiation of the existing agreements contained therein" [op. par. 6]. This "ground rule" is particularly important in light of the problems encountered when negotiating agreed conclusions at recent CSW sessions, and in view of the divisive efforts of some participants at Cairo + 5 in July 1999 to renegotiate parts of that document dealing with reproductive health, abortion, and the right of the individual to freely decide the number and spacing of offspring, among other human rights issues.

The enabling resolution calls for circulating a questionnaire among member states to identify "good practices" and "lessons learned"—a means of measuring progress and overcoming obstacles to achieving the goals of the PFA—and for convening a variety of preparatory meetings in different regions of the world. The DAW secretariat focused the debate at the CSW on five categories: political will and commitment to creating an enabling environment for the implementation of the PFA; capacity-building for the advancement of women and gender mainstreaming; accountability for and assessment of the implementation of the strategies and actions outlined in the PFA; cooperation in implementing the PFA; and assistance to women currently subjected to discrimination. **Four cross-cutting themes** were also proposed for consideration at the June Special Session: globalization and the economic empowerment of women; women, science, technology, and the new information age; women's leadership; and human security and social protection.

The resolution, as voted, offers a simpler set of plans and priorities. The Special Session, it says, should review the implementation of the PFA, the development of good practices and indicators of progress; and the obstacles encountered and strategies for overcoming them. Suggestions for "further actions and initiatives" would also be enlisted at the Special Session.

The **modalities of NGO participation** were left to the next CSW session. Many NGOs want to see as broad a list of participants as possible, but many governments prefer to restrict NGO participation to those already in consultative status with ECOSOC or that attended the Beijing conference itself. Initial attempts to include NGOs that have applied for consultative status but are yet to receive it were turned aside, but this could change later on [see S. Fried and C. Bunch in *Global Center News* (published by Center for Women's Global Leadership), no. 6, 1999; and see IWTC Women's Globalnet 123, 5/21/99].

Gender Mainstreaming

The Commission continued its drive to "mainstream" a gender perspective into all policies and programs of the U.N. system, and the 53rd General Assembly took up the call. ECOSOC, which emphasized mainstreaming in 1998, adopted as the theme of the high-level segment of its 1999 session "The role of employment and work in poverty eradication: The empowerment and advancement of women." Other U.N. bodies have studied the mainstreaming of a gender perspective in the work of the human rights treaty bodies themselves, and the Commission on Human Rights has a number of special rapporteurs—including, for the first time, several new women appointees—who now address various gender-related violations of the human rights principles that fall within their mandate. Another first for the Commission on Human Rights is a separate agenda item to address issues related to the human rights of women and to a gender perspective [for more on this subject, see the "Human Rights" section of the present chapter].

Afghanistan

The **treatment of women in Afghanistan** affects the U.N.'s very presence and role in that country, and it offers important insights into the institutional and cultural difficulties of mainstreaming gender into operational activities of the U.N. system.

In July 1998, U.N. Emergency Relief Coordinator Sergio Vieira de Mello characterized Afghanistan as "probably the most difficult place to work on earth," citing the hostile security environment, extreme chronic poverty, recurrent natural disasters, an ongoing armed conflict, and a discriminatory human rights regime [press briefing, U.N. Office for the Coordination of Humanitarian Affairs, 7/22/98; available on Reliefweb]. Yet the United Nations does work there. Its efforts continue to focus on promoting a peaceful settlement to the country's civil war, stemming the flow of narcotics from Afghanistan (the world's single largest producer), and providing humanitarian aid to the internally displaced and others. Cease-fire talks (unsuccessful) and armed conflict also continue in 1999, and so do the **repressive measures against women decreed by the Taliban,** the warring faction that controls an estimated 80 percent of the country [Agence France-Presse, 6/27/99]. The U.N. Secretary-General and other key officials, including the Special Rapporteur of the Commission on Human Rights, have reported on conditions in Afghanistan during the year, and both can be expected to report again during the 54th General Assembly.

The Secretary-General reported to the 53rd General Assembly that

> The situation of women and girls in Afghanistan, which has deteriorated in all areas under the control of the Taliban movement, continues to be of serious concern. Women and girls continue to be denied access to adequate health care, to all levels and types of education, to employment and at times to humanitarian assistance. In addition, a number of women and girls were reportedly abducted and raped during the tragic events which took place in northern Afghanistan in August 1998. [A/53/695-S/1998/1109, 11/23/98, par. 56]

His conclusions were based on almost two years of intensive U.N. scrutiny of the measures adopted by the Taliban faction against women and the worldwide condemnation that has followed. Violations of the human rights of Afghan women are nothing new, but it is the Taliban whose actions (in the words of Amnesty International) "have imposed a new form of repression against women in Kabul, Herat, Kandahar and other areas they control" [AI Index: ASA 11/03/99, 2/17/99]. Among the abuses against women in Afghanistan perpetrated by all the warring factions, says Amnesty, are abductions and rapes—women "often being treated as the spoils of war." Furthermore, "thousands of women have been indiscriminately killed in fighting . . . and hundreds of thousands of women and children have been displaced or forced to flee the country as a result of systematic human rights abuses" [ibid.].

Taliban rule has restricted women to their homes under edicts that ban women from seeking employment or education, or from leaving the house unaccompanied by a male relative. These and other measures (e.g., decrees on appropriate coverings for women, with bans even on certain socks and shoes) have been rigidly enforced, and the women who fail to conform to exacting standards have been beaten by Taliban guards in detention centers or in such public places as shops, streets, and bus stops [AI Index: ASA 11/01/98, 2/5/98]. Amnesty International itself considers any women so "detained or physically restricted on account of their gender" to be prisoners of conscience [ibid.; and AI Index: ASA 11/03/99, 2/17/99].

In late 1996, after the Taliban's repressive measures came into force, then-U.N. Secretary-General Boutros Boutros-Ghali and numerous other U.N. officials spoke out against the restrictions on women's rights and against the denial of U.N. aid to women. Some U.N. programs were suspended, others reevaluated and redesigned. In June 1997 the U.N.'s Executive Committee on Humanitarian Affairs (ECHA) **recommended that all U.N. agencies adopt a principle-centered approach to the gender issue** in Afghanistan. Under its terms, U.N. agencies would continue to engage in life-sustaining activities that benefited any Afghans in need, male and female, but would not contribute to the Afghan authorities' institution-building efforts while the discriminatory practices continued. These agencies were also asked to keep up a dialogue with Afghan authorities, with a view to bringing about their adherence to the principles of the Universal Declaration of Human Rights [Appendix to Report of the U.N. Interagency Gender Mission to Afghanistan, . . . Recommendations of the ECHA, 6/3/97]. The Secretary-General "fully" endorsed the principle-centered approach [ibid.].

In November 1997 the United Nations dispatched a seven-member **"Inter-agency Gender Mission to Afghanistan"** under the leadership of Assistant Secretary-General Angela King, U.N. Special Advisor on Gender Issues and Advancement of Women. The "gender mission" team examined the condition of women in Afghanistan and recommended ways in which the international community could address gender concerns in the delivery of aid.

The Inter-agency Gender Mission to Afghanistan, by its own account, "resulted in the development of a coherent set of guidelines for field staff for implementing a principle-centered approach to humanitarian and development assistance." But its report also revealed that U.N.

agencies and their implementing partners in Afghanistan have done little to promote gender equality. Indeed, "most programmes and projects [it wrote] ignore women at all at stages of their design and implementation. Even women-specific projects are not designed in consultation with women," and "UN staff are notably unprepared to confront the challenges of reversing gender discrimination" [Report, pp. 13–14]. Despite the new U.N. concern over gender-related abuses, the situation continued to deteriorate.

In May 1998 the United Nations tried to balance principle and pragmatism in the field by negotiating **a memorandum of understanding with the Taliban** on security, privileges, immunities, and obligations of U.N. staff; participation of international and national female staff in U.N. assistance programs; access to health and education for women and girls; and coordination and follow-up [U.N. OCHA press briefing, 7/22/98, "U.N. Humanitarian Policy in Afghanistan"]. According to reports, the United Nations made significant compromises in the course of those negotiations—for example, by agreeing that access to health care and education for girls would be "gradual" and by failing to obtain assurances that girls could even attend schools or travel freely [Human Rights Watch Annual Report 1999, "Afghanistan: The Role of the International Community"]. De Mello acknowledged the lack of "tangible, measurable, demonstrable progress," particularly in the matter of equal access to health and education.

Taliban authorities declared that no Muslim female employee of the United Nations—from *any* country—could travel to or within Afghan territory under their control unless accompanied by a male relative. As the year progressed, threats to the security of U.N. personnel and to foreign NGOs grew as well. Compromises were worked out, but harassment of U.N. officials continued, and eventually even Kabul's home-based schools for girls and women were closed.

The security situation became increasingly untenable for foreign personnel, particularly after the U.S. air strikes on alleged training camps associated with terrorist Osama bin Laden in retaliation for the bombings of U.S. embassies in Africa. In August 1998, Taliban forces captured the city of Mazar-i-Sharif. Massive abuses, and worse, followed, including detentions "of thousands of men from various ethnic communities" and a massacre directed against members of the Hazara ethnic group—a "killing frenzy" believed to be in retaliation for the killing of some 2,000 Taliban soldiers after their surrender 15 months earlier [Human Rights Watch, 11/1/98, "HR Watch Urges U.N. Investigation of Massacre"].

In July 1998, de Mello **questioned the efficacy of cutting U.N. aid programs because of gender concerns**. "[Is] it better in view of unacceptable violations of human rights, to withdraw and condemn, or [is] it better to remain engaged and to try to make a small difference on the ground however tenuous the chances of success might be?" he asked, adding: "At what point should humanitarian agencies draw the line and withdraw? There was another increasingly central question too: "What level of security risks to . . . staff was acceptable?" [press briefing, 8/22/98, "U.N. Humanitarian Policy in Afghanistan"; available on Reliefweb].

The answer came soon enough. After the **shooting of U.N. personnel serving in Kabul**, the capital, with one dead, the Organization evacuated its staff from the country, as did most NGOs. They were gone by November. Yet, almost immediately, they began negotiating the terms of their return, and indeed, by March 1999, the United Nations was returning to Afghanistan. In June 1999, de Mello explained to the Security Council that the return to Kabul and elsewhere has been "a difficult and painstaking process," but "I am confident that we are well on the way to posting staff in all six locations agreed to earlier" ["Briefing of the Security Council on emergency situations outside the Federal Republic of Yugoslavia," 6/3/99; available on OCHA-Online Homepage].

In the spring of 1999, reports by the U.N.'s Special Rapporteur on Afghanistan and the *Washington Post* suggested that restrictions on women had eased somewhat in Kabul. Newly appointed Rapporteur Kamal Hossain, a former Foreign Minister of Bangladesh, said after visiting the capital that he had "observed some relaxation of the restrictions imposed on the rights of women, as a few women doctors and nurses were seen at work in a hospital attending to female patients." Further: "A more flexible attitude was expressed by Taliban representatives with regard to the access of girls to education, and a recent edict granted exemption to needy widows from the restriction against the employment of women in urban areas" [E/CN.4/1999/40]. Visiting the capital two months later, *Post* reporter Pamela Constable related that the burqa is said to be only a partial covering in Kabul; some women doctors are permitted in a few hospitals, some religious schools were said to exist for girls; and the United Nations has signed agreements to build four colleges for women at some appropriate future point. She added that during the entire time she was told about or shown such "improvements" in Kabul, she was accompanied by two male officials, who often answered in place of the person she questioned, and that other restrictions had been placed on her ability to investigate actual conditions. Constable concluded that the changes, however modest, were in response to outside pressure on the Taliban [*Washington Post*, 5/11/99].

At a press briefing in Geneva [4/7/99; available on High Commissioner for Human Rights Web site], the Special Rapporteur sought to make clear that "the situation was very negative in all fields regarding women," that clear-cut indicators of improvement were lacking, and that "the emergence of a framework for building peace . . . aimed at establishing a broad-based multiethnic and fully representative government" was needed to improve the overall human rights situation in Afghanistan. Both the Commission on the Status of Women and the Commission on Human Rights arrived at the same negative assessment of the condition of women, and the 54th General Assembly will no doubt pronounce on this situation again, perhaps asking the Secretary-General for added reporting on the status of women in Afghanistan.

The CSW's 1999 resolution on Afghanistan, adopted by consensus, was introduced by U.S. Ambassador Linda Tarr-Whelan, who noted that "Few practices of the Taliban have aroused more worldwide condemnation than their treatment of women and girls" [speech, 3/11/99]. (Only a week before, First Lady Hillary Rodham Clinton, speaking at a global teleconference on violence against women, had condemned the Taliban's treatment of women and girls and described their actions as criminal, not cultural.) Ambassador Tarr-Whelan said that "it was crucial to highlight the denial of women's and girls' access to health care in Afghanistan" and that the resolution would condemn "continuing grave violations of the human rights of women and girls, especially their right to an adequate standard of living, including health care, and their rights to education and employment" [U.S. Mission to the U.N. press release, 3/11/99].

The resolution on Afghanistan was unusual in the context of the CSW, since other resolutions and actions adopted by the Commission are traditionally global in scope, save for the annual political resolution on Palestinian women. (For seasoned observers of the United Nations it was even more unusual to hear an American official citing as human rights a group of economic and social rights, including the right to an adequate standard of living. Only a few years ago the United States argued bitterly in various U.N. venues that such matters were "social policies," not rights.)

The CSW resolution "condemns the continuing grave violations of the human rights of women and girls . . . in all areas of Afghanistan, particularly in areas under control of the Taliban"; condemns its denial of access to health care, denial of access to education, employment outside the home, freedom of movement, and freedom from violence; urges the Taliban and other parties in Afghanistan "to recognize, protect, promote, and act in accordance with all human rights and fundamental freedoms, regardless of gender, ethnicity or religion" in accord with international human rights instruments and humanitarian law; and calls for urgent measures to ensure: the repeal of legislative measures that discriminate against women; participation of women in all aspects of Afghan life; respect for the right of women to work (the 1998 resolution had added "outside the home"); the equal right of women to education, freedom of movement, and equal access to health care; and respect for the right to security of the person. Acknowledging the importance of accountability for human rights violations, the resolution also speaks of the need to see that "those responsible for physical attacks on women are brought to justice" [E/CN.6/

1997/L.7]. Missing from these lists is any direct reference to the killings, rape, torture, or other physical maltreatment of women during the Afghan civil war.

As in 1998, the CSW resolution asks the United Nations as well as other donors to ensure that U.N.-assisted programs in Afghanistan are formulated and coordinated to promote and secure participation of women in those programs, and that women benefit equally with men. It goes on to urge that all humanitarian aid—including the U.N.'s own programs—be "based on the principle of non-discrimination, incorporates a gender perspective, and actively attempts to promote the participation of both women and men." Calling on member states to "mainstream a gender perspective into all aspects of their policies and actions related to Afghanistan," it welcomes the **new posts of Gender Coordinator and Human Rights Coordinator in the U.N.'s Office for Coordination of Humanitarian Assistance for Afghanistan** and urges implementation of the 1997 Gender Mission recommendations [E/CN.6/1999/L.7].

The absence from the CSW resolution of a request for an ongoing investigation of the situation, or even for reports from other bodies, illustrates the difference in approach to the human rights of women by the CSW, which generally fields broad issues but does not examine specific cases of violations, and the CHR, which vests special independent experts with the authority to investigate, intervene, gather facts, analyze the situation, and make recommendations in public reports. The calling to accountability those who perpetrate violence against women in Afghanistan is arguably a sign that the CSW may be ready to change its approach. Elsewhere in the resolution the CSW calls upon the CHR's Special Rapporteur on Afghanistan to stress in his report the importance of ensuring the human rights of women and girls.

Afghanistan has been on the **agenda of the Commission on Human Rights** since 1984—although attention to the human rights of women is comparatively recent. The CHR's 1999 resolution addressed most of the issues touched on by the CSW while offering a bit more detail.

Reflecting upon the conclusions of both former Special Rapporteur Choonh Hyun-Paik and new Rapporteur Kamal Hossain, the human rights body condemns the widespread pattern of human rights violations, including violations of the human rights of women and girls, particularly in areas under Taliban control. In other paragraphs focusing on women and girls it went on to urge all parties to put an end to all violations of the human rights of women and girls, and, getting down to specifics, called for urgent measures to ensure the repeal of discriminatory legislative measures; effective participation of women in numerous spheres, including the economy; respect for the right of women to work (the CSW called for "the *equal* right of women to work"), including reintegration into their jobs; fulfillment of the right to education (the CSW spoke of "the *equal* right . . . to education"); the reopening of schools and admission of women at all levels; respect for a woman's right to security of the person and freedom of movement; and equal access to facilities that protect her right to the highest attainable level of physical and mental health. As for follow-up, the CHR reappointed its Special Rapporteur for another year, asking him to continue paying attention to the human rights of women and children. It encouraged the Secretary-General to investigate fully all reports of mass killings, rape, and "other cruel treatment" and make a concerted effort to ensure a gender perspective in the selection of staff for the U.N. Special Mission to Afghanistan [res. 1999/9].

In Stockholm in mid-June 1999, at a **meeting of the Afghan Support Group (ASG)**—this is a group of states that contribute to programs in the country—participants "took stock of the progress in integrating gender considerations into assistance activities." The nature of that progress is not indicated in the summary of the meeting (which was *not* convened by the United Nations), other than a brief reference to the group's support for "rights-based programming and in particular the recruitment by the U.N. Coordinator's Office of a human rights advisor and a gender advisor" [Chairman's Summary, Afghanistan Support Group, Stockholm, 6/21–22/99].

Still, various U.N. officials continue to resist the idea of giving any serious attention to gender-related issues in their decisions and programming for humanitarian assistance in Afghanistan, as their written reports demonstrate. For example, a paper on "Gender Issues in Afghanistan" delivered at the Stockholm ASG meeting by the office of the U.N. Coordinator in Islamabad argued that

> Any underestimation of the influence of the cultural, socio-economic factors contributing to shaping the status quo of Afghan society and economy will lead either to the failure of these interventions to achieve their objectives or worse, to reduce the very narrow margin of access to social services and employment women have at present. . . . There is a great need for the donor community . . . if they wish to create a climate conducive to gender equity in Afghanistan, to make a more intensive effort to look into Afghan society rather than to look at it.

The gender paper goes on to note that a senior gender advisor has joined the office in Islamabad and will be responsible for "the engagement, follow-up, and coordination, through the principled common programming approach, of gender mainstreaming in Afghanistan." A gender action plan, outlined in the document, calls for dialogue with the local community, with technical departments affecting women, and with political and religious leaders. It also calls for sensitization workshops and related training on the capacity of the U.N. system for gender mainstreaming, advising the U.N. system on gender-related policies and guidelines, and working closely on gender-related issues with the NGOs involved in Afghan-related matters ["Gender Issues in Afghanistan," U.N. Coordinator's Office, Islamabad, 6/12/99]. Notably, what it does *not* call for—or even mention—are any actions to implement gender non-discrimination policies.

Another indication that **gender-related concerns have been relegated to a low level in U.N. programming for Afghanistan and in the donor community** as well can be gleaned from two U.N. documents issued in June 1999. One is a press release issued in Islamabad by the U.N. Spokesman for Afghanistan, Stephanie Bunker, who noted the three major concerns of donors to Afghan programs expressed at the Stockholm meeting: the lack of national reconciliation, the need for a political solution to the conflict, and concern over forced repatriation of refugees from Iran. Discrimination against women is mentioned nowhere in the press release, whether as a reason for the "relatively low level of response" to the 1999 appeals for funding or in any other context [AFG/98, 6/25/99].

Gender-related concerns also take a back seat in the Secretary-General's quarterly report on the **U.N.'s Special Mission to Afghanistan** [S/ 1999/698, 6/20/99]—a report mandated by the 53rd General Assembly. It addresses military, political, humanitarian, human rights, and other aspects of the Afghan situation without even mentioning gender-related issues. A brief reference to education mentions female education in passing. Reportedly, the gender advisor attached to the United Nations in Afghanistan has visited Kandahar and Kabul without an accompanying "male relative" and not wearing a burqa, and has met with top Taliban officials.

The overall devastation in Afghanistan—physical, economic, social, and political—presents enormous problems at many levels for those seeking to provide aid and assistance of many kinds, and gender may well be downplayed deliberately at present. The security situation is another major obstacle to the presence of the United Nations and other groups seeking to assist in this complex emergency. A lack of program resources merely compounds the problems involved in implementing policy and planning operational activities.

The Afghan Support Group called for the U.N. Coordinator's Office to present a Human Rights Plan of Action for the next ASG meeting in Ottawa in December 1999. It also noted how vital resources are to any attempt at implementing "principled programming" on gender and human rights but noted that "progress from a rights-based perspective would require a long-term engagement and a broad interpretation of priorities in terms of human rights in Afghanistan" [Chairman's Summary, ASG, 6/ 21–22/99, par. 17]. Women have never been a priority in such assistance programs in this region in the past, and an emphasis on the "long-term" rarely means a focus on the status of women. The 54th General Assembly will have an opportunity to call for more attention to these issues when it turns its attention once again to the situation in Afghanistan.

Women in the Secretariat

For many years the General Assembly has asked the United Nations to live up to its own broad pronouncements on gender by improving the status of women employed by the United Nations Secretariat [see E/CN.6/ 1999/5]. A speech by Gender Advisor/Assistant Secretary-General Angela King at the 1999 CSW updated statistics that the 53rd General Assembly had considered only a few months earlier [A/53/376]. Since January 1, 1998, King advised, and despite the 50–50 gender distribution goals that the Assembly has set for all posts in the U.N. system by the year 2000, the **increase in the percentage of women has been only marginal**, rising from 36.8 percent to 37.1 percent. She drew attention to "notable progress at the senior and policy-making levels"—particularly at the rather high D-1 level, where the proportion of women has increased from 24.3 percent to 31.3 percent over the same period. (A U.N. press release indicates that there were 65 women in D-1 level posts as of November 30, 1998, up from 51 the previous year [WOM/1099, 3/5/99].) However, there were fewer women at other levels of senior management, which means that there is a smaller pool for future top-level appointments of women. King also updated information about the recently approved special measures for achieving gender equality, including the **introduction of gender action plans in every U.N. department** to improve accountability and performance in recruitment and promotion [speech by the Gender Advisor at the 1999 CSW; available at www.un.org/womenwatch].

NGOs and Women

The **treatment of NGOs at the Beijing + 5 review** in the year 2000 is still uncertain and will be finalized only as the special session draws nearer. The Beijing conference itself was notable for the energy of the NGO participants from around the globe and the sense of empowerment it generated among them.

The treatment of NGOs at the Cairo + 5 meeting in June 1999 offers an ominous prognosis for NGO participation in the Special Session on Women in June 2000. At Cairo + 5, NGOs were locked out of plenary sessions until the last part of the last day—and then only after news of their protest about exclusion appeared in the *New York Times* and all the conference newspapers. Three NGOs were allowed to speak, apparently selected to offer balance on the controversial issues.

NGOs participated fully and effectively in the conference, outside the speakers' platforms. "They supported government delegates with technical expertise and in-depth knowledge of national policies and achievements in implementing the Cairo Programme of Action," notes Adrienne Germain, President of the International Women's Health Coalition and herself a member of the U.S. delegation. "This was truly democracy in action." Indeed, she said, the "clear and progressive agreements" reached at the Special Session "would not have happened without the full participation of NGOs throughout the PrepCom process" [statement, International Women's Health Coalition, 7/2/99].

The CSW session back in March will be remembered for another NGO-related incident. A Canadian woman, Losang Rabgey, had been asked to speak before the Commission on behalf of the NGO Caucus/Committee on the Status of Women's Health but was prevented from doing so by Secretariat officials apparently fearful that she, a person of Tibetan ethnicity, might offend or provoke complaints from Beijing. China, a permanent member of the Security Council, has in the past challenged NGOs that come from China, Tibet, or Taiwan or incorporate the name of these places in its own. What shocked in this instance was the idea that **the Secretariat itself prevented an individual from taking the floor.** (According to a statement by the U.S. delegate to the CSW, the Secretariat staff member who called off Ms. Rabgey's appearance told the organizer of the NGO speakers list that she "was through; that NGOs would be barred from further participation in the meeting, and that she was responsible.") Negative publicity and public protests by the Canadian and U.S. delegates led Assistant Secretary-General King to apologize to the CSW on behalf of her staff. Said U.S. Ambassador Tarr-Whelan: "Judging a person's eligibility to speak in the United Nations on the basis of her name is no more acceptable than doing so on the basis of her skin color, nationality, religion, or the substance of her statement" [U.N. press release WOM/1099, 3/5/99].

Ms. Rabgey later returned to New York and stood on the speaker's podium to thank the United Nations for its apology.

A Balance Sheet

At the 1999 CSW meeting, Assistant Secretary-General/Special Advisor on Gender Issues King assessed a half-century's efforts on behalf of the advancement of women and anticipated the challenges of the next:

- Much legislation on gender equality and the elimination of violence against women has been enacted, but practical application is far from the norm;
- A greater incidence of awareness of the growing phenomenon of violence against women particularly domestic violence exists but coping mechanisms are rare and precise data scant;
- There is a failure to regard women as part of the solution to eradicating extreme poverty for them and their families, [*sic*] little has

been done to incorporate them into [the] decision-making . . . process;

- There is a worsening in women's access to health care facilities, yet on balance we note a growing awareness of the inhumanity of traditional practices which are harmful to the health of women and girls such as female genital mutilation and the growing impact of HIV/AIDS, particularly in Africa;
- In the field of education despite the fact that women and girls are entering secondary . . . education more than ever before in some countries yet in others drop out rates particularly for adolescent girls continue to increase;
- While more and more women enter the labour market, their role in the informal sector, particularly in agriculture, is ignored and [the] issue of their unpaid work unresolved;
- In the area of decision-making there has been some regression overall in the political arena. . . . [introductory statement by Angela E.V. King; available at www.un.org/womenwatch/daw/csw/akspeech.htm]

3. Crime and Drugs
By Fiona Shukri

Organized Crime

An increase in international travel, improvements in communications technology, and globalization of the world economy have created transnational opportunities for individual entrepreneurs and businesses—both legal and criminal. Moving people, money, and drugs across borders has become easier, as has coordinating the effort with cohorts in other countries. International crime is "increasing in scope, intensity, and sophistication," according to the United Nations Centre for International Crime Prevention [CICP Web site, www.ifs.univie.ac.at/~unjin/CICP/Index.html].

Areas undergoing transition to a market economy, such as republics of the former Soviet Union, are particularly vulnerable to organized criminal activity. As the disparity in socio-economic strata has grown, so have opportunities for enterprising criminals in decentralizing economies. Drug money is believed to account for half of Moscow's real estate market, for example [UNESCO *Sources*, 4/99]. Such corruption can damage an entire national economy. A corrupt country is likely to achieve aggregate investment levels of almost 5 percent less than a relatively uncorrupt country and to lose about half a percentage point of gross domestic product growth per year [ibid.].

As criminal activity internationalizes, the effects of corruption in such places as Moscow reach far beyond Russia's borders. The result is what economist Guilhem Fabre calls "the **progressive criminalisation of the world economy**" [ibid.]. Organized crime groups gross about $1.6 trillion a year, $400 billion of that from the sale of illegal narcotics, according to the U.N. Development Programme's 1999 Human Development Report [UN Wire, 7/6/99]. Multinational criminal syndicates have taken full advantage of advancing communications technology and open borders, significantly broadening the range of their operations from drug and arms trafficking to money laundering. Estimates of laundered money run as high as $500 billion a year [U.N. Office for Drug Control and Crime Prevention, *United Nations Global Progamme against Money Laundering*]; and traffickers move as many as 4 million illegal migrants each year, generating gross earnings of between $5 and $7 billion [CICP Web site].

The **Naples Political Declaration and Global Action Plan Against Organized Crime**—as approved in 1994 by the highest-level gathering ever called by the United Nations on transnational crime—has guided all subsequent U.N. efforts in multinational cooperation to fight crime. Approved by the 49th General Assembly, the Naples Plan emphasizes the harmonizing and strengthening of national legislation to facilitate extradition [A/Res/49/159]. In 1998 the 53rd General Assembly passed a resolution requesting that the Secretary-General "intensify his efforts to identify and allocate within the overall budget of the United Nations adequate resources for strengthening the capacity of the Centre for International Crime Prevention in order to assist Member states in the full implementation of the Naples Political Declaration and Global Action Plan" [A/Res/53/111]. This same resolution, passed December 9, 1998, also established the **Ad Hoc Committee on the Elaboration of a Convention against Transnational Organized Crime**. A separate resolution passed that day charged the Ad Hoc Committee with elaborating instruments to address trafficking in women and children, the illicit manufacturing of and trafficking in firearms, their parts and components and ammunition, and illegal trafficking and transporting of migrants [A/Res/53/114].

States have committed themselves to ensure that the Ad Hoc Committee completes its work by the year 2000. To date, the Ad Hoc Committee has met four times in Vienna and has additional meetings scheduled for October 4–15 and December 6–10, 1999, the latter of which is subject to the availability of extrabudgetary resources. Further meetings are planned for 2000, depending on the pace of negotiations.

In other activity, the **Centre for International Crime Prevention (CICP)**, jointly with its research arm, the United Nations Interregional Criminal Justice and Research Institute, based in Rome, has prepared proposals for three global programs. The **Global Programme against Corruption** will provide technical assistance to a selection of developing and transitional countries. The **Global Programme against the Trafficking** in **Human Beings** addresses smuggling of migrants and trafficking in women and children. **Assessing Transnational Organized Crime Groups: Dangerousness and Trends** will attempt to forecast the future developments and strategies of organized crime groups and develop pre-emptive action. In another effort to strengthen the United Nations Crime Prevention and Criminal Justice Programme, the General Assembly supported the efforts of the CICP to obtain executing agency status with the U.N. Development Programme [ibid.].

In April 2000 the Centre will host the Tenth United Nations Congress on the Prevention of Crime and the Treatment of Offenders, with the theme "Crime and justice, meeting the challenges of the 21st century." The 53rd Session of the General Assembly approved the agenda for the Congress [A/Res/53/110], which will assemble government representatives, academics, nongovernmental organizations, and media in Vienna to discuss how to promote the rule of law and strengthen the criminal justice system; international cooperation in combating transnational organized crime: new challenges in the 21st century; effective crime prevention that keeps pace with new developments; and accountability and fairness in the justice process.

The Congress will also feature workshops on combating corruption; crimes related to the computer network; community involvement in crime prevention; and women in the criminal justice system. The 53rd Session requested that the Congress prepare a single declaration with recommendations to submit to the Commission on Crime Prevention and Criminal Justice at its ninth session. The declaration will help to define an international agenda for crime prevention and criminal justice and outline the future work of both the United Nations Crime Prevention and Criminal Justice Programme and national governments.

In a resolution aimed at improving mutual assistance and cooperation in criminal matters, the 53rd Session asked member states to establish a central authority within their own national systems to process outside requests for assistance [A/Res/53/112]. The Secretary-General was asked to prepare a database of these authorities and develop training materials for mutual assistance law for the states. The resolution also requests that states assess the effectiveness of their own treaties on mutual assistance in criminal matters. Addressing transnational crime fighting measures, the resolution recommends that states contribute forfeited criminal proceeds to programs to improve crime fighting in developing countries and countries with economies in transition, and recommends too the use of video-conferencing for consultation between authorities and the taking of testimonies [ibid.].

The International Convention against Transnational Organized Crime will provide the legal framework for harmonizing different legal systems and stress the importance of a legally binding instrument to over-come the problems traditionally associated with international cooperation and mutual assistance. Three protocols to the Convention will address the illicit manufacturing of and trafficking in firearms, the illegal trafficking in and transport of migrants, and the international trafficking in women and children. The Convention will be submitted for adoption to the Millennium General Assembly in 2000.

Terrorism

The **bombings of the U.S. embassies in Kenya and Tanzania in August 1998** were responsible for the record number of terrorism casualties in 1998—killing more than 700 people and injuring nearly 6,000 [U.S. Department of State Web site, www.statev/www/global/terroris/1998Report]. However, **the number of international terrorist attacks actually fell,** as it has for the past several years—from 404 in 1997 to a 27-year low of 273 [ibid.]. Terrorism made headlines in the United States again in April 1999 when U.N. representatives delivered to Dutch authorities two suspects accused of killing 270 people in the 1988 bombing of Pan Am flight 103. The suspects will be tried before a Scottish court sitting in the Netherlands [U.S. Mission Web site, www.undp.org/missions/usa/terror, 4/5/99]. In a public statement, U.S. Secretary of State Madeleine Albright thanked U.N. Secretary-General Kofi Annan, "who worked tirelessly to implement the Security Council resolutions [against Libya]." The ten-year delay in bringing the suspected bombers to trial demonstrates, however, the difficulty of prosecuting transnational cases.

The **Ad Hoc Committee** established by the 51st General Assembly in December 1996 **to draft an international convention for the suppression of acts of nuclear terrorism and of terrorist financing** concluded its third session in March 1999 [U.N. press release L/2918, 3/26/99]. The proposed convention attempts to prevent future terrorist suspects from avoiding justice under the principle "prosecute or extradite." The convention provides investigators with ways to address those who supply funding or otherwise sponsor terrorist activities—something the draft's sponsor country, France, maintains is not adequately established in the 11 existing international anti-terrorist conventions. Potential methods include the seizure or freezing of property or assets used to commit the offense.

The Ad Hoc Committee's work on the document will continue when it meets from September 27 to October 8, 1999, within the Working Group of the General Assembly's Sixth (Legal) Committee. The Committee will report to the 54th General Assembly. Informal consultations have also been taking place among interested delegations on the other instrument being elaborated by the Ad Hoc Committee: a draft convention for the suppression of acts of nuclear terrorism, submitted by the Russian Federation.

The 54th Session will also address **the question of convening a high-level conference** in 2000 to formulate a joint, organized response of the international community to terrorism [A/Res/53/108].

Trafficking People for Prostitution

Trafficking people for prostitution brings in $8 billion a year, according to the *Observer* of London [UN Wire, 7/6/99]. The U.N. Development Fund for Women (UNIFEM) estimates that roughly 2 million girls between the ages of 5 and 15 are trafficked, sold, coerced into prostitution, or otherwise introduced into the commercial sex market each year [www.unifem.undp.org/campaign/violence/mediafac.htm]. The number appears to be growing. In February 1998 the General Assembly passed a resolution on the trafficking of women and girls that acknowledges an increase in the crime—particularly in developing countries and countries with economies in transition [A/Res/53/116]. The United Nations Foundation's daily online service reports a growing coerced prostitution industry, with the largest number in South and Southeast Asia [UN Wire, 4/14/99]. The increase appears to be due to failing economies in such countries as Bolivia, reported by the *Economist* to have a 70 percent poverty rate [ibid., 5/18/99], and South Africa, where children "are rented out by their own mothers in return for food and shelter," according to the May 1999 issue of *New African* magazine [ibid., 4/30/99].

Opportunities for trafficking in people and drugs have multiplied with the increasing ease and frequency of international travel and the growing trend of temporary migration for work. Trafficking networks in drugs and people have expanded into trafficking for the purpose of prostitution and other forms of exploitation. The Internet is also used by those peddling prostitution and pornography. A resolution of the 53rd Session expresses concern about the "unabated use of new information technologies, including the Internet, for purposes of prostitution, child pornography, paedophilia, trafficking in women as brides and sex tourism." [A/Res/53/116]. In response, the resolution "invites Governments to encourage Internet service providers to adopt or strengthen self-regulatory measures to promote the responsible use of the Internet with a view to eliminating trafficking in women and girls." [ibid.]. It also calls upon governments to criminalize trafficking in women and girls in all its forms, and requests that the Secretary-General compile a reference guide of successful programs (both U.N. and non-U.N.) to combat the problem and submit a report to the 55th Session of the General Assembly.

In June 1999 the U.N. Educational, Scientific and Cultural Organization (UNESCO) launched **"Innocence in Danger"**—a campaign to combat the misuse of the Internet by child pornographers and child abusers. The campaign aims to coordinate cyber law-enforcement agencies around the world and allow them to share information [U.N. press briefing, 6/15/99]. The U.S.'s National Action Committee will include the Department of Justice, the New York Attorney-General's Office, and other experts in cyberspace crimes, children's Web sites, and child advocacy groups [ibid.].

"While child abusers had existed before the Internet, they had previously been isolated and lonely. Today the Internet has made it possible for them to communicate easily with each other," said Homayra Sellier, president of Innocence in Danger [press conference on Child Safety on Internet, 6/15/99]. A UN Wire story [6/16/99] announcing the campaign includes an Associated Press statistic that approximately 23,000 of 3.8 million Web sites on the Internet advocate sex with children. Innocence in Danger plans to launch a "watchdog" Web site by next year to track pedophilia around the world—something UNESCO had proposed at a conference in January 1998 [ibid.].

In other activity, UNICEF Executive Director Carol Bellamy announced in April that the agency would give Chinese police financial and technical support to capture kidnappers and reunite abductees with their families. "This project will rescue and save the lives of many young children who are abducted, trafficked, and sold for commercial sex. . . . It will also rescue young women who are abducted or trafficked as unwilling wives or taken away to brothels as virtual sex slaves" [UN Wire, 4/27/99]. UNIFEM argues that trafficking must be prevented by reducing both demand and supply. Demand reduction should be handled through the criminal justice system and law enforcement. And supply reduction may be achieved through the provision of alternative employment and income-earning opportunities for women and girls and through campaigns targeting parents on the long-term advantages of girls' education [UNIFEM Web site, www.unifem-eseasia.org/Gendiss/Gendiss2.htm].

Country initiatives to eliminate trafficking appear to be largely educational, including a campaign in Russia to educate orphans and at-risk young girls about the dangers of trafficking and sexual slavery and how to obtain help if they are abducted. In Nepal a fictional film will raise awareness among potential victims and their families by highlighting the consequences of the practice, including the health risks, such as contracting HIV/AIDS and other infectious diseases [www.unifem.undp.org/campaign/violence/mediafac.htm].

Money Laundering

Estimates of laundered money run as high as $500 billion a year, of which law enforcement agencies currently recover approximately $500 million a year—a mere 0.1 percent. The crime has been made easier in some respects by technological developments that have facilitated the quick transfer of money across international borders. With a few strokes of a computer keyboard, vast sums of money can be moved electronically 24 hours a day. Criminals, along with legitimate financiers, are taking advantage of both improved technology and increasing globalization of the world economy. The **Political Declaration and Action Plan against Money Laundering,** adopted in June 1998 at the 20th **Special Session of the General Assembly,** devoted to countering the **World Drug Problem,** is the latest agreement to counter money laundering. It contains a series of measures intended to improve international cooperation between member states and to institute bank safety practices—notably the removal of bank secrecy measures that impede investigation and punishment of money laundering.

In March 1999 the **U.N. Global Programme against Money Laundering** launched the "Offshore Initiative," a proposal to create a league of internationally approved offshore centers that would adhere to accepted standards of control. Governments responsible for centers that fail to meet standards would face international pressure to close them [*Financial Times*, 3/5/99]. Offshore centers—traditional tax havens—have multiplied as communications technology has allowed the financial industry to globalize. In May **the Cayman Islands** became the first offshore center to agree to U.N. review under the Initiative [*Toronto Star*, 5/25/99]. The Offshore Initiative will provide training to these centers, many of which are located in the Caribbean and Central America, as they have few people technically qualified to ensure that legal standards are met.

The Global Programme against Money Laundering also launched the **International Money Laundering Information Network (IMoLIN).** Available over the Internet, IMoLIN is a network developed with several other anti-money laundering organizations to assist states by providing a secure News Forum, an electronic library, a database on laws and regulations (AMLID), and a calendar of events in the anti-money laundering field [www.imolin.org].

Illegal Drugs

With annual revenues of over $400 billion, the illegal drug industry is a major employer, political actor, and financial force [UNESCO *Sources*, 4/99]. The past 20 years have seen an increase in the industry as organized crime has taken full advantage of an increasingly open world market, global banking systems, and improved technology in communications and transportation.

In a resolution designed to strengthen international cooperation in combating the illegal drug trade, the General Assembly acknowledged that, despite increased efforts by the states, there has been global expansion of the drug problem [A/Res/53/115]. The resolution notes "growing and spreading violence and economic power of criminal organizations and terrorist groups engaged in drug trafficking activities and other criminal activities such as money laundering and illicit traffic in arms, precursors and essential chemicals, and by the increasing transnational links between them. . . ." The resolution further recognizes that "the Internet poses new opportunities and challenges to international cooperation in combating drug abuse and illicit production and trafficking" [ibid.].

In an effort to combat the problem, the **Commission on Narcotic Drugs (CND)**—the principal U.N. policy-making body on drug control issues—adopted a resolution to set up a **high-technology monitoring network,** including ground surveys and remote satellite sensing. The system is part of an effort to eradicate the coca bush, cannabis plant, and opium poppy by the year 2008 [U.N. press release SOC/NAR/796, 4/24/99]. Sponsored by Colombia at the CND's annual meeting in Vienna in March, the resolution requests that the Office for Drug Control and Crime Prevention (ODCCP) assist nations with the investigation of causes and consequences of drug abuse, the establishment of national monitoring systems, and the assessment of the impact of intervention programs. National monitoring would form the backbone of an international network to stamp out illicit drug crops. A **joint database** that has been in the works for several years was announced in June 1999 by the U.N. International Drug Control Programme (UNDCP), the International Criminal Police Organization (Interpol), and the World Customs Organization (WCO) [U.N. press release SOC/NAR/803, 6/14/99]. The database, which combines information collected by each organization about global drug seizures, contains over 10,000 records and will be updated by the three agencies as new information comes in. It is hoped that the database will help to illuminate the scale and dynamics of drug trafficking as well as to identify trends and routes worldwide. "The international community now has an instrument that will accurately measure all progress to eradicate illicit crops and promote alternative development," said Pino Arlacchi, Executive Director of ODCCP. "The next step will be to begin implementing the monitoring programme by providing adequate resources" [ibid.].

In other business at the Vienna meeting, the 53-member Commission approved a revised UNDCP budget for 1998–99, up from $50 million in 1998 to $70 million in 1999. It also set up several cross-border projects to train law enforcement officials, promote information exchange between regions, and provide needed equipment [ibid.].

The **CND's targeting of both supply and demand** is in keeping with the conclusions of the General Assembly's 1998 Special Session, at which President Bill Clinton and other world leaders agreed to a program to cut off drug production at its source while reducing demand for drugs in developed countries. This approach is necessary, since southern supply countries and northern demand countries have spent much time blaming each other for the world's drug problem. **UNESCO's Management of Social Transformations Programme (MOST)** will examine societal forces that cause some people to take drugs and others to cultivate them. The **second annual Conference of the International Research Project on the Economic and Social Transformations Connected with the International Drug Problem** was held in Rio de Janeiro, October 19–22, 1998. The meeting was convened to analyze progress and data since the inception of MOST in April 1997. The third meeting will be held in New Delhi in October 1999, and UNDCP will host the final conference in 2000. As part of the U.N. attempt to reduce both supply and demand, a five-part General Assembly resolution calls upon the international community and relevant U.N. agencies, particularly UNDCP, to provide drug-producing countries with financial and technical aid for alternative development. International financial institutions and regional development banks should also be encouraged to provide financial assistance for alternative development programs [U.N. press release UNIS/NAR/658, 3/25/99].

At the Rio conference, member countries also committed themselves to establishing drug-reduction strategies and programs; setting up and strengthening national legislation and programs to combat illicit manufacture, trafficking, and abuse of amphetamine-type stimulants and their precursors; eradicating illicit drug crops; and promoting alternative development—all by the year 2003. The Declaration on Guiding Principles contains standards to help governments set up drug demand-reduction programs by the target date and encourage the establishment of prevention, treatment, and rehabilitation programs [ibid.].

On June 25, World Anti-Drug Day, U.N. Secretary-General Kofi Annan said that despite progress by U.N. programs, 3 to 4 percent of the world's population uses illicit drugs regularly, and noted that intravenous drug use is a main contributor to the spread of AIDS. The **International Narcotics Control Board,** an independent panel that monitors the implementation of U.N. drug control treaties, reported in its annual survey an upsurge in the use of prescribed sedatives and stimulants in developing countries and the spread of "designer" drugs, such as ecstasy, into most countries in Latin America, Asia, and the former Soviet Union [*Financial Times*, 2/24/99].

But if demand is up, **crop production appears to be going down,** according to the United Nations. Arlacchi told the *New York Times* that the plan he proposed at the 53rd Session to eliminate opium poppy and coca leaf cultivation within ten years is ahead of schedule [6/11/99]. He cited success in Bolivia, which eradicated 34,000 acres of coca in the past year—

and-a-half, and Peru, which has destroyed more than 50,000 acres. Arlacchi also told the *Times* that the $5 billion 10-year plan includes money from international donations, cooperation by local governments, and "a modest degree of coercion" to make farmers switch to legal crops. An earlier *Times* article [5/9/99] reported that Bolivia has slashed its coca production from 25 percent of its land, replacing much of it with legal crops with the help of the United Nations. This pace means that Bolivian President Hugoi Banzar could fulfill his pledge to eradicate the crop by the end of his term in 2002.

Arlacchi has been working directly with several countries on drug-control initiatives. In April 1999, Tajik President Emomali Rakhmanov signed an agreement with Arlacchi to set up a drug-control agency to document and curb local drug trafficking and "collect and analyze incoming data" [U.N. press release UNIS/CP/369, 4/27/99]. President Rakhmanov, who gave a formal address at the annual meeting of the **Commission on Crime Prevention and Criminal Justice**—the first president ever to do so—told the Commission that 58 percent of the world's opium production comes from Afghanistan and that much of it travels through Tajikistan on its way to Europe. The Tajik Drug Control Agency will be under the direct supervision of President Rakhmanov and will receive support and technical assistance from the ODCCP, which will assist in hiring and paying up to 350 employees for three years, provide communications and other equipment, and help the Agency set up contacts with other states and organizations. In April, Arlacchi pledged $6.4 million to Tajikistan to help it curb the drug trade.

4. Health
By Daniel Guss Butenschøn

Gro Harlem Brundtland, who became Director-General of the World Health Organization (WHO) in July 1998, has created a small revolution at Geneva headquarters and in the world health community. She is in the process of changing how this specialized agency works and how it interacts with other parts of the U.N. system as well as with national ministries, whole governments, universities, and the private sector. In recent years the Health Assembly—WHO's governing and policy-making body—and its Executive Board have expressed the need for changes in the WHO secretariat and budget to make the organization more transparent and accountable.

A sense of excitement and expectation surrounds the new reforms. Dr. Brundtland, a physician and former Prime Minister of Norway who earned a master's degree in public health at Harvard University, reports that she has been asked many times: "Is it possible to reform a U.N.

agency?" To this she replies: "Yes it is possible and we are doing it" [press release WHO/82, 11/9/98].

A conventional criticism of U.N. agencies is that they have evolved at a slower pace than the world around them. The U.S.-based publication *Public Health Reports* calls WHO's reform plan the first **serious attempt to rethink a complex agency of the U.N. system** and make it work in a world vastly different from that of 1948, WHO's founding year [Anthony Robbins in *Public Health Reports*, 1/99]. One of the more significant differences, in fact, is the relative importance of health care systems—today, a large fraction of the gross domestic product in every industrial country and, increasingly, in newly industrialized countries as well. The developing world, however, has failed to keep pace, presenting WHO with its greatest challenge. In 1990, for example, when health services accounted for 8 percent of the total world product, industrialized countries spent an average of $1,500 per capita, developing countries a mere $41 [Julio Frenk et al., "The Future of World Health," *British Medical Journal*, 1997].

The Focus

Often perceived as a development agency specializing in health, WHO now aims **to become a global health agency.** To achieve this—that is, "to give the best advice; support and develop the best policies; trigger and stimulate the best research"—Dr. Brundtland's reform plan begins with an emphasis on WHO's "core functions" rather than on its "supportive functions" [address to WHO staff in Geneva, 7/21/98]. Supportive functions (rendering assistance during a famine is one example) are intended to compensate for a government's failure to provide for its citizens, while core functions look beyond the individual nation-state, addressing global problems and developing global solutions to them. As explained by Dean Jamison, Julio Frenk, and Felicia Knaul, writing in the British medical journal *The Lancet* [1998]: "The ultimate goal of supportive functions is to help countries move from dependence to independence, whereas the goal of core functions is to help them move from independence to interdependence, which represents a higher level of international cooperation—and the only way to meet the challenges of the global era." (The first two authors are members of Brundtland's "new team.")

Although the core functions will be played up, Brundtland does not downplay the importance of supportive functions in the business of WHO. After all, the aim of these activities is to help countries develop effective preventive and curative services, and they certainly require the expertise of WHO professionals. But they also require resources—material and professional—beyond WHO's means. Here, Dr. Brundtland envisions even closer collaboration with the U.N. system's true development agencies—prominently, the World Bank, UNICEF, and the U.N.

Development Programme—than in the past. Three other intergovern-mental agencies—the World Trade Organization, the World Intellectual Property Organization, and the United Nations Commission on Trade and Development—will also be important players in the health sector, since their policies affect the availability and price of pharmaceuticals, vac-cines, diagnostics, and medical devices.

The Strategy

To **expand WHO's core functions** requires a higher level of involvement and commitment by member governments than they give today, when the domestic body responsible for WHO-related affairs is apt to be the relatively low-ranking ministry of health. Right now, WHO is trying to enlist the support of presidents, prime ministers, and ministers of finance and planning for its **"Roll Back Malaria"** initiative, in order to make it a global priority—the better to assure its success. The disease, an ever-pres-ent threat to almost 2 billion inhabitants of Asia, Africa, and the Ameri-cas, and responsible for the death of 1.5 million to 2.7 million people a year, has grown resistant to traditional drug therapy. Eradication will re-quire the development of new therapies and a commitment to undertake decisive preventive measures. The WHO campaign stresses the wide-spread use of anti-mosquito insecticide-impregnated bednets and vector control [WHO, The World Health Report 1998].

If the malaria campaign is successful, WHO plans to adopt a similar approach to controlling tobacco use, eradicating polio, caring for ageing populations, and developing services for individuals suffering from men-tal illness.

The Cluster System

The major internal reform is a linking of WHO's 50-plus programs to improve transparency, accountability, efficiency, and the cooperation among them—in short, to make the best use of limited resources. Dr. Brundtland has gathered a new senior management team to supervise the reorganization, which takes the form of nine clusters, whose executive directors form the "Cabinet." The clusters themselves fall into four broad categories that correspond to WHO's main goals, which are unchanged: "building healthy populations and communities, combating ill health, sustaining health activities, and supporting internal work and reaching out to others" [WHO, *World Health Forum*, vol. 19, no. 4, 1998].

The WHO Web site [specifically, www.who.org/inf.dg/structure] is the source of the information that follows.

Building Healthy Populations and Communities

Cluster on Sustainable Development and Healthy Environment, aimed at ensuring that the health aspect in sustainable development and poverty reduction is properly addressed in formulating and implementing public policies, strategies, and programs at all levels. Among the programs in this cluster are

- Health in Sustainable Development (the impact of development policies on health, policy issues related to globalization and global change, and health-related aspects of poverty-reduction strategies).
- Nutrition for Health and Development (nutrition planning, alleviation of malnutrition, support to countries, and formulation of nutrition norms and standards).
- Protection of the Human Environment (risk-assessment and planning activities in such areas as food and water, sanitation and chemical safety, radiation and occupational health).
- The WHO Department of Emergency and Humanitarian Action (responsible for coordinating WHO's response to humanitarian emergencies).

Cluster on Social Change and Mental Health, addressing the health consequences of social change and global demographic trends through promotion of mental and physical health; prevention of violence; prevention of disabilities and injuries (and rehabilitation too); and the prevention and treatment of substance abuse. It is expected that by 2020 over 70 percent of premature deaths among adults will be caused by behaviors initiated during childhood and youth, prominently smoking, alcohol/substance abuse, unsafe sex, bad dietary patterns, and lack of physical activity. Mental disorders, including depression and schizophrenia, constitute another 10.5 percent of the global burden of disease, mainly because of the disability associated with them. Urbanization, the ageing of populations, and increasing levels of violence also pose complex challenges to health in all countries.

Cluster on Health Systems and Community Health—one of WHO's largest—uniting many of the WHO divisions that deal with health care systems and access to health care, placing special emphasis on the health status of women, adolescents, and children. WHO's new HIV/AIDS and Sexually Transmitted Infections Initiative falls in this cluster. The initiative supports national efforts at developing and implementing programs to reduce the spread of the disease; coordinates WHO's HIV-related activities; and serves as a link with the Joint U.N. Programme on AIDS (UNAIDS) to ensure that WHO fulfills its mandate as a co-sponsor—a position it shares with UNICEF, the U.N. Development Programme, the U.N. Population Fund (UNFPA), UNESCO, and the World Bank. (The agencies in UNAIDS, each with its own expertise, were brought together to pool resources, coordinate fund-raising, and reduce overlaps in the U.N. system's efforts to combat AIDS.)

Also falling in this cluster is the Special Programme of Research, Development, and Research Training in Human Reproduction, which in June 1999 received word of a $10 million grant from Microsoft founder **Bill Gates,** to be disbursed by the William H. Gates Foundation in annual installments of $2 million. The program, a joint effort of UNDP, UNFPA, the World Bank, and WHO, is the only research program in the U.N. system dedicated to sexual and reproductive health. The grant will support studies "on men's responsibility and related cross-cutting issues in sexual and reproductive health" [press release WHO/34, 6/16/99].

Combating Ill Health

Cluster on Communicable Diseases, to reduce the global impact of tuberculosis (TB), malaria, cholera, lymphatic filariasis ("elephantiasis"), dracunculiasis ("guinea-worm disease"), dengue fever, and intestinal parasitic and other diseases through prevention and control, surveillance, and research and development. Whether the task is to prevent or to cure, the numbers are alarming: TB, for example, kills an estimated 2 million to 3 million people a year, and 120 million people in 73 countries are at risk of contracting lymphatic filariasis.

Before the restructuring, WHO's communicable disease activities were overwhelmingly organized along disease-specific lines. The new orientation is function-specific.

Cluster on Noncommunicable Diseases, to provide leadership in surveillance, prevention, and the management of efforts to reduce cardiovascular diseases, cancer, chronic rheumatic and lung diseases, diabetes mellitus, and degenerative disorders, which account for 75 percent of all deaths in developed countries and 40 percent in developing countries. It is expected that by 2020 "three-quarters of all deaths in the world" will result from such diseases. (Departing from past practice here too, WHO activities in the area of noncommunicable diseases will be function-specific.)

WHO's Tobacco-Free Initiative falls under this cluster, tobacco having been identified as a significant cause of lung disease and of cancer. By 2025 there will be 10 million smoking deaths a year, according to current estimates—7 million in developing countries alone.

Sustaining Health

Cluster on Evidence and Information for Policy and **Cluster on Health Technology and Pharmaceuticals.** The first of these is aimed at strengthening the scientific and ethical foundations of health policies and programs, the better to serve the needs of individuals. The second puts WHO's work on drugs, vaccines, and health technologies under one umbrella containing three "struts"—that is, there will be a unit to deal with drugs, another with vaccines, and the third with clinical technology.

Support Services and Reaching Out

Cluster on External Relations and Governing Bodies and **Cluster on General Management.** The first of these, working closely with WHO's governing bodies, will build and maintain partnerships and alliances with other key players in the health field, including civil society and industry as well as multilateral organizations. The actual restructuring of WHO, and oversight of that process, falls to the General Management cluster. Restructuring is expected to continue into the biennium 2000–01.

Every cluster assumes substantial responsibility for its own administration, budget, and personnel, giving it a good deal of autonomy. The Management cluster will guide and assist the clusters where needed, but its main focus is intended to be WHO's management policy overall.

On the Ground

Although WHO does not look upon itself as a field agency, with large numbers of personnel working in member countries, it recognizes that the ultimate test of health programs is how well they work. The agency's **six regional offices** are closest to the field—and farthest from headquarters' control. In fact, the directors of these offices are appointed not by the WHO Director-General but by joint decision of the ministers of health in the region itself.

To increase contacts and communications between headquarters and those "out there," Brundtland has asked the regional directors to help her find vacant regional or country positions for some WHO professionals currently working in Geneva—the first time headquarters has asked to be involved in regional personnel decisions [Robbins in *Public Health Reports*, 1/99].

These WHO reforms are carried out in a **climate of relative optimism.** Major advances in health during the 20th century have laid the foundation for further dramatic progress in the years ahead, notes The World Health Report 1998; and although these health gains are most visible in industrialized countries, they are slowly materializing in many poorer countries. To anchor and build on those gains will require **a sus-**

tained investment in the health of women, counsels the Report: The health of women largely determines the health of their children—the adults of tomorrow.

Tempering that optimism is the indication that developing countries are now facing a double threat: from noncommunicable diseases (heart disease, cancer, diabetes, and other "lifestyle" diseases"), which are expected to become more prevalent in the Third World in the 21st century, and from infectious diseases, which will simply hold their own [The World Health Report 1998]. (In the latter group, HIV/AIDS will continue to earn the title "deadliest menace.") This double threat imposes the need for difficult decisions about allocating scarce resources—especially difficult when, as experience shows, reduced spending on the control of communicable diseases can result in their returning home with a vengeance. And international travel and trade increase the risk of global spread [ibid.].

Even as WHO sets its own priorities for the end of this biennium and the beginning of the millennium, money is tight, but relief could come in January of the year 2000.

Back in January 1999, WHO's Executive Board was presented with a budget for 2000–01 that required an increase of nearly one-fifth in voluntary contributions to the organization. The new budget is intended to be more transparent, reflecting the new structure of WHO, and Dr. Brundtland believes that the reforms already under way within the organization—as well as growing recognition that health in one region affects well-being in all others—will attract that further support from member states. Getting the United States to pay its dues is a top priority.

5. Children and Youth
By Lara E. Saxman

One of the highest profile and arguably most effective U.N. agencies is the United Nations Children's Fund (UNICEF), a powerful advocate for a child's right to health, education, and fundamental well-being. Since its inception in 1946, child survival rates have doubled worldwide; and UNICEF's dedicated efforts on behalf of this vulnerable population earned it the Nobel Peace Prize in 1965. For all the successes of UNICEF and other members of the U.N.'s community of humanitarian and development agencies, though, over 12 million children die in the developing world each year—this from largely preventable causes. UNICEF itself maintains eight regional and 130-plus field offices in developing regions, and 84 percent of its staff works in the field [UNICEF Annual Report 1998]. In each country of operation, the under-five mortality rate, income level (GNP per capita), and size of the child population determine the size of UNICEF's program budget.

UNICEF is dependent on voluntary contributions from governments as well as from the private sector, including the national committees that sell the well-known "UNICEF cards" among their other fund-raising efforts. Projected resources for 1998–99 are $1.9 billion, reflecting a 6 percent drop from the previous two-year budget. This is believed to be the result of decreasing contributions in a period of falling resources for development, as well as of a strong U.S. dollar, which devalues donations made in other currencies [UNA-USA, *InterDependent*, Spring 1998].

A needed boost came in May 1998, with the announcement by businessman and philanthropist Ted Turner of the first round of grants from his $1 billion gift to the United Nations. Nearly three-quarters of the initial $22 million disbursed by Turner's **United Nations Foundation** goes to women and population stabilization and to children's health—two of the Foundation's broad priorities. Among the specific targets of the initial grants are the eradication of many childhood killer diseases in various nations of Africa, the disarmament of child soldiers in Sierra Leone, and the provision of vitamin supplements for mothers in the Indonesian province of West Timor [*New York Times*, 5/20/98]. The Foundation plans to distribute $100 million per year over a decade.

UNICEF is a member of both the U.N. Secretariat's **Executive Committee on Humanitarian Affairs** and the **Executive Committee of the U.N. Development Group**—one of the Secretary-General's latest efforts to reform and coordinate the operations of the numerous U.N. funds, programs, and other bodies in these areas [see "The United Nations and Development" in Chapter III of the present volume]. Building a more unified country approach has also been a goal of U.N. reform, and UNICEF participated in the pilot phase of a project that employed a provisional **U.N. Development Assistance Framework (UNDAF)**—newly formulated common guidelines—in 18 country programs, where its main partners are the United Nations Development Programme (UNDP), the United Nations Population Fund (UNFPA), and the World Food Programme (WFP). Shared indictors for monitoring progress toward development goals were the desired result of the exercise, with considerable savings and more efficient operations to follow. The pilot has now been completed and evaluated and the provisional UNDAF guidelines finalized. Twenty more countries were scheduled to begin the exercise in June 1999 [U.N. press release DSG/SM/56, 6/8/99].

Rights of the Child

The most widely accepted human rights document in history is the one that spells out the rights of the child—from the right to a name and nationality, to economic and social rights (education and health care, for example) and civil and political rights (freedom of expression and freedom of religion, among them), to special rights and protections (refugee children and disabled children are named). Adopted by the General Assembly in 1989, the Convention on the Rights of the Child has been ratified by every country but the United States and anarchic, war-torn Somalia.

Monitoring the progress of the 191 states parties in implementing the convention, and recommending the means of improvement, is the **Committee on the Rights of the Child**—ten independent experts "of high moral standing and recognized competence" in convention-related fields. A proposed amendment would expand that number to 18 to accommodate a "rapidly growing workload" [U.N. press release HR/4410, 5/12/99]. At the 20th session of the Committee, held in Geneva, January 11–29, 1999, the Committee considered six reports on the state of children's rights, two from developed countries (Austria, Sweden), and four from developing ones (Belize, Barbados, Guinea, and Yemen) [HR/4403, 1/29/99]. (Reports are due two years after ratification and every five years after that.) The 53rd General Assembly "recogniz[ed] that [domestic] legislation alone is not enough to prevent violations of the rights of the child" and recommended that, "within their mandates," all U.N. agencies and mechanisms of the U.N. system "pay attention to particular situations in which children are in danger and where their rights are violated, and that they take into account the work of the Committee on the Rights of the Child." It welcomed, without specifying, "the positive results of the cooperation" between the Committee and UNICEF [A/Res/53/128].

At the UNICEF-organized **World Summit for Children** held in September 1990, representatives of over 150 countries made a significant commitment to meet 27 specific goals on a wide range of development issues by the year 2000, fleshing out the principles and provisions of the Convention. During this pre-millennial decade, UNICEF has been working at the country level with nongovernmental organizations and its U.N. partners to meet as many of these ambitious goals as possible. They include universal access to basic education, a one-third reduction in under-five mortality, and immunization of 90 percent of the world's children against six child-killer diseases.

For UNICEF and others helping to ensure that children receive the legal and other protections the Convention promises them before and after birth, the 21st century will be no less demanding.

Education

As the new century opens, almost a billion people, two-thirds of them women, will be unable to read a book or even sign their name, and over 130 million children of primary school age in the developing world will still be without access to a basic education [*The State of the World's Children 1999*], viewed as the mortar of a productive, healthy, and tolerant society. The most recent of UNICEF's annual *State of the World's Children* speaks of bringing about an "education revolution," whose bywords are learning for life; accessibility, quality, and flexibility; gender sensitivity and girls' education; the state as key partner; and care for the young child. The aim is not only to give children basic numeracy and literacy skills but also to equip them to appreciate their own rights, respect the rights of others, and take control of their own lives.

One of the obstacles cited as blocking the road to education for all is instruction in the former colonial language, despite evidence that children learn more quickly when first taught in their native tongue. UNICEF is currently sponsoring projects in Australia, Latin America, and Southeast Asia that offer native tongue and bilingual education [ibid.]. Another obstacle is the fact that, in many parts of the world, girls continue to suffer discrimination and prejudice, no less in education than in any other realm. In fact, girls make up nearly two-thirds of the primary school-age children in the developing world who are *not* in school; and even for those who are able to attend, both curriculum and the environment usually contribute to their sense of inferiority. UNICEF's Girls' Education Initiative is implementing measures in over 50 countries to promote "girl-friendly" schools and teaching material, and to ensure that girls feel safe and appreciated in the classroom.

An example of the education revolution at work is supplied by the Pratham Mumbai Education Initiative in Mumbai, India—a collaboration among education activists, preschool instructors, community groups, and government officials to make school accessible to disadvantaged children, help them enroll in school, and stay there. UNICEF contributed at the outset by facilitating a dialogue on education, bringing together city officials and representatives from diverse communities. By 1997, the Initiative was running schools in slums and other disadvantaged areas for 38,000 children [UNICEF Annual Report 1998].

Health and Nutrition

"The most sustainable investment we can make in healthy populations is to take proper care of our children's health," U.N. Secretary-General Kofi Annan is quoted as saying. "That investment—be it in terms of proper primary care facilities, access to vaccines and treatment or simply access to care—will continue to yield throughout life" [www.unfoundation.org/ issues/children/children.cfm]. UNICEF has worked tirelessly on this front— today it supports programs in 138 countries aimed at providing health care, nutrition, and access to safe water and sanitation—often with impressive results. Despite such efforts, however, an estimated 2 million children die each year from vaccine-preventable illnesses: diphtheria, measles, pertussis, polio, tuberculosis, and tetanus [UNICEF Facts & Figures 1998].

Immunization campaigns are particularly important in the fight against these diseases, and require the close collaboration of governments, UNICEF, UNDP, the World Health Organization, and NGOs to conduct them. In an earlier era, such campaigns contributed to the eradication of smallpox; today, they are close to winning the war against polio. China's President Jiang Zemin kicked off a drive on polio in his country, for example, by helping to administer vaccine; 82 million children are said to have been immunized during that single, day-long effort [www.unfoundation. org/issues/children/polio.cfm]. In civil war-afflicted areas, such as Sudan and Afghanistan, "Days of Tranquility" have been negotiated to allow the immunizations to go forward.

The fight against malnutrition and the efforts to provide safe water and sanitation require the same sort of dedication and collaboration. Three of the nutritional problems high on the UNICEF agenda are those brought about by iodine, iron, and vitamin A deficiencies, affecting an estimated 2 billion people around the world, mostly women and children, and threatening mental retardation, blindness, and anemia [ibid.]. Malnutrition is particularly acute in sub-Saharan Africa where, thanks to years of political instability, armed conflicts, and abnormal weather patterns, it is a cause of about half of all deaths of children under five years of age. Here, UNICEF tries to develop and promote long-term solutions that nurture and develop links between food and health care for children and their mothers.

HIV/AIDS. Despite the impression in the industrialized world that the threat of HIV/AIDS is receding at the close of the 1990s, the disease is responsible for an increasing number of deaths in many parts of the developing world, with girls and women the most numerous victims. "What was once a predominantly male disease has become a heterosexually-spread pandemic which is now consigning tens of millions of girls to a cruel, slow death," reports UNICEF Executive Director Carol Bellamy [www.unicef.org/newsline/99pr9.htm]. In western Kenya, for example, almost one in four girls between 15 and 19 is now infected with HIV, the virus that causes AIDS, compared to only one in 25 boys in the same age group. Social norms, poverty, anatomy, the nature of HIV transmission, and the persistence of misinformation about the disease have conspired to make this so.

At the same time, *any* infant, male or female, whose mother is HIV-positive may be infected through her breast milk—a 1-in-7 risk, according to UNICEF's *Progress of Nations 1997*. This fact presents the World Health Organization, UNICEF, and the Joint U.N. Programme on AIDS (UNAIDS—"a U.N. family response" to the disease) with a difficult choice: Do they counsel infected women to breastfeed, and risk passing the disease to their children, or do they recommend breast-milk substitutes, which can expose the infant to lethal diarrhea and other health hazards? Both WHO and UNICEF continue to proclaim the nutritional and health benefits of breast milk but have sought to offer health care providers "guidance when advising infected mothers" [www.who.int/dsa/cat98/aids8. htm]. Three guides recently published by WHO identify factors that influence HIV transmission from mother to child and discuss a variety of measures that government officials and health care professionals can take to reduce the risk of infection ["HIV and Infant Feeding: Guidelines for Decision-Makers," "A Guide for Health Care Managers and Supervisors," and "HIV and Infant Feeding: Review of HIV Transmission Through Breastfeeding"].

HIV/AIDS is likewise responsible for huge numbers of orphaned children, who may themselves be infected with the virus. In 1997, 1.7 million children were orphaned by the disease, more than 90 percent of them in sub-Saharan Africa [*New York Times*, 9/18/98]. Although many of these youngsters have been absorbed into extended families, they often face prejudice and discrimination and, some observers say, are likely to suffer physical and sexual abuse *and* to suffer from malnutrition and generally poor health [ibid.]. UNICEF is working at many levels to address the often complex issues surrounding AIDS—from promoting the rights of women to organizing shelters for orphaned children.

Bangkok—a destination for thousands of girls from rural Thailand each year, many of whom end up becoming prostitutes and contracting AIDS—offers one success story. Back in 1995, UNICEF teamed up with a top Bangkok hotel to launch the Youth Career and Development Program, training young women, age 17 to 19, in the basics of the hotel trade (hospitality, housekeeping, floral arrangement, cooking, and English). The hotel provided three meals a day, uniforms and shoes, and a small daily stipend; UNICEF was responsible for lodging, travel expenses, and health insurance as well as workshops on rights and education. Seven other top hostelries in the city have since signed on as sponsors, and in 1998 major hotels in the Philippines launched a version of their own [UNICEF Annual Report 1998].

Sexual and Reproductive Health. The work of the U.N. family in preventing the spread of HIV/AIDS is complemented by efforts of U.N. agencies and NGOs in the area of sexual and reproductive health. The United Nations Population Fund (UNFPA) and International Planned Parenthood Federation (IPPF), for example, are the major players in a campaign to publicize the lack of family planning and other health care services for women and girls in many areas of the world. UNFPA-IPPF's "Face to Face" campaign confronts a traditional practice in regions of Africa and the Middle East, female genital mutilation (FGM), involving the excision of part or all of the external female genitalia, and sometimes the stitching or narrowing of the vaginal opening (infibulation). The operation, usually performed on young girls and under less than hygienic conditions, places an estimated 2 million children at risk of physical and emotional injury each year [*CaribWoman*, 10/7/97]. A Somalian-born supermodel, Waris Dirie (herself infibulated at age 5), was named in 1997 as spokesperson for the international campaign. "I was strong enough to survive and I want to make a difference," she said. "I can talk because I have experienced the pain" [IPPF press release, 2/28/98].

In January 1999, Senegal passed legislation banning FGM, following in the footsteps of Egypt, which had renewed its ban on the practice in December 1997. The Senegalese legislation owes much to a movement of village women, who had taken part in a nationwide program conducted by a local NGO and funded by a UNICEF program to educate them about their rights. President Abdou Diouf threw his support behind the movement, helping to spread the campaign to other villages and to give the campaign weight [www.unicef.org/newsline/99pr1.htm]. Over recent years FGM has been officially outlawed in Burkina Faso, Central African Republic, Djibouti, Ethiopia, Ghana, Guinea-Conakry, and Togo, but it will take more than legislation to end a traditional practice.

Children and Armed Conflict

The Convention on the Rights of the Child calls on the states parties to "ensure protection and care of children who are affected by an armed conflict," and for some years now the U.N. Secretary-General has appointed a Special Representative on that very subject (today, Olara A. Otunnu). The decade's toll on young lives and limbs is 2 million killed; 6 million maimed, injured, or permanently disabled; and 1 million orphaned or separated from parents [U.N. press release HR/4338, 11/9/98]. Child soldiers are no less the victims of their countries' wars. And at an estimated 300,000 today [ibid.], they are certainly no rarity—this despite pledges by the parties to the Geneva Conventions of 1949, the Convention on the Rights of the Child, and the Statute of the International Criminal Court (ICC) to refrain from recruiting or conscripting under-15-year-olds (a war crime in the eyes of the ICC).

In acknowledgment of "the harmful impact of armed conflict on children," the Security Council conducted a special session in June 1998 to explore the problem and indicate its concern. A Presidential Statement issued after the session condemned the targeting of children in armed conflicts, urged nations to comply with the provisions of international conventions, and advised that the Council would be in close contact with Special Representative Otunnu [S/PRST/1998/18].

UNICEF, while working through diplomatic and political channels to eliminate the conscription of child soldiers (it is, for example, attempting to garner support for an optional protocol to the Children's Rights Convention that would raise to 18 the minimum age of military recruitment), has been doing some of its most important work in demobilizing these youthful forces and reintegrating them into civil society. And in company with other agencies, UNICEF is employing such interrelated strategies as family reunification, mobilization of the child care support system, psycho-social healing, medical screening and treatment, and school and vocational training to help the war-scarred children recover their lives and their health ["UNICEF and Humanitarian Crises: An Overview of Operational and Program Strategies," 1998]. In Liberia, for example, UNICEF aids the Support to War-Affected Youth Program, which helps roughly 6,000 children each year. In Sierra Leone, a UNICEF-supported network that receives the help of ECOMOG, the peacekeeping arm of the West African economic community, has seen an encouraging response to its efforts at reuniting children with their families. In March 1999 rebel forces released 51 abducted children into the care of UNICEF aid workers, who then helped to reunite them with their families. A total of 92 children had been returned as of mid-April 1999 [www.unicef.org/newsline/99pr12.htm].

Exploitation of Children

The Convention recognizes the right of children to be protected from all forms of exploitation prejudicial to their welfare, naming child labor; sexual exploitation; drug abuse; sale, trafficking, and abduction; and, indeed, "any aspects . . . not covered" in specific articles. The first on this list, **child labor,** gets particular play today, when media exposés and celebrity-led campaigns are publicizing the use of child labor to produce many of the consumer products popular in the industrialized world. International Labour Organization (ILO) statistics indicate that almost 250 million of the world's children are working simply to ensure the family's survival; and of these, at least 120 million work full time and at jobs that are dangerous and exploitive [see *A Global Agenda: Issues Before the 53rd General Assembly of the United Nations*, p. 248]. The largest number work in agriculture, the service sector, and small-scale manufacturing; the majority of these working children are to be found in Asia, Africa, and Latin America (in descending order).

At the International Labour Conference in June 1999—the annual meeting of delegates from all ILO member states—the representatives of government, labor, and business (the ILO's "tripartite" membership) adopted unanimously a **Worst Forms of Child Labour Convention,** targeting "child slavery, forced labor, trafficking, debt bondage, serfdom, prostitution, pornography, . . . exploitive work in industries using dangerous machinery and hazardous substances," and forced military recruitment of those under 18 [Stephanie Nebehay for Reuters, 6/17/99]. A separate recommendation (these have less weight than the provisions of the convention itself) urges ratifying states to criminalize these practices and impose penalties on the perpetrators [ibid.]. (The convention enters into force after two states have ratified it.) The ILO's Statistical Information and Monitoring

Project on Child Labor continues to collect information on child labor, its scale and type, and plans to compile an extensive database over the next few years [www.dol.gov/dov/ilab/public/media/reports/iclp/sweat5/execsum.htm]—information that will be useful to governments when devising national policies to implement the convention.

Researchers have identified universal primary education as one of the best weapons against child labor. Acting on this finding in the Asian subcontinent, for example, UNICEF and the Nepal Rugmark Foundation joined forces in 1997 to provide child carpet workers with "non-formal" schooling through local NGOs. UNICEF pays for the schooling as well as for the running of the Rugmark offices, staff salaries, and promotional campaigns. A similar UNICEF-Rugmark program has since been initiated in India to help loom workers attend school, and the Indian Human Rights Commission has started its own programs to promote compulsory primary education and elimination of child labor [UNICEF Annual Report 1998].

Evidence of the persistence and global nature of **sexual exploitation** comes by way of children's charities around the world, their reports indicating that roughly a million children enter the sex market (willingly and unwillingly) each year. In Asia alone more than 650,000 children under the age of 16 work as prostitutes; UNICEF cites a lesser but still significant number (100,000–300,000) in North America; and in many regions of the world women and children are abducted and sold into sexual slavery or used in the "sex tourism" industry. Currently, more than 100 Web sites are promoting teenage commercial sex in Asia alone [www.missingkids.com/html/ncmec_default_ec_tourism_background.html], adding to the difficulty of containing the problem and undermining the effectiveness of national legislation outlawing the sexual exploitation of children. One country that appears to have taken decisive action is China, which in April 1999 joined with UNICEF in developing a program that gives the police the technical and financial support it needs to capture and jail kidnappers and to reunite stolen children with their families [UN Wire, 4/26/99].

Refugee and Displaced Children

Refugee children—52 percent of the world's large and growing population uprooted by civil conflicts—are among those singled out for special protection by the Child's Rights Convention. The United Nations High Commissioner for Refugees (UNHCR) does have a specific set of policies and guidelines for dealing with refugee and displaced children, but following through can be a near-impossibility in the chaos of the refugee camps or other crisis-driven locale. And even when humanitarian organizations disaggregate refugees, notes the Senior Coordinator for Refugee Children at UNHCR, the particular needs of children often remain "invisible," since they are apt to be made dependents of their parents or are grouped with women ["On the Record Excom '98," 10/5/98, an advocacy group's report on the UNHCR Executive Committee meeting]. Additional problems arise in the case of those who are orphaned or separated from their families. The hundreds of thousands of Kosovar men, women, and children fleeing the campaign of "ethnic cleansing" by Serbian armed forces in the province presented UNHCR, UNICEF, and other humanitarian aid providers with their greatest refugee challenge of recent months. UNICEF typically sought to provide clothing, blankets, shelter, and essential drugs to all refugees to combat acute respiratory infections, which were widespread. There were food supplements for children, who were also immunized upon entering the camps—this based on estimates that more than half had not received all their shots, given the instability in Kosovo over the previous year [www.unicef.org/kosovo/stat1.htm]. UNICEF has helped to support a network of local trauma centers for refugee children too. The humanitarian aid givers now turn to the growing population of refugees from, for example, the war between Ethiopia and Eritrea—an exodus that will overwhelm crisis-ridden and already impoverished border states like Somalia.

Youth

A major yet often overlooked demographic group is the world's 1 billion youth. Today one in six persons falls into the 15 to 24 age range and roughly 85 percent of them live in the developing world. No longer children, yet not quite adults, youth have special concerns and face special challenges. The social and economic changes of the past decade have intensified many of the pressures on youth in both the industrialized world and the developing world, and so too the recent economic crisis that began in Asia and has spread to different regions. Other demographics also contribute to the situation of youth—for example, the declining fertility rates and increased life expectancy that make for an ageing population, and sometimes make for social and economic policies that favor the latter ["United Nations Report on Global Situation of Youth Shows Changing Trends," www.un.org/events/youth98/backinfo/yrefort.htm]. Some pressures may be felt unequally by different portions of the youth population, a World Health Organization study has found. In the developing world, for example, the suicide rate of females 15–24 is 75 percent greater than the suicide rate for males in the same age category [ibid.].

The Youth Unit

The United Nations Youth Unit, founded in 1946 and today part of the Division for Social Policy and Development (itself part of the Department of Social and Economic Affairs) is working to enhance awareness of the global situation of youth and of the rights of youth; to promote the development of national youth policies and plans for action with the cooperation of nongovernmental youth organizations; and to strengthen participation of youth in all aspects of society, increasing their impact on national development and international cooperation [UNDPI, "The United Nations Youth Agenda," 11/97]. A networker on a grand scale, it not only acts as liaison between and consultant to U.N. agencies that deal with youth in various contexts but also acts as liaison/consultant between and among U.N. agencies, "outside" NGOs, and youth groups. It reports to the General Assembly through the Economic and Social Council and the Commission for Social Development.

The U.N. Declaration on the Promotion among Youth of the Ideals of Peace, Mutual Respect and Understanding Between Peoples, adopted by the General Assembly in 1965, recognized the value of harnessing the ideals and energy of young people for the benefit of society—the first official U.N. document on youth concerns. International Youth Year 1985, proclaimed by the General Assembly, called attention to youth "as a major human resource for development and key agents for social change, economic development and technological innovation" at home. In that same year the Assembly gave its approval to "guidelines for further planning and suitable follow-up in the field of youth" [A/Res/40/103] and, a decade later, approved the World Programme of Action for Youth to the Year 2000 and Beyond. Several years in the drafting, it offers policy guidelines and practical suggestions for national and international action to improve the situation of youth and realize their potential for "full, effective, and constructive participation in society" [A/Res/50/81, and see www. un.org/esa/socdev/unyin/content.htm]. Education, employment, hunger and poverty, health, environment, drug abuse, juvenile delinquency, leisure-time activities, girls and young women, and the participation of youth are identified as "priority areas." The U.N. Secretary-General will be reporting to the 54th General Assembly on the progress made in carrying out the suggested actions [A/Res/52/83].

World Youth Forum

Broadening and strengthening communication between the U.N. system and nongovernmental youth organizations is seen as one of the most important steps toward carrying out the world action program, and a series of World Youth Forums is facilitating the networking process. The third and latest of these forums—held in Braga, Portugal, August 2–6, 1998— focused on "youth participation for human development" and went on to adopt a Braga Youth Action Plan that the U.N. Secretary-General has described as "a joint commitment to Youth Participation for Human Development made by youth NGOs, the United Nations System and other international organizations in partnership" [A/53/378]. Education, youth participation in political decision-making, and the effects on youth of structural adjustment (among other economic policies) are a few of the issues addressed. The 500 delegates from 150 countries recommended that the United Nations organize an ad hoc event on youth rights, to take the form of a world conference or a special session of the General Assembly. World Youth Forum number four will be held in Senegal in the year 2000.

In nearby Lisbon, at the close of the Braga forum, came the first-ever World Conference of Ministers Responsible for Youth (August 8–12, 1998)—like the forum, a bid to raise the profile of youth issues. Joined by representatives of NGOs from around the world, the ministers discussed strategies and national policy objectives for increasing the role of young people in political and civil society and approved a Lisbon Declaration on Youth Policies and Programmes, which it presented to the U.N. General Assembly [interview with William D. Angel, Officer in Charge of the U.N. Youth Unit, 3/28/99].

6. Ageing
By Susana Urra Calzada

A demographic revolution is under way. Better nutrition, improved living conditions, and expanded health care have extended the average life span, while declining fertility rates (particularly in developed countries) have been reducing the proportion of young people. This **"graying of the planet"** amounts to nothing less than a radical restructuring of society.

The figures are telling. In 1955, newborns had a global life expectancy of 48. Their own great-grandchildren, born in 2030, can look forward to an additional 25 years of life. By then, the number of elderly people in China will exceed the entire population of the United States right now [The World Health Report 1998]. Today, one out of every ten people is 60 or older; by 2050 the ratio will be one in five. And the older population itself is ageing. The "eldest of the old"—people aged 80 and over—are currently the fastest-growing group in the world. Now estimated at 11 percent of the over-60 population, in just half a decade they will make up 27 percent of that same age group [ibid.; *New York Times*, 2/11/99; Report of the Expert Group Meeting on Care Giving and Older Persons, Malta, 11/30–12/2/97].

But even though ageing is a global phenomenon, it is not occurring evenly in all parts of the world. Some developing nations still have significantly younger populations than do the developed countries; today one out of five Europeans is 60 or older versus one out of 20 Africans. By 2025, however, an estimated 70 percent of older persons will be living in developing regions [E/CN.5/1997/4].

Many national governments are beginning to feel the **political, economic, and social effects of these demographic changes.** Policy-makers are confronting such matters as the contraction of the working population, the rising demand for publicly supported pension systems and other safety nets, the changing role of state and family in caring for the elderly, and the integration of the elderly in the country's economic and social life. Of particular concern are the prevention of disease and disability among the elderly and the provision of specialized health care on a large scale. Some of the wealthier countries admit they have trouble meeting the needs of their present population of elderly citizens [The World Health Report 1998]. Developing regions in particular—where poverty is endemic and the social service infrastructures inadequate—will have even more trouble dealing with the consequences of rapidly growing older populations. Many developing countries are anticipating a need for direct technical, educational, and financial aid from the developed nations to establish or expand their programs for the elderly [Fourth Review and Appraisal of the Implementation of the IPPA]. Yet the volume of aid to developing countries, now at 0.22 percent of GDP of the industrialized countries, has been decreasing throughout the 1990s [Report of the Secretary-General on the Work of the Organization, 1998].

The elderly may comprise an ever-larger segment of society, but national and international law has so far tended to overlook their specific needs. Although two other vulnerable groups, women and children, are by now the subject of comprehensive global conventions, **the rights of older persons** are only implicitly acknowledged in one international legal document: the International Covenant on Economic, Social and Cultural Rights, whose article 9 recognizes a right to social security, including social insurance. In 1982, acknowledging the importance of current demographic trends and the need for guidance in setting up national programs on ageing, the United Nations organized a **World Assembly on Ageing** in Vienna, which drafted an **International Plan of Action on Ageing** that was adopted by the General Assembly in the same year [A/Res/37/51]. This Plan of Action established priorities for governments—in infrastructure, health, housing, family, education, social welfare, and income security for the elderly. The overall objective of the Plan, as stated in the General Assembly's set of **Principles for Older Persons (1991)**, is to promote the independence, participation, care, self-fulfillment, and dignity of this population [A/Res/46/91]. The following year the General Assembly issued a Proclamation on Ageing that designated 1999 the International Year of Older Persons (IYOP) [A/Res/47/5]. The Proclamation urged the international community to find a new and active role for the elderly, both in post-industrial societies driven by a technology-based work culture and in developing societies beginning to experience the dissolution of traditional family structures.

The initiatives developed through the IYOP are intended to encourage U.N. member states, the U.N. system, other intergovernmental bodies, and nongovernmental organizations to develop projects that implement the International Plan of Action on Ageing, employing the Principles for Older Persons. **Preparations for the IYOP** have been coordinated by the Department of Economic and Social Affairs (DESA), which is in charge of the permanent activities on ageing at the United Nations. DESA and its Division for Social Policy and Development have set up a special Programme on Ageing for 1999 that is run by the IYOP secretariat. An intergovernmental Support Group, later redesignated the Consultative Group, was created in 1996 to serve as an informal forum for member states to discuss their individual progress in the development of programs on ageing. The IYOP secretariat deemed it a good sign that, by the time of the official launching of the Year, half the member states had established national committees or focal points to develop initiatives in observance of the Year.

The **International Year of Older Persons** was officially launched on October 1, 1998, at a day-long event organized by the NGO Committee on Aging, in cooperation with the U.N. Programme on Ageing and the U.N. Department of Public Information. In his opening address, Secretary-General Kofi Annan (recently turned 60, and thus qualifying as an "older person," he noted) explored the Year's theme, "Towards a Society for All Ages"—described as a society that "does not caricature older persons as patients and pensioners. Instead, it sees them as both agents and beneficiaries of development" [Countdown to 1999, 11/98].

The overall goal of the Year is to promote the Plan and Principles for Older Persons by encouraging "active ageing," that is, the participation and integration of older persons in the social, economic, and cultural life of their nation. The IYOP program seeks to involve family and community as well as government in this process [Recommendations, Conceptual and Operational Frameworks, IYOP 1999 Web site: www.un.org/esa/socdev/iyop]. Among the specific targets are children and youth, in the interest of fostering early life-long development of good health, work skills, and family/community networks [Raising Awareness: The Society for All Ages, Operational Framework, IYOP 1999 Web site]. To reach so broad an audience, the IYOP program is reaching out to the media and the business sector as well as promoting research and information exchange on ageing-related matters at the local, national, regional, and international levels.

On the IYOP list of **recommended initiatives** at the local level are cultural activities such as fairs and exhibits, and information campaigns on topics ranging from rural and urban ageing to technology for the elderly and from caregiving structures to multigenerational relationships within the family. At the national level, governments are being urged to take into account the needs of older people when drafting policies dealing with unemployment, social security, consumption, poverty, and social exclusion [IYOP 1999 Web site]. On the international calendar for 1999 and 2000 are conferences on ageing-related themes sponsored by NGOs, various

U.N. bodies, and other intergovernmental organizations—sometimes alone, more often in partnership.

U.N. Headquarters in New York, for instance, was the venue for an exploration of the specific demands posed by a rapidly ageing population on such infrastructural elements as housing, transportation, and recreation facilities ("Caring Communities for the 21st Century: Villages and Cities for All Generations—Towards a Society for All Ages," February 10–11, 1999), enlisting as co-sponsors the U.N. Programme on Ageing, the U.N. Department of Public Information, the International Council for Caring Communities, and the U.N. Center for Human Settlements (Habitat). The New York-based NGO Committee on Ageing, for its part, is sponsoring a four-part series of "Age Quake Debates," the first of which, held on March 4, 1999, dealt with ageing and gender; the others will take up ageing and the media, relationships between the elderly and younger generations, and different generations of peacemakers (the debates are dedicated to Ambassador Julia T. De Alvarez, Alternate Permanent Representative of the Dominican Republic to the United Nations and a leading spokesperson on ageing issues at the Organization) [Calendar of events for 1999 and beyond, IYOP 1999 Web site]. Other conferences scheduled in observance of the IYOP take up such issues as ageing in Africa, global trends in care and services for the elderly, and the human rights of older persons [ibid.].

The 53rd Session of the General Assembly inaugurated its IYOP activities with a discussion of the Secretary-General's report on "Preparations for the International Year of Older Persons" [A/53/294], outlining country-specific activities. Between October 5 and 7, 43 member state representatives took the floor to explore the implications of ageing populations on national policy-making and the reasons why developing countries in particular should establish national strategies on ageing. The General Assembly also spoke of the need to pay special attention to older women in their role as caregivers for the elderly—a function that will be in greater demand as the number of older persons increases worldwide.

The Assembly's resolution in support of the IYOP called upon the United Nations and institutions of civil society to incorporate into national legislation the right of older persons to equal access to social services and to avoid age and gender bias in their treatment of older women [A/53/615]. The IYOP program itself stresses income security and health care strategies for older women who, because of greater longevity, already make up the majority of the population of elderly persons.

World Health Day 1999—the most recent of the annual observances sponsored by the World Health Organization (WHO)—was tailored to IYOP's "active ageing" theme, encouraging individuals and communities to adopt healthy life-styles early on and calling on governments to promote policies that reduce social inequalities and poverty. "Older people are often viewed as a homogenous group from mainly industrialized countries, who no longer contribute to their families and societies, and may even be a burden," said WHO Director-General Gro Harlem Brundtland. "The truth could not be more different." WHO is launching its own Global Movement for Active Aging, which will be inaugurated on October 2, 1999, with a global walk, the "Global Embrace" [UN Wire, 4/7/99]. A high point of the IYOP (observed until December 31) will be a Special Session of the General Assembly, October 1, to assess the Year's achievements and plan future activities on ageing.

The international community's ongoing work in this area includes the **periodic reviews of progress in implementing the International Plan of Action on Ageing** that are undertaken by the U.N.'s Commission for Social Development, an intergovernmental body. The fifth of these quadrennial reviews, which is scheduled for 2001, will assess the impact of ageing on national budgets, pension systems, and health care through data provided by member states and appraise their projects intended to integrate the elderly into society. Currently being readied is a two-year project aimed at developing a **"Research Agenda on Ageing for the 21st Century,"** to be conducted by the U.N. Secretariat in association with the International Association of Gerontology. Viewed as a major initiative, it is "intended to influence the development of national policy and research on ageing in the next decade" [Countdown, 11/98]. The Commission for Social Development, for its part, has been encouraged to **mainstream the issue of older persons** into the preparatory work for the General Assembly's year 2000 review of the progress made in implementing the recommendations of the 1995 World Summit for Social Development at which heads of state pledged to "put people at the center of development" by, among other things, promoting social integration [A/Res/53/109]. A further evaluation of the IYOP itself is scheduled for the year 2001 ["Looking Ahead Beyond 1999," Operational Framework; available on IYOP Web site].

Of continuing concern to many bodies of the U.N. family is the fact that, even as the average life span increases, there is a **big gap between the health status—and the life expectancies—of the rich and of the poor.** Today, three out of every four people in the least developed countries will die before the age of 50, the average life span of half-a-century ago [The World Health Report 1998]. In Africa, a third of the population is not expected to survive past age 40 [Report of the Secretary-General on the Work of the Organization, 1998]. Still, reports WHO, the overall trend is toward longer, healthier lives— this thanks to social and economic advances that began in the industrialized world and are now slowly taking root in developing countries—and it offers the reminder that "increased longevity without increased quality of life is an empty prize" [The World Health Report 1998].

7. Disabled Persons

By Nina Stechler Hayes and Elizabeth A. Lynch

More than 500 million people around the globe have a mental or physical disability, and the United Nations has "sought to advance the status of disabled persons and to improve their lives"—an agenda rooted in the Organization's founding principles of human rights and equality [www.un.org/esa/socdev/disun]. The 54th Session of the General Assembly will review the Secretary-General's report on the **implementation of the World Programme of Action Concerning Disabled Persons (WPA).** Adopted by the Assembly at the end of 1981 (the International Year of the Disabled Person, IYPD) and updated in 1997, the WPA continues to influence disability policies and national programs aimed at equalization of opportunity as well as at prevention and rehabilitation.

The IYDP—which inaugurated the U.N.'s Decade on Disabled Persons, 1982–92—followed a decade of increased U.N. attention to the needs of disabled populations. The General Assembly's "Declaration on the Rights of Mentally Retarded Persons" (1971) and its "Declaration on the Rights of Disabled Persons" (1975) embraced "the growing international concept of human rights of persons with disabilities and equalization of opportunities for them" [ibid.], with the aim of accelerating their social integration. Both of the declarations marked a departure from earlier social welfare approaches by emphasizing "the need to protect disabled persons from exploitation and provide them with proper legal procedures" [ibid.].

Among the resources available to member states in developing disability policies are the **Standard Rules on the Equalization of Opportunities for Persons with Disabilities** ("Standard Rules," 1994), a guide to legislative action affecting every aspect of national life—from education, employment, and social security to recreation, sports, and culture [A/Res/48/96]. In the same year the Standard Rules were approved, the Secretary-General appointed a **Special Rapporteur, Bengt Lindqvist of Sweden,** for a three-year term to monitor member states' legislative progress in these areas. In his report to the Commission on Social Development in 1997, Lindqvist noted the growing awareness of "disability issues in all regions, an observed rethinking of policies, and the introduction of national legislation based upon the Rules" [United Nations, *Disabled Persons Bulletin,* 1997]. The Commission voted to renew Lindqvist's appointment for an additional three years, to the year 2000. **Accessibility** has become the rallying cry of his second term, and he has encouraged member states to adopt policies to increase disabled persons' access to public transport, housing, and other facilities.

Complementing these efforts are the activities of the Economic and Social Commission for Asia and the Pacific (ESCAP), which proclaimed the period 1993–2002 as the **Asian and Pacific Decade of Disabled Persons.** The ESCAP agenda aims to promote "barrier-free societies," ensuring that disabled persons will have freedom of movement in public places. ESCAP created a draft guide on training disabled persons to train others to make use of newly accessible environments, and preparations are being made for a "training-of-trainers" seminar in late 1999 [E/CN.5/1999/5].

The **U.N.-sponsored world conferences of the 1990s** have also been instrumental in integrating disability-related issues into the global policy-making agenda. The heads of state who came together for the 1993 World Conference on Human Rights agreed that discrimination based on disability is a violation of human rights, the 1995 World Summit for Social Development directed special attention to the needs of disabled persons in such areas as employment, and the 1995 World Conference on Women addressed a variety of areas in which gender and disability issues intersect [A/49/435].

A small **Persons with Disabilities unit** in the Division for Social Policy and Development of the Secretariat assists "in the promotion of effective measures for prevention of disability, rehabilitation, . . . and . . . equality" [www.un.org/esa/socdev/disabled.htm]. The Secretary-General, in conjunction with the unit, administers the **U.N. Voluntary Fund on Disability** (founded 1993), which is designed to finance "field-based action related to the [WPA], with special emphasis directed to least developed and low-income developing countries and to especially disadvantaged groups of society" [www.un.org/esa/socdev/disunvf.htm]. Such countries are home to more than three-quarters of the world's disabled persons, and in many of these places 10 percent of the population has a physical or sensory impairment while an additional 15 percent serves as their caretakers. War, environmental pollution, and epidemic diseases are among the major cause of disabilities in these regions, preying on a population mired in poverty, already weakened by malnutrition, and with only limited access to medical care and health education.

Indeed, **prevention of disability** has become the focus of many U.N. health-related programs. Improvement of hygiene, better access to food and information on nutrition, and increased attention to prenatal and child health care are among the goals. "Programmes to prevent impairment or to ensure that impairments do not escalate into more limiting disabilities are less costly to society in the long run than having to care later for disabled persons," notes the **"Persons with Disabilities" U.N. Web page** [www.un.org/esa/socdev/diswpa04].

All such efforts call on the special interests and expertise of a variety of U.N. bodies—prominently the United Nations Educational, Scientific and Cultural Organization, World Health Organization (WHO), International Labour Organization (ILO), and United Nations Children's Fund (UNICEF). The **ILO,** for example, responding to the "growing difficulties in finding and keeping employment experienced by people with disabilities," has launched a Vocational Rehabilitation Programme [www.ilo.org/public/english/60empfor/dis/index.htm]. The program works with countries to provide vocational skills training for the disabled and to develop policies that will provide incentives for employers to hire disabled workers. **WHO,** among the most active promoters of improved quality of life for disabled people, sponsors a Disability and Rehabilitation Team (DAR) as part of its "Health-for-All by the Year 2002" strategy. During 1999–2000, DAR is joining up with **UNICEF** for a program aimed at the early detection of and intervention in pediatric disabilities. Another DAR program focuses on rehabilitation of especially vulnerable groups, including refugees; and still another encourages the mainstreaming of rehabilitation by primary health care centers [www.who.int/hpr/rhb/index.html].

The theme of the most recent **Day of the Disabled Person** (December 3, 1998) was "Arts, Culture and Independent Living." The celebration at U.N. Headquarters in New York sought to "ensure that persons with disabilities have opportunities to utilize their creative, artistic and intellectual potential to the enrichment of society as a whole" [www.un.org/esa/socdev/disid98.htm].

VI
Legal Issues
By Mark A. Drumbl

Much Ado about Something

In 1989 the 44th General Assembly declared **1990–99 the United Nations Decade of International Law** to encourage further efforts at codifying the principles of international law and at ensuring wider appreciation of them [A/Res/44/23]. The 53rd General Assembly, spanning the final year of that U.N. Decade, was an extraordinarily busy time for international lawyers—and saw breakthroughs in international humanitarian and criminal law that pushed the frontiers of international law beyond what was contemplated by even the most enthusiastic supporters of the 1989 resolution.

The international community has created a permanent International Criminal Court and has seen its ad hoc criminal tribunals for the former Yugoslavia and Rwanda hand down significant judgments. Nor have the year's international legal developments been confined to the *supra*-national: Judicial validation by Britain's House of Lords of Spain's request to extradite Chile's Augusto Pinochet to face torture charges could be a bellwether of national court involvement in coordinating the prosecution of international crimes. It could also herald the emergence of an international legal order in which claims of national sovereignty are secondary to the protection of human rights. In the area of dispute settlement, the year saw increased recourse by national governments to the International Court of Justice—an indication, perhaps, of an emerging "law habit" among states.

As the activities of international tribunals increase, so should the involvement of judges in formulating international law. Although this is traditionally (and still) the role of the treaty-drafting and inter-state negotiating process, judicial interpretation could begin "filling the gaps." The active participation of nongovernmental interest groups at all levels of international humanitarian law also reveals an important trend: the opening up of international law, once the preserve of states and diplomats, to grass-roots organizations and individual citizens.

In the end, an important challenge for the international legal community is to assess the limits of international law in promoting peace among citizens and nations. Law alone is unlikely to deter human rights abuses and promote national reconciliation in societies torn by such abuses in the past. In the absence of economic development, democratization, and social reform, the sanction of law can have little long-term effect.

1. Armed Intervention Outside U.N. Auspices

The Security Council has addressed many of the conflicts—both international and internecine—the world has seen this past year, but NATO's bombardment of the Federal Republic of Yugoslavia (FRY) and United States/United Kingdom sorties over Iraq have occurred without Security Council approval. This raises questions about both the political effectiveness of the Security Council and the legitimacy of such interventions. Ironically, these military actions in the name of promoting human rights may drive not only against the notion of state sovereignty but also against the international rule of law.

Former Yugoslavia: Kosovo

At the end of 1998, as the U.N. continued to search for a peaceful resolution to the conflict between the FRY and Kosovar Albanians, Belgrade's protracted noncompliance with a series of Security Council resolutions led NATO to threaten direct intervention. These resolutions—1160 [3/31/98], 1199 [9/23/98], 1203 [10/24/98], and 1207 [11/17/98]—adopted under Chapter VII of the Charter of the United Nations, call for the cessation of violence in Kosovo and call upon the FRY to ensure the safety of humanitarian personnel in Kosovo (whose monitoring Belgrade is to make possible); to withdraw its military and internal security forces from Kosovo; and (as explicitly stated in Resolution 1199) to facilitate the safe return of Kosovar refugees to their homes. They also require the FRY to cooperate fully with the International Criminal Tribunal for the Former Yugoslavia by allowing investigators access to Kosovo, enforcing arrest warrants, and transferring suspects.

In January 1999, as proof emerged of continued massacres of ethnic Albanians in Kosovo, the threat of NATO involvement escalated. Kosovar rebels also broke the terms of the same Security Council resolutions by ambushing Serb police patrols and otherwise failing to cease all terrorist actions. Ultimately, FRY President Slobodan Milosevic's twin decisions to reject the Rambouillet peace plan for Kosovo [see "Making and Keeping the Peace: The Former Yugoslavia" in the present volume] and to continue to raze Kosovar villages—all undertaken, in Secretary-General Annan's words, while "persist[ing] in rejection of a political settlement"—brought Operation Allied Force, NATO's extensive aerial bombardment of the FRY [Judith Miller in *New York Times*, 3/25/99].

None of the Security Council resolutions directly authorizes the use of force to ensure compliance with its terms. As a result, Operation Allied Force may raise questions about the effectiveness of the United Nations in determining the legitimate use of force under the international law of armed conflict. The Charter of the United Nations orders member states to refrain from the use of force against the territorial integrity of any state unless such force is used in self-defense or expressly authorized by the Security Council. Does NATO's decision to launch offensive military attacks to promote respect for human rights or compliance with cease-fire agreements without Security Council approval amount to a breach of the U.N. Charter? The fact that the alliance is a coalition of 19 nations may give its actions greater legitimacy than any unilateral action by a single state. **Operation Allied Force, however, was not an *international* intervention but a *multilateral* one.** This begs the question whether the Security Council can simply be bypassed when determining whether it is legitimate to use force. And what happens if another military alliance intervenes or opposes the other's intervention? Without the United Nations as a coordinating center, there is a risk that any intervention might escalate to international conflict on a wider scale. Concern about escalation of the conflict may well have prompted Secretary-General Annan's muted support of the NATO attacks. "It is indeed tragic that diplomacy has failed, but there are times when the use of force may be legitimate in the pursuit of peace," he said, but hastened to add: "As Secretary-General I have many times pointed out, not just in relation to Kosovo, that under the [U.N.] Charter, the Security Council has primary responsibility for maintaining international peace and security" [CNN, 3/24/99].

On March 24, 1999, Operation Allied Force began bombing selected military targets in Serbia, Montenegro, and Kosovo—FRY air defenses, command and control capability, government institutions, and military forces—but sometimes striking civilian installations, causing significant numbers of civilian casualties. The attacks escalated in intensity and breadth and, by late April 1999, had been joined by a NATO-led oil and trade embargo. The bombing drew to a close in June 1999 when the FRY agreed to an international civil and security presence endorsed and adopted by the United Nations [S/Res/1244, 6/10/99].

Simultaneous with the NATO attacks the **FRY undertook a "broad-based ethnic cleansing campaign across Kosovo,"** resulting in the massacre of approximately 10,000 ethnic Albanians (and the displacement of a million others) [Jane Perlez in *New York Times*, 3/28/99 and 4/10/99; and John Kifner in ibid., 7/18/99]. Prior to the Serb campaign, Kosovo was populated by an estimated 1.8 million ethnic Albanians and 200,000 Serbs. The arrival of peacekeepers in Kosovo triggered an exodus of over 80,000 of the 200,000 Kosovar Serbs. One challenge peacekeepers face is preventing reprisal killings of Serbs.

The fact that the Security Council did not approve military intervention in Kosovo or pass any resolution authorizing the use of force does not (and should not) constitute a principled basis for bypass. Although, arguably, there may be some justification in international law for the NATO involvement—the principle that nations may violate the sovereignty of another nation to stop widespread human rights abuses—**it is unclear whether the situation immediately *preceding* March 24 constituted such a humanitarian crisis.** (Tragically, there is no doubt that the situation in which the Kosovo Albanians found themselves after March 24 fit anyone's definition of humanitarian crisis [see S/Res/1239, 5/14/99].) In the end, Operation Allied Force might create within the scope of state practice or customary international law a broader future legal precedent for armed intervention with asserted humanitarian objectives.

No one believes that the members of a political body like the Security Council will see eye to eye on all future occasions when human rights are seriously threatened. For certain players committed to action this leaves no recourse but unilateral (or multilateral) armed intervention—a situation that feeds **the fears of U.N. Commissioner for Human Rights Mary Robinson, among others, that "war-making has become a tool of peace-making"** [AP, 5/1/99]. Institutional reform aimed at depoliticizing the treatment of humanitarian crises is a tall order, but international lawyers might take up the challenge, working to develop rules and criteria of humanitarian intervention that could be enforced by a non-political U.N. body.

Iraq

The United States and United Kingdom conducted **systematic attacks on Iraqi military installations** from December 16 to December 19, 1998; and military interventions, mostly in the form of **policing the "no-fly zones" in northern and southern Iraq,** continued throughout the winter and spring of 1999. Iraq has repeatedly questioned the international legitimacy of these zones, claiming that no U.N. Security Council resolution mandates their enforcement [BBC News, 12/29/98, 1/5/99, 3/4/99, and 4/2/99].

The December 1998 intervention, Operation Desert Fox—carried out by cruise missiles, designed to knock out key command-and-control elements and air-defense sites, as well as by manned bombers—was not approved by the Security Council, distinguishing this intervention from the use of force authorized by the Security Council in 1991 to expel Iraq from Kuwait [S/Res/678, 11/20/90]. Operation Desert Fox was criticized by the Russian, the Chinese, and continental European governments. Much of this criticism is similar to that arising out of NATO's involvement in the

FRY, namely, that no nation or group of nations should act unilaterally as the "world's policeman." In response, **the United States and Britain pointed out that the terms of Security Council Resolution 678 could accommodate the use of force to uphold "all subsequent relevant" Security Council resolutions,** thereby creating an ongoing basis for military intervention. It was also argued that a similar justification could be seen to flow from Security Council Resolution 1154 [3/2/98], which calls for "severest consequences" should Iraq not comply with the obligations imposed by the Security Council [BBC News, 12/17/98].

The **justification for the attacks was Iraq's chronic failure to cooperate with the mandate of the United Nations Special Commission (UNSCOM)** to disarm Iraq's weapons of mass destruction, together with a failure to respect a series of Security Council resolutions commanding this disarmament [S/Res/687, 4/3/91; S/Res/1194, 9/9/98; and S/Res/1205, 11/5/98]. Iraqi noncompliance has essentially been the norm since the 1991 Gulf War first exposed Iraq's arsenal of weapons of mass destruction. In refusing to allow UNSCOM arms inspectors to enter sites, review documents, or conduct investigations, Baghdad took the position that UNSCOM was simply a disguise permitting the international community in general, and the U.S. in particular, to spy on Iraq. Not long after the bombing of Iraq came the first news reports suggesting that some American members of UNSCOM weapons inspection teams were in fact spying on behalf of the United States [BBC News, 1/7/99] and that these spies used UNSCOM missions to gather intelligence aimed at toppling Iraqi President Saddam Hussein. These allegations were initially denied by Washington and by the United Nations [BBC News, 1/6/99; and see "Making and Keeping the Peace: The Middle East" in the present volume].

On March 27, 1999, a U.N. review of Iraq's disarmament record concluded that there was still a need for the United Nations in general and UNSCOM in particular to conduct a comprehensive and intrusive monitoring, inspection, and investigation of Iraq's weapons programs [Judith Miller in *New York Times*, 3/28/99]. Assuredly, UNSCOM will not be able to fulfill its mandate until the Security Council finds a way to persuade Iraq to provide access to international inspectors. Since the December 1998 bombing and ongoing aerial monitoring, Iraq has refused all cooperation with UNSCOM and demands an end to the inspections, sanctions, and no-fly zones. This puts the United Nations and Iraq at an impasse, since the Security Council resolutions state that UNSCOM must certify that Iraq is rid of all nuclear, biological, chemical, and other weapons of mass destruction before it will replace the investigation with a less intrusive long-term monitoring regime. Meanwhile, U.N. economic sanctions against Iraq show no signs of being lifted. In the interim, however, the Security Council continues to permit distribution of humanitarian supplies to the people of Iraq [S/Res/1242, 5/21/99].

The **work of the United Nations Compensation Commission (UNCC) continues.** Created in 1991 as a subsidiary organ of the Security Council, it is charged with processing claims and ordering compensation for losses and damages suffered as a direct result of Iraq's unlawful invasion and occupation of Kuwait [S/Res/687, 4/3/91]. The UNCC is a unique initiative: Part court of law, part arbitral tribunal, it adopts mass tort litigation approaches to restitution of harm. Iraq is to pay reparations out of its frozen international assets as well as out of its future oil export earnings. Some 2.6 million claims have been filed thus far, among them Kuwait's claims regarding damage to its natural environment and to public health.

In a July 1, 1998, decision on contractual and corporate claims, the UNCC limited many of the asserted contractual losses on the basis that the claimants had not established a sufficiently direct causal link to Iraqi aggression. More particularly, the UNCC required "specific proof that the failure to perform [the contract] was the direct result of Iraq's invasion and occupation of Kuwait" [Jay Austin and Carl Bruch, "The Greening of Warfare," *Environmental Forum*, 11–12/98]. Such rigorous requirements of causality and directness of damage may make it quite difficult for environmental and public health claims to succeed.

2. The Sixth Committee and the International Law Commission

The **Sixth Committee**'s work for the 53rd General Assembly focused on five issues: the International Criminal Court; a convention on jurisdictional immunities of states and their property; measures to eliminate international terrorism; amending the statute of the Administrative Tribunal of the United Nations as it relates to the status and terms of members of the tribunal; and drafting a set of principles and guidelines for international negotiations [Summaries of the Work of the Sixth Committee, www.un.org/law/fiftythr.htm; see also A/C.6/53/L.10 and U.N. press release GA/L/3092, 11/10/98]. The Sixth Committee also heard from the Special Committee on the Charter of the United Nations and on Strengthening the Role of the Organization on the subject of U.N. economic sanctions—specifically, the provision of assistance to third-party states affected by the application of sanctions—and on the drafting of a declaration on basic principles and criteria for peacekeeping [see A/AC.182/L.102, and www.un.org/law/charter.htm].

The **International Law Commission (ILC)** was established by the U.N. General Assembly in 1947 to promote the progressive development of international law and its codification. The ILC, during its 1998 session, adopted 17 draft articles (with commentaries) on the issue of preventing transboundary damage from hazardous activities—activities "which involve a *risk* of causing significant transboundary harm through their physical consequences" [emphasis added]. These articles may contribute to the codification of preventive tort and nuisance principles with the public policy goal of, inter alia, promoting environmental welfare. Further work in this area was encouraged by the General Assembly [A/Res/53/102].

The ILC also adopted seven draft guidelines on reservations to treaties. The specific topics considered are: object of reservations, instances in which reservations may be formulated, reservations having territorial scope, reservations formulated when a party gives notification of territorial application, reservations formulated jointly, and the relationship between definitions and admissibility of reservations. Work also continued on issues as varied as state responsibility, diplomatic protection, unilateral acts of states, and nationality in relation to the succession of states [see the ILC Report, A/53/10, available at www.un.org/law/ilc/reports/1998; and see A/Res/53/102].

3. The International Criminal Court

The Negotiations

From June 15 to July 17, 1998, representatives of 160 states and observers from intergovenmental organizations and a large number of nongovernmental organizations gathered in Rome for the United Nations Conference of Plenipotentiaries on the Establishment of an International Criminal Court (Rome Conference) [see A/Conf.183/10, Annexes III and IV, for a list of observer organizations]. It was widely hoped that this would constitute the final set of negotiations on a statute creating a permanent International Criminal Court (ICC). Behind this international tribunal is the belief that crimes against humanity and genocide are crimes against the international community at large—and that it makes sense to have available an international mechanism to prosecute and punish those who perpetrate such crimes.

The basis for the negotiations at the Rome Conference was a **draft statute prepared by the International Law Commission (ILC)** between 1990 and 1994. The ILC's input into the creation of an international criminal court was officially invited by the General Assembly in 1989 [A/Res/44/30] and restated in subsequent years. The draft statute was reviewed by the Ad Hoc Committee on the Establishment of an International Criminal Court [A/Res/49/53], which was later transformed by the General Assembly into a **Preparatory Committee on the Establishment of an International Criminal Court** [A/Res/50/46]. The Preparatory Committee met on several occasions in 1996 and 1997 with a view to preparing a consolidated text that would be widely acceptable to the U.N. member states. At the final meeting of the Preparatory Committee (March 16–April 3, 1998) a draft Convention on the Establishment of an International Criminal Court was adopted, and the General Assembly directed that it be forwarded to the Rome Conference [A/Res/51/207. See A/Conf.183/2/Add. 1 for the original Preparatory Committee draft]. This draft was a complex document containing 116 articles, 1,300 words of which appeared in brackets, indicating problems yet to be resolved.

The large number of delegates at the Rome Conference, and the relatively short period of time available for reaching agreement on a final text, made it necessary to form committees—there were four: the General Committee, the Committee of the Whole, the Drafting Committee, and the Credentials Committee—and coordinate them. The Committee of the Whole, under the chairmanship of Philippe Kirsch of Canada, quickly became the locus of activity [Records of the Conference, A/Conf.183/SR.1 to SR.9; and Records of the Committee of the Whole, A/Conf.183/C.1/SR.1 to SR.42]. It was the Committee of the Whole that coordinated the final consensus that resulted in the adoption of the Rome Statute of the International Criminal Court [A/Conf.183/9 (hereinafter Rome Statute)].

On July 17, 1998, the final day of the Conference, 120 nations voted in favor of the Rome Statute, 7 voted against and 21 abstained. Although no official record of the electronic vote was taken, opponents of the Rome Statute included the United States, China, Libya, Israel, Iraq, Qatar, Yemen, India, Russia, and Algeria. In the main, those who did not support the Rome Statute were concerned that an independent court might encroach on national sovereignty, might make it difficult for a crackdown on movements of self-determination, or might place under a microscope the conduct of military forces stationed on foreign soil.

The Rome Statute will enter into force when ratified by 60 countries (Article 126); no reservations are allowed (Article 120). Senegal was the first to ratify the Statute, on February 2, 1999. San Marino, Italy, and Trinidad and Tobago followed suit. Eighty-three other nations have signed the Rome Statute, and many of these are moving swiftly toward ratification.

An Overview of the ICC

Jurisdiction

The Rome Statute creates **jurisdiction for the ICC over "the most serious crimes of concern to the international community as a whole,"** as enumerated in Article 5: genocide, crimes against humanity, war crimes, and aggression. Articles 1 and 26 limit the ICC's jurisdiction to persons 18 years or older at the time the offense was alleged to have been committed. As a result, states, institutions, and non-natural legal persons cannot be subject to the sanction of the ICC [see also Article 25]. In all cases, the ICC's jurisdiction is only prospective: **Mass political or ethnic violence that occurred before the coming into force of the Rome Statute will not be**

covered by the ICC [Article 11; see also Article 22 on *nullum crimen sine lege* and Article 24 on nonretroactivity]. For this reason, the response of international law to past crimes in regions as disparate as Cambodia, East Timor, and Guatemala would still have to be engaged on an ad hoc basis. The time-limited jurisdiction of the ICC also precludes the transfer of cases from the ad hoc Tribunals investigating violence in Rwanda and the former Yugoslavia.

Article 12 notes that states that become parties to the Rome Statute accept the ICC's jurisdiction over the crimes enumerated in Article 5. **States that have not signed the Rome Statute can opt in to the ICC's jurisdiction on a case-by-case basis.** The ICC will exercise jurisdiction when one of three events occurs (Article 13): a state party refers a matter to the ICC; the Security Council, acting under Chapter VII, refers a matter to the ICC; or the Prosecutor acting independently has initiated an investigation. The **ability of the Prosecutor to initiate an investigation**—a controversial issue at the Rome Conference—is circumscribed in Article 15: The Prosecutor must first conclude there is a "reasonable basis to proceed with an investigation" and then must obtain the authorization of a Pre-Trial Chamber of the ICC (based on its determination that there is a reasonable basis to proceed and apparent jurisdiction). Individuals subject to prosecutorial investigation are given considerable due process rights, including a privilege against self-incrimination (Article 55[1][a]), freedom from coercion (Article 55[1][b]), the assistance of an interpreter (Article 55[1][c]), and freedom from arbitrary arrest or detention (Article 55[1][d]). Additional rights accrue to an individual about to be questioned by the Prosecutor (or by national authorities) during the course of an investigation (Article 55[2]). These include the right to remain silent, the right to free legal assistance (or legal assistance of one's own choosing), and the right to be questioned only in the presence of counsel unless that right has been waived voluntarily.

The **relationship of the Security Council to the ICC** concerned many delegates to the Rome Conference. Some feared that a presumption that Security Council approval was necessary to authorize a prosecution would create a least-common denominator situation in which one member of the Security Council, acting alone, could negate the ICC's exercise of jurisdiction. These fears led to the inclusion of Article 16, which creates a reverse presumption: The Security Council can interfere with proceedings only by adopting a resolution requesting that an investigation or prosecution be dropped or deferred.

When a state party or the Prosecutor refers a case to the ICC, the Court can exercise jurisdiction (Article 12) only when the state in which the alleged conduct occurs is a party to the Rome Statute (or has informed the Registrar that it wishes to accept the ICC's jurisdiction regarding the crime in question) or when the state of which the accused is a national is a party to the Statute (or has informed the Registrar, as above). **It is thus possible for the ICC to obtain jurisdiction in a case involving a na-**

tional of a state that refuses the ICC's jurisdiction, should that individual's alleged criminal conduct occur in a state that *is* party to the Statute or accepts ICC jurisdiction.

None of the crimes within the jurisdiction of the ICC is subject to any statute of limitations. Each crime is defined for the purpose of the Rome Statute alone and does not constitute the codification of international criminal law. Of course, should the Statute be ratified widely, the scope and definitions of the crimes it prohibits may well inform the spirit of customary international law.

Crimes

Drawing from the 1948 Genocide Convention, Article 6 **defines genocide** as any of the following acts committed with intent to destroy, in whole or in part, a national, ethnic, racial, or religious group:

  a. killing members of the group
  b. causing serious bodily or mental harm to members of the group
  c. deliberately inflicting on the group conditions of life calculated to bring about its physical destruction in whole or in part
  d. imposing measures intended to prevent births within the group
  e. forcibly transferring children of the group to another group.

Of course, there is always room for judicial interpretation to define more precisely the contours of the definition of genocide—Article 21(2) permits the ICC to apply principles and rules of law from its previous decisions—and ICC pronouncements will also likely be guided by precedents set by today's ad hoc tribunals. Delegates to the Rome Conference chose not to add "political" or "social" groups to the list of groups protected from genocide—a matter under debate for over 50 years. Persecution on political grounds is treated as a crime against humanity under Article 7.

The *chapeau* to Article 7 provides—in a somewhat awkward definition—that **"crime against humanity"** means any of a series of acts that form part of a "widespread or systematic attack directed against any civilian population, with knowledge of the attack." These acts include murder, extermination, enslavement, deportation, torture, persecution, enforced disappearance, and apartheid. **Certain forms of gender-based violence**—rape, sexual slavery, enforced prostitution, forced pregnancy, enforced sterilization, or any other form of sexual violence of comparable gravity—are specifically included within the scope of crimes against humanity (Article 7[1][g]). Explicit reference to gendered violence is due largely to the efforts of nongovernmental organizations invited to participate in the Rome Conference.

Returning to the language of the *chapeau*, "attack directed against any civilian population" means a "course of conduct involving the multiple commission of [prohibited] acts against any civilian population, pursuant to or in furtherance of a state or organizational policy to commit such attack" (Article 7[2][a]). In the end, there are numerous hurdles the Prosecutor would have to overcome in order to obtain a conviction for crimes against humanity. One is the fact that seemingly isolated criminal acts could fall outside the ambit of Article 7.

War crimes are addressed by Article 8. The ICC has jurisdiction over war crimes "in particular" when committed as part of a plan or policy or as part of a large-scale commission of such crimes—the exact meaning of "in particular" remaining unclear. The Statute creates two subsets of such crimes: those arising out of international conflicts and those arising out of "armed conflict[s] not of an international character." In an international conflict, war crimes are defined as: (1) grave breaches of the Geneva Conventions on the Laws of War of August 12, 1949; and (2) "other serious violations of the laws and customs applicable in international armed conflict within the established framework of international law." Article 8(2)(a) provides a seemingly exhaustive list of crimes against persons and property that constitute specific breaches of the 1949 Geneva Convention. Article 8(2)(b) adds to this list of war crimes by enumerating 26 serious violations of the law and customs of international armed conflict. These include crimes against soldiers, civilians, humanitarian aid workers, property, the natural environment, and historic monuments. The same article also prohibits the use of poison and poisoned weapons and the conscription of children. In each case the use of the word "namely" before the list of examples suggests that the list is exhaustive as opposed to illustrative. If the list is in fact closed, the use of chemical, biological, and nuclear weapons and landmines may not be sanctioned as a war crime by the ICC unless and until the Rome Statute is amended (for amendment procedures see Article 121).

War crimes committed during armed conflicts "not of an international character" are treated in a more limited manner by the Rome Statute (Articles 8[2][c–f]). Nonetheless, the fact that the ICC has some jurisdiction over internal conflicts is a major breakthrough, insofar as this jurisdiction can be perceived as a major incursion into state sovereignty. In terms of internal conflicts, the ICC will assume jurisdiction over serious violations of Article 3 common to the four Geneva Conventions of August 12, 1949. This refers to mutilation, torture, outrages upon personal dignity, hostage-taking, and execution without judgment by a regularly constituted court when these crimes are committed against persons taking no active part in the hostilities, a category that includes armed personnel who have surrendered or who are *hors de combat*. In an important limitation whose scope will have to await judicial interpretation, Article 8(2)(d) states that Article 8(2)(c) will not apply to "situations of internal disturbances and tensions, such as riots, [or] isolated or sporadic acts of violence." The ICC will *also* assume jurisdiction over "serious violations of the laws and customs applicable in armed conflicts not of an international character within the framework of international law" (Article 8[2][e]). These include a significantly more limited array of crimes than is provided in Article 8(2)(b) but will cover pillaging, sexual violence, conscription of children, certain types of property damage, and intentional attacks against civilian populations (once again, as in the case of Article 8[2][c], the use of the term "namely" creates a seemingly exclusive list). Article 8(2)(f) specifies that Article 8(2)(e) applies "to armed conflicts that take place in the territory of a State when there is protracted armed conflict between governmental authorities and organized armed groups or between such groups," thereby limiting the definition of armed conflict supplied in (c). It is unclear how the adjective "organized" will be interpreted—whether militarily "organized," politically "organized," or both.

In sum, **internal conflicts are treated more narrowly than international armed conflicts.** These limitations illustrate the extent to which war crimes proved to be a controversial element of the Rome Conference negotiations. This controversy also accounts for the fact that jurisdiction over war crimes can immediately be assumed, although—in an important limitation—**any signatory state may, for seven years, opt out of the ICC's jurisdiction over war crimes alleged to have been committed by that state's nationals or on that state's territory** (Article 124). Another limitation holds that, in cases of war crimes, soldiers may not be held responsible if they were obeying orders, if they did not know the orders were unlawful, and if the order was not obviously unlawful (Article 33). These limitations do not apply to genocide or crimes against humanity.

Article 5(1)(d) explicitly accords the ICC jurisdiction over **the crime of aggression**—although a definition of the crime and the conditions under which the ICC would exercise jurisdiction in this regard have yet to be finalized. To do so will require an amendment to the Rome Statute. (The Preparatory Commission responsible for providing a draft proposal on the crime of aggression is discussed later on.) A similar, although more reserved, stance was taken by the parties regarding terrorism and drug trafficking. Instead of using the text of the Rome Statute to foreshadow the integration of such crimes within the mandate of the ICC, the Rome Conference simply passed a resolution recommending a review conference to "consider the crimes of terrorism and drug crimes with a view to arriving at an acceptable definition and . . . inclusion in the list of crimes" [Final Act, Annex I.E, A/Conf.183/10]. Deferring drug crimes to a future date is somewhat ironic, given the history of the ICC: It was at the suggestion of Trinidad and Tobago, concerned with narcotics trafficking, that the idea of an international criminal court was revisited by the Sixth Committee in 1989.

Article 21 determines **the sources of law the ICC is to apply.** The ICC will, in the first place, apply the Rome Statute and the Elements of Crimes and Rules of Procedure that the parties will elaborate over time. In the second place, the ICC will apply treaties and the principles and rules of international law (Article 21[1][b]); subsequently, recourse may be had to the general principles of law derived from national laws of legal systems of the world, including national laws of the states that would normally exercise jurisdiction over the crime (provided these national laws are not inconsistent with the Rome Statute and with international law) (Article 21[1][c]). This latter provision may allow the ICC to demonstrate sensitivity to local law, custom, and usage, and thereby perhaps increase the legitimacy of international intervention within the society affected by the crime(s).

Principles of Criminal Law

Articles 22 to 33 of the Rome Statute set out the general principles of criminal law the ICC is to apply. Article 22(1) provides that criminal responsibility under the Rome Statute will arise only should the impugned conduct constitute, at the time it is committed, a crime within the jurisdiction of the ICC (see also Article 24). The accused is entitled to the benefit of strict construction of the definition of a crime (Article 22[2]), of favorable interpretation of ambiguous definitions (Article 22[2]), and of the principle of nonretroactivity (Article 24). Article 27 provides that the Rome Statute will apply equally to all individuals regardless of any distinction based on official capacity—in particular, official capacity as a head of state or government—thereby eliminating sovereign immunity as a defense. Article 28 addresses **the doctrine of command responsibility.** It imputes criminal responsibility to military commanders and persons acting as military commanders for crimes committed by forces under that commander's effective command, authority, and control when the crimes result from that commander's failure to properly exercise control over such forces. In the case of commanders, criminal responsibility attaches both subjectively and objectively: Article 28 holds criminally accountable commanders who know or should know that their forces are committing or are about to commit the crimes and, notwithstanding, fail to take all necessary and reasonable measures to prevent or repress the commission of these crimes. Article 28(2) holds criminally accountable superiors other than commanders. In the case of superiors other than commanders, criminal responsibility attaches to those who subjectively knew or consciously disregarded that the crimes were about to be committed; this is a higher evidentiary standard than is applied to commanders, who may also face sanction when they simply "should have known" that forces were committing or about to commit crimes. Notwithstanding the operation of command responsibility on a limited objective standard, the Rome Statute provides that the general presumption is that an individual will be criminally responsible and liable for punishment only if the crime was committed with intent and knowledge (Article 30). This accords with most theories of criminal law in which an individual is only culpable if there is proof of a guilty mind (*mens rea*).

In this vein, Article 25(3) determines that **criminal responsibility** will attach to an individual who: (1) commits a crime (either individually, jointly with another person, or through another person); (2) orders, solicits, or induces the commission of a crime that did in fact occur; or (3) aids, abets, or assists in the commission or attempted commission of a crime, which includes providing the means for committing it. Criminal responsibility will also attach to an individual who intentionally contributes to the commission or attempted commission of a crime by a group of persons acting with a common purpose, provided the individual acted to further the criminal purpose of the group and did so with knowledge of the intention of the group to commit the crime (Article 25[3][d]). Article 25(3)(e) criminalizes the act of directly and publicly inciting others to commit genocide—a provision that may prove instrumental in prosecuting those who disseminate hate propaganda—although it is unclear whether those whose actions do not actually result in genocidal violence come under the ICC's jurisdiction. At the same time, the language of Article 25(3)(f) does give the ICC jurisdiction over attempts to commit a crime when an individual takes action that commences the execution of that crime by means of a "substantial step," even if the crime did not occur because of circumstances out of the individual's control.

Some **defenses to criminal responsibility** are set out in Article 31. These include: incapacity arising out of mental disease or defect; intoxication that destroys capacity, unless that intoxication was voluntary and undertaken under circumstances in which the person knew or disregarded the risk that a criminal act was likely to result; reasonable defense of self, of another person, or (in more limited circumstances and only in the case of war crimes) of property essential for survival; and duress resulting from threat of imminent death or of continuing or imminent serious bodily harm against the accused or another person. The range of defenses is not closed, and the ICC may incorporate defenses that draw from principles of international law or from the national legal system of the relevant state. Article 32 discusses mistake of fact (can absolve criminal responsibility if it negates the mental element [criminal intent]) and mistake of law (or legal error, not a ground for excluding criminal responsibility unless the mistake negates the mental element or involves a situation in which a person is following superior orders). For the most part, Articles 31 and 32 parallel criminal defenses common to many national legal systems.

Article 33 addresses **the situation of an individual following orders.** This has always been a controversial area of criminal justice, and so it was during the negotiations leading to the Rome Statute. Article 33 provides that when an individual commits a crime pursuant to an order of a government or superior (either military or civilian), this fact will not relieve the individual from criminal responsibility unless all of the following can be proved: (1) that individual was under a legal obligation to obey orders of the government or the superior; (2) the individual did not know the order was unlawful (i.e., did not know it violated the Rome Statute); and (3) the order was not manifestly unlawful. Article 33(2) expressly states that orders to commit crimes against humanity or genocide are manifestly unlawful. As a result, the defense of superior orders can surface only in situations of war crimes or, when it is ultimately defined, aggression. Eliminating the defense of superior orders in cases of genocide and crimes against humanity might well narrow the scope of this defense beyond its present form in much domestic criminal law [see, e.g., the decision of the Canadian Supreme Court in *Regina* v. *Finta*, [1994] 1 S.C.R. 701, 3/24/94]. At Nuremberg obedience to superior orders was considered a mitigating circumstance (not a defense) with regard to both war crimes and crimes against humanity, including persecution. However, since the ICC is intended to prosecute "major" international criminals, it is unclear how frequently "superior orders" will be offered as a defense at trials.

Administration, Structure, and Finances

The Rome Statute provides that the ICC will be located in The Hague (Article 3); that it will have 18 judges (Article 36[1]), each to serve a non-renewable nine-year term (Article 36[9][a]); and that it will be comprised of the Presidency, an Appeals Division, a Trial Division, a Pre-Trial Division, the Office of the Prosecutor, and the Registry (Article 34). Detailed provisions as to the qualification, nomination, election, and terms of service of the judges are provided in Articles 35–41. The judges are to elect by absolute majority from their ranks a President and two Vice-Presidents (Article 38). The President plus four other judges will comprise the Appeals Chamber; and the Pre-Trial and Trial chambers will have at least six judges each (Article 39). Judicial independence is guaranteed by Article 40, which also requires that judges refrain from engaging in any activity likely to interfere with their judicial functions or to affect confidence in their independence (see also Article 40[2] regarding judicial impartiality). The scope of this requirement—for example, whether it may exclude judges with connections to or background in human rights organizations—will be determined over time in accordance with the procedure established by Article 40(4) or Article 41(2)(c). Removal of judges (as well as of the Prosecutor, Registrar, and deputies) can occur in cases of "serious misconduct," "serious breach," or an inability to exercise functions (Article 46).

The **Office of the Prosecutor,** established in Article 42, is to act independently and is accorded investigatory as well as prosecutorial functions. The non-judicial administration and servicing of the ICC is left to the Registry (Article 43). Both the Prosecutor and the Registrar will appoint such qualified staff as may be required (Article 44), and the Prosecutor may appoint investigators (Article 44[1]; specifics regarding investigations are found in Part 5, Articles 53 to 55 of the Rome Statute).

The official languages of the ICC are Arabic, Chinese, English, French, Russian, and Spanish; its working languages English and French; and additional languages may be added as needed for individual cases (Article 50).

The **expenses of the ICC** will be paid out of assessed contributions by the states party to the Rome Statute (Article 115[a]). Funds will also be provided by the United Nations, "in particular" in relation to expenses arising from cases referred by the Security Council (Article 115[b]). Voluntary contributions from governments, international organizations, individuals, corporations, and other entities are encouraged as well (Article 116).

Relationships with National Courts and Governments

Article 1 of the Rome Statute provides that the ICC "shall be complementary to national criminal jurisdictions," and Article 17 provides some specifics about what is meant. In certain circumstances the Rome Statute permits the ICC to try an accused over the objections of a national government that has the jurisdiction for such a trial and is seeking to prosecute (or otherwise hold accountable) that same individual.

Article 17(1) obliges the ICC itself to determine that, in the following situations, a case properly referred to it is inadmissible:

a. the case is being investigated or prosecuted by a state that has jurisdiction, unless the state is unwilling or unable genuinely to carry out the investigation or prosecution;
b. the case has been investigated by a state that has jurisdiction and the state has decided not to prosecute the person concerned, unless the decision resulted from the unwillingness or inability of the state genuinely to prosecute;
c. the accused has already been tried for conduct that is the subject of the complaint, unless, as provided by Article 20(3), the domestic prosecutions were for the purpose of shielding the accused from

criminal responsibility or were not conducted independently or impartially in accordance with the norms of due process recognized by international law;

d. the case is not of sufficient gravity.

Two types of situations thus arise in which **the ICC is to decline jurisdiction:** (1) when local investigations or prosecutions are ongoing or have been disbanded; and (2) when the accused has already been tried. Situation (1) would tend to flow more from concerns over comity between national and international institutions, whereas (2) would flow from the core principle of double jeopardy, namely, that no one should be tried twice for the same offense. As regards (2), the ICC will, of course, have to determine, inter alia, whether a domestic proceeding was conducted "impartially in accordance with the norms of due process recognized by international law." This will involve a review of the judicial process in the relevant national court.

The exercise of this judicial review accords the ICC ultimate say over whether a national process conforms with the "norms of due process" and, thus, whether a given case falls under its jurisdiction. Of great importance will be emerging definitions of what constitutes the "norms of due process recognized by international law." Given the enormous cultural and sociological differences between societies, it is unclear whether such a definition can ever be worked out.

Besides deciding whether a domestic legal system's trial meets the norms of due process, the ICC has further discretion in determining its jurisdiction through other conditions stated in Article 17. **The ICC can assume jurisdiction** should it determine that the state in question is or was "unwilling or unable genuinely to carry out the investigation or prosecution." These are broad terms, and the parties to the Rome Conference made them more precise in Article 17(2). Here, the ICC is instructed to consider, having regard once again to the "principles of due process recognized by international law," whether "one or more of the following exists": (1) the proceedings were undertaken for the purpose of shielding the person responsible from criminal responsibility; (2) there has been an unjustified delay inconsistent with an intent to bring the accused to justice; and (3) the proceedings were not or are not being conducted independently or impartially. For the most part, these guidelines go to whether a state is "willing" to undertake investigations or prosecutions. As for those who are simply "unable" to do so, the ICC shall, in its determination of "inability," consider whether a "total or substantial collapse or unavailability of its national judicial system" renders the state "unable to obtain the accused or the necessary evidence and testimony or [is] otherwise unable to carry out its proceedings" (Article 17[3]). The Statute says nothing about assisting states willing yet presently unable to prosecute to become "able" to do so in accordance with the "principles of due process recognized by international law." By positioning the ICC to assume jurisdiction of a case if the state with jurisdiction "is unwilling or unable genuinely" to investigate or prosecute, Article 17 suggests the primacy of the adversarial trial model to "prevent and punish" serious international crimes. Thus it is possible that a state that establishes a truth commission, for example, or other non-prosecutorial or extrajudicial means of dealing with a legacy of violence, may not satisfy the ICC's requirements, leaving open the door to the ICC's assumption of jurisdiction.

Article 18 requires the Prosecutor to notify concerned states when the Court has determined that there is a reasonable basis to initiate an investigation. Articles 18 and 19 provide procedural details for challenging the ICC's assumption of jurisdiction. These procedures are quite complicated—no surprise, given the difficulty in negotiating an appropriate balance between national sovereignty and international accountability.

Article 20(2) provides explicitly that no person shall be tried before "another court" for a crime referred to in Article 5 for which that person has already been convicted or acquitted by the ICC. Still, the question arises as to what may happen to an individual who has been charged by the Prosecutor only to have the charges dropped.

The Rome Statute addresses issues of international cooperation, judicial assistance, surrender of defendants, and enforcement, in all cases emphasizing the role of national governments and institutions. Clearly, without active involvement of national actors, there can be no nuts-and-bolts implementation of ICC judgments, not to mention such procedures as assuming custody over the accused. Recognizing the importance of domestic involvement, Article 86 stipulates that parties must cooperate fully with the ICC in its investigation and prosecution of crimes—though whether Article 86 is hortatory or will bring compliance remains to be seen. Article 90, dealing with competing requests for the surrender of an accused by a state party to the Rome Statute and the ICC, states that, when the accused is physically present in a second state, the ICC's request takes precedence.

From Investigation to Trial to Appeal

At any time after the initiation of an investigation, the Prosecutor has the power to apply to the **Pre-Trial Chamber** for a warrant of arrest (Article 58). The warrant will be granted should the Pre-Trial Chamber be satisfied that there are reasonable grounds for believing the named individual has committed a crime and should be detained. Alternatively, the Pre-Trial Chamber may simply issue a summons for the named individual to appear. The Rome Statute then turns to national authorities to actually arrest and deliver individuals against whom warrants have been issued (Article 59).

After an accused person is surrendered to the ICC, the Pre-Trial Chamber will schedule preliminary hearings to confirm the charges (Article 61) and provide an opportunity to set bail (Article 60). Should the matter continue beyond the preliminary stage, Article 62 provides that the trial will take place at The Hague. The Statute also provides important guarantees of due process: The accused will be present during the trial (Article 63), which must be fair and expeditious (Article 64[2]) and held in public (Article 64[7]). The accused will also benefit from the presumption of innocence and, in a direct extraction from Anglo-American common law, will be convicted only if the ICC is convinced of the guilt of the accused beyond a reasonable doubt (Article 66; further rights of the accused set out in Article 67). **The judges will serve as triers of both fact and law;** the absence of juries is a departure from American common law (but not as marked a departure from British or Canadian common law). The rights of the accused are balanced against the need to protect witnesses and victims (Articles 64[2], 68), and it will be up to **subsequent Preparatory Commission meetings to draw up the Rules of Procedure and Evidence of the ICC** and establish the precise balance between the accused's rights and victims' needs. This balance may be especially difficult in matters of sexual violence or violence against children. The Trial Chamber is authorized to accept a guilty plea (Articles 64[8] and 65) only under certain conditions (Article 65[1]).

Articles 69, 72, and 73 provide a fairly comprehensive regime governing the **admissibility and weight to be attached to evidence** once a matter goes to trial. Eventually, this regime will also be supplemented by the Rules of Procedure and Evidence. The ICC is empowered to sanction offenses against the administration of justice, such as giving false evidence and influencing witnesses (Articles 70, 71).

At the end of the trial, **the Trial Chamber issues a decision.** This is to be in writing and will contain a full and reasoned statement of the findings on the evidence and conclusions (Article 74). The judges are instructed to attempt to achieve unanimity in their decision. Should this prove unattainable, the majority will rule (Articles 74[3], 74[5]). Both the majority and the minority decision (or a summary thereof) will be delivered in open court (Article 74[5]). The ability of judges to dissent and to do so publicly flows from the advocacy of the common law delegations (including the United States, England, Australia, Canada, and New Zealand) at the Rome Conference, as most civilian jurisdictions simply do not accord judges a right to dissent. In **sentencing,** the Trial Chamber is to consider "the appropriate sentence to be imposed" at an independent sentencing hearing (Article 76).

The Rome Statute sets out **a detailed appellate scheme.** Both Prosecutor and defendant may make an appeal against the ICC's decision (Article 81). Their appeals may be based on procedural error, error of fact, error of law, or any other ground that affects the fairness or reliability of the proceedings or decision (Article 81[1]). Sentences may also be appealed on the ground of disproportion between the crime and the sentence (Article 81[2]). The presumption is that a convicted person will remain in custody pending an appeal (Article 81[3]). Yet another article governs appeals against what will generally be interlocutory decisions, often of the Pre-Trial Chamber or of the Trial Chamber on evidentiary matters, and also permits an appeal from an order for reparations (Article 82).

The appeals will be heard by the **Appeals Chamber,** which has the power to reverse or amend the decision or sentence or order a new trial before a different Trial Chamber (Article 83). It can do so if it finds that "the proceedings appealed from were unfair in a way that affected the reliability of the decision or sentence, or that the decision or sentence appealed from was materially affected by error of fact or law or procedural error" (Article 83[2]). In the case of a sentence appeal, the Appeals Chamber is able to "vary" the sentence, should it find that the original sentence is disproportionate to the crime (Article 83[3]). Article 84 creates a procedure to revise a conviction or sentence (in the ostensibly exceptional situation in which there may be new exculpatory evidence or there is evidence that inculpatory evidence had been falsified). Article 85 accords a victim of unlawful arrest or detention a right to compensation.

Penalties

Article 77(1) limits penalties to:

a. a fixed term of imprisonment up to a maximum of 30 years; or
b. a term of life imprisonment when justified by the extreme gravity of the crime and the individual circumstances of the convicted person.

The ICC is not empowered to apply the death penalty.
The time a convict will have served in detention while awaiting trial will be deducted from the aggregate sentence (Article 78[2]). Issues that arise when a person has been convicted of more than one crime are dealt with in Article 78(3). In such a situation, the ICC will pronounce a sentence for each crime and a joint sentence specifying the total period of imprisonment—a period no less than the highest individual sentence pronounced and not to exceed a period of 30 years unless the "extreme grav-

ity" criteria of Article 77(1)(b) are met, in which case a life sentence may be issued.

Article 77(2) provides that "in addition to imprisonment" the ICC may order a fine, as well as a forfeiture of proceeds, property, and assets derived directly or indirectly from the crime. The language of Article 77 suggests that the fines or forfeitures cannot substitute for imprisonment or be awarded without a term of imprisonment.

Article 79 is an important part of the Rome Statute, for it goes beyond the retributive justice model encapsulated in Articles 77 and 78. It allows fines and assets collected under Article 77(2) to be transferred to a Trust Fund for the benefit of victims of crime and their families. This Trust Fund can be accessed through claims, made under Article 75, which permits the ICC to make an order specifying appropriate reparations to victims for such purposes as restitution, compensation, and rehabilitation. Alternatively, this order can also be made against a convict directly. In terms of procedure, the order can be made either on independent motion by the victims or, in exceptional situations, at the ICC's own behest. In either case, the ICC will invite legal representations from the convicted person, victims, or other interested parties. In this sense, a proceeding under Article 75 is akin to an ex post facto civil claim. This may offer victims possibilities for restitution. Broadening the types of penalties the ICC can award is important, since this may accord it the finesse to promote reparative, transformative, or rehabilitative justice.

One area in which the parties may contemplate future discussion involves developing a sentencing policy that may represent the complexities of transitional societies moving past mass political violence. Article 75(1), which calls upon the Court to establish principles relating to reparations, restitution, compensation, and rehabilitation, may provide the impetus for the development of such a policy. Nonetheless, the Rome Statute remains unflinching in its mandatory use of criminal trials to redress serious international crimes, as opposed to blending this approach with public inquiries, truth commissions, or other mechanisms to allocate responsibility and ensure accountability.

Sentences are to be served in a state designated by the ICC, and the imprisonment will be subject to the supervision of the ICC (Articles 103, 106). The conditions of imprisonment are to be consistent with widely accepted international treaty standards governing the treatment of prisoners (Article 106[2]). It is the ICC alone that has the right to decide any reduction of sentence (Article 110). Such reductions may be implemented upon review of the ICC when the convict has served two-thirds of the sentence, or 25 years in the case of life imprisonment (Article 110[3]). **Criteria for sentence reduction** are enumerated in Article 110(4), and cover most of the basic grounds for which parole is awarded in national penal systems: willingness to cooperate with the court in its investigation; providing information and/or reparations; and establishing a "clear and significant change of circumstances sufficient to justify the reduction of sentence."

Bringing the Dissenters on Board

From the perspective of a political realist, the ICC will be truly effective only if all members of the global community support it. The participation of such nations as the United States, India, Russia, and China is especially important. The U.S. decision not to support the Rome Statute gave rise to considerable criticism at home, since American nongovernmental organizations were among the most dynamic forces propounding the Rome Statute. Ironically, the U.S. government had been one of the principal advocates of the idea of an international criminal court, and continues to be a major supporter of the existing ad hoc tribunals. In the months following adoption of the Statute, the United States continued to express hope that it would sign on. However, the U.S. would sign only were several important changes to be made to the text [U.N. press release GA/L/3077, 10/21/98]—principally to provide safeguards that would protect American troops serving overseas from political or frivolous prosecutions [Betsy Pisik in *Washington Times*, 2/26/99]. Regarding the U.S. position, it would seem that the current language of the Rome Statute, which permits the Prosecutor and, subsequently, the Pre-Trial Chamber to proceed only when there is a "reasonable basis," already drives against politically motivated or frivolous prosecutions. Nonetheless, U.S. ratification would be conditional upon Senate approval. Such approval does not seem likely at present, since Senate Foreign Relations Committee Chair Jesse Helms has warned that the Rome Statute would be "dead on arrival" [Paul Lewis in *New York Times*, 7/25/99].

Subsequent Preparatory Commission Negotiations

The Rome Conference foresaw that many key details of the implementation and structure of the ICC remained to be worked out. In order to provide a coherent structure for future discussions, delegates at the Rome Conference established a **Preparatory Commission for the International Criminal Court (Preparatory Commission)** [Final Act, Annex I.F, s. 1, A/CONF.183/10]. The Preparatory Commission consists of representatives of all states invited to attend the Rome Conference (the United States is therefore still a member). The mandate of the Preparatory Commission is to "prepare proposals for practical arrangements for the establishing and coming into operation of the Court" [Final Act, s. 5]. It is to report to the first meeting of the Assembly of States Parties to the Rome Statute, after which it will cease to exist. The Assembly of States Parties is to act as a kind of managerial secretariat. One important task of the Preparatory Commission is to make proposals for the definition of the crime of aggression and the situations in which the ICC might exercise jurisdiction regarding this crime [see Final Act, s. 7]. The Preparatory Commission is also to pay attention to the following specific areas:

a. Rules of Procedure and Evidence
b. Elements of Crimes
c. The Relationship Between the Court and the U.N.
d. Negotiating a Headquarters Agreement Between the Host Country [i.e., the Netherlands] and the Court
e. Financial Regulations
f. Privileges and Immunities of the Court
g. Budget for the First Financial Year
h. The Rules of Procedure of the Assembly of States Parties

The Rome Conference gave priority to the drafting of the Rules of Procedure and Evidence as well as to the Elements of Crimes. In both cases, a draft text is to be finalized before June 30, 2000 [see Final Act, s. 6]. It therefore comes as no surprise that, at the First Meeting of the Preparatory Commission, held in New York, February 16–26, 1999, these two sets of issues dominated the agenda [Preparatory Commission for the International Criminal Court, Proceedings of the Preparatory Commission at its first session, PCNICC/1999/L.3/Rev.1 (hereinafter Proceedings)]. The parties had before them proposals from working groups in the major areas delegated to the Preparatory Commission by the Final Act. Nongovernmental organizations were invited to the first meeting and played an active role.

In the area of **Rules of Procedure and Evidence,** the parties agreed to focus on the investigation, prosecution, trial, appeal, and revision portions of the Rome Statute [Proceedings, Summary par. 11], designating specific coordinators for each of these issue areas [Proceedings, Summary par. 12 and 13]. In the end, the Working Group on Rules of Procedure and Evidence proposed discussion papers for the next session of the Preparatory Commission on: (1) the commencement of investigations and proceedings; (2) the procedure to be followed in the event of an application for review of a decision by the Prosecutor not to proceed with an investigation or not to prosecute as well as review by the Pre-Trial Chamber of these prosecutorial decisions; (3) proceedings with regard to the confirmation of charges; and (4) disclosure of evidence (at the confirmation-of-charges hearing and on a pre-trial basis more generally). These discussion papers take the form of draft rules in each of these areas [Proceedings, Annex II].

In the area of the **Elements of Crimes,** the parties agreed to designate Herman van Hebel of the Netherlands as Coordinator of the Working Group. This Working Group is to consider refining the definitions of the crimes within the ICC's jurisdiction and clarifying the elements the Prosecutor will have to demonstrate under each crime to secure a conviction. Discussions in this area were more heated than in the case of the

Rules of Procedure, since there was concern that, by creating stringent elements to these crimes, they might become quite difficult to prove and, as a result, weaken the effectiveness of the Rome Statute. During this First Meeting, the Working Group considered the elements of the crime of genocide and of certain war crimes that arise from grave breaches of the 1949 Geneva Conventions. Its views were then presented in the form of discussion papers [Proceedings, Annex III].

On the **issue of genocide,** the Working Group closed the discussion paper with a list of "suggested comments" relating to genocide and without prejudice to their potential integration within the elements for the crime in the future. These comments, perhaps owing to the active intervention of nongovernmental organizations, extend the definition of genocide. For example, it is suggested that rape and sexual violence may on their own constitute an act of genocide (on this point, see the International Criminal Tribunal for Rwanda's decision in the Akayesu case, infra). This may be important to ensure that sexual violence is treated as seriously as other manifestations of genocide. Additionally, it is noted that the "deliberate infliction of conditions of life" calculated to destroy a group could include systematic expulsion from homes. This latter proviso could capture more clearly the patterns of forced deportation and migration characteristic of ethnic cleansing.

Subsequent meetings of the Preparatory Commission were scheduled for July 26–August 13, 1999, and November 29–December 17, 1999.

4. Ad Hoc War Crimes Tribunals

Since the jurisdiction of the ICC operates only prospectively, covering crimes committed after the Statute enters into force, violations of international humanitarian law that occurred before that time do not fall within its mandate. The U.N. Security Council, however, may choose to deal with pre-existing violations through the creation of geographically limited ad hoc international criminal tribunals. Two such tribunals—for the former Yugoslavia and for Rwanda—have already been created by resolution of the Security Council. Both ad hoc tribunals have their own statutes establishing jurisdiction and mandate. Over 1998–99 there has also been discussion of the creation of a new ad hoc tribunal for Cambodia and, more distantly, for the Democratic Republic of Congo. Assuredly, the international community's experiences with these tribunals has played (and will continue to play) an important role in determining the structure of the ICC.

The International Criminal Tribunal for the Former Yugoslavia (ICTY)

Established by Security Council Resolution 827 [5/25/93], the ICTY is mandated to prosecute persons responsible for serious violations of international humanitarian law committed in the former Yugoslavia. As evidence mounts of atrocities in Kosovo, the number of ICTY indictments has increased. FRY President Slobodan Milosevic now figures among the accused. At the same time, the departure of **ICTY/ICTR Chief Prosecutor Justice Louise Arbour** (who will have served three years of her four-year term) and **ICTY President Judge Gabrielle Kirk MacDonald** may portend an uncertain future for the ICTY. Justice Arbour has accepted an appointment to the Supreme Court of Canada, effective September 15, 1999. Judge MacDonald will leave the ICTY as of November 1999. She will be replaced by Judge Patricia M. Wald of the U.S. District of Columbia federal appeals court.

Events of this past year reveal **weaknesses of the ICTY as a mechanism for enforcing international humanitarian law.** FRY violence in Kosovo not only stands as a tragedy but indicates defiance of the threat of ICTY prosecution. In addition, FRY refusal to grant visas or otherwise allow ICTY investigators unimpeded access to massacre sites reveals the dependence of any international tribunal on national cooperation, even the cooperation of the nation whose actions may be investigated [Marlise Simons in *New York Times*, 10/8/98]. Repeated attempts by the ICTY to secure FRY cooperation have been unsuccessful, resulting in charges by the ICTY President that the FRY is a "rogue state" [ICTY press releases JL/PIU/359-E, 11/5/98, and JL/PIU/371-E, 12/8/98].

Security Council Resolutions 1160 [3/31/98] and 1203 [10/24/98] urge the ICTY to gather information on the violence in Kosovo and investigate all atrocities, although the FRY government maintains that the ICTY does not actually have jurisdiction over Kosovo [ICTY press release CC/PIU/351-E, 10/7/98]. In response, the ICTY points to Articles 1 and 8 of its Statute, which extend its jurisdiction over violations of international humanitarian law on the "territory of the former Yugoslavia" as of January 1, 1991. This clearly includes Kosovo. In March 1999, in light of evidence of FRY-sponsored atrocities in Kosovo, Justice Arbour warned the FRY leadership of its accountability for the commission of serious violations of international humanitarian law [press release CC/PIU/391-E, 3/31/99; see also statements of ICTY President Judge McDonald, press release JL/PIU/394-E, 4/8/99]. These warnings were followed up by the historic indictments of Milosevic and four other leading Serb officials on May 27, 1999 [press release JL/PIU/404-E, 5/27/99]. With the arrival of an international peacekeeping force in Kosovo, access to massacre sites became easier. The United States, United Kingdom, and Germany have pledged to provide to the ICTY classified surveillance and intelligence information regarding the atrocities in Kosovo [Marlise Simons in *New York Times*, 4/18/99; ICTY press release CC/PIU/398-E, 4/21/99]. This information was originally gathered for the purposes of and through the NATO military intervention in the FRY. ICTY investigators are in fact building a "massive database" of evidence of war crimes by Serbian forces in Kosovo

[Geoffrey York in *Globe and Mail*, 5/7/99]. At the time of writing, NATO military police have detained 12 people suspected, yet not indicted, of war crimes [Carlotta Gall in *New York Times*, 7/8/99].

Indictments

Since its inception, the ICTY has indicted 84 individuals, most of them Serbs. Of these indictees, 6 have died, 18 have seen their charges dropped, 8 have been convicted, and 1 has been acquitted. Of the remaining 51 individuals, only 20 are actually in custody. Numerous indictees remain subject to international arrest warrants. Some of these international warrants have been issued against such well-known individuals as Bosnian Serbs Radovan Karadzic and Ratko Mladic, who continue to avoid capture [Thomas Sancton and Gilles Delafon in *Time*, 8/10/98]. By far **the most well-known indictees are Milosevic, Milan Milutinovic (President of Serbia), Nikola Sainovic (FRY Deputy Prime Minister), Dragoljub Ojdanic (Chief of Staff of the FRY Army), and Vlajko Stojiljkovic (Minister of Internal Affairs of Serbia).** This joint indictment was issued on May 27, 1999. It charges each accused with three counts of crimes against humanity and one count of violating the laws or customs of war. The charges stem from the persecution and deportation of Kosovar Albanians as of January 1, 1999. Each indictee is charged with, among other things, the murder of over 340 persons identified by name in an annex to the indictment. This is the first indictment to charge a head of state during an ongoing armed conflict with the commission of serious violations of international humanitarian law [ICTY press release JL/PIU/403-E, 5/27/99]. Arrest warrants have been transmitted to the FRY Ministry of Justice, all U.N. member states, and Switzerland. These warrants are accompanied by an ICTY order requesting all states to search for and freeze any and all assets of the accused under their jurisdiction. This order may "prevent foreign assets being used for the purpose of evading justice, and permit effective restitution to be made upon conviction" [press release JL/PIU/404-E, 5/27/99].

Acquiring custody over indictees is a major problem faced by the ICTY. Milosevic will be no exception, nor will the other recently indicted Serb leaders. Since it lacks its own police force, the ICTY must rely on the cooperation of national authorities or NATO forces to capture those accused.

In fact, it is suspected that many other indictees remain at liberty in Serbia or in Serb-held Herzegovina, and Justice Arbour has criticized the lack of cooperation the ICTY receives from governments in the region—specifically the FRY and, to a lesser extent, the Republika Srpska [press briefing, 3/5/99]. ICTY President McDonald has levied similar criticisms, for example in her address to the U.N. General Assembly on November 19, 1998 [ICTY press release JL/PIU/373-E, 12/14/98, see also Kevin Sullivan in *Christian Science Moni-*

tor, 12/29/98, and ICTY press release JL/PIU/402-E, 5/13/99]. Most graphically, *all* existing public indictments accompanied by arrest warrants remain outstanding in the FRY [ICTY press briefing, 3/5/99]. In the Republika Srpska, authorities have issued false identification papers to persons indicted by the ICTY so as to shield them from its jurisdiction [ICTY press release CC/PIU/336-E, 7/24/98]. The FRY has been recalcitrant in failing to issue visas to permit ICTY investigators to complete their mandates, specifically in Kosovo [press release CC/PIU/362-E, 11/11/98]. In fact, the ICTY has repeatedly sought the aid of the Security Council in obtaining FRY compliance and discouraging obstructionism; and numerous appeals for Security Council intervention have been made by both Justice Arbour and Judge McDonald. These have resulted in the adoption of Security Council Resolutions 1160, 1199, 1203, and 1207 reaffirming the Prosecutor's right to investigate in Kosovo and confirm the FRY's (and Kosovo Albanians') legal obligation to cooperate fully with the ICTY. When the FRY did not comply, NATO used this noncompliance with the ICTY as one justification for military intervention.

On December 7, 1998, **Bosnian Serb Major General Radislav Krstic** pleaded not guilty to charges of genocide, extermination, murder, and persecution for his alleged role in the 1995 massacre of Muslims in the U.N.-protected enclave of Srebrenica. Krstic is the highest-ranking military officer in the Bosnian Serb army to appear before the ICTY. He was arrested by the NATO-led Stabilization Force (SFOR, the peacekeeping operations in Bosnia) earlier that month [Jacqueline Pietsch for Agence France-Presse, 12/7/98]. Krstic had been secretly indicted by the ICTY on October 30, 1998 [ICTY press release JL/PIU/368-E, 12/2/98]. ICTY prosecutors intend to prove that Krstic was one of the main organizers of the Srebrenica massacre—one of the bloodiest in the 1992–95 Bosnian war, in which an estimated that 7,000 Muslims, mostly civilians, were killed. It is rumored that Krstic may provide the ICTY with information regarding the involvement of Radovan Karadzic and Ratko Mladic in the Srebrenica tragedy [Kevin Sullivan in *Christian Science Monitor*, 12/29/98]. It is also believed that Krstic is "capable, if he is willing to testify, of implicating . . . Milosevic" [Steven Erlanger in *New York Times*, 12/3/98].

In mid-March 1999, investigators at the ICTY concluded that **the Croatian Army** had carried out summary executions, indiscriminate shelling of civilian populations and "ethnic cleansing" during an August 1995 military offensive called Operation Storm [Raymond Bonner in *New York Times*, 3/21/99]. Specifically, the investigators allege that the Croatian armed forces and special police shelled the city of Knin, summarily executed at least 150 Serbs, forced the departure of 100,000 Serbs from their ancestral homes, and engaged in looting and burning. They recommended indicting three **Croatian generals—Mirko Norac, Ante Gotovina, and Ivan Cermak**—on all but the Knin charges. These are the first recommendations to indict Croat officers. Since Operation Storm was tacitly supported by the United States, there are concerns that such indictments may create political tensions between Washington and the ICTY. These tensions may arise from allegations that the United States has failed to provide critical evidence requested by the Tribunal regarding Operation Storm [ibid.]. On another note: Because these investigators' reports were improperly leaked confidential internal documents of the ICTY Prosecutor, the Tribunal must now be concerned over the secrecy of its process [ICTY weekly press briefing, 3/24/99]. The Office of the Prosecutor has emphasized that the contents of these investigations do not represent the official conclusions of the Prosecutor.

Other indictments over the past year include **Mladen Naletilic** and **Vinko Martinovic for involvement in the Croatian army's ethnic cleansing of the Mostar municipality** [ICTY press release CC/PIU/377-E, 12/22/98]. On March 31, 1999, the ICTY disclosed that it was seeking the arrest of **Serbian paramilitary leader Zeljko Raznjatovic ("Arkan")** for crimes committed in Croatia and Bosnia, and possibly for recent allegations of involvement in the Kosovo violence [BBC News, 3/31/99]. The ICTY has also been urged to consider investigating **NATO's conduct in bombing the FRY.** On May 6, 1999, several Canadian law professors filed a formal request that the ICTY Prosecutor investigate and indict the leaders of the nations participating in the NATO attacks for serious violations of international humanitarian law.

Activities of the Trial and Appeals Chambers

As this volume went to press, the ICTY Appeals Chamber released its decision in the matter of **Dusko Tadic, the first individual brought before and tried by the ICTY Trial Chamber** [*Prosecutor v Tadic*, Case No. IT-94-1-A, 7/15/99]. Tadic, a Bosnian Serb, was a reserve police officer and café owner in northwestern Bosnia. The thrust of the charges against him involve the murder, torture, and beating of local Bosnian Muslims in villages as well as in prison camps he visited. On May 7, 1997, Tadic was found guilty of nine, and guilty in part on two, counts (out of 31) of violating the laws or customs of war and crimes against humanity. He was sentenced to 20 years' imprisonment on July 14, 1997. Both Tadic and the Prosecution appealed the verdict, and the Appeals Chamber convicted Tadic of nine additional crimes for which he had been acquitted at trial. In a decision that could have wide repercussions for the prosecution of those who committed atrocities against civilians in Bosnia, the Appeals Chamber held that the conflict between Bosnia and Herzegovina on the one hand and the FRY on the other was, in fact, an international armed conflict (the Trial Chamber had held that the conflict was an internal one). Characterizing the conflict as international means that civilians may be protected by the 1949 Geneva Conventions, and therefore the commission of atrocities against civilians can be punished under Article 2 of the Statute of the ICTY. This interpretation accounts for six of the nine substituted convictions [*New York Times*, 7/16/99].

The Appeals Chamber also convicted Tadic of involvement in the murder of five men from the village of Jaskici, whereas the Trial Chamber had acquitted him of these charges (finding there to be reasonable doubt that Tadic had played any part in their killing). In the Tadic decision the Appeals Chamber also issued important pronouncements on the doctrine of common purpose as well as on the elements of crimes against humanity. On this latter point it was held that an act carried out for purely personal motives can constitute a crime against humanity; additionally, a discriminatory intent is not required for all crimes against humanity, only for crimes relating to persecution. The Appeals Chamber deferred to a separate sentencing phase its decision whether Tadic's sentence should be lengthened.

Over the past year, the Trial Chamber released three significant decisions: the Celebici case, the Furundzija case, and the Aleksovski case. The Celibici case involved allegations of war crimes at a prison camp run by Bosnian Muslims and Bosnian Croats and resulted in three convictions and one acquittal. Anto Furundzija was found guilty of two counts of violating the laws or customs of war (specifically as a co-perpetrator of torture and for aiding and abetting rape) and was sentenced to ten years' imprisonment. The Celebici and Furundzija decisions, if read together, contribute to the development of international criminal law in the areas of rape and torture. The Celebici decision and the judgment in the matter of Zlatko Aleksovski offer an important elucidation of command responsibility in international law.

The **Celebici trial** began on March 10, 1997, and continued through to October 15, 1998. It was a complex affair with 122 witnesses and 691 exhibits. Four defendants—Zdravko Mucic, Hazim Delic, Esad Landzo, and Zejnil Delalic—were charged with numerous counts of breaching the Geneva Conventions and violating the laws or customs of war. In the end, three of these defendants were found guilty: Mucic (sentenced to seven years' imprisonment), Delic (20 years) and Landzo (15 years). The fourth defendant, Delalic, was acquitted of all charges. Appeals and cross-appeals (against sentence and judgment) have been filed in all cases.

All of the Celebici defendants were accused of actual or imputed involvement with killings, torture, sexual assault, and cruel and inhuman treatment at the prison camp located at Celebici in central Bosnia. This area of Bosnia, largely inhabited by Bosnian Serbs, was taken over in 1992 by Bosnian Muslim and Bosnian Croat forces; many of the local Bosnian Serbs were held at the Celebici prison camp. Given the complexity of the issues and the number of defendants, it is no surprise that the final decision is approximately 500 pages long. However, the salient jurisprudential contributions of the Celebici judgment can be distilled to **four points.**

First, the ICTY was careful to set out a detailed historical record of the conflict in Bosnia and Herzegovina. It concluded that this conflict must be recognized as international in nature throughout 1992. There is no question, it reasoned, that FRY forces were involved in the hostilities. Attempts by the FRY to create the appearance its forces were no longer involved were deliberately designed to mask the actual involvement. This finding dovetails with the reasoning of the Appeals Chamber in the Tadic case. **Second,** the ICTY addressed the doctrine of command responsibility (when superiors in a chain of command bear legal responsibility for the misdeeds of their subordinates). Application of command responsibility is important, since commanders are not usually direct participants in the atrocities and may in fact be unaware that they are being committed. In situations in which commanders do not know about such activities, how should they be judged? Can a commander be convicted because he or she "should have known" or because he or she created conditions in which it could be reasonably expected that the atrocities would ensue? The ICTY held that command responsibility encompasses "not only military commanders, but also civilians holding positions of authority." This is an important extension of command responsibility as a basis for liability. The ICTY also held that responsibility extends not only to those in de jure command (in other words, those who have the official titles and rankings) but also those in de facto command (those who may not have the official titles but who exert authority in the field). Such individuals may be held criminally responsible if they knew or had reason to know that offenses had been or were about to be committed by their subordinates and failed to take the necessary and reasonable measures to prevent or punish such offenses.

It was owing to the application of command responsibility that Delalic was acquitted: He was found not to have had command and control over the prison camp and the guards who worked there. Mucic, on the other hand, was implicated solely because he was derelict in his duty as commander of the prison camp: He allowed those under his authority to commit the most heinous of offenses without taking any disciplinary action; he also bore responsibility for the inadequate food, water supplies, and medical and sleeping facilities as well as for the atmosphere of terror in the prison camp.

The **third important contribution of the Celebici judgment** is that it was the first conviction for rape as torture. The ICTY was unequivocal on this point: "There can be no question that acts of rape may constitute torture under customary law." The **fourth** and last contribution of Celebici was in sentencing policy: Here, the ICTY recognized that age, impressionability, immaturity, and the effects of an armed conflict on an individual's personality can serve to mitigate a sentence. However, the ICTY did emphasize that, even in the face of chaos and social breakdown during an armed conflict, all individuals must act morally and responsibly.

The **Furundzija trial** began on June 8, 1998, and drew to a close on November 12—quite a bit shorter than the Celebici affair but not without its own procedural difficulties. Furundzija was a commander of the Jokers, a Croatian paramilitary unit that took part in a campaign to drive Muslims out of central Bosnia. In this capacity he and another soldier interrogated Witness A, the lead witness at trial. Witness A told the ICTY that she (and another individual, Victim B) had been locked up in a house in May 1993, where she was repeatedly beaten and raped by the other soldier. Furundzija failed to intervene and, in fact, continued to interrogate her. After the initial testimony, the ICTY on motion by the defense held that the Prosecution had improperly withheld information that Witness A had been treated for post-traumatic stress disorder [Marlise Simons in *New York Times*, 7/29/98]. As a result, the ICTY ordered that the defense had the right to further cross-examine Witness A and to call or recall relevant witnesses [ICTY press release, CC/PIU/332-E, 7/14/98]. The Prosecution had also been ordered to hand over certain medical documents about the victim that it sought to keep private. The trial was then adjourned until September so that these procedural rulings could be accommodated.

In this sense the Furundzija trial revealed the complexities in the procedures required for prosecuting wartime crimes against women while maintaining a balance with a defendant's due process rights. These complexities are in need of resolution, given the widespread prevalence of rape in all stages of the Balkans wars. In the Bosnian conflicts it is estimated that at least 20,000 women [mostly Muslim] were rape victims [Marlise Simons in *New York Times*, 7/29/98]. Allegations of rape and other sexual brutalities by FRY soldiers and Serb militia also arose during the recent Kosovo violence [R. Jeffrey Smith in Washington Post Foreign Service, 4/13/99].

After the proceedings were reopened in September, Furundzija was found guilty of two counts of violating the laws or customs of war. On December 10, 1998, he was sentenced concurrently to ten years' imprisonment. He has indicated he will appeal. In an important ruling regarding future prosecutions of all crimes, the ICTY held that a person's testimony may be reliable notwithstanding proof that he or she is suffering from post-traumatic stress disorder. The ICTY also held that the prohibition of torture had attained the status of a norm of international law from which no derogation is possible (*jus cogens*). **It defined torture as:**

> The intentional infliction, by act or omission, of severe pain or suffering, whether physical or mental, for the purpose of obtaining information or a confession or of punishing, intimidating, humiliating or coerc-

ing the victim or a third person, or of discriminating on any ground against the victim or a third person. For such an act to constitute torture, one of the parties thereto must be a public official or must, at any rate, act in a non-private capacity.

In the Furundzija decision the ICTY affirmed and applied the Celebici judgment's finding that rape may amount to torture. **As for the offense of rape, the Furundzija bench held that its elements included:**

> The sexual penetration, however slight, either of the vagina or anus of the victim by the penis of the perpetrator, or any other object used by the perpetrator, or of the mouth of the victim by the penis of the perpetrator, where such penetration is effected by coercion or force or threat of force against the victim or a third person.

This definition—still hinged on proof of some sort of penetration—should be contrasted with the somewhat broader definition of rape (and sexual violence) established by the International Criminal Tribunal for Rwanda (see *infra*). The ICTY further noted that aiding and abetting the commission of such an offense would entail practical assistance, encouragement, or moral support having a substantial effect on the perpetration of the crime and knowledge that such acts assist the commission of the offense. Co-perpetrating an offense entails a higher level of involvement (participating in an integral part) and a shared purpose.

Judgment in the **Aleksovski case** was delivered on May 7, 1999, and the written opinion issued on June 25. Aleksovski was the commander of the prison facility at Kaonik prior to becoming the Head of the District Croatian Defense Council. He is alleged to have accepted hundreds of detained Bosnian Muslim civilians into his custody at Kaonik. Many of the detainees under Aleksovski's control were subjected to inhumane treatment, including excessive and cruel interrogation, physical and psychological harm, forced labor, and being used as human shields [ICTY press release JL/PIU/400-E, 5/7/99]. Some detainees were murdered or otherwise killed.

In the end, Aleksovski was found not guilty of grave breaches of the 1949 Geneva Conventions (Article 2 of the Statute of the ICTY). The ICTY held that Article 2 did not apply to the offenses allegedly committed against these Bosnian Muslim detainees, since the alleged offenses did not take place during an international armed conflict [ICTY press release CC/PIU/413-E, 6/25/99]. However, Aleksovski *was* found guilty—as both an individual participant and a commander—of violating the laws or customs of war (namely, perpetrating outrages upon personal dignity) pursuant to Article 3 of the Statute of the ICTY. The Trial Chamber imposed a sentence of two-and-a-half years' imprisonment. Since Aleksovski had already served nearly two years and 11 months in prison pending trial, he was immediately released. The Prosecution intends to appeal. It may well be assisted in this regard by the broader approach to the applicability of

Article 2 espoused by the Tadic Appeal Chamber decision (although there are important factual differences between Aleksovski's armed involvement and Tadic's).

In another important matter, that of **Goran Jelisic,** a guilty plea was forthcoming on 31 of the 32 counts of the indictment [ICTY press release JL/PIU/357-E, 10/29/98]. All of these counts pertained to crimes against humanity and violations of the laws or customs of war. Jelisic's trial on the sole remaining count—genocide—began on November 30, 1998. Jelisic's sentencing on the guilty pleas will be determined after a verdict is issued on the **genocide charge.** By pressing on with a genocide trial, ICTY Prosecutors hope to be able to call additional evidence on the background of the violence in Bosnia and have judicial notice taken of its ethnic animus. Proceeding with the genocide charge against Jelisic is especially important from a precedential point of view, given the fact that the first genocide trial initiated by the ICTY, involving **Dr. Milan Kovacevic,** was never completed. Kovacevic was a Bosnian Serb official alleged to have played a key role in organizing three notorious prison camps in Prijedor and coordinating ethnic cleansing during the Bosnian wars. He died of a heart attack on August 1, 1998, in his cell in The Hague (Kovacevic's trial had begun on July 6) [ICTY press release CC/PIU/337-E, 8/3/98; see also Marlise Simons in *New York Times,* 8/2/98]. **His death** prompted a review by the ICTY of its Rules of Detention and the implementation of certain measures to ensure that medical care provided to detainees in an emergency is not unnecessarily delayed (although no fault was found in the Kovacevic death) [ICTY press release CC/PIU/343-E, 9/7/98].

Kovacevic was the third person held and indicted by the ICTY to have died. On June 29, 1998, Slavko Dokmanovic (a Serb mayor) hanged himself in his cell [ICTY press release CC/PIU/334-E, 7/23/98]. In 1996 another indictee, terminally ill with cancer, was released to die at home. It is also reported that at least five individuals suspected of war crimes by the ICTY (but not in custody) have been killed [Dejan Anastasijevic in *Time,* 8/24/98].

Several other trials are ongoing before the Trial Chamber: that of Tihomir Blaskic (commenced June 24, 1997), Zoran Kupreskic and five others (August 17, 1998), and Dario Kordic and Mario Cerkez (April 12, 1999); in some of these cases interlocutory evidentiary rulings have been made by the Trial and Appeals Chambers. Several other individuals in custody find themselves at various stages of pre-trial procedure. Most immediately, initial appearances continued in the Omarska and Keraterm cases (consolidated into one single indictment on November 9, 1998), and in the Bosanski Samac case (in which a fourth defendant, Stevan Todorovic, was detained on September 27, 1998). The Prosecutor also continued to seek jurisdiction over the defendants in the Vukovar Hospital case, in which FRY military courts purport to have initiated domestic proceedings [ICTY press releases CC/PIU/370-E, 12/7/98, and CC/PIU/374-E, 12/15/98]. This attempt to seek jurisdiction was reinforced by U.N. Security Council Resolution 1207 [11/17/98], which requires the FRY to surrender immediately and unconditionally to the ICTY the three indicted individuals (Mile Mrksic, Veselin Sljivancanin and Moroslav Radic) and to defer their prosecution to the ICTY. These indictments were issued by the ICTY on November 7, 1995, and relate to the murder of 260 unarmed individuals during an attack on the city of Vukovar in 1991 [ICTY press release JL/PIU/376-E, 12/15/98]. Neither the indictments nor the arrest warrants that followed have been respected by the FRY. The ICTY is concerned that purported legal proceedings in the FRY are designed to shield these accused from international criminal responsibility.

Finances and Administration

For 1999 the ICTY's budget rose to $94,103,800, up considerably from the 1998 budget of $64,775,300 [ICTY Fact Sheet, www.un.org/icty/glance/fact.htm]. The ICTY's budget has increased significantly every year since its creation (the original budget in 1994, its first full year of operation, was $10,800,000). These large increases have been criticized at meetings of the Fifth (Administrative and Budgetary) Committee of the General Assembly [U.N. press release GA/AB/3271, 11/23/98].

On May 13, 1998, a **Third Trial Chamber** was created by virtue of Security Council Resolution 1166. As a result, the number of judges was increased by three to 14, and on October 16, 1998, the Assembly elected the three to fill those spots: David Hunt (Australia), Mohamed Bennouna (Morocco), and Patrick Robinson (Jamaica) [ICTY press release CC/PIU/363-E, 11/13/98]. A list of nominees was provided by the Security Council in Resolution 1191 [8/27/98].

International Criminal Tribunal for Rwanda (ICTR)

Established in 1994 [S/Res/955, 11/8/94] to hold accountable perpetrators of the massacre of approximately 800,000 mainly Tutsi Rwandans, the ICTR rendered its first sentences in 1998 and continues its activities in 1999. In addition, it delivered its first judgment, issued in the matter of Jean-Paul Akayesu [ICTR Case No. 96-4-T]. This judgment is one of the most important contributions to judge-made international criminal law since the Nuremberg trials. The ICTR also issued judgment in the matter of Clément Kayishema and Obed Ruzindana, both of whom had been cited in the very first indictment issued by the ICTR on November 28, 1995. The two men were convicted of genocide.

Two Guilty Pleas and Two Judgments

Jean-Paul Akayesu is the former *bourgmestre* (mayor) of the Taba commune. He was charged with numerous counts of genocide, crimes against humanity, and war crimes. The nub of the charges related to Akayesu's failure to prevent the killing of Tutsi in Taba or otherwise call for assistance to quell the violence, despite the fact that he had the authority and responsibility to do so. Many Tutsi had sought refuge at the local government offices. It was there that the atrocities took place, allegedly facilitated by Akayesu's decision to allow them to occur. There were also charges that Akayesu himself had ordered beatings and killings.

Akayesu's **principal line of defense** was that he did not commit or participate in any of the beatings or killings and, responding to the facilitation charge, that he was helpless to prevent the massacres of Tutsi. Regarding the latter, Akayesu sought to rely on the testimony of Major-General Roméo Dallaire of Canada as to the unstoppable nature of the Rwandan genocide. Ultimately, this line of argumentation was rejected and Akayesu was found to have "ordered, committed, or otherwise aided and abetted" these crimes. In fact, his failure to prevent genocide constituted "tacit encouragement" of genocide, which, in turn, led to individual criminal responsibility for genocide.

On September 2, 1998, Akayesu was found guilty of nine counts of genocide and crimes against humanity, although acquitted of war crimes charges, since it had not been proved his acts were committed in conjunction with the armed conflict (which the ICTR distinguished from genocide) in Rwanda. Sentenced shortly thereafter to three life terms, plus 80 years, Akayesu is vigorously seeking to appeal both the sentence and the conviction [press release ICTR/INFO-9-2-168, 11/25/98].

In pursuing these appeals, Akayesu has gone through many lawyers, and this has led the ICTR to reassess, and confirm, that under international law it may assign a detainee defense counsel should that detainee be unable to retain a lawyer. In so doing, it used as persuasive authority the ICTY's decision in the Delalic case according to which **the right to assigned counsel does not mean the right to assigned counsel of the accused's own choosing.** Administratively speaking, this discussion has also prompted the ICTR to implement a temporary moratorium on defense counsel from Canada and France in order to achieve a better geographic balance and representation of the principal legal systems of the world [ICTR Update and Bulletin, ICTR/INFO, 2/22/99].

The **ICTR's judgment in the Akayesu matter** gave judicial notice to the pervasiveness of the violence during the Rwandan genocide, to the fact that it was both organized and planned, and to the fact that it was ethnically motivated. The ICTR held that the massacres "had a specific objective, namely the extermination of the Tutsi, who were targeted especially because of their Tutsi origin" and that "genocide was committed in Rwanda in 1994 against the Tutsi as a group." This was an important finding, since there is ethnographic uncertainty as to whether Hutu and Tutsi in fact constitute ethnic groups. After all, as was noted by the ICTR,

Hutu and Tutsi share the same language, religion, music, art, culture, and territory. Indeed, as Philip Gourevitch reports in his recent book: "Ethnographers and historians have lately come to agree that Hutus and Tutsis cannot properly be called distinct ethnic groups" [We wish to inform you that tomorrow we will be killed with our families: Stories from Rwanda, New York: Farrar, Straus and Giroux, 1998, p. 48]. In an important jurisprudential development, the ICTR held that ethnicity can, in fact, be constructed and, in the case of Rwanda, that this construction can be linked to Belgian colonial intervention, most notably the infamous distribution of "ethnic identity" cards. In so doing, the ICTR imported some elasticity into the definition of genocide. The ICTR was quick to point out, however, that genocide could target only "stable groups"—those that were "constituted in permanent fashion" and "membership of which is determined by birth." As a result, destroying "mobile groups which one joins through individual voluntary commitment, such as political and economic groups," would not fall within the ambit of genocide. The Tutsi were found to be a "stable and permanent" group within the context of the Rwandan violence.

The ICTR was also careful to draw a distinction between the genocidal acts of violence against the Tutsi and the military conflict between the Rwandan Armed Forces and the Rwandese Patriotic Army (an emigré Tutsi force based in Uganda that eventually seized control of Rwanda and put an end to the genocide). The ICTR went on to conclude that there was an "armed conflict" between the Rwandese Patriotic Army and the Rwandan Armed Forces—a finding necessary to ground liability for the violation of the laws or customs of war.

The Akayesu judgment also clarified the law surrounding whether an individual can be convicted of crimes against humanity, genocide, and war crimes arising out of the same set of facts. The ICTR held that, as a general matter, multiple convictions were indeed possible in one of three circumstances: (1) where the offenses have different elements; (2) where the provisions creating the offenses protect different interests; or (3) where it is necessary to record a conviction for both offenses in order fully to describe what the accused did. In terms of the crime of inciting genocide, the ICTR held that incitement can be implicit as well as direct; and that public incitement to commit genocide can be punished even when such incitement was unsuccessful. This latter ruling is important in discouraging the incitement of hatred by characterizing it as an independent offense regardless of its effects.

The Akayesu decision is also notable for having set out a comprehensive historical narrative of sexual violence in the Taba commune, for concluding that systematic sexual abuse can constitute genocide, and for developing the definition of rape in international law. Drawing from its enabling Statute, the ICTR held that rape is a "physical invasion of a sexual nature, committed on a person under circumstances which are coercive"—an invasion that, if undertaken with the specific intent to destroy, in whole or in part, a particular group, can constitute genocide. The Court went beyond the "physical invasion" definition, however, in concluding that "sexual violence is not limited to physical invasion of the human body and may include acts which do not involve penetration or even physical contact." As a result, it found that Akayesu's ordering militia forces to undress a student and force her to do gymnastics naked in front of a crowd constituted sexual violence. In this sense, the Akayesu decision may offer an approach to gendered violence that is more progressive than the approach of the ICTY in the Celebici and Furundzija judgments. In regard to proving that the circumstances were "coercive," the Tribunal held that "coercive circumstances need not be evidenced by a show of physical force . . . threats, intimidation, extortion and other forms of duress which prey on fear or desperation may constitute coercion, and coercion may be inherent in certain circumstances, such as armed conflict or the military presence of *Interahamwe* [Hutu militia] among refugee Tutsi women at the *bureau communal*."

On another note, **the joint trial of Dr. Kayishema and Mr. Ruzindana** closed in November 1998. Judgment was issued on May 21, 1999 [press release ICTR/INFO-9-2-184, 5/21/99]. Kayishema, a *préfet* of Kibuye, and Ruzindana, a businessman, were accused of a variety of barbarities committed in Kibuye *préfecture*, including having directed *Interahamwe* and civilians to attack and kill Tutsi seeking refuge in Kibuye and having taken part in these attacks themselves. Many of the massacres took place at churches and at the Kibuye stadium. Over half of the victims of the 1994 genocide were killed in Kibuye prefecture [press release ICTR/INFO-9-2-183, 5/13/99].

The ICTR convicted both of genocide. Kayishema was sentenced to life imprisonment and Ruzindana to a term of 25 years. Both were acquitted of crimes against humanity: Drawing from the reasoning in the Akayesu decision, the ICTR found these charges to be based upon the same conduct and evidence as the genocide charges. As a result, these charges were found to be subsumed under the crime of genocide.

In other matters before the ICTR, **Jean Kambanda, Rwanda's Prime Minister at the time of the 1994 genocide,** pleaded guilty on May 1, 1998, to charges of genocide and crimes against humanity. On September 4, 1998, Kambanda was sentenced to life imprisonment; his lawyers had suggested he receive a term of two years [IRIN News Update no. 495, 9/4/98]. The life sentence was issued in part because Kambanda occupied a high ministerial post at the time of the genocide and, as result, abused a position of trust; these considerations negated any mitigating circumstances, such as promptly pleading guilty, cooperating with authorities, and remorse [ICTR Case No. 97-23-S, 9/4/98]. The Kambanda sentencing decision provides a helpful overview of ICTR sentencing policy, part of which derives from domestic legislation in Rwanda. The incorporation of domestic law into the Tribunal's work can help bridge the gap between international institutions and national audiences.

On February 5, 1999, the ICTR sentenced **Omar Serushago** to 15 years' imprisonment [press release, ICTR/INFO-9-2-160, 2/5/99]. Serushago, a Hutu militia leader in Gisenyi *préfecture*, had previously pled guilty (on December 14, 1998) to one count of genocide and three counts of crimes against humanity. He was the first genocide convict at the ICTR to receive less than a life sentence. Judge Laïty Kama held that Serushago deserved a degree of clemency because he had surrendered voluntarily, had cooperated with the ICTR, and had expressed remorse for his crimes. Originally, Serushago had been charged with a fifth count: rape. He denied this charge, and it was withdrawn by the Prosecution at the time he agreed to plead guilty to the genocide and crimes against humanity charges. Although the Akayesu judgment successfully demonstrated the prevalence of rape as a tool of genocide in Rwanda, the withdrawing of the Serushago charges, together with the fact that Akayesu was not charged with rape until well after the original indictment was filed, may justify concerns that the ICTR Prosecutor's office is not taking gender-based charges such as rape as seriously as it could [see the Amicus Brief Regarding Rape in Rwanda in the ICTR Trial Chamber, *Re* Akayesu, www.hri.ca/doccentre/violence/amicus-brief.shtml]. Serushago has appealed his sentence.

Ongoing Activities and Indictments

On January 25, 1999, the **trial of Alfred Musema** began before the Trial Chamber. During the genocide, Musema was director of the Gisovu tea factory in western Rwanda, a location at which thousands of Tutsi were massacred. Although not a government official, Musema is accused of using his influential position as a businessman to carry out the government's policy of murder and ethnic hatred [press release ICTR/INFO-9-2-161, 2/8/99]. The Musema trial drew to a close on June 28 [ICTR/INFO-9-2-193, 6/29/99]. The trial of **another high-profile accused, George Rutaganda**—a former vice president of the *Interahamwe* militia—was completed on June 17 [ICTR/INFO-9-2-190, 6/18/99]. No date has been fixed for delivery of judgment in either the Musema or the Rutaganda cases. The ICTR intends to complete these two cases before January 31, 2000 [S/Res/1241, 5/19/99]. The trial of **Laurent Semanza**—a former *bourgmestre* of Bicumbi now charged with 14 counts of genocide, crimes against humanity, and war crimes—was scheduled to begin in early February but was postponed due to his counsel's request for replacement [press release ICTR/INFO-9-2-159, 2/3/99]. On April 7, 1999, **five senior officials of the 1994 Rwandan government,** including two ministers, pleaded not guilty to 11 joint counts, including conspiracy to commit genocide and genocide [ICTR/INFO-9-2-177, 4/7/99]. On April 19,

Emmanuel Bagambiki, the former *préfet* of Cyangugu, pleaded not guilty to seven counts of genocide and crimes against humanity [ICTR/ INFO-9-2-179, 4/19/99]. The charges against Bagambiki involve **publicly expressing anti-Tutsi sentiments** and preparing lists of people to eliminate that were given to soldiers and militia.

The ICTR has received considerable **cooperation from other African nations** in terms of turning over individuals accused of crimes during the 1994 genocide. Mathieu Ngirumpatse, a former Rwandan Minister of Justice, was arrested in Mali on June 11, 1998, and transferred to the ICTR [ICTR/INFO-9-2-163, 2/12/99]. Arrests (and transfers) in February 1999 by Kenya and South Africa of genocide suspects Dr. Casimir Bizimungu, Eliezer Niyitegeka, and Ignace Bagilishema are further examples of this cooperation [ICTR/INFO-9-2-167, 2/23/99, -162, 2/11/99, -165, 2/21/99]. **Niyitegeka,** Minister of Information in the 1994 Rwandan government, made his initial appearance before the ICTR on April 15, 1999, and pleaded not guilty to six counts, including genocide and conspiracy to commit genocide [ICTR/INFO-9-2-178, 4/15/99]. **Bagilishema** made his initial appearance on April 1, 1999, pleading not guilty to 13 counts principally involving massacres in churches and the stadium in Kigali [ICTR/INFO-9-2-175, 4/1/99]. **Bizimungu** remains in custody and has not yet made a court appearance. Cameroonian officials weighed in on April 6, 1999, with the arrest of three former Rwandan ministers suspected of involvement in the genocide: **Jerome Bicamumpaka** (foreign affairs), **Prosper Mugiraneza** (civil service), and **Justin Mugenzi** (commerce) [ICTR/INFO-9-2-176, 4/6/99]. The active participation of many countries in the transfer of suspects to the ICTR bodes well for the future viability of the Tribunal. In an important public interview, **Justice Arbour contrasted this cooperation with the "tolerated noncompliance" accorded the ICTY** [press briefing, 3/5/99].

The ICTR has been supportive of **European attempts to try individuals involved in the Rwandan genocide** whose conduct may have affected European citizens. For example, on March 20, 1999, Belgium urged Tanzania to extradite **Bernard Ntuyahaga,** a former major in the Rwandan army, to face murder charges in Belgium. These charges date from 1994 and pertain to the killing of Agathe Uwilingiyimana, a former Rwandan Prime Minister, and ten Belgian peacekeepers. The ICTR had previously granted the Prosecutor's request to withdraw the indictment against Ntuyahaga in favor of trial in Belgium [ICTR Update 014, 3/18/99]; Ntuyahaga was released only to be arrested by Tanzania [IRIN News Update no. 640, 3/30/99]. Rwanda has also filed an independent, and apparently competing, extradition request [IRIN News Update nos. 637, 3/25/99, and 641, 3/31/99]. These transfers and requests strike at the heart of issues of complementarity between national and international tribunals. They also squarely address such issues as double jeopardy and Rwanda's interest in prosecuting its citizens who committed atrocities on Rwandan soil. Ntuyahaga had voluntarily surrendered to the ICTR on July 10, 1998, and was indicted by the ICTR on one count of crimes against humanity (murder) on September 29, 1998. As of June 1, 1999, the ICTR has 38 suspects in custody. For the most part, these individuals were high-ranking political, military, media, and civilian leaders in Rwanda at the time of the genocide. In recognition of the growing ranks of detainees awaiting trial, the Security Council established a **Third Trial Chamber** at the ICTR [S/Res/1165, 4/30/98], and on November 3 the General Assembly elected three judges to fill it: Lloyd George Williams (Jamaica), Dionysios Kondylis (Greece), and Pavel Dolenc (Slovenia). All three were sworn in on February 22, 1999 [ICTR/INFO-9-2-166, 2/23/99]. Judge Kondylis subsequently resigned for personal reasons [ICTR/INFO-9-2-172, 3/24/99]. Six other judges—some of them new, others renewing their terms— were also elected in November to serve in the Trial Chambers [U.N. press release GA/9495, 11/3/98].

U.N. Secretary-General Annan has requested **$80.6 million gross appropriation for the ICTR for 1999** [GA/AB/3271, 11/23/98]. There has been a reduction in the number of complaints about the fiscal and administrative management of the ICTR, although the Fifth Committee still has concerns in the areas of efficient hiring and procurement [GA/AB/3271, 11/23/98].

The Rwandan Courts and Genocide Prosecutions

The Rwandan domestic courts continue to deliver verdicts. In some cases those found guilty are sentenced to death—22 prisoners were executed on April 24, 1998 [James C. McKinley Jr. in *New York Times*, 4/25/98]—although most of those convicted receive prison terms. There are an estimated 125,000 individuals in prison in Rwanda still awaiting trial for alleged involvement in the 1994 massacres [Irinwire, 3/9/99]. Approximately 4,500 of these detainees were between the ages of 14 and 18 at the time of their arrest [ibid.]. Most were arrested in the summer and fall of 1994 and, thus, have been in prison for about five years [see Mark Drumbl, "Rule of Law Amid Lawlessness: Counseling the Accused in Rwanda's Domestic Genocide Trials," 29 *Columbia Human Rights Law Review* 545 (1998)]. In an attempt to accelerate the judicial process, the Rwandan government has proposed **community-based mediations—called** *gacaca***—to deal with those accused of intermediate and less serious offenses** [IRIN News Update no. 642, 4/1/99; and Ian Fisher in *New York Times*, 4/21/99].

Future Tribunals: Cambodia?

Between 1975 and 1979, 1.7 million Cambodians were killed during the rule of Pol Pot and the Khmer Rouge. Cambodians have spent much of the last two decades coming to terms with this legacy of violence. In 1998, questions of accountability and national reconciliation came to the forefront when two former Khmer Rouge leaders, Nuon Chea and Khieu Samphan, emerged from hiding and surrendered to authorities. Both issued ambiguous statements of regret. Khieu Samphan, for his part, remarked: "I am very sorry. . . . Actually we are very sorry, not just for the lives of the people, but also for the lives of animals that suffered in the war. . . . If we have to say who was wrong and who was right, we cannot have national reconciliation" [quoted by Ker Munthit in *Globe and Mail*, 12/30/98].

Many Khmer Rouge leaders desire reintegration into Cambodian society without trials or judicial intervention. This presents the current Cambodian government as well as the international community with a delicate situation. (For discussion of the Cambodian and the international community's response to calls for an international tribunal see "Making and Keeping the Peace: Cambodia" in the present volume.)

In contemplating the creation of a tribunal, the international community would do well to draw from its experiences in Rwanda. **One important consideration is the location of the tribunal.** Choosing not to locate an international tribunal in the affected country may undermine the legitimacy of that country's nascent political structures (as opposed to building them up). It may further disempower victims by reinforcing the perception that they are unable to hold accountable their own aggressors. The decision to locate the ICTR in Arusha, Tanzania, may have had such an effect on the Rwandan government and the victims of the genocide, creating some tensions between the ICTR and the Rwandan government. **A second consideration is who, exactly, should be tried.** Involving only a handful of select elites in the proceedings may not effectively promote collective memory or meet individual victims' potential need for individualized justice [see José Alvarez, "Crimes of State/Crimes of Hate: Lessons from Rwanda," *Yale Journal of International Law*, Summer 1999]. In poor countries like Rwanda and Cambodia, where the vast proportion of the population has no access to coverage of the trials, international processes may hold only limited promise of contributing to national reconciliation [ibid.].

There are further **parallels between the Rwandan situation and that of Cambodia.** In both cases, many leaders of the factions that perpetrated crimes against humanity seem to have little remorse; in Cambodia the only public exception is Kang Kek Ieu ("Duch"), the head of the Khmer Rouge secret police and commandant of Tuol Sleng prison. Also in both cases, the involvement of the international community in propping up abusive regimes when there was some outside knowledge of the barbarities being committed needs to be fleshed out and critically assessed. In the case of Cambodia, for example, the Khmer Rouge was given the right to occupy Cambodia's U.N. seat. Then there is the matter of U.S. involvement in the Vietnamese war, which had an extraterritorial effect upon Cambodia and may have consolidated the Khmer Rouge's accession to power. In exploring these issues, courts may promote some self-reflection, but a truly searching truth commission could be more effective. On this point, U.N. Secretary-General Kofi Annan has proposed (and the Security Council has approved) an independent inquiry into the actions of the U.N. before and during the Rwandan genocide [IRIN News Updates nos. 635, 3/23/99, and 641, 3/31/99; Judith Miller in *New York Times*, 3/24/99].

The Cambodian government has initiated three **domestic war crimes trials of former Khmer Rouge leaders.** On June 7, 1999, Nuon Paet, a Khmer Rouge commander and the first senior leader to face trial, was sentenced to life imprisonment for his participation in the murder of 13 people during a 1994 train ambush [BBC News, 6/7/99]. The proceedings, however, lasted less than one day, affording little opportunity for the trial to establish a judicially sanctioned historical narrative of the atrocities perpetrated by the Khmer Rouge. Two other Khmer leaders await trial: Kang Kek Ieu and Ta Mok. Nonetheless, many Khmer leaders remain at large, living freely under **surrender deals negotiated with the Cambodian government.** Should trials be systematically pursued on an international level, these surrender deals may have to be undone. This raises complex questions of who should be tried, how the guilty should be punished, and what other forms of restitution and reparation should be awarded to victims. Trials may be conjoined with a U.N. Commission of Inquiry into the Crimes of the Khmer Rouge to establish a historical narrative that what happened in Cambodia was not a "war," as Khieu Samphan states, but a coercive pattern of forced collectivization in which innocent civilians were the victims of brutal crimes against humanity. These crimes included rape and expropriation of assets; many Vietnamese in Cambodia were also subject to genocidal persecution. Forced marriage was also widespread [Laura McGrew, "Cambodian Women at Year Zero," *On the Record*, 3/9/99]. As neither the ICTY, ICTR, or ICC has jurisdiction to prosecute forced marriage (the ICC has jurisdiction over forced impregnation, all three have jurisdiction over rape), the prevalence of this practice in the Cambodian "killing fields" may suggest expanding the list of gender-based crimes.

5. Domestic Courts and International Crimes: Pinochet as Precedent?

General Augusto Pinochet Ugarte was the military dictator of Chile from 1973 to 1990. He was also a participant in Chile's transition to democracy from 1988 to 1990, agreeing to relinquish power (after he lost a public plebiscite), although only in exchange for the promise of immunity from prosecution, a full amnesty for his actions as leader of Chile's junta, and a permanent appointment as Senator. An estimated 3,000 people were killed or "disappeared" under Pinochet's regime [*Globe and Mail*, 3/24/99]. Much of this evidence was collected in 1991 by the Chilean National

Commission on Truth and Reconciliation, which produced an authoritative document (the Rettig Report) listing many victims and abuses but no abusers.

On October 16, 1998, Pinochet, in London recovering from back surgery, was arrested by British authorities on a provisional warrant—the result of an extradition request from Baltasar Garzón, a judge of Spain's National Court. Spain was seeking to try Pinochet on charges of crimes against humanity, genocide, terrorism, hostage-taking, and torture. These charges made specific reference to Spanish citizens targeted by this violence but also invoked international humanitarian law to capture incidents involving non-Spaniards. Since Chile had decided not to prosecute Pinochet, Judge Garzón issued the charges and extradition request while Pinochet was in the United Kingdom.

It is unclear where the basis for a genocide charge may lie. Judge Garzón alleged that Pinochet tried to destroy an entire group of people, namely, his opponents, but political groups are not covered by the Genocide Convention. There is, however, significant factual evidence supporting the legal claim that Pinochet committed torture, terrorism, and crimes against humanity during his rule [*Economist*, 11/28/98]. France, Switzerland, and Belgium joined Spain in seeking Pinochet's extradition for crimes committed against their citizens [Tim Weiner in *New York Times*, 12/2/98].

Pinochet's spirited attempt to use the courts to quash the arrest warrant and prevent his extradition has given rise to an important body of judge-made international law. It was argued, for example, that the amnesty given Pinochet by Chile, the society affected by his rule, must be respected as a rightful exercise of national sovereignty. It was also argued that because the allegations against Pinochet involved his conduct while Head of State, he was immune to prosecution for such actions under the doctrine of sovereign immunity. It was argued too that Pinochet had diplomatic immunity because he is a Senator in Chile, even though his visit to the United Kingdom was not for official diplomatic reasons. Challenges were also brought to the United Kingdom's ability to assume jurisdiction over crimes that did not occur within its own borders.

Pinochet's arguments were successful before the High Court of Justice on October 28, 1998. According to its decision, Pinochet had absolute sovereign immunity for actions made while carrying out the functions of Head of State and therefore could not be tried for these crimes in a British court—or be extradited to Spain to face trial there. The High Court's decision was appealed to the judicial committee of the House of Lords. **On November 25, 1998, the House of Lords, in a split decision, held that the Pinochet arrest warrant was, in fact, proper** [*Regina* v *Bartle, ex parte Pinochet*, House of Lords, 11/25/98, (1998) 3 WLR 1456]. Sovereign immunity could not apply to Pinochet's situation, said the Lords, since that doctrine covers only legitimate official acts of former Heads of State. Pinochet's crimes, committed in secret, were not legitimate official acts of the Chilean government but were undertaken in a personal capacity. More broadly, the judicial committee of **the House of Lords held that the sovereign immunity doctrine could never shield a Head of State from charges of murder, extrajudicial executions, torture, and hostage-taking.** Lord Steyn observed that such absolute immunity would have protected Adolf Hitler against prosecution for ordering the "Final Solution" and orchestrating the Holocaust—an unacceptable result.

Taking up the matter of jurisdiction, the judicial committee of the House of Lords discussed but did not rely on the principle that all states have jurisdiction over crimes prohibited by customary international law ("universal jurisdiction"). Lord Nicholls, for his part, focused on international conventions that the U.K. has signed in the areas of torture and hostage-taking and incorporated into domestic legislation. These conventions stipulate that commission of such offenses is punishable by the courts of individual states—indeed, that there is an *obligation* to try alleged perpetrators or to extradite them. Lord Steyn, although noting that by 1973 genocide, torture, hostage-taking, and crimes against humanity had already been condemned as high crimes by customary international law, nonetheless referred to the statutes and conventions detailed by Lord Nicholls when discussing jurisdiction. In this case, then, **international convention established extraterritorial jurisdiction and Pinochet could be held in the U.K. while the extradition request was considered.**

As for the political argument involving Chilean national sovereignty, the House of Lords held that this was not a matter for it to decide but, rather, for the executive branch of government—specifically, the Office of the Home Secretary, which would evaluate the validity of the charges as part of the decision whether or not to extradite Pinochet. Since extradition decisions are subject to judicial review, the Home Secretary's decision in this matter could ultimately return to the House of Lords [Warren Hoge in *New York Times*, 12/10/98].

In an odd twist, **Pinochet requested a new hearing,** alleging that Lord Hoffman, one of the Law Lords judging his appeal and upholding the extradition request, was biased, since he was chairman of Amnesty International's charitable arm and his wife had worked for the organization for over 20 years. Even though Amnesty International had intervened in the appeal, presenting arguments to the Law Lords, Lord Hoffmann had failed to disclose his connection. **On December 17, 1998, the judicial committee of the House of Lords ordered a fresh hearing on the issues of immunity and jurisdiction** [Reuters, 12/17/98], and on January 15, 1999, the Lords' November decision was set aside [(1999) 2 WLR 272]. This was the very first time the Lords had reviewed one of their own rulings [Warren Hoge in *New York Times*, 3/25/99].

In its second series of deliberations on the matter, **the House of**

Lords ruled six to one that the extradition request was legally valid
[*Regina v Bartle, ex parte Pinochet*, House of Lords, 3/24/99]. However, in an important
caveat, the Lords decided that the extradition request could be based on
allegations of torture committed only after December 8, 1988. The
Lords reached this conclusion through a circuitous path; in fact, seven
separate judgments were issued—one by each Lord—although it is possible to trace some areas of jurisprudential consensus. The Lords began
with the reasoning on jurisdiction that had led to their first decision,
namely, that jurisdiction was based on the pertinent international conventions. The Lords agreed that the International Convention against Torture
gave the U.K. courts extraterritorial jurisdiction to adjudge allegations of
torture. This Convention stipulates that any signatory must put an alleged
offender on trial if the offender is present on its territory or, failing to try
the offender, must extradite the offender to a country that will—Spain,
for example. The Lords reasoned further that, because the United Kingdom did not incorporate the Torture Convention into its domestic legislation until September 29, 1988, the nation's courts would have extraterritorial jurisdiction over crimes committed only after that date. In the words
of Lord Browne-Wilkinson: "Torture outside the United Kingdom was
not a crime under the law of the United Kingdom until the 1988 Criminal
Justice Act, section 134 came into force on 29 September 1988."

In fact, torture may also be precluded by customary international
law. If that is the case, universal jurisdiction might well permit Pinochet
to be tried for acts of torture committed before 1988. A persuasive argument could be made that the judicial committee of the House of Lords
failed to give sufficient weight to the fact that universal jurisdiction to
prosecute the crimes with which Pinochet is charged can be traced back
to the Nuremberg and Tokyo tribunals and subsequent U.N. General Assembly resolutions. What is more, torture was firmly prohibited in Chilean law, British law, and Spanish law before Pinochet seized power in
1973. Such were the suggestions of Lord Hutton who, dissenting on this
point, concluded that the U.K. courts did not require the authority of a
statute to exercise jurisdiction over all the allegations of torture, since
such extraterritorial jurisdiction existed by virtue of the operation of customary international law. Lord Hutton buttressed this conclusion with a
reference to the ICTY's recent decision in the Furundzija matter, in
which it was held that the prohibition of torture is a *jus cogens*, thereby
entitling every state to investigate, prosecute, and punish or extradite offenders. The integration of the ICTY's decisions into municipal case law
is certainly an important jurisprudential development.

In the end, based upon its reasoning regarding jurisdiction, the
Lords dismissed all but three of the 32 charges in the arrest warrant
[BBC News, 3/29/99]. Although the Lords continued to hold that Pinochet's
status as a former Head of State did not give him immunity, they now

noted that the immunity he once had came to an end on December 8, 1998, the date on which the United Kingdom finally ratified the Torture Convention, joining Spain and Chile, which had ratified earlier. The logic of the House of Lords was that, by ratifying the Convention, each party agreed that none of its former heads of state could ever claim immunity in cases of alleged torture.

Shortly after the Lords' decision, Judge Garzón sent British prosecutors 33 new charges of human rights abuses involving Pinochet, all of them alleged to have occurred after 1988 [Warren Hoge in *New York Times*, 3/28/99]. (By mid-June the number of charges reached 108 [ibid., 6/18/99].) **On April 15, 1999, the Home Secretary issued an Authority to Proceed,** allowing the extradition case against Pinochet (on the previous charges—torture and conspiracy to commit torture— and potentially the ones added by Judge Garzón) to go forward [BBC News, 4/15/99]. In this regard, the Home Secretary chose not to follow the obiter dicta of the House of Lords. In the second Pinochet decision, the Law Lords actively entered the political fray by suggesting that, owing to the substantial reduction in the number of charges, the Home Secretary should reconsider whether the extradition request should proceed. This judicial activism vis-à-vis the decision-making authority of the executive branch of government is something the first Pinochet decision was careful to avoid. As Pinochet is entitled to a legal hearing to challenge the extradition proceedings (which may eventually be appealed to the House of Lords), these comments may foreshadow the activist approach the Lords could take in adjudicating the merits of the extradition itself. **In May 1999, Pinochet in fact launched an application for judicial review of the Authority to Proceed with the extradition.** Chile, for its part, remains deeply divided as to whether Pinochet should face these charges in Spain.

Despite the narrowness of the legal reasoning in the Lords' final decision, it nonetheless **sets the stage for trying abroad former heads of state who are alleged to have been involved in torture at home.** This raises the broader question of whether ghosts of past oppression should indeed be exposed, and, if the decision is made to expose them, whether foreign national courts constitute an appropriate forum. The issue is anything but abstract: A number of former dictators with long records of gross abuse of human rights now live in exile. These include Uganda's Idi Amin (currently in Saudi Arabia), Paraguay's Alfredo Stroessner (in Brazil), and Haiti's Jean-Claude Duvalier (in France). Might the Pinochet affair give rise to a unilateralism that could roil international comity? Could Iraq, for example, indict George Bush on charges of war crimes arising out of the Gulf War? Should France have indicted DRC President Laurent Kabila on torture charges while in Paris for a diplomatic conference in November 1998? [see Craig R. Whitney in *New York Times*, 11/28/98].

There are certainly ways in which national courts could help enforce international law, but in the absence of a coordinating mechanism, there is apt to be confusion as well as the charge that particular national efforts are politically motivated. The complementarity provisions of the ICC could—notwithstanding their current shortcomings—help set rules of the game. Without such rules, the United States could have something more immediate to fear than the overreach of the ICC: unilateral charges arising at the national level against a broad array of military and political leaders.

From a political realist perspective, however, prosecuting Pinochet may give rise to what journalist Charles Krauthammer identifies as a perverse incentive. "For any tyrant, the best protection from justice is to continue to tyrannize," he writes, and "Pinochet would never have been arrested if he had not done the right thing: giving up power to a democratic government" [*Time*, 12/14/98]. Of course, one can make the equally persuasive argument that the ease with which political leaders can escape the consequences of their brutality may encourage more of them to seize power and commit atrocities; the threat of legal sanction—either from the ICC or coordinated national proceedings—can act as a deterrent. In the end, political realities, from which law can never be disentangled, should urge us to be thorough, yet thoughtful, about the manner in which legal norms are enforced.

Although a watershed, the Pinochet case is **not the only example of domestic courts actively involved in punishing transnational crimes.** The extradition to Scottish courts of suspects in the **Lockerbie affair** (discussed later in this chapter) shows the ability of national institutions to fill the void created by the absence of an international regime to punish terrorism. On another note, **Kuwait Airways** has used the British courts to claim up to $1 billion in damages from Iraqi Airways for the loss of aircraft and spare parts seized during the 1990 invasion of Kuwait. A decision in Kuwait Airways' favor by the High Court constitutes the first firm legal precedent for making claims against the state-owned entities that a foreign government may use to seize another country's commercial assets [John Mason in *Financial Times*, 12/1/98]. Owing to significant breaches of international law on the part of Iraq, it was held the seizure of the aircraft by Iraqi Airways could not be protected by any act of state doctrine. As a result, Iraq faces the threat that civil aircraft belonging to Iraqi Airways may be seized when international service recommences at such time as sanctions against the country are lifted.

6. The International Court of Justice (ICJ)

The ICJ, or World Court, the principal judicial organ of the United Nations, is located in The Hague. Its enabling statute allows it to hear disputes only when both parties agree to participate in the proceedings. States alone can be parties to a contentious proceeding, although authorized international organizations may refer legal questions to the ICJ for advisory opinions.

Over the course of 1998–99 the ICJ has seen an increase in its workload. Accounting for this activity are several new cases as well as the counterclaims, preliminary objections, and requests for provisional measures in pre-existing cases that create "cases within cases." This increase in the activities of the ICJ has yet to be matched with a corresponding increase in its resources. Concerns over the ICJ's budget prompted President Judge Schwebel to request from the U.N. General Assembly the allocation of appropriate resources so that the ICJ could work "with full effectiveness and despatch" [International Court of Justice (ICJ) press communiqué 98/33, 10/27/98].

In terms of **new cases,** on April 29, 1999, the **Federal Republic of Yugoslavia initiated proceedings against ten states involved in the NATO bombings,** alleging that they violated their international obligations not to use force against other states, infringed on the FRY's sovereignty, and breached, inter alia, their obligations to protect civilian populations and the environment and refrain from using prohibited weapons [ICJ press communiqué 99/17, 4/29/99]. The FRY sought provisional relief in the form of an injunction halting the bombings and compensation for the damage already done. Hearings on the request for provisional relief closed on May 12, 1999.

On June 2 the ICJ denied the requests for provisional relief [ICJ press communiqué 99/23, 6/2/99], holding that it lacked the jurisdiction to issue provisional measures. It also held that, since the ICJ cannot have jurisdiction without the consent of the states involved in the litigation, the Court manifestly lacked jurisdiction vis-à-vis the claims brought by the FRY against the United States and Spain, both of which had made declarations and reservations to the jurisdiction of the ICJ. These two cases (**Legality of Use of Force [*Yugoslavia* v *United States of America* and *Yugoslavia* v *Spain*]**) were consequently removed from the ICJ's docket. As for the claims against the eight other nations, the ICJ remained seized of the jurisdictional question but held that it did not have the prima facie jurisdiction to ground an award for provisional measures. To this end, the ICJ may eventually adjudicate the substantive issues raised by these eight claims. Time limits for the filing of pleadings have been established. The ICJ express profound concern about the use of force in Yugoslavia, which "under the present circumstances . . . raises very serious issues of international law." The Court also held that, whether or not states consent to the jurisdiction of the ICJ, they remain "in any event responsible for acts attributable to them that violate international law, including humanitarian law."

On March 2, 1999, Germany instituted proceedings in the **LaGrand case (*Germany* v *United States of America*)**. Germany alleges violations of the Vienna Convention on Consular Relations with respect to Karl and Walter LaGrand, two German nationals convicted of murder in Arizona. Germany submits that these individuals were tried and sentenced to death without being advised of their rights to consular assistance, as required by the Convention. Germany requests, inter alia, reparations arising out of the breach by the United States of its international legal obligations to Germany as well as a declaration of assurance to Germany that the United States will not disregard the Convention again [press communiqué 99/7, 3/2/99]. On March 3, the ICJ issued an urgent order calling upon Washington to "take all measures at its disposal" to ensure that Walter LaGrand was not executed while a final decision in the ICJ proceedings was pending [Order, General List No. 104, 3/3/99]. Notwithstanding notification of this order, U.S. authorities executed Walter LaGrand on that same date. His brother had been executed on February 24. The U.S. decision not to follow the provisional order in the LaGrand matter hearkens back to a similar decision it took in April 1998, when Paraguay brought a request to the ICJ for provisional relief staying the execution of Angel Breard, a Paraguayan national (also not informed of his rights under the Convention) in the United States (State of Virginia) [see Vienna Convention on Consular Relations (*Paraguay* v *United States of America*); and see also ICJ press communiqué 98/22, 6/9/98]. The ICJ's order of April 9, 1998, to prevent the execution while the ICJ case was pending was not followed by the government of the United States, the State of Virginia, or the U.S. Supreme Court. The ICJ remains seized of the LaGrand matter and has fixed time limits for the filing of written pleadings [press communiqué 99/12, 3/8/99]. As for the Breard matter, Paraguay requested that it be removed from the list of the ICJ [press communiqué 98/36, 11/11/98]. The ICJ ordered the discontinuance of the proceedings and removed the case from the list on November 10, 1998.

In another new matter, **Eritrea initiated proceedings against Ethiopia** concerning the alleged violation of the premises and diplomatic immunities of the staff of Eritrea's diplomatic mission in Addis Ababa [ICJ communiqué 99/4, 2/16/99]. These violations are alleged to have begun during the week of February 8, 1999, when widescale hostilities opened between the two neighbors. Eritrea alleges that some staff members of its mission are still being detained incommunicado, taken hostage by Ethiopia. Ethiopia, however, has not given its consent to the jurisdiction of the ICJ, and unless it gives such consent, the ICJ cannot take any action, even provisional, in the case. Two months earlier, **the Republic of Guinea had brought a case against the Democratic Republic of Congo (DRC)** [ICJ press communiqué 98/46, 12/30/98] in which it requests that the ICJ condemn the DRC for the grave breaches of international law allegedly perpetrated upon Ahmadou Sadio Diallo, a Guinean national resident of the country. Diallo, says the application, was unlawfully imprisoned by DRC authorities, divested of his properties, and then expelled from the DRC on February 2, 1996. Both parties have accepted the jurisdiction of the ICJ. In another new case, Indonesia and Malaysia jointly seized the ICJ of a dispute concerning sovereignty over Pulau Ligitan and Pulau Sipadan, two islands in the Celebes Sea [press communiqué 98/35, 11/2/98]. Memorials are due on November 2, 1999, and countermemorials by March 2, 2000 [press communiqué 98/37, 11/11/98].

On June 23, 1999, **the DRC instituted proceedings against Burundi, Uganda, and Rwanda** for "acts of armed aggression committed . . . in flagrant breach of the United Nations Charter and of the Charter of the Organization of African Unity" [press communiqué 9934, 6/23/99]. The DRC contends that the alleged invasion of Congolese territory by Burundi, Uganda, and Rwanda constitutes a violation of the DRC's sovereignty and territorial integrity. It asks the ICJ to declare the three guilty of aggression, compel the withdrawal of their forces, and order restitution.

On April 29, 1999, judgment was issued in **the one advisory case before the ICJ: Difference Relating to Immunity from Legal Process of a Special Rapporteur of the Commission on Human Rights** [press communiqué 99/16, 4/29/99]. The request for an advisory opinion was brought on August 5, 1998, by the Economic and Social Council (ECOSOC), one of the six principal organs of the United Nations. ECOSOC wanted the ICJ to advise on the immunity of Param Cumaraswamy, a Malaysian jurist, in the face of private lawsuits filed in Malaysia alleging he used defamatory language in an interview he gave in 1995. The Secretary-General maintained that Mr. Cumaraswamy had spoken in his official capacity as Special Rapporteur of the Commission on Human Rights and was thus immune from legal process by virtue of the Convention on the Privileges and Immunities of the United Nations. Notwithstanding the pronouncements of the Secretary-General, the Malaysian government did not intervene in the proceedings pending before the Malaysian courts. The emerging difference between the United Nations and the government of Malaysia on the immunity issue prompted ECOSOC's request for an advisory opinion. The ICJ held 14 to 1 that the Convention was applicable, that Mr. Cumaraswamy was entitled to immunity from legal process for the words spoken by him during the impugned interview, and that the government of Malaysia should have informed the Malaysian courts of the decision of the Secretary-General. As a result, Mr. Cumaraswamy should not be liable for any costs imposed upon him by the Malaysian proceedings. The Malaysian government was obliged to communicate the advisory opinion to the Malaysian courts so that the immunity could be respected.

The ICJ issued **two important judgments**—regarding jurisdiction, admissibility, and requests for interpretation—in two pre-existing con-

tentious cases. On December 4, 1998, the Court ruled that it had no jurisdiction to adjudicate the **Fisheries Jurisdiction case** (*Spain* v *Canada,*
initiated by Spain March 28, 1995). Hearings in this case had concluded
on June 17, 1998 [press communiqué 98/24, 6/17/98]. Spain alleged that the boarding
on the high seas of a Spanish fishing boat, the *Estai,* on March 9, 1995, by
a Canadian patrol boat amounted to a violation of certain principles of
international law, namely, freedom of navigation and fishing on the high
seas as well as the right of exclusive jurisdiction of the flag state (in this
case Spain) over its ships on the high seas [press communiqué 98/41, 12/4/98]. When
Canada accepted the jurisdiction of the ICJ on May 10, 1994, however, it
excluded the ICJ from "disputes arising out of or concerning conservation and management measures taken by Canada with respect to vessels
fishing in the Northwest Atlantic Fisheries Organization's Regulatory
Area and the enforcement of such measures." The ICJ ruled 12 to 5 in
favor of Canada's preliminary objection that this reservation removed jurisdiction. Although only a decision on a preliminary objection, the ICJ's
judgment is important because it called upon the Court to characterize
Canada's conduct (as well as the legislation authorizing it) as a matter of
state sovereignty or a matter of fisheries conservation/management. In
opting for the latter, the ICJ may adumbrate a broader understanding
of conservation regulation and strengthen the ability of nations to act
extraterritorially in promoting environmental welfare. This judicial interpretation may reflect a trend away from enforcing state sovereignty or
freedom of navigation in matters of transnational concern, such as the
environment. This same trend may well form part of the paradigm that
supports the jurisdiction of ad hoc tribunals over human rights violations,
notwithstanding the concomitant erosion of state sovereignty.

The second of these contentious cases—the **Land and Maritime
Boundary case** (*Cameroon* v *Nigeria,* initiated on March 29, 1994)—
involves a dispute over the delimitation of the Cameroon/Nigeria border
in the area of the oil-rich Bakassi Peninsula in the Gulf of Guinea. That
border, which runs 1,680 kilometers from Lake Chad to the Gulf of
Guinea, has never been established using contemporary geographical
techniques, and Cameroon claims that the Bakassi Peninsula is unlawfully
occupied by Nigeria's military. There have been intermittent clashes
along the border since 1994. Thus far in the hearings, Nigeria has filed
numerous preliminary objections to admissibility as well as to the ICJ's
jurisdiction over the dispute [Reuters, 3/25/99].

On June 11, 1998, the ICJ decided to proceed with the consideration
of the merits of this case by assuming jurisdiction. It admitted Cameroon's claims, including those for internationally unlawful acts by Nigeria
involving incursions of its armed forces into Cameroonian territory [ICJ
press communiqué 98/25, 7/1/98; see also *I.C.J. Reports 1998*, p. 318, par. 98–100]. On March 25,

1999, the ICJ, in a 13–3 decision, confirmed its position that Cameroon may introduce evidence that Nigeria bore responsibility for incidents occurring along the border. This decision arose out of Nigeria's October 1998 request for interpretation of the June judgment [ICJ press communiqué 98/ 34, 10/29/98]. This was the first time that the ICJ had been called upon to rule on a request for interpretation of a judgment on preliminary objection [press communiqué 99/14, 3/25/99; see also Judgment, General List No. 101, 3/25/99]. Nigeria submitted that the June judgment did not specify which border incidents were to be considered as part of the merits of the case, and, thus, the meaning and the scope of the judgment required interpretation.

The ICJ held that it has jurisdiction to entertain requests for reinterpretation of any judgment, but that such a request must relate to the operative part of the judgment—namely, the final paragraph, containing the ICJ's actual decision—and cannot call into question the effect of a judgment rendered as final and without appeal. The objective of a request for reinterpretation, said the Court, "must be solely to obtain clarification of the meaning and the scope of what the Court has decided with binding force." It cannot serve as a basis to reargue a prior decision. Since Nigeria's request would call into effect the June 11, 1998, judgment by rearguing settled points, thereby infringing on the principle of *res judicata*, it was declared inadmissible. The ICJ's substantive deliberations in this matter continue.

Proceedings continue in a variety of other cases on the ICJ docket. March 5, 1999, marked the **conclusion of hearings in the Kasikili/Sedudu Island case (*Botswana/Namibia*)** [ICJ communiqué 99/10, 3/5/99]. The ICJ is ready to consider judgment in this boundary and equitable maritime delimitation dispute. Also continuing is another case involving **Maritime Delimitation and Territorial Questions (*Qatar v Bahrain*)**. On March 30, 1998, the ICJ ordered Qatar to file an interim report on the question of the authenticity of each of 82 documents it had filed with the ICJ in 1997 as annexes to its memorial. The legitimacy and validity of these documents were challenged by Bahrain. Qatar's report, filed on a timely basis, stated that it would no longer rely on the disputed documents. On February 17, 1999, the ICJ placed on record Qatar's decision to disregard these 82 documents [ICJ press communiqué 99/5, 2/18/99]. Replies to the initial memorials were to be filed by May 30, 1999.

In the case concerning the **Application of the Genocide Convention (*Bosnia and Herzegovina* v *Yugoslavia*,** filed March 20, 1993), Yugoslavia's time limit for filing its rejoinder (a form of written pleading) was extended to February 22, 1999 [press communiqué 98/44, 12/17/98]. This case derives from Bosnia and Herzegovina's request that the ICJ declare that Yugoslavia "has killed, murdered, wounded, raped, robbed, tortured, kidnapped, illegally detained, and exterminated the citizens of Bosnia and Herzegovina." The claimant is also seeking reparations. Yugoslavia has filed counterclaims asking the Court to find Bosnia and Herzegovina responsible for acts of genocide committed against Serbs in its territory. **Yugoslavia also faces proceedings initiated by Croatia on July 2, 1999, for violations of the Genocide Convention** allegedly committed between 1991 and 1995 [press communiqué 99/38, 7/2/99].

Since both sets of claims derive from Yugoslav policies of "ethnic cleansing" during the wars in the Balkans, they overlap somewhat with the mandate of the International Criminal Tribunal for the Former Yugoslavia (ICTY). It will be interesting to see how the ICJ harmonizes its findings in these matters with those of the tribunal. The combined use of both courts may allow the criminal, interstate, and civil aspects of the violence to be addressed. In fact, as more nations turn to the ICJ to adjudicate humanitarian disputes (or order restitutionary and declaratory relief in such situations), it may be important to develop a memorandum of understanding with the International Criminal Court.

Time limits for the filing of written pleadings were extended in the **Oil Platforms case (*Iran* v *United States of America*, filed November 2, 1992)** [press communiqué 98/42, 12/9/98]. In the **Gabcíkovo-Nagymaros Project case (*Hungary/Slovakia*, originally submitted July 2, 1993),** Slovakia requested the ICJ to issue an additional judgment [press communiqué 98/31, 10/7/98]. The original judgment, delivered by the ICJ on September 25, 1997, found both countries in breach of their international obligations related to the construction and operation of dams on the Danube river and required them to negotiate in good faith. Slovakia submits that an additional judgment is necessary because of the unwillingness of Hungary to implement the September 25, 1997 judgment.

The successful transfer in April 1999, of two suspects from Libya to a Scottish court sitting in the Netherlands may well affect the continuation of the **Lockerbie case (*Libya* v *United Kingdom, United States*)** [see more detailed discussion in "International Terrorism," section 7 of the present chapter]. Libya claimed that it was entitled to try the suspects of the 1988 terrorist bombing of Pan Am flight 103, which exploded over the town of Lockerbie, Scotland. The United States and the United Kingdom, whose nationals were killed in the bombing, had sought the extradition of the suspects for trial in British or American courts. On February 27, 1998, the ICJ ruled that it had jurisdiction to deal with the merits of this dispute, and welcomed the continued submission of written pleadings [press communiqué 98/45, 12/18/98]. The voluntary transfer, arranged through diplomatic means, may render academic the resolution of this legal dispute. For the moment, however, the proceedings continue [press communiqué 99/36, 7/1/99].

7. International Terrorism

The **Ad Hoc Committee on Instruments to Combat International Terrorism** [established by A/Res/51/210] began its Third Session on May 15, 1999. Its work, encouraged by the Sixth Committee, involves drafting an international convention on the suppression of acts of nuclear terrorism and another on terrorist financing. **Nuclear terrorism** is defined in draft documents as including the use of or threat to use nuclear material, nuclear fuel, radioactive products or waste, or any other radioactive substances with toxic, explosive, or other dangerous properties [U.N. press releases GA/L/ 3094, 11/11/98, and GA/L/2914, 3/10/99; see also A/C.6/53/L.4]. The use of nuclear weapons by military forces is excluded from the scope of the draft convention. It is unclear to what extent legal sanction (as opposed to consensual cooperation) will operate as a device to enforce compliance.

In the area of **terrorist financing,** a draft working document submitted by France actively contemplates a penal justice regime, defining as an "offence" the unlawful and intentional financing of a person or organization that is known to commit, or is prepared to commit, a broad series of offences, including taking hostages, hijacking, or causing death or serious bodily injury to a civilian [Working Document A/AC.252/L.7, cited in U.N. press release L/ 2914, 3/10/99]. The draft does not consider establishing an international adjudicative body—or linking these crimes to the emerging jurisdiction of the ICC. Instead, it would require states to establish as criminal offenses under their domestic law the offenses outlawed by the convention. A more *supra*-national perspective may emerge in upcoming years as the Committee's mandate expands: General Assembly Resolution 53/108 requests it to address in future sessions the development of a comprehensive legal framework dealing with international terrorism writ large. Such discussions may be important, since only 24 states have signed the **International Convention for the Suppression of Terrorist Bombings,** adopted by the General Assembly in December 1997, and no state has ratified it yet [U.N. press release GA/L/3103, 11/24/98]. The work of the Ad Hoc Committee on Instruments to Combat International Terrorism will continue during the 54th Session within the framework of a working group of the Sixth Committee [ibid.].

The Security Council has also underscored the **linkages between terrorism and illegal arms sales.** Resolution 1209 [11/19/98] welcomed the negotiation of an international convention against transnational organized crime, including a protocol to combat illicit manufacturing of and trafficking in firearms. Import, export, and re-export controls would figure prominently in such a regime.

The Lockerbie affair—involving the bombing of Pan Am flight 103, which killed 270 people over Lockerbie, Scotland, in December 1988—attests to the difficulties inherent in prosecuting terrorism through national courts—and the importance of developing *supra*-national institutions.

However, more **recent developments in the Lockerbie case** also make clear that national prosecutions *can* be coordinated, although requiring considerable persistence and a large investment in diplomacy. On April 5, 1999, Libya, after protracted negotiations, transferred to the Netherlands suspects Al-Amine Khalifa Fhimah and Abdel Basset Ali al-Megrahi. The suspects will be tried by Scottish prosecutors under Scottish law before a three-judge Scottish court sitting at the converted U.S. Camp Zeist Airbase in the Netherlands. If found guilty, the suspects will serve prison sentences in Barlinnie prison in Glasgow under U.N. supervision [Mark Huband in *Financial Times*, 3/20–21/99]. Libya, concerned that information arising out of the trial or subsequent interrogations could implicate its government or leadership in the bombing, also received assurances that the proceedings would not be used for such purposes.

The U.N. Security Council and Secretary-General have played a major role in orchestrating the transfer of the suspects [see S/Res/731, 1/21/92; S/Res/742, 3/31/92; S/Res/883, 11/11/93; and S/Res/1192, 8/27/98]. In fact, the transfer represents a major success for the United Nations; South Africa and Saudi Arabia also played key roles in the negotiation. The economic sanctions against Libya that the Security Council imposed to enforce compliance were suspended shortly after the suspects reached the Netherlands [*New York Times*, 4/11/99].

VII
Finance and Administration
By Anthony Mango

1. The Financial Situation of the United Nations

The financial situation of the Organization was on the agenda of the 53rd Session of the General Assembly under the optimistic title "Improving the financial situation of the United Nations." In actual fact little if any improvement had taken place. Joseph Connor, Under-Secretary-General for Management, submitted two reports to the Fifth Committee: the first on the situation as of the end of September 1998, the second on the situation in early March 1999. His second report indicated that, despite a substantial decrease in the total amount of unpaid contributions to the regular budget, the United Nations still had no capital and no reserves, and was obliged to resort to borrowings [A/C.5/53/SR.50]. In his first report, Mr. Connor had indicated that the total amount of unpaid assessments at the end of September 1998 had been $2.5 billion, of which $683 million related to the regular program budget, over $1.8 billion to peacekeeping operations, and $22 million to the International Tribunals for former Yugoslavia and Rwanda. Of the 185 members states, only 100 had paid in full their regular-budget assessments for 1998 and for all prior years. Mr. Connor estimated that at the end of 1998, $864 million would be owed to troop- and equipment-contributing countries [A/C.5/53/SR.4].

The **U.N. financial regulations** provide that "Contributions and advances shall be considered as due and payable in full within thirty days of the receipt of the communication of the Secretary-General." For the regular program budget these communications are sent out early in January. In practice, many countries, including regular payers, remit their assessed contributions after the 30-day period, because of their parliamentary or other domestic procedures. In assessing the Organization's financial situation, it is therefore necessary to differentiate between outstanding assessments for the current year and "arrears," i.e., unpaid assessments for prior years. The total amount of such **arrears as of December 31, 1998,** for the regular program budget was $417 million, as against $473.6 million a year earlier. The decrease of $56.6 million occurred because in the course of 1998 the United States had reduced its indebtedness under the regular program budget by $57.5 million, from $373.2 million to $315.7 million. Ukraine had also substantially reduced its arrears under the regular program budget—from $17.7 million at the end of 1997 to $6.4 million at the end of 1998. On the other hand, the arrears owed by Brazil and Argentina increased by $14 million and $4.3 million respectively. Of the 15 largest contributors, three had arrears on December 31, 1998, related to unpaid assessed contributions for 1998 and prior years: the United States, $315.7 million (75.7 percent of the total); Brazil, $30.7 million (7.4 percent of the total); and Argentina, $8.4 million (2 percent of the total). Sixty-five other member states had arrears totaling $62.2 million (14.9 percent of the total arrears of $417 million). One hundred and seventeen member states were fully paid up on their regular-budget assessments.

The **regular-budget assessments for 1999,** which became due in January, amount to a total of $1,083.7 million, of which $387.1 million was paid (or credited through adjustments) during the first two months of the year, and a further $104.4 million in March and April. Sixty member states paid off all their regular-budget assessments by April 30, 1999, among them four of the five permanent members of the Security Council (China, France, Russia, and the United Kingdom) as well as the Organization's second and third largest contributors (Japan and Germany). **Contributions to the regular budget outstanding on April 30, 1999,** totaled $985.6 million, consisting of $592.2 million for 1999 assessments and $393.4 million for prior years. As of that date, seven member states owed more than $10 million each for regular-budget assessments, as follows:

United States	$620.1 million (62.9% of all outstanding contributions)
Japan	$155.7 million (15.8%)
Germany	$51 million (5.1%)
Brazil	$44.3 million (4.5%)
Argentina	$19 million (1.9%)
Yugoslavia	$11 million (1.1%)
Mexico	$10.2 million (1%)

Three of the above, namely Germany, Japan, and Mexico, had paid all their assessed contributions for prior years, and the fact that they still had outstanding contributions for 1999 was attributable to their domestic procedures.

Outstanding assessed contributions for prior periods in respect of peacekeeping operations totaled $1,593.9 million as of January 1, 1999, of which $975.6 million (61.2 percent) was owed by the United States, $125.9 million (7.9 percent) by the Russian Federation, and $98.4 million (6.2 percent) by Japan. Two completed operations accounted for the bulk of these arrears, namely UNPROFOR ($675.3 million) and UNOSOM ($284.6 million). **Total peacekeeping assessments outstanding as of April 30, 1999,** amounted to $1,584.2 million. Only three member states (Colombia, New Zealand, and the United Kingdom) had no outstanding contributions for peacekeeping operations as of that date.

Total outstanding contributions in respect of the International Tribunals for former Yugoslavia and for Rwanda stood at $73.2 million as of April 30, 1999. Twenty-four member states had no outstanding contributions.

As of April 30, 1999, 183 member states owed the United Nations a total of $2,643.1 million by way of assessments under the regular budget, the International Tribunals, and peacekeeping operations. Taken together, $803.9 million was owed for the current period and $1,839.2 million in arrears. Only two member states (New Zealand and the United Kingdom) were fully paid up. Of the total amount of assessed contributions outstanding on that date, the United States owed $1,637.4 million (61.9 percent) [ST/ADM/SER.B/539 and 541].

Unlike previous years, when the Organization's precarious financial situation had generated lengthy debates in the Fifth Committee, the member states' reaction at the 53rd Session was muted, largely because everybody realized that everything that could be said on this topic had already been said. General Assembly Resolution 52/215 D had left open the possibility of a compromise whereby the Assembly would agree to **lower the current 25 percent ceiling** for assessments to the regular budget, as requested by the United States, provided the United States paid off its arrears. But such a compromise was foreclosed by the lack of the necessary action on the part of the U.S. Congress [see *A Global Agenda: Issues Before the 53rd General Assembly*]. Criticism of the U.S. position was voiced by the representative of Austria (speaking on behalf of the European Union, and also of Bulgaria, Cyprus, Czech Republic, Estonia, Hungary, Iceland, Latvia, Liechtenstein, Lithuania, Norway, Poland, Romania, and Slovakia), who noted that the United States, as the largest contributor to the United Nations, a permanent member of the Security Council, and the sole beneficiary of the existence of a ceiling that reduced the level of its assessment below its capacity to pay, should bear in mind its responsibility for the financial health of the Organization. [A/C.5/53/SR.4]. The representative of China said that the United States, using the excuse of its domestic legislation and disregarding the Charter and the relevant regulations, had accumulated colossal sums of arrears over a long period of time, as a result not of economic difficulties, but of its desire to achieve certain political objectives [ibid.]. The failure of the **High-Level Open-Ended Working Group on the Financial Situation of the United Nations** to come up with a solution was regretted.

The General Assembly again took no action on the recommendation made by the Secretary-General in his report on "Renewing the United Nations: a programme for reform" that a **revolving credit fund** in the amount of $1 billion be established to ensure the Organization's financial solvency and meet cash-flow problems pending receipt of assessed contributions. Instead, it decided to resume consideration of the question at the 54th Session.

The only penalty prescribed by the U.N. Charter in case of nonpayment of assessed contributions is contained in **Article 19,** which states: "A Member of the United Nations which is in arrears in the payment of its financial contributions to the Organization shall have no vote in the General Assembly if the amount of its arrears equals or exceeds the amount of the contributions due from it for the preceding two full years. The General Assembly may, nevertheless, permit such a Member to vote if it is satisfied that the failure to pay is due to conditions beyond the control of the Member."

At the beginning of February 1999, the Secretary-General informed the General Assembly that 42 member states were in arrears under the terms of Article 19. Twenty-one were African countries, 7 were Asian, 8 were from Latin America and the Caribbean, 5 from Europe, and 1 from the Pacific [A/ES-10/33]. Member states facing the loss of their vote in the General Assembly normally pay the minimum amount necessary to avoid application of Article 19.

At the 53rd Session, the procedures of implementing the second sentence of Article 19 were discussed at considerable length in the Fifth Committee. In the case of two countries, the recommendation that the penalty of loss of the vote be waived for the duration of the main segment of the Session had come from the Committee on Contributions; in two other cases, the decision was made by the Assembly itself without any input from the Committee on Contributions. But when the Fifth Committee found itself having to deal with several other requests—including one from Iraq—that had been submitted directly to it, differences of opinion emerged. Some delegations expressed preference for all requests for waivers to be considered first in the **Committee on Contributions,** which had a technical role to play in providing advice to the Assembly. A decision on the outstanding requests was postponed, and the Assembly requested the Committee on Contributions to hold a special session early in 1999 to analyze the requests for waivers and to report to it at the resumed 53rd Session [A/Res/53/36]. The Committee on Contributions held its special session in early February 1999. Its report dealt not only with the requests for waivers of Article 19 but with the practice of some states to pay just enough to avoid being deprived of the vote—a question to which it would revert at its next regular session. The Committee recommended that of the four states that had applied for exemptions, three be granted such exemptions until June 30, 1999. With regard to the fourth state, Iraq, the Committee concluded that the political issues involved went beyond its technical advisory role.

For purposes of the application of Article 19, each member state's arrears are aggregated regardless of whether the assessments relate to the regular budget, peacekeeping operations, or the International Tribunals. The calculations are made once a year, in January, on the basis of the arrears for the preceding two calendar years. During periods of declining budgets (and, thus, of lower assessments for the current year, compared to those in the preceding two years) Article 19 comes into play earlier than is the case in periods of rising budgets, and it becomes necessary for a member state to make payments larger than the amount assessed for the current year in order to avoid the application of Article 19. The United States faced this situation in 1998, and will likely face it again in 1999.

During 1998 the **U.S. Congress** needed to approve both authorizing and appropriating legislation in order to provide resources for the country's contributions to the U.N. regular budget, peacekeeping operations, and other requirements for the U.S. financial year (FY) 1999, which began on October 1, 1998. The Congress did approve a State Department authorization bill (H.R. 1757) in April 1988, but delayed sending it to President Clinton, who had threatened to veto it because it contained an unrelated provision dealing with restrictions on international family planning aid. The Congress failed to complete work on the related appropriation legislation by October 1, 1998, and it became necessary for Congress to approve a FY1999 omnibus appropriation bill (H.R. 4328) to ensure continued funding of U.S. government activities. When the State Department authorization bill was finally sent to the President in October 1998, he vetoed it, as expected. The omnibus appropriation bill did not contain language concerning arrears payments, which made it possible for the administration and Congress to reach an understanding that permitted the payment to the United Nations of a sum sufficient to save the United States from losing its vote in 1999 under Article 19 [*Washington Weekly Report*, XXIV-28, 10/22/98]. Payments by the United States in 1998 for the regular budget, peacekeeping operations, and the International Tribunals totaled $586 million [A/C.5/53/SR.19].

Authorization bill H.R. 1757 contained a series of conditions and certification requirements to which payment of U.N. arrears would have been subject, had the President not vetoed the bill. Among them were the more than three dozen conditions laid down in the so-called Helms-Biden agreement [see *A Global Agenda: Issues/53*], including the requirement that the U.S. contribution rate to the regular budget be lowered first from 25 percent to 22 percent and then to 20 percent, and that a 25 percent ceiling be imposed on the U.S. contribution to peacekeeping operations (currently about 31 percent). On June 22, 1999, the Senate overwhelmingly (99 to 1) approved a bill authorizing the payment of $819 million in U.S.

arrears to the United Nations, which once again included provisions for a reduction in the U.S. assessment rates. This time, however, the administration indicated that it would not object to the presence of this provision in exchange for Senate approval of the President's candidate for U.S. Ambassador to the United Nations, Richard Holbrooke.

As the *New York Times* was quick to point out [6/23/99], the Senate action did "not mean the United Nations was about to get a big check from Washington. Far from it." In a repeat of the 1998 scenario, the bill still faced the stiff opposition of conservative Republicans in the House, who made it clear that they intended once again to attach a provision banning international family planning aid—the same provision that provoked the President's veto a year earlier. It remained to be seen whether the administration could overcome the House opposition this time around.

2. Scale of Assessments

The scale of assessments for the U.N. regular budget in 1998–2000 was approved by the General Assembly on December 22, 1997 [A/Res/52/215 A], after long and acrimonious discussions. The next scale, for the years 2001–03, will be approved in 2000. Meantime, in response to General Assembly requests, the Committee on Contributions has been **reviewing the assessment process.** In its report to the General Assembly at the 53rd Session, the Committee stated that, having examined the implications of using gross domestic product (GDP) rather than gross national product (GNP) in preparing future scales, it had concluded that GNP should continue to be used because it was the least unsatisfactory income measure for the purposes of the scale. A consolidated set of recommendations on other elements of the scale methodology will be submitted to the Assembly at its 54th Session in 1999.

While the debate under this agenda item at the 53rd Session focused mainly on the best procedure for the consideration of requests for the waiver of the Charter provision regarding loss of vote by member states in arrears, several delegations also touched upon the **scale methodology** as a whole. The representative of Indonesia, speaking on behalf of the Group of 77 and China, said that the fundamental criterion for the apportionment of U.N. expenses was the principle of "capacity to pay." The Organization's difficult financial situation would not be solved by revising the scale methodology; and even if the methodology was changed, there would be no guarantee that future assessments would be paid promptly and in full. Once the scale was fixed by the General Assembly, it should not be subject to a general revision for at least three years, unless it was clear that there had been substantial changes in relative capacity to pay [A/C.5/53/SR.14]. Comments on individual aspects of the scale methodology were made by several delegations, and support was expressed for shortening the base period to three years. The representative of China said that his delegation categorically rejected any principle or concept, such as that of responsibility to pay, that was contrary to the principle of capacity to pay [ibid]. The representative of Singapore recalled that even though the vast majority of member states had found unacceptable the U.S. delegation's proposal that the ceiling be lowered, the Fifth Committee had agreed to consider it if the United States paid its arrears to the Organization. He regretted that nearly a year after that offer had been made, the United States was still heavily indebted to the United Nations [A/C.5/53/SR.15]. The U.S. representative expressed concern that, once again, the Committee on Contributions had failed to acknowledge the existence of any scale of assessments dealing with peacekeeping operations. After some 25 years such assessments were still determined on an ad hoc basis, and it was incumbent on the Committee to begin to examine the issue. The representative of Indonesia, speaking on behalf of the Group of 77 and China, disagreed, saying that the Committee on Contributions did not have a mandate to discuss the special scale for peacekeeping operations [A/C.5/53/SR.44].

3. Revised Program Budget for the Biennium 1998–99

Having considered the Secretary-General's first performance report on the program budget for 1998–99, the General Assembly approved a **net decrease** of $48.2 million in appropriations and a net decrease of $4.6 million in the estimates of income [A/Res/53/214 and 215]. The decreases were attributable largely to the higher-than-expected vacancy rate and to the strength of the U.S. dollar in 1998. The Assembly requested the Secretary-General immediately to intensify recruitment efforts, so as to reduce the number of vacant posts. It reviewed progress of work on the Integrated Management Information System, for which it approved an additional appropriation of $3.3 million. The Assembly took note of the estimate of $1.4 million (net of staff assessment) for the U.N. political office in Bougainville, Solomon Islands, and it approved increases in the remuneration and pensions of the judges of the International Court of Justice (ICJ) and of the International Tribunals for former Yugoslavia and Rwanda.

4. Program Budget for the Biennium 2000–01

The 53rd General Assembly determined the amount of the **budget outline** within which the Secretary-General's program budget proposals for the biennium 2000–01 would have to be accommodated [A/Res/53/206]. The three main issues discussed were (a) whether the outline should exclude or include the estimated cost of special political missions that were likely to be continued into the biennium even though their extension depended on future decisions of the Security Council or the General Assembly; (b) the Secretary-General's proposal that the outline should identify $20 million in compensating economies to offset the estimated $20 million that would be required for conferences and other activities; and (c) the level of the contingency fund, which the Secretary-General proposed be left unchanged at 0.75 percent of the overall level of resources for the outline. The **Advisory Committee on Administrative and Budgetary Questions (ACABQ)** recommended that the requirements for special political missions, which were estimated at $112.6 million, be included in the outline, with a consequential revision of the estimate to $2,568.8 million for the biennium at 1998–99 rates. The ACABQ was also of the opinion that the $20 million in compensating economies should not be identified in the outline; the savings should be reflected instead in the performance report. The Committee supported the retention of the 0.75 percent level for the contingency fund [A/C.5/53/SR.39].

The ACABQ's recommendation that provision for special political missions be included in the outline was supported by the representatives of Austria, speaking on behalf of the European Union and a number of Central and East European countries; of Indonesia, who spoke on behalf of the Group of 77 and China; of New Zealand, speaking on behalf also of Australia and Canada; and of Japan, the Republic of Korea, the Russian Federation, and Bangladesh. No delegation opposed the recommendation. The ACABQ's recommendation regarding the $20 million in expected economies was supported by the representatives of Cameroon, Indonesia (speaking on behalf of the Group of 77 and China), the Republic of Korea, Cuba, Norway, the Russian Federation, and Bangladesh. The recommendation was opposed by the representatives of Japan, New Zealand (who spoke also on behalf of Australia and Canada), and the United States [A/C.5/53/SR.40; SR.41]. In their statements, the representatives of Panama and China, in supporting the ACABQ recommendation, pointed out that savings resulting from efficiency measures should in any case be transferred to the Development Account [A/C.5/53/SR.39-41].

As to the amount of resources to be included in the budget outline, the U.S. representative said that it must not exceed that of the budget for 1998–99; his government could show no flexibility on that score. He also questioned why the ACABQ had endorsed the 0.75 percent level for the contingency fund, since additional requirements over and above the agreed budget level could and should be financed with savings. The representative of Norway, on the other hand, said that the setting of prior budget ceilings and the absorption of all additional requirements through compensating economies had no part in the practice of program budgeting in the United Nations. The outline was a planning tool and not a numerical straightjacket. His delegation found the proposed program budget outline for the biennium 2000–01 to be less than satisfactory in several respects, among other things because it implied negative real growth and even negative nominal growth, and because it revealed no effort to make up for the persistent underfunding of core peacekeeping, human rights, and humanitarian activities [ibid.].

The draft resolution on the proposed budget outline was adopted in the Fifth Committee without a vote. It specified a total preliminary estimate of $2,545 million at revised 1998–99 rates, which included $86.2 million for special political missions and excluded the anticipated reduction related to compensating economies—both in line with ACABQ recommendations. The level of the contingency fund was set at 0.75 percent of the preliminary estimate. Before the adoption of the draft resolution, the representatives of the United States and Japan indicated that they could not agree with the total preliminary estimate [A/C.5/53/SR.45.Add.1].

The Secretary-General's proposed program budget for the biennium 2000–01 [A/54/6] amounts to $2,535.6 million before recosting (which reflects inflation expected in 2000 and 2001 and rates of exchange prevailing in 1998), and is thus nearly $10 million less than the preliminary estimate [A/Res/53/206]. The reduction reflects lower estimates for major conferences and special sessions and for special political missions. According to the Secretary-General, it reflects an increase in real terms of 0.2 percent compared with the revised appropriations for the biennium 1998–99. After recosting, the amount for 2000–01 becomes $2,655.4 million. A comparison with the budgets of the previous three biennia is given below:

1994–95 (revised appropriation)	$2,608.3 million
1996–97 (revised appropriation)	$2,603.3 million
1998–99 (revised appropriation)	$2,529.9 million
2000–01 (estimates before recosting)	$2,535.6 million
2000–01 (estimates after preliminary recosting)	$2,655.4 million

A comparison between the revised appropriations for 1998–99 and the estimates for 2000–01, broken down by part and section, is given in Table VII-1.

On a section-by-section basis, the largest increases in percentage terms have been proposed by the Secretary-General for jointly financed administrative activities (40.3 percent); capital expenditures (26.2 percent); international drug control (15.6 percent); administration, Nairobi (15.2 percent); Africa: New Agenda for Development (15.0 percent); and crime prevention and criminal justice (11.2 percent). The largest decrease in per-

Table VII-1

Part/Section	1998–99 Appropriations	2000–01 Estimates Before recosting	2000–01 Estimates After recosting
	$ million	*$ million*	*$ million*
PART I: Overall policy-making, direction, and coordination	469.0	469.5	489.9
1. Overall policy-making, direction, and coordination	42.0	45.9	48.7
2. General Assembly affairs and conference services	427.0	423.6	441.2
PART II: Political affairs	239.6	225.8	241.6
3. Political affairs	142.1	127.9	134.6
4. Disarmament	13.0	13.5	14.2
5. Peacekeeping operations	80.6	80.4	88.6
6. Peaceful uses of outer space	3.9	4.0	4.2
PART III: International justice and law	53.1	54.7	57.6
7. International Court of Justice	20.7	21.3	22.3
8. Legal affairs	32.4	33.4	35.3
PART IV: International cooperation for development	266.7	271.8	283.5
9. Economic and social affairs	107.0	107.3	113.8
10. Africa: New Agenda for Development	5.2	6.0	6.3
11A. Trade and development	93.3	93.7	95.3
11B. International Trade Centre UNCTAD/WTO	19.8	19.8	20.2
12. Environment	8.8	8.7	9.5
13. Human settlements	12.6	13.3	14.6
14. Crime prevention and criminal justice	5.4	6.0	6.2
15. International drug control	14.7	17.0	17.6
PART V: Regional cooperation for development	355.9	356.6	381.2
16. Economic and social development in Africa	80.6	80.8	83.5
17. Economic and social development in Asia and the Pacific	56.7	56.5	64.5
18. Economic development in Europe	43.5	43.6	44.3
19. Economic and social development in Latin America and the Caribbean	82.7	83.1	90.8
20. Economic and social development in Western Asia	49.8	50.0	53.0
21. Regular program of technical cooperation	42.7	42.7	45.1

Table VII-1 (continued)

PART VI: Human rights and humanitarian affairs		125.3	128.5	132.5
22.	Human rights	40.8	42.4	43.4
23.	Protection of and assistance to refugees	45.1	45.0	45.7
24.	Palestine refugees	21.8	21.8	23.4
25.	Humanitarian assistance	17.6	19.3	20.0
PART VII: Public information		135.6	137.6	145.7
26.	Public information	135.6	137.6	145.7
PART VIII: Common support services		446.3	442.1	460.1
27.	Management and central support services:			
A.	Office of the USG for Management	11.1	11.0	11.6
B.	Office of Program Planning, Budget, and Accounts	20.9	21.5	22.8
C.	Office of Human Resources Management	44.7	46.3	48.8
D.	Office of Central Support Services	226.9	221.3	231.3
E.	Administration, Geneva	99.8	98.7	99.7
F.	Administration, Vienna	30.7	29.3	29.9
G.	Administration, Nairobi	12.2	14.0	16.0
PART IX: Internal oversight		17.9	18.9	20.1
28.	Internal oversight	17.9	18.9	20.1
PART X: Jointly financed administrative activities and special expenses		58.5	57.8	62.3
29.	Jointly financed administrative activities	5.8	8.2	8.5
30.	Special expenses	52.7	49.6	53.9
PART XI: Capital expenditures		34.2	43.1	45.7
31.	Construction, alteration, improvement, and major maintenance	34.2	43.1	45.7
PART XII: Staff assessment		314.7	316.0	322.2
32.	Staff assessment	314.7	316.0	322.2
PART XIII: Development account		13.1	13.1	13.1
33.	Development account	13.1	13.1	13.1
TOTAL, REGULAR BUDGET		2,529.9	2,535.6	2,655.4

Source: A/Res/53/206 and A/54/6.

centage terms has been proposed for political affairs (− 10 percent). The Secretary-General is proposing a total staffing table of 8,933 regular-budget posts, including 11 temporary posts, an increase of 58 posts over 1998–99. The number of professional posts is to increase by 67, and that of general service posts is to be reduced by 9.

The real-terms increase of 5.3 percent proposed by the Secretary-General for section 28, internal oversight, was criticized by the representatives of Indonesia, speaking on behalf of the Group of 77 and China, and of Panama on the ground that internal oversight is not one of the priority areas identified by the General Assembly in the medium-term plan for the period 1998–2001 [A/C.5/53/SR.40; SR.41]. The representative of the United States, on the other hand, referred to internal oversight as a priority activity [A/C.5/53/SR.41]. The debates at the 53rd Session on the **activities of the Office of Internal Oversight Services (OIOS)**, which were conducted in the context of the evaluation and review of the Office (as mandated by A/Res/48/218 B), revealed continuing differences of opinion as to the role of the OIOS. The representative of Indonesia, speaking on behalf of the Group of 77 and China, pointed out that it was the responsibility of the Secretary-General to ensure that the reports of the Office did not contain any recommendations that transgressed the mandates approved by member states. The OIOS should make recommendations on matters of internal management, whereas programs and activities approved by the member states could be modified only by the competent intergovernmental bodies [A/C.5/53/SR.17]. The representative of the Syrian Arab Republic said that the operational independence of the OIOS did not mean that it was not accountable to the member states. The latter should review the role of the Office in order to spell out what had not been stated clearly in A/Res/48/218 B. The Syrian delegation categorically rejected the interference of the Office in political matters that were not part of its mandate [ibid.]. In a subsequent statement, the Syrian representative criticized the OIOS for failure to reflect in its report the comments of program managers. He also took exception to the proposal by the OIOS for a reduction in the staffing of the U.N. Truce Supervision Organization (UNTSO); any such proposals should be considered in the context of the program budget in accordance with established procedure. Several representatives disagreed with the OIOS proposal concerning reduction of the staff of the Office to Combat Desertification and Drought [A/C.5/53/SR.27]. Improved cooperation between the OIOS, on the one hand, and the Joint Inspection Unit (JIU) and the Board of Auditors on the other, was welcomed. Several delegations stressed the importance of the functions assigned to the OIOS and praised the performance of the Office. The representative of the United States, responding to criticism by developing countries that the Office had overstepped its mandate by dealing with questions that were within the province of the General Assembly, said that that situation had arisen in only a few cases, and that in any case it was the role of the Office to draw the attention of member states to instances of insufficient productivity or poor results [A/C.5/53/SR.26]. Continued discussion of the OIOS at the resumed 53rd Session in 1999 showed that the differences of opinion had not been resolved, and further consideration was accordingly deferred to the Assembly's 54th Session.

Other questions deferred to the 54th Session were the Joint Inspection Unit (JIU) reports on procurement and outsourcing and on U.N. system common services at Geneva; and the Secretary-General's reports on developments in the post structure of the Secretariat, the implementation of pilot projects, and the construction of additional conference facilities at Addis Ababa and Bangkok.

Section 33 of the proposed program budget for the biennium 2000–01 contains $13.1 million for the **Development Account,** the same amount as was contained in section 34 of the program budget for the biennium 1998–99. The creation of this account, to be financed from efficiency savings, had been proposed by the Secretary-General, who had forecast that some $120 million would become available within two biennia. At the 52nd Session, several delegations were skeptical about the sustainability of the account. The view was also expressed that savings should be returned to member states [see *A Global Agenda: Issues/53*]. In A/Res/52/235 of June 26, 1998, the General Assembly requested the Secretary-General to submit proposals on the use of the funds available in section 34 of the 1998–99 budget. When discussion of the Development Account was resumed at the 53rd Session, the representative of Indonesia, speaking on behalf of the Group of 77 and China, said that questions about the sustainability of the account had not been dispelled by the Secretary-General's report [A/53/7/Add.1]. It now seemed that sustainability was to be achieved not only through savings but also by way of appropriations; the originally proposed target had also been dropped in favor of the idea that member states should determine the ultimate level of the Development Account and the timeframe for achieving it. It remained to be seen whether savings could be achieved without a negative impact on the level and quality of Secretariat services; the Secretariat should submit to the Assembly biannual reports on the impact of efficiency measures on the implementation of mandated programs and activities [A/C.5/53/SR.4]. Several other delegations also voiced doubts about the operation and sustainability of the account. The representative of the Russian Federation agreed with the ACABQ that neither gains from currency fluctuations and inflation nor savings resulting from postponement of activities and programs should be transferred to the account. A far more logical procedure would be to consider the question in the context of the performance reports, which would show the level of efficiency gains, he said. His delegation saw no good reason to create a separate budget section for the account in future program budgets. The Syrian representative said that the achievement of savings through efficiency measures was not an end in itself, the first priority being to ensure optimum implementation of mandated programs. The representative of China said that since savings achieved through efficiency measures would not be limitless, it would be difficult in the long run to rely on them to fund the Development Account [ibid.].

In response to the request addressed to him in A/Res/52/235, the Secretary-General submitted a report with proposals for eight projects that could be funded from the Development Account at a total cost of $12.3 million [A/53/374]. In a statement made on behalf of the Group of 77 and China, the representative of Indonesia voiced doubts about four of the eight proposals. He said that the resources in the Development Account should be used to fund new projects only for developing countries in accordance with the development priorities set in the medium-term plan, and they should be selected by applying six criteria: (a) projects should have a multiplier effect and promote capacity-building; (b) they should promote regional and inter-regional economic and technical cooperation between developing countries; (c) they should complement and not replace existing program activities; (d) they should relate to new activities not already mandated under the program budget; (e) they should not involve the transfer of resources from the regular budget to extrabudgetary activities; and (f) they should have a strong South-South cooperation content [A/C.5/53/SR.40]. In a subsequent statement on behalf of the Group of 77 and China, the representative of Indonesia said that the sustainability of the Development Account should not be pursued through unjustifiable and unsound measures that took no account of the views of the developing countries, and the proposed economy measures should not result in a reduction in staffing or in the overall level of the regular budget; adequate resources should be provided for full implementation of mandated programs and activities [A/C.5/53/SR.45/Add.1]. Further consideration of the question having been deferred to the resumed 53rd Session, four of the Secretary-General's proposals were approved during the first part, and the other four, after reformulation, during the second part of the resumed session. At the time of writing it remained to be seen whether the four approved projects would be launched in 1999 and, if so, what effect, if any, that would have on the estimated size of the Development Account in section 33 of the program budget for 2000–01.

Consideration and approval of the program budget for 2000–01 will be the main item on the agenda of the Fifth Committee at the 54th Session.

5. Budgets of Peacekeeping Operations and of International Tribunals

The financial year of peacekeeping operations runs from July 1 to June 30. In recent months the number of such operations has declined following the decision to withdraw the U.N. Observer Mission in Angola because of the deteriorating security situation in the country, and the failure of the Security Council to extend the mandate of the U.N. Preventive Deployment Force in the Former Yugoslav Republic of Macedonia as a result of a Chinese veto. The estimated requirements for these two missions in the financial year 1999/2000 relate to costs of winding up the missions. The budgetary requirements of the U.N.'s continuing peacekeeping operations in the financial years 1998/1999 and 1999/2000 are summarized in Table VII-2.

The **Support Account** finances the posts and related expenses in various departments at U.N. Headquarters providing backstopping for peacekeeping operations in the field. The related budgetary requirements and those for the U.N. Logistics Base at Brindisi are allocated pro rata to those operations.

On June 10, 1999, the Security Council authorized the Secretary-

Table VII-2
U.N. Peacekeeping Operations
(In U.S. $ millions)

	1998/1999	*1999/2000*
U.N. Peacekeeping Force in Cyprus (UNFICYP)	42.7	43.6
U.N. Disengagement Observer Force (UNDOF)	33.4	33.3
U.N. Interim Force in Lebanon (UNIFIL)	134.7	139.9
U.N. Iraq-Kuwait Observation Mission (UNIKOM)	49.1	50.8
U.N. Mission in the Central African Republic (MINURCA)	45.5	31.4
U.N. Operation in Sierra Leone (UNOMSIL)	22.0	16.4
U.N. Mission for the Referendum in Western Sahara (MINURSO)	58.7	49.0
U.N. Civilian Police Mission in Haiti (MIPONUH)	16.7	17.5
U.N. Observer Mission in Georgia (UNOMIG)	19.8	29.2
U.N. Mission of Observers in Tajikistan (UNMOT)	19.5	19.1
U.N. Mission in Bosnia and Herzegovina (UNMIBH)	178.5	168.2
U.N. Observer Mission in Angola (MONUA)	130.4	7.0
U.N. Preventive Deployment Force in the Former Yugoslav Republic of Macedonia (UNPREDEP)	48.8	0.2
Support Group	7.0	—
Subtotal	806.8	605.6
U.N. Logistics Base at Brindisi	5.1	6.4
Support Account	31.9	32.2
TOTAL	843.8	644.2

Source: A/C.5/53/50 and 60.

General to establish "an international civil presence in Kosovo in order to provide an interim administration for Kosovo," and to appoint a Special Representative to control the implementation of the international civil presence [S/Res/1244]. At the time of writing, the financial implications of these decisions were not known, but it was safe to assume that, given the scope and complexity of the responsibilities of the international civil presence and its likely duration, the new peacekeeping operation would cost several hundred million dollars a year. Further considerable costs would arise if a decision were taken to send a U.N. peacekeeping force to the Democratic Republic of Congo once all the parties to the civil war there agreed to a cease-fire.

The expenses of peacekeeping operations are assessed on member states on a case-by-case basis ("an *ad hoc* arrangement") using a special scale, the methodology for which was approved by the General Assembly in A/Res/3101 (XXVIII) of December 11, 1973. Under this method the assessments of the poorer countries are reduced compared to the regular-budget scale, and the reduction is added to the assessments of the permanent members of the Security Council because of their special responsibilities under the Charter. However, domestic legislation (Public Law 103–236) enacted by the U.S. Congress in 1995 limits U.S. contributions to peacekeeping operations to not more than 25 percent, effective October 1 of that year, compared with approximately 31 percent under the peacekeeping scale, thereby contributing to the U.S. indebtedness to the world organization. Unless a solution is found, the problem will become more acute in light of the likely costs of the international civil presence in Kosovo.

By A/Res/53/212, the General Assembly approved for the **International Tribunal** for the Prosecution of Persons Responsible for Serious Violations of International Humanitarian Law Committed in the Territory of the **Former Yugoslavia** since 1991 an amount of $103.4 million gross ($94.1 million net) for the financial period January 1 to December 31, 1999. By the same resolution it approved revised appropriations for the 1998 financial year in the amount of $68.3 million gross ($61.9 million net). The appropriations for the International Criminal Tribunal for the Prosecution of Persons Responsible for Genocide and Other Serious Violations of International Humanitarian Law Committed in the Territory of **Rwanda** and Rwandan Citizens Responsible for Genocide and Other Such Violations Committed in the Territory of Neighbouring States for the period January 1 to December 31, 1999, amounted to $75.3 million gross ($68.5 million net) [A/Res/53/213]. The revised appropriations for the 1998 financial year, as approved in the same resolution, amounted to $52.3 million gross ($48.0 million net). The increase in the requirements of both tribunals in 1999, as compared to 1998, was attributable in the main to the hiring of additional judges for the additional (third) Chambers of the

Tribunals. Half of the appropriations for the Tribunals are assessed on member states on the basis of the regular-budget scale, and the other half on the basis of the scale for peacekeeping operations.

6. Personnel and Administration

Personnel and administration are considered in depth by the Fifth Committee in **even-numbered years**. At its 53rd Session the General Assembly discussed these matters under three main agenda items: human resources management; the U.N. common system; and the U.N. pension system.

The debate on **human resources management** dealt with delegation of authority and responsibility and the related role of the **Office of Human Resources Management (OHRM)**; the planning of human resources, including recruitment and placement, performance appraisal, and career development; the use of gratis personnel and of consultants and individual contractors; the composition of the Secretariat from the point of view of geographical representation; and the status of women in the Secretariat. The item was introduced by the Secretary-General himself, who placed it in the context of U.N. reforms. The Secretary-General said that, as authority in personnel matters was delegated to program managers, OHRM would be responsible for setting strategy, developing policies, providing guidelines to managers, and monitoring their performance. Certain core functions, such as the geographical distribution of staff, would remain with OHRM. Staff development and mobility would be stressed. Best practices would be sought wherever they might be found, while recognizing that what was tried and true on the outside was not necessarily applicable to an international organization. The Secretary-General pointed out that human resources management reform was not an exercise in budget-cutting or staff-cutting, and was certainly not a way to fund the Development Account [A/C.5/53/SR.14].

In the ensuing debate several delegations, including those of Austria (speaking on behalf of the European Union), Japan, New Zealand (speaking on behalf also of Australia and Canada), and the Republic of Korea, regretted that the staff recruitment procedure was inordinately lengthy and took an average of 461 days, thereby discouraging potential applicants, including successful candidates in national competitive examinations. In this connection, the representative of New Zealand ascribed the delay partly to the involvement of staff representatives in the selection process [A/C.5/53/SR.14; SR.22; SR.26]. Responding to the debate, the Assistant Secretary-General for Human Resources Management said that the average time needed for recruitment had been reduced to 260 days, and that efforts were under way to reduce it even further [A/C.5/53/SR.38].

The importance of **career development** was addressed by several delegations. The representative of New Zealand, speaking on behalf also of Australia and Canada, said that the **expected retirement of 1,223 staff members over the next five years** presented the Secretary-General with both challenges and opportunities, including increasing the number of women in senior posts—a point also made by the representative of the Republic of Korea. Currently, 57.5 percent of the staff approaching retirement are men. The representative of Austria, who spoke on behalf of the European Union and of associated Central and East European countries, expressed concern at the fact that there were more resignations than retirements from the United Nations; the number of resignations of P-2 and P-3 staff revealed an intolerable level of frustration that must be addressed urgently. The representative of Mozambique felt that the high number of resignations of P-2 and P-3 staff was indicative of the lack of career prospects. Concern at the high number of resignations was also voiced by the representative of Indonesia, speaking on behalf of the Group of 77 and China, and the representatives of Japan, Romania, and Croatia [A/C.5/53/ SR. 22; SR.24; SR.26]. The representative of Austria, speaking on behalf of the European Union and associated countries, also said that the high average age of newly hired staff was undesirable, and that more efforts should be made to attract younger people. The representative of Croatia, after noting that the overall average age of staff was 45.5 years, and that the average age in the Director category was 53.9 years, said that, in the interest of reform, the Organization must attract young, ambitious men and women, rather than discourage them [A/C.5/53/SR.22; SR.26]. The representative of Norway said that the maintenance and development of a strong and independent international civil service, which his government favored, called for more attractive and competitive conditions of service [A/C.5/53/SR.22]. Responding to these concerns, the Assistant Secretary-General for Human Resources Management said that interviews with resigning P-2 staff members indicated that there were many reasons why they had decided to resign, including employment of spouses; dissatisfaction with compensation and/or career development prospects; the attractiveness of outside opportunities; and inability to adjust to a multicultural environment [A/C.5/53/SR.38].

The representative of Jamaica referred to the link between career development and the contractual status of staff; she expressed concern about the maintenance of fixed short-term contracts and stressed the need for their conversion to permanent contracts and for greater movement from the General Service to the Professional category [A/C.5/53/SR.28]. The importance of job security through permanent contracts was stressed by the President of the United Nations Staff Union [A/C.5/53/SR.22]. The Fifth Committee was informed that in 1998, 70.3 percent of the posts subject to geographical distribution were held by staff with permanent contracts, and that the Secretariat was continuing its efforts to reduce that proportion to 70 percent. The representative of the Russian Federation, on the other hand, strongly favored reducing the proportion of career appointment to less than 70 percent, because fixed-term contracts provided greater flexibility. In the meantime, he supported the extension for a few more years of the freeze on career appointments, which had been introduced in order to achieve the reduction of the proportion of permanent appointments to 70 percent of posts subject to geographical distribution. Both he and the representative of Ukraine supported the practice of seconding personnel to the United Nations [A/C.5/53/SR.26].

The representative of New Zealand, speaking on behalf also of Australia and Canada, felt that Article 101 of the Charter could not be fully observed in the absence of a performance-based culture that rewarded and promoted staff solely on the basis of merit; the **tolerance of underperformance** that the Organization had displayed in the past could no longer be accepted [A/C.5/53/SR.22]. In response, the Assistant Secretary-General for Human Resources Management said with reference to staff who were not considered sufficiently productive, that it was intended, in the new culture, that seniority-based advancement would give way to career progression based on merit, productivity, achievement, and continuous professional growth. Underperformance would be addressed first through remedial action, and thereafter through appropriate sanctions [A/C.5/53/SR.38].

With regard to **geographical distribution,** the representative of Austria, speaking on behalf of the European Union, pointed out that 10 of the Union's 15 member countries were below the midpoint of their desirable range, including three that fell into the underrepresented category. Meanwhile, 11 of the 13 overrepresented countries were developing countries. The representative of Japan said that his country was well below the lower limit of the desirable range [A/C.5/53/SR.22].

The Fifth Committee continued its consideration of the agenda item "Human resources management" at its resumed 53rd Session when it adopted Resolution 53/221, which runs to 104 operative paragraphs. In that resolution:

- It decided that OHRM would remain the central authority for the monitoring and approval of the recruitment and placement of staff and for the interpretation of the rules and regulations of the Organization and the enforcement of their application.
- It expressed concern at the growing number of resignations, particularly those in the Professional category, and requested the Secretary-General to carry out a study on the causes thereof.
- It regretted the high vacancy rate at some regional commissions and other duty stations, particularly those in developing countries.

- It called for enhanced staff mobility.
- It requested the Secretary-General to ensure, before authority was delegated to program managers, that well-designed mechanisms of accountability are put in place, including a mechanism for reviewing the decisions of program managers.
- It gave the Secretary-General detailed instructions relating to recruitment and placement of staff, including that all appointments to P-2 posts and to posts requiring language competence and most appointments to P-3 level posts should be made through competitive examinations; that staff selected through such examinations should be considered for permanent appointments after they had successfully completed their period of probationary service; and that he should continue his efforts to increase the share of fixed-term appointments.
- It requested the Secretary-General to implement a transparent promotion policy, augmented by the effective use of a simplified and appropriate performance appraisal system.
- It reiterated that the Secretary-General should refrain from using consultants to carry out functions assigned to established posts; and noted with concern that 31 percent of contract personnel were hired from only four member states.
- It noted with concern that 24 member states were unrepresented and 10 were underrepresented in the Secretariat as of June 30, 1998; and that there had been a significant reduction in the number of P-2 and P-3 level posts subject to geographical distribution, whereas the number of such posts at the D-2 and ASG levels had increased.
- It reaffirmed the goal of 50/50 gender distribution by the year 2000 in all categories of posts within the United Nations system, especially at the D-1 level and above.

The Secretary-General was requested to submit a number of reports to the Assembly at its 55th Session in 2000, the next occasion when personnel questions will again be considered in depth. However, he is to submit to the Assembly at its 54th Session a consolidated and comprehensive compendium of all administrative circulars on delegation of authority. This request was made in the context of the concern that some administrative instructions on this question do not conform to the provisions of General Assembly resolutions and decisions.

On the question of **gratis personnel,** to which considerable attention had been paid at the 51st and 52nd Sessions, the Secretary-General was requested not to extend the current contracts of 17 such personnel who had been recruited for service with the International Tribunals on former Yugoslavia and Rwanda in contravention of A/Res/51/226. In a separate resolution [A/Res. 53/218], the General Assembly decided to revisit the question of gratis personnel at its 54th Session.

Under the agenda item **"United Nations common system,"** the Fifth Committee considered a report submitted by the **International Civil Service Commission (ICSC)**. The Assembly adopted A/Res/53/209, in which the Commission's recommendations were generally supported. With regard to the conditions of service of staff in the Professional and higher categories, the Assembly reconfirmed the continued application of the Noblemaire principle, which states that the salaries of internationally recruited staff should be such as to attract nationals of the country with the highest-paid civil service. For technical reasons, the ICSC has retained the U.S. federal civil service as the comparator, even though it appeared that the German federal civil service now had a higher remuneration. The Assembly accepted the ICSC recommendation for a small upward adjustment in U.N. Professional salary scales, which was justified on the basis of the evolution of the margin between U.N. and U.S. levels of remuneration. The General Assembly also approved an increase in the children's allowance and in the secondary dependant's allowance, effective January 1, 1999, and in the maximum reimbursement level of the education grant, as recommended by the Commission. The Commission's recommendation that the language allowance be replaced by a non-pensionable lump-sum payment was referred back to the Commission for further study. The questions of the working methods of the ICSC, and of the selection and appointment of the members of the Commission (there had been criticism that not all the Commission members had the necessary expertise and qualifications) were deferred.

Consideration of the report of the **U.N. Joint Staff Pension Board (UNJSPB)** under the agenda item "United Nations pension system" led to the adoption of A/Res/53/210. The **U.N. Joint Staff Pension Fund,** which covers all the organizations in the U.N. system, currently serves more than 110,000 active participants and beneficiaries, and pays out more than $78 million in 26 currencies in benefits each month. In its resolution, the General Assembly took note with satisfaction of the improvement in the actuarial situation of the Fund from an actuarial deficit of 1.46 percent of pensionable remuneration as of December 31, 1995, to an actuarial surplus of 0.36 percent of pensionable remuneration as of December 31, 1997. It also noted that the Board would await the results of the actuarial valuation as of December 31, 1999, before any action was taken on the proposed improvements in the adjustment of benefits. The Assembly approved the revised cost-sharing arrangements between the United Nations and the Fund regarding services and facilities provided by the former. It decided to terminate membership in the Fund of the Interim Commission for the International Trade Organization, as requested by the Interim Commission. The General Assembly also approved proposals by the Board for amendment of the Fund's Regulations that:

a. eliminated the provision whereby a surviving spouse's benefit was discontinued upon his or her remarriage;
b. introduced, subject to certain conditions, a benefit for a surviving divorced spouse; and
c. made it possible for the Fund, pursuant to a settlement agreement, or an order of a court, to pay a portion of a benefit to a beneficiary's former spouse or a spouse from whom he or she is separated.

Index

www.unausa.org

Whether you're interested in UNA-USA's 54-year-old history or our very latest programs and publications, it's all a fingertip away on our state-of-the-art Web Page. Accessed by thousands of visitors every month, the UNA Web Page—like UNA itself—has become identified as the ultimate source for timely and reliable information on the United Nations, its specialized and related agencies, and on the vital relationship between the United States and the world organization.

Join the Nationwide Movement for a
More Effective United Nations

For more than 50 years the United Nations has been working to prevent conflict, promote economic and social development, and preserve the environment. Since 1945 the U.N. and its family of agencies have:

♦ wiped out smallpox and river blindness, and immunized 80% of the world's children against measles, diphtheria, and other killers;

♦ forged agreement on over 300 treaties, including those committing nations to the peaceful uses of outer space, protection of the earth's ozone layer, and the rights of women and children;

♦ cooled hot wars and defused heated conflicts through mediation, fact-finding missions, and some 30 peace-keeping operations; and

♦ moved the environment, sustainable development, and human rights to the top of the international agenda.

As the world organization enters its second half-century, nations *must* work together to address these and other challenges. No nation can go it alone. Therefore, the United States and other countries must cooperate in making the world body work even better.

The United Nations Association of the USA (una-usa) is the nation's largest foreign policy organization, building public support for constructive U.S. leadership in a more effective United Nations.

UNA-USA is an incubator of new ideas on such issues as conflict resolution, nuclear non-proliferation, and sustainable development.

UNA-USA is a constructive critic of the U.N. and of U.S. policy at the U.N. We believe that the U.N. is so important that we must point out problems and offer alternative solutions.

UNA-USA is a force for change. Through the work of its 175 community-based Chapters, its 145 affiliated national organizations, and its vigorous Washington/ New York-based staff, UNA-USA is creating a powerful national constituency for an even better U.N.

UNA-USA is building for tomorrow. The Association's programs, including the renowned Model United Nations program for high school and college students, are preparing new members of all ages for active participation in a world of global change and challenge.

The bottom line is this: one country alone cannot solve the world's problems. The organization best suited to affect global problem-solving is the United Nations, and no other group is doing more to make the U.N. stronger than is UNA-USA.

M E M B E R S H I P A P P L I C A T I O N

❏ $25 .............................INTRODUCTORY *(1st year only)*
❏ $35 ....INDIVIDUAL
❏ $40 ....FAMILY
❏ $40 .............................ORGANIZATION/SCHOOL/BUSINESS
❏ $10 ....STUDENT
❏ $20 ....LIMITED INCOME INDIVIDUAL
❏ $25 ....LIMITED INCOME FAMILY
❏ $100 ....SPONSOR
❏ $500 ....PATRON
❏ $1,000 ....BENEFACTOR

Status: ❏ New ❏ Renewal
Membership type:
❏ Personal
❏ Local Organization/School/Business

NAME *(please print)*

ADDRESS

CITY   STATE   ZIP

HOME PHONE

BUSINESS PHONE

Please return this form, along with your check payable to UNA-USA, to:

UNA-USA Membership Services
801 Second Avenue
New York, NY 10017-4706
Phone: 212 907-1300
Fax: 212 682-9185